Get the eBook FREE!

(PDF, ePub, Kindle, and liveBook all included)

We believe that once you buy a book from us, you should be able to read it in any format we have available. To get electronic versions of this book at no additional cost to you, purchase and then register this book at the Manning website.

Go to https://www.manning.com/freebook and follow the instructions to complete your pBook registration.

That's it!
Thanks from Manning!

T0100143

Bayesian Optimization in Action

QUAN NGUYEN

FOREWORDS BY LUIS SERRANO AND DAVID SWEET

MANNING

SHELTER ISLAND

For online information and ordering of this and other Manning books, please visit
www.manning.com. The publisher offers discounts on this book when ordered in quantity.
For more information, please contact

Special Sales Department
Manning Publications Co.
20 Baldwin Road
PO Box 761
Shelter Island, NY 11964
Email: orders@manning.com

Manning Publications Co.   Development editor: Marina Michaels
20 Baldwin Road   Technical editor: Kerry Koitzsch
PO Box 761   Review editor: Aleks Dragosavljević
Shelter Island, NY 11964   Production editor: Andy Marinkovich
                                    Copy editor: Christian Berk
                                     Proofreader: Melody Dolab
                           Technical proofreader: James Byleckie
                                      Typesetter: Dennis Dalinnik
                                   Cover designer: Marija Tudor

ISBN: 9781633439078
Printed in the United States of America

To my dear best friend, Nhung.

brief contents

v

contents

forewords

As the complexity of problems we face in machine learning and related fields continues to increase, it is more and more important to optimize our use of resources and make informed decisions efficiently. Bayesian optimization, a powerful technique for finding the maxima and minima of objective functions that are expensive to evaluate, has emerged as a very useful solution to this challenge. One reason is that the function can be taken as a black box, which enables researchers and practitioners to tackle very complicated functions with Bayesian inference as the main method of optimization.

Due to its complexity, Bayesian optimization has been more out of reach for beginner ML practitioners than other methods. However, a tool like Bayesian optimization must be in the toolkit of any ML practitioner who wants to get the best results. To master this topic, one must have a very solid intuition of calculus and probability.

This is where *Bayesian Optimization in Action* comes to the rescue. In this book, Quan beautifully and successfully demystifies these complex concepts. Using a hands-on approach, clear diagrams, real-world examples, and useful code examples, he lifts the veil off the complexities of the topic, both from the theoretical and the practical point of view.

Quan uses his extensive experience as a data scientist and educator to give the reader a very clear picture of these techniques and how they can be applied to solve real-world problems. Starting from the principles of Bayesian inference, the book gradually builds up the concepts of Bayesian optimization and the Gaussian process model. It teaches state-of-the-art libraries, such as GPyTorch and BoTorch, exploring their use in several domains.

This book is an essential read for any data science or ML practitioner who wants to harness the true power of Bayesian optimization to solve real-world problems. I highly recommend it to anyone looking to master the art of optimization through Bayesian inference.

—LUIS SERRANO, PhD, AI Scientist and Popularizer,
Author of *Grokking Machine Learning*

Engineers and scientists face a common challenge, essential to capturing the value of their research and creativity. They need to optimize. A machine learning engineer finds the hyperparameters that make models generalize. A group of physicists tunes a free electron laser for maximal pulse energy. A software engineer configures the garbage collector of the JVM to maximize throughput of a server. A materials science engineer selects a microstructure morphology that maximizes the light absorption of a solar cell. In each example, there are design decisions that cannot be made based on first principles. They are instead made by experimental evaluation.

To evaluate something experimentally, one might execute software, run hardware, or build a new object, simultaneously measuring its performance. To find a good design, one needs to make multiple evaluations. These evaluations take time, cost money, and may incur risk. It is, therefore, imperative that one make as few experimental evaluations as are necessary to find an optimal design. That's what Bayesian optimization is all about.

I have used Bayesian optimization, and related precursor methods, in my work over the past 20 years. In that time, academic research and reports of industrial application have improved the performance and expanded the applicability of Bayesian optimization. There now exist high-quality software tools and techniques for building project-specific optimizers.

One may think of the current state as analogous to that of prediction with linear models. An engineer who wants to build a linear model will find that software tools like sklearn enable them to design models for various types (e.g., continuous or categorical) and numbers of input and output variables, to perform automated variable selection, and to measure the quality of generalization. Similarly, an engineer who wants to build a Bayesian optimizer will find that BoTorch, which is built on GPyTorch, pyro, and PyTorch, provides tools for optimizing over different variable types, maximizing multiple objectives, handling constraints, and more.

This book teaches Bayesian optimization, starting from its most basic components—Gaussian process regression and numerical optimization of an acquisition function—to the latest methods for handling large numbers of evaluations (aka observations) and exotic design spaces. Along the way, it covers all the specializations you might need for a given project: constraint handling, multiple objectives, parallelized evaluation, and evaluation via pairwise comparison. You'll find enough technical depth to make you comfortable with the tools and methods and enough real code to enable you to use those tools and methods for real work very quickly.

For all the success of Bayesian optimization, there is little literature aimed at the newcomer. This book fills that niche excellently.

—DAVID SWEET, adjunct professor, Yeshiva University, author of *Experimentation for Engineers*, Cogneato.xyz

preface

In the fall of 2019, I was a first-year PhD student unsure of what problem to work on for my research. I knew I wanted to focus on artificial intelligence (AI)—there was something appealing about automating thinking processes using computers—but AI is an enormous field, and I was having a hard time narrowing my work down to a specific topic.

All that uncertainty disappeared when I took a course titled Bayesian Methods for Machine Learning. At this point, I had had brief encounters with Bayes theorem in my undergrad, but it was during the first lectures of this course that everything started to click! Bayes' theorem offered an intuitive way to think about probability, and to me, it is an elegant model of human beliefs: Each of us has a prior belief (about anything) that we start with, which is updated as we observe evidence for or against that prior, and the result is a posterior belief reflecting both the prior and data. The fact that Bayes' theorem brings this elegant way of maintaining beliefs to AI and finds applications across many problems was a strong signal to me that Bayesian machine learning is a topic worth pursuing.

By the time we got to the lecture on Bayesian optimization (BayesOpt), my mind was made up: the theory was intuitive, the applications were numerous, and there was just so much possibility in what could be built. Again, something innate in me was (and continues to be) attracted to automating thinking or, more specifically, decision-making, and BayesOpt was the perfect attraction. I got myself into the research lab of Roman Garnett, the professor teaching the course, and my BayesOpt journey began!

Jumping to 2021, I had spent some time researching and implementing BayesOpt solutions, and my appreciation for BayesOpt only grew. I would recommend it to friends and colleagues to handle difficult optimization problems, promising that BayesOpt would work well. There was only one issue: there wasn't a good resource I could point to. Research papers were heavy on math, online tutorials were too short to provide substantial insight, and tutorials of BayesOpt software were disjointed and didn't offer a good narrative.

Then, an idea came to mind, in the form of Toni Morrison's quote, "If there's a book that you want to read, but it hasn't been written yet, then you must write it." How very true! The prospect excited me for two reasons: I could write a book on something near and dear to my heart, and writing would undoubtedly help me gain even deeper insights. I put together a proposal and contacted Manning, the publisher of my favorite books with the style I was envisioning.

In November 2021, my acquisition editor, Andy Waldron, sent me an email, marking the very first communication from Manning. In December 2021, I signed my contract and began writing, which would later prove to require more time than I initially thought (as is the case for every book, I'm sure). In April 2023, I wrote this preface as one of the last steps before publication!

acknowledgments

It takes a village to raise a child and no less to write a book. The following are only a small part of my own village, who helped me immensely during the writing process.

My first and foremost thanks are for my parents Bang and Lan, whose constant support has allowed me to fearlessly explore the unknown: studying abroad; pursuing a PhD; and, of course, writing a book. And I'd like to sincerely thank my sister and confidante, Nhu, who is always there to help me through the toughest of times.

Bayesian optimization is a large part of my PhD research, and I'd like to thank the people in the program who truly have and continue to make my PhD experience invaluable. Special thanks go to my advisor Roman Garnett, who effortlessly convinced me to pursue research in Bayesian machine learning. You're the one who started all this. I also thank my friends from the Active Learning lab: Yehu Chen, Shayan Monadjemi, and Professor Alvitta Ottley. They say that a PhD has very sparse rewards, and working with you all has been what makes up most of those rewards.

Next, I gratefully acknowledge the amazing team at Manning. I thank my development editor, Marina Michaels, who has stewarded this ship, from day one, with the highest level of professionalism, care, support, and patience. I completely lucked out getting matched with you for our project. Thanks to my acquisition editor, Andy Waldron, for having faith in the idea, even though a much better author was already working on a book with a similar topic, and Ivan Martinović for helping me with AsciiDoc questions and patiently fixing my markup code.

I'd like to thank the reviewers who devoted time and energy to significantly improve the quality of the writing: Allan Makura, Andrei Paleyes, Carlos Aya-Moreno,

Claudiu Schiller, Cosimo Attanasi, Denis Lapchev, Gary Bake, George Onofrei, Howard Bandy, Ioannis Atsonios, Jesús Antonino Juárez Guerrero, Josh McAdams, Kweku Reginald Wade, Kyle Peterson, Lokesh Kumar, Lucian Mircea Sasu, Marc-Anthony Taylor, Marcio Nicolau, Max Dehaut, Maxim Volgin, Michele Di Pede, Mirerfan Gheibi, Nick Decroos, Nick Vazquez, Or Golan, Peter Henstock, Philip Weiss, Ravi Kiran Bamidi, Richard Tobias, Rohit Goswami, Sergio Govoni, Shabie Iqbal, Shreesha Jagadeesh, Simone Sguazza, Sriram Macharla, Szymon Harabasz, Thomas Forys, and Vlad Navitski.

One, inevitably, has blind spots while writing a book, and it's the reviewers who help fill in those blind spots and keep the author focused on what's truly important. Dedicated thanks to Kerry Koitzsch for his insightful feedback and James Byleckie for his excellent suggestions on both the code and the writing.

Finally, I thank the teams behind the incredible GPyTorch and BoTorch libraries, the main workhorses of the code developed for this book. I have sampled various libraries for Gaussian processes and Bayesian optimization, always finding myself coming back to GPyTorch and BoTorch. I hope this book can play a part in building an already-wonderful community around these libraries.

about this book

It used to be that to learn about Bayesian optimization, one would need to look for online articles and tutorials in the documentation of a relevant library, which are scattered and, due to their nature, don't go deeply into the specifics. You could also turn to technical textbooks, but they are usually too dense and math heavy, posing a challenge if you are a practitioner who would like to hit the ground running right away.

This book fills the gap by offering a blend of hands-on discussions, references to more in-depth materials for the interested reader, and ready-to-use code examples. It works by first building intuition for the components of Bayesian optimization and then implementing them in Python using state-of-the-art software.

The spirit of the book is to provide an accessible introduction to Bayesian optimization grounded in high-level intuitions from math and probability. The interested reader can, further, find more technical texts that are referenced throughout the book for a deeper dive into a topic of interest.

Who should read this book?

Data scientists and ML practitioners who are interested in hyperparameter tuning, A/B testing, or experimentation and, more generally decision-making, will benefit from this book.

Researchers in scientific fields such as chemistry, materials science, and physics who face difficult optimization problems will also find this book helpful. While most background knowledge necessary to follow the content will be covered, the audience should be familiar with common concepts in ML, such as training data, predictive models, multivariate normal distributions, and others.

How this book is organized: A roadmap

The book comprises four main parts. Each part contains several chapters that cover the corresponding topic:

- Chapter 1 introduces Bayesian optimization using real-world use cases. It also includes, without going into technical details, a visual example of how Bayesian optimization could accelerate finding the global optimum of an expensive function.

Part 1 covers Gaussian processes as the predictive model of the function we wish to optimize. The central thesis is that Gaussian processes offer calibrated quantification of uncertainty, which is essential in our Bayesian optimization framework. This part is composed of two chapters:

- Chapter 2 shows that Gaussian processes are a natural solution to the problem of learning a regression model from some observed data. A Gaussian process defines a distribution over functions and can be updated to reflect our belief about the function's value, given some observed data.
- Chapter 3 introduces the two main ways we incorporate prior information into a Gaussian process: the mean function and the covariance function. The mean function specifies the general trend, while the covariance function specifies the smoothness of the function.

Part 2 enumerates Bayesian optimization policies, which are decision procedures for how function evaluations should be done so that the global optimum may be identified as efficiently as possible. While different policies are motivated by different objectives, they all aim to balance the tradeoff between exploration and exploitation. This part is composed of three chapters:

- Chapter 4 discusses a natural way of deciding which function evaluation is the most beneficial to make: considering the improvement that would be gained from the current best function value. Thanks to the Gaussian process–based belief about the function, we may compute these improvement-related quantities in closed form and cheaply, enabling two specific Bayesian optimization policies: Probability of Improvement and Expected Improvement.
- Chapter 5 explores the connection between Bayesian optimization and another common class of problems, called the *multi-armed bandit*. We learn how to transfer multi-armed bandit policies in the Bayesian optimization setting and obtain corresponding strategies: Upper Confidence Bound and Thompson sampling.
- Chapter 6 considers a strategy that reduces the most uncertainty in our belief about the function's global optimum. This constitutes entropy-based policies, which use a subfield of mathematics called *information theory*.

Part 3 presents some of the most common use cases that don't fit neatly into the work-flow developed thus far in the book and shows how Bayesian optimization may be modified to tackle these optimization tasks:

- Chapter 7 introduces batch optimization, in which to increase throughput, we allow experiments to run in parallel. For example, one may train multiple instances of a large neural network simultaneously on a cluster of GPUs. This requires more than one recommendation to be returned at the same time by an optimization policy.

- Chapter 8 discusses safety-critical use cases, where we cannot explore the search space freely, as some function evaluations may have detrimental effects. This motivates the setting in which there are constraints on how the function in question should behave and our need to factor in these constraints in the design of optimization policies.

- Chapter 9 shows that when we have access to multiple ways of observing the function's values at different levels of cost and accuracy—commonly known as *multifidelity Bayesian optimization*—accounting for variable costs can lead to increased optimization performance.

- Chapter 10 covers pairwise comparisons, which have been shown to reflect one's preference more accurately than number evaluations or ratings, as they are simpler and pose a lighter cognitive load on the labeler. Chapter 10 extends Bayesian optimization to this setting, first by using a special Gaussian process model and then by modifying existing policies to fit into this pairwise compari-son workflow.

- One may aim to optimize multiple, potentially conflicting objectives at the same time. Chapter 11 studies this problem of multiobjective optimization and shows how Bayesian optimization can be extended to this setting.

Part 4 deals with special variants of the Gaussian process models, demonstrating their flexibility and effectiveness at modeling and providing uncertainty-calibrated predic-tions, even outside of the Bayesian optimization context:

- In chapter 12, we learn that in some cases, obtaining the closed-form solution of a trained Gaussian process is impossible. However, high-fidelity approxima-tions may still be made using sophisticated approximate strategies.

- Chapter 13 demonstrates that thanks to the Torch ecosystem, combining PyTorch neural networks with GPyTorch Gaussian processes is a seamless process. This allows our Gaussian process models to become more flexible and expressive.

A beginner will benefit a great deal from the first six chapters. Experienced practi-tioners looking to fit Bayesian optimization into their use case might find value in chapters 7 through 11, which can be read independently and in any order. Long-time users of Gaussian processes will most likely be interested in the last two chapters, where we develop specialized Gaussian processes.

About the code

You can get executable snippets of code from the liveBook (online) version of this book at https://livebook.manning.com/book/bayesian-optimization-in-action. The code is available for download from the Manning website at https://www.manning.com/books/bayesian-optimization-in-action and GitHub at https://github.com/KrisNguyen135/bayesian-optimization-in-action; the latter of which will accept issues and pull requests.

You will be using Jupyter notebooks to run the code accompanying the book. Jupyter notebooks offer a clean way to dynamically work with the code, allowing us to explore how each object behaves and interacts with other objects. More information on how to get started with Jupyter notebooks can be found on their official website: https://jupyter.org. The ability to dynamically explore objects is specifically helpful in our case, as many components of the Bayesian optimization workflow are implemented as Python objects by GPyTorch and BoTorch, the main libraries we'll be using.

GPyTorch and BoTorch are the premiere libraries for Gaussian process modeling and Bayesian optimization in Python. There are other choices, such as the scikit-optimize extension of scikit-Learn or GPflow and GPflowOpt, which extend the TensorFlow framework for Bayesian optimization. However, the combination of GPyTorch and BoTorch makes up the most comprehensive and flexible codebase, which includes many state-of-the-art algorithms from Bayesian optimization research. I have found in my own experience using Bayesian optimization software that GPyTorch and BoTorch achieve a good balance between being beginner-friendly and providing state-of-the-art methods.

One thing is important to note: it's exactly because these libraries are being actively maintained that the APIs shown in the book might change slightly in newer versions, and it's important that you install the library versions specified in the `requirements.txt` file to run the code without errors. You can find more instructions on how to create a Python environment using a `requirements.txt` file in, for example, the official Python documentation at https://packaging.python.org/en/latest/guides/installing-using-pip-and-virtual-environments. With that said, to work with newer versions, you will most likely only need to make minor modifications to the code.

You will notice as you go through the book that the text tends to focus on only the key components of the code, leaving out many details, such as library imports and bookkeeping code. (Of course, the first time a piece of code is used, it will be properly introduced in the text.) Keeping our discussions concise helps us stay focused on what's truly new in each chapter and avoid having to repeat ourselves. The code in the Jupyter notebooks, on the other hand, is self-contained, and each notebook can be run on its own, without any modification.

liveBook discussion forum

Purchase of *Bayesian Optimization in Action* includes free access to liveBook, Manning's online reading platform. Using liveBook's exclusive discussion features, you can attach comments to the book globally or to specific sections or paragraphs. It's a snap to make notes for yourself, ask and answer technical questions, and receive help from the author and other users. To access the forum, go to https://livebook.manning.com/book/bayesian-optimization-in-action/discussion. You can also learn more about Manning's forums and the rules of conduct at https://livebook.manning.com/discussion.

Manning's commitment to our readers is to provide a venue where a meaningful dialogue between individual readers and between readers and the author can take place. It is not a commitment to any specific amount of participation on the part of the author, whose contribution to the forum remains voluntary (and unpaid). We suggest you try asking the author some challenging questions lest their interest stray! The forum and the archives of previous discussions will be accessible from the publisher's website for as long as the book is in print.

about the author

QUAN NGUYEN is a Python programmer and machine learning enthusiast. He is interested in solving decision-making problems that involve uncertainty. Quan has authored several books on Python programming and scientific computing. He is currently pursuing a PhD in computer science at Washington University in St. Louis, where he does research on Bayesian methods in machine learning.

About the technical editor

The technical editor of this book is Kerry Koitzsch. Kerry is an author, and software architect with over three decades of diverse experience in the implementation of enterprise applications and information architecture solutions. Kerry is the author of a book on distributed processing as well as many shorter technical publications and holds a patent for innovative OCR technology. He is also a recipient of the U.S. Army Achievement Medal.

about the cover illustration

The figure on the cover of *Bayesian Optimization in Action* is captioned "Polonnois," or "Polish Man," taken from a collection by Jacques Grasset de Saint-Sauveur, published in 1797. Each illustration is finely drawn and colored by hand.

In those days, it was easy to identify where people lived and what their trade or station in life was just by their dress. Manning celebrates the inventiveness and initiative of the computer business with book covers based on the rich diversity of regional culture centuries ago, brought back to life by pictures from collections such as this one.

Introduction to Bayesian optimization

1

This chapter covers

- What motivates Bayesian optimization and how it works
- Real-life examples of Bayesian optimization problems
- A toy example of Bayesian optimization in action

You've made a wonderful choice in reading this book, and I'm excited for your upcoming journey! On a high level, *Bayesian optimization* is an optimization technique that may be applied when the function (or, in general, any process that generates an output when an input is passed in) one is trying to optimize is a black box and expensive to evaluate in terms of time, money, or other resources. This setup encompasses many important tasks, including hyperparameter tuning, which we define shortly. Using Bayesian optimization can accelerate this search procedure and help us locate the optimum of the function as quickly as possible.

While Bayesian optimization has enjoyed enduring interest from the machine learning (ML) research community, it's not as commonly used or talked about as other ML topics in practice. But why? Some might say Bayesian optimization has a steep learning curve: one needs to understand calculus, use some probability, and be an overall experienced ML researcher to use Bayesian optimization in an application. The goal of this book is to dispel the idea that Bayesian optimization is difficult to use and show that the technology is more intuitive and accessible than one would think.

Throughout this book, we encounter many illustrations, plots, and, of course, code, which aim to make the topic of discussion more straightforward and concrete. You learn how each component of Bayesian optimization works on a high level and how to implement them using state-of-the-art libraries in Python. The accompanying code also serves to help you hit the ground running with your own projects, as the Bayesian optimization framework is very general and "plug and play." The exercises are also helpful in this regard.

Generally, I hope this book is useful for your ML needs and is an overall fun read. Before we dive into the actual content, let's take some time to discuss the problem that Bayesian optimization sets out to solve.

1.1   *Finding the optimum of an expensive black box function*

As mentioned previously, hyperparameter tuning in ML is one of the most common applications of Bayesian optimization. We explore this problem, as well as a couple of others, in this section as an example of the general problem of black box optimization. This will help us understand why Bayesian optimization is needed.

1.1.1   *Hyperparameter tuning as an example of an expensive black box optimization problem*

Say we want to train a neural network on a large dataset, but we are not sure how many layers this neural net should have. We know that the architecture of a neural net is a make-or-break factor in deep learning (DL), so we perform some initial testing and obtain the results shown in table 1.1.

Table 1.1   **An example of a hyperparameter tuning task**

Number of layers	Accuracy on the test set
5	0.72
10	0.81
20	0.75

Our task is to decide how many layers the neural network should have in the next trial in the search for the highest accuracy. It's difficult to decide which number we should try next. The best accuracy we have found, 81%, is good, but we think we can do better with a different number of layers. Unfortunately, the boss has set a deadline to finish implementing the model. Since training a neural net on our large dataset takes several days, we only have a few trials remaining before we need to decide how many layers our network should have. With that in mind, we want to know what other values we should try so we can find the number of layers that provides the highest possible accuracy.

This task, in which we want to find the best setting (hyperparameter values) for our model to optimize some performance metric, such as predictive accuracy, is typically called *hyperparameter tuning* in ML. In our example, the hyperparameter of our neural net is its depth (the number of layers). If we are working with a decision tree, common hyperparameters are the maximum depth, the minimum number of points per node, and the split criterion. With a support-vector machine, we could tune the regularization term and the kernel. Since the performance of a model very much depends on its hyperparameters, hyperparameter tuning is an important component of any ML pipeline.

If this were a typical real-world dataset, this process could take a lot of time and resources. Figure 1.1 from OpenAI (https://openai.com/blog/ai-and-compute/) shows that as neural networks keep getting larger and deeper, the amount of computation necessary (measured in petaflop/s-days) increases exponentially.

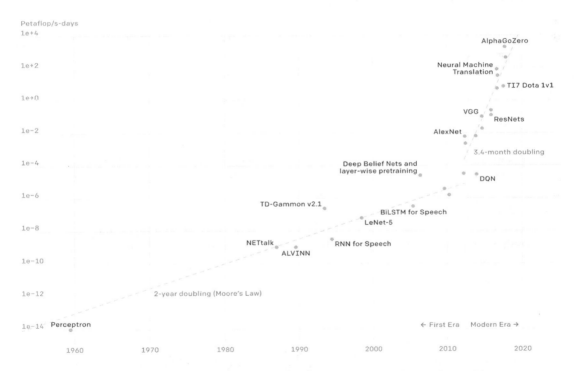

Figure 1.1 **The compute cost of training large neural networks has been steadily growing, making hyperparameter tuning increasingly difficult.**

This is to say that training a model on a large dataset is quite involved and takes significant effort. Further, we want to identify the hyperparameter values that give the best accuracy, so training will have to be done many times. How should we go about choosing which values to use to parameterize our model so we can zero in on the best combination as quickly as possible? That is the central question of hyperparameter tuning.

Getting back to our neural net example in section 1.1, what number of layers should we try next so we can find an accuracy greater than 81%? Some value between 10 layers and 20 layers is promising, since at both 10 and 20, we have better performance than at 5 layers. But what exact value we should inspect next is still not obvious since there may still be a lot of variability in numbers between 10 and 20. When we say *variability*, we implicitly talk about our uncertainty regarding how the test accuracy of our model behaves as a function of the number of layers. Even though we know 10 layers lead to 81% and 20 layers lead to 75%, we cannot say for certain what value, say, 15 layers would yield. This is to say we need to account for our level of uncertainty when considering these values between 10 and 20.

Further, what if some number greater than 20 gives us the highest accuracy possible? This is the case for many large datasets, where a sufficient depth is necessary for a neural net to learn anything useful. Or, though unlikely, what if a small number of layers (fewer than 5) is actually what we need?

How should we explore these different options in a principled way so that when our time runs out and we have to report back to our boss, we can be sufficiently confident that we have arrived at the best number of layers for our model? This question is an example of the *expensive black box optimization* problem, which we discuss next.

1.1.2   *The problem of expensive black box optimization*

In this subsection, we formally introduce the problem of expensive black box optimization, which is what Bayesian optimization aims to solve. Understanding why this is such a difficult problem will help us understand why Bayesian optimization is preferred over simpler, more naïve approaches, such as grid search (where we divide the search space into equal segments) or random search (where we use randomness to guide our search).

In this problem, we have black box access to a function (some input–output mechanism), and our task is to find the input that maximizes the output of this function. The function is often called the *objective function*, as optimizing it is our objective, and we want to find the *optimum* of the objective function—the input that yields the highest function value.

Characteristics of the objective function

The term *black box* means that we don't know what the underlying formula of the objective is; all we have access to is the function output when we make an observation by computing the function value at some input. In our neural net example, we don't know how the accuracy of our model will change if we increase the number of layers one by one (otherwise, we would just pick the best one).

The problem is expensive because in many cases, making an observation (evaluating the objective at some location) is prohibitively costly, rendering a naïve approach, such as an exhaustive search, intractable. In ML and, especially, DL, time is usually the main constraint, as we already discussed.

Hyperparameter tuning belongs to this class of expensive black box optimization problems, but it is not the only one! Any procedure in which we are trying to find some settings or parameters to optimize a process without knowing how the different settings influence and control the result of the process qualifies as a black box optimization problem. Further, trying out a particular setting and observing its result on the target process (the objective function) is time-consuming, expensive, or costly in some other sense.

DEFINITION   The act of trying out a particular setting—that is, evaluating the value of the objective function at some input—is called *making a query* or *querying the objective function*. The entire procedure is summarized in figure 1.2.

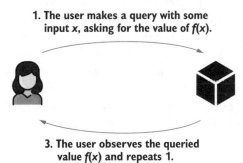

1. The user makes a query with some input x, asking for the value of $f(x)$.

2. The function value $f(x)$ is computed in an expensive procedure hidden from the user.

3. The user observes the queried value $f(x)$ and repeats 1.

Figure 1.2   The framework of a black box optimization problem. We repeatedly query the function values at various locations to find the global optimum.

1.1.3   *Other real-world examples of expensive black box optimization problems*

Now, let's consider a few real-world examples that fall into the category of expensive black box optimization problems. We will see that such problems are common in the field; we often find ourselves with a function we'd like to optimize but that can only be evaluated a small number of times. In these cases, we'd like to find a way to intelligently choose where to evaluate the function.

The first example is drug discovery—the process in which scientists and chemists identify compounds with desirable chemical properties that may be synthesized into drugs. As you can imagine, the experimental process is quite involved and costs a lot of money. Another factor that makes this drug discovery task daunting is the decreasing trend in the productivity of drug discovery R&D that has been robustly observed in recent years. This phenomenon is known as *Eroom's Law*—a reverse of *Moore's Law*—which roughly states that the number of new drugs approved per billion US dollars halves over a fixed period of time. Eroom's Law is visualized in figure 1 of the Nature paper "Diagnosing the Decline in Parmaceutical R&D Efficiency" by Jack W. Scannell, Alex Blanckley, Helen Boldon, and Brian Warrington (https://www.nature.com/articles/nrd3681). (Alternatively, you can simply search for images of "Eroom's Law" on Google.)

Eroom's Law shows that drug discovery throughput resulting from each billion-dollar investment in drug research and development (R&D) decreases linearly on the logarithmic scale over time. In other words, the decrease in drug discovery throughput for a fixed amount of R&D investment is exponential in recent years. Although there are ups and downs in the local trend throughout the years, the exponential decline is obvious going from 1950 to 2020.

The same problem, in fact, applies to any scientific discovery task in which scientists search for new chemicals, materials, or designs that are rare, novel, and useful, with respect to some metric, using experiments that require top-of-the-line equipment and may take days or weeks to finish. In other words, they are trying to optimize for their respective objective functions where evaluations are extremely expensive.

As an illustration, table 1.2 shows a couple of data points in a real-life dataset from such a task. The objective is to find the alloy composition (from the four parent elements) with the lowest mixing temperature, which is a black box optimization problem. Here, materials scientists worked with compositions of alloys of lead (Pb), tin (Sn), germanium (Ge), and manganese (Mn). Each given combination of percentages of these compositions corresponds to a potential alloy that could be synthesized and experimented on in a laboratory.

Table 1.2   Data from a materials discovery task

% of Pb	% of Sn	% of Ge	% of Mn	Mixing temp. (°F)
0.50	0.50	0.00	0.00	192.08
0.33	0.33	0.33	0.00	258.30
0.00	0.50	0.50	0.00	187.24
0.00	0.33	0.33	0.33	188.54

Source: Author's research work.

As a low temperature of mixing indicates a stable, valuable structure for the alloy, the objective is to find compositions whose mixing temperatures are as low as possible. But there is one bottleneck: determining this mixing temperature for a given alloy generally takes days. The question we set out to solve algorithmically is similar: Given the dataset we see, what is the next composition we should experiment with (in terms of how much lead, tin, germanium, and manganese should be present) to find the minimum temperature of mixing?

Another example is in mining and oil drilling, or, more specifically, finding the region within a big area that has the highest yield of valuable minerals or oil. This involves extensive planning, investment, and labor—again an expensive undertaking. As digging operations have significant negative effects on the environment, there are regulations in place to reduce mining activities, placing a limit on the number of *function evaluations* that may be done in this optimization problem.

The central question in expensive black box optimization is this: What is a good way to decide where to evaluate this objective function so its optimum may be found at the end of the search? As we see in a later example, simple heuristics—such as random or grid search, which are approaches implemented by popular Python packages like scikit-learn—may lead to wasteful evaluations of the objective function and, thus, overall poor optimization performance. This is where Bayesian optimization comes into play.

1.2 *Introducing Bayesian optimization*

With the problem of expensive black box optimization in mind, we now introduce Bayesian optimization as a solution to this problem. This gives us a high-level idea of what Bayesian optimization is and how it uses probabilistic ML to optimize expensive black box functions.

> **DEFINITION** Bayesian optimization (BayesOpt) is an ML technique that simultaneously maintains a predictive model to learn about the objective function *and* makes decisions about how to acquire new data to refine our knowledge about the objective, using Bayesian probability and decision theory.

By *data*, we mean input–output pairs, each mapping an input value to the value of the objective function at that input. This data is different, in the specific case of hyperparameter tuning, from the training data for the ML model we aim to tune.

In a BayesOpt procedure, we make decisions based on the recommendation of a BayesOpt algorithm. Once we have taken the BayesOpt-recommended action, the BayesOpt model is updated based on the result of that action and proceeds to recommend the next action to take. This process repeats until we are confident we have zeroed in on the optimal action.

There are two main components of this workflow:

- An ML model that learns from the observations we make and makes predictions about the values of the objective functions on unseen data points
- An optimization policy that makes decisions about where to make the next observation by evaluating the objective to locate the optimum

We introduce each of these components in the following subsection.

1.2.1   *Modeling with a Gaussian process*

BayesOpt works by first fitting a predictive ML model on the objective function we are trying to optimize—sometimes, this is called the surrogate model, as it acts as a surrogate between what we believe the function to be from our observations and the function itself. The role of this predictive model is very important as its predictions inform the decisions made by a BayesOpt algorithm and, therefore, directly affect optimization performance.

In almost all cases, a Gaussian process (GP) is employed for this role of the predictive model, which we examine in this subsection. On a high level, a GP, like any other ML model, operates under the tenet that similar data points produce similar predictions. GPs might not be the most popular class of models, compared to, say, ridge regression, decision trees, support vector machines, or neural networks. However, as we see time and again throughout this book, GPs come with a unique and essential feature: they do not produce point estimate predictions like the other models mentioned; instead, their predictions are in the form of *probability distributions*. Predictions, in the form of probability distributions or probabilistic predictions, are key in BayesOpt, allowing us to quantify uncertainty in our predictions, which, in turn, improves our risk–reward tradeoff when making decisions.

Let's first see what a GP looks like when we train it on a dataset. As an example, say we are interested in training a model to learn from the dataset in table 1.3, which is visualized as black *x*s in figure 1.3.

Table 1.3   An example regression dataset corresponding to figure 1.3

Training data point	Label
1.1470	1.8423
-4.0712	0.7354
0.9627	0.9627
1.2471	1.9859

We first fit a ridge regression model on this dataset and make predictions within a range of –5 and 5; the top panel of figure 1.3 shows these predictions. A *ridge regression model* is a modified version of a linear regression model, where the weights of the model are regularized so that small values are preferred to prevent overfitting. Each prediction made by this model at a given test point is a single-valued number, which does not capture our level of uncertainty about how the function we are learning from behaves. For example, given the test point at 2, this model simply predicts 2.2.

We don't need to go into too much detail about the inner workings of this model. The point here is that a ridge regressor produces point estimates without a measure of uncertainty, which is also the case for many ML models, such as support vector machines, decision trees, and neural networks.

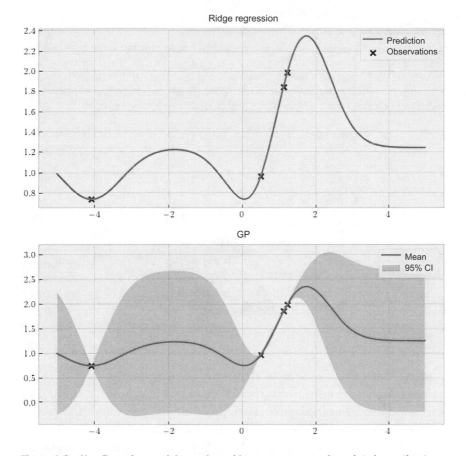

Figure 1.3 Non-Bayesian models, such as ridge regressors, make pointwise estimates, while GPs produce probability distributions as predictions. GPs thus offer a calibrated quantification of uncertainty, which is an important factor when making high-risk decisions.

How, then, does a GP make its predictions? As shown on the bottom panel of figure 1.3, predictions by a GP are in the form of probability distributions (specifically, normal distributions). This means that at each test point, we have a mean prediction (the solid line) as well as what's called the 95% credible interval, or CI (the shaded region).

Note that the acronym *CI* is often used to abbreviate *confidence interval* in frequentist statistics; throughout this book, I use *CI* exclusively to denote *credible interval*. Many things can be said about the technical differences between the two concepts, but on a high level, we can still think of this CI as a range in which it's likely that a quantity of interest (in this case, the true value of the function we're predicting) falls.

GP vs. ridge regression

Interestingly, when using the same covariance function (also known as the *kernel*), a GP and a ridge regression model produce the same predictions (mean predictions for the GP), as illustrated in figure 1.3. We discuss covariance functions in greater depth in chapter 3. This is to say that a GP receives all the benefits a ridge regression model possesses, while offering the additional CI predictions.

While the mean represents the *most likely* value, the 95% credible interval shows the range of values that are probable, in the sense that this range makes up 95% of the probability mass of the distribution.

Effectively, this CI measures our level of uncertainty about the value at each test location. If a location has a large predictive CI (at −2 or 4 in figure 1.3, for example), then there is a wider range of values that are probable for this value. In other words, we have greater uncertainty about this value. If a location has a narrow CI (0 or 2, in figure 1.3), then we are more confident about the value at this location. A nice feature of the GP is that for each point in the training data, the predictive CI is close to 0, indicating we don't have any uncertainty about its value. This makes sense; after all, we already know what that value is from the training set.

Noisy function evaluations

While not the case in figure 1.3, it's possible that the labels of the data points in our dataset are noisy. It's very possible that in many situations in the real world, the process of observing data can be corrupted by noise. In these cases, we can further specify the noise level with the GP, and the CI at the observed data points will not collapse to 0 but, instead, to the specified noise level. This goes to show the flexibility modeling with GPs offers.

This ability to assign a number to our level of uncertainty, which is called *uncertainty quantification*, is quite useful in any high-risk decision-making procedure, such as BayesOpt. Imagine, again, the scenario in section 1.1, where we tune the number of layers in our neural net, and we only have time to try out one more model. Let's say that after being trained on those data points, a GP predicts that 25 layers will give a mean accuracy of 0.85, and the corresponding 95% CI is 0.81 to 0.89. On the other hand, with 15 layers, the GP predicts our accuracy will also be 0.85 on average, but the 95% CI is 0.84 to 0.86. Here, it's quite reasonable to prefer 15 layers, even though both numbers have the same expected value. This is because we are more *certain* 15 will give us a good result.

To be clear, a GP does not make any decision for us, but it does offer us a means to do so with its probabilistic predictions. Decision-making is left to the second part of the BayesOpt framework: the policy.

1.2.2 *Making decisions with a BayesOpt policy*

In addition to a GP as a predictive model, in BayesOpt, we also need a decision-making procedure, which we explore in this subsection. This is the second component of BayesOpt, which takes in the predictions made by the GP model and reasons about how to best evaluate the objective function so the optimum may be located efficiently.

As mentioned previously, a prediction with a 95% CI of 0.84 to 0.86 is considered better than a 95% CI of 0.81 to 0.89, especially if we only have one more try. This is because the former is more of a sure thing, guaranteed to get us a good result. How should we make this decision in a more general case in which the two points might have different predictive means and predictive levels of uncertainty?

This is exactly what a BayesOpt policy helps us do: quantify the usefulness of a point, given its predictive probability distribution. The job of a policy is to take in the GP model, which represents our belief about the objective function, and assign each data point with a score denoting how helpful that point is in helping us identify the global optimum. This score is sometimes called the *acquisition score*. Our job is then to pick out the point that maximizes this acquisition score and evaluate the objective function at that point.

We see the same GP in figure 1.4 that we have in figure 1.3, where the bottom panel shows the plot of how a particular BayesOpt policy called *Expected Improvement* scores each point on the *x*-axis between –5 and 5 (which is our search space). We learn what this name means and how the policy scores data points in chapter 4. For now, let's just keep in mind that if a point has a large acquisition score, this point is valuable for locating the global optimum.

In figure 1.4, the best point is around 1.8, which makes sense, as according to our GP in the top panel, that's also where we achieve the highest predictive mean. This means we will then pick this point at 1.8 to evaluate our objective, hoping to improve from the highest value we have collected.

We should note that this is not a one-time procedure but, instead, a *learning loop*. At each iteration of the loop, we train a GP on the data we have observed from the objective, run a BayesOpt policy on this GP to obtain a recommendation that will hopefully help us identify the global optimum, make an observation at the recommended

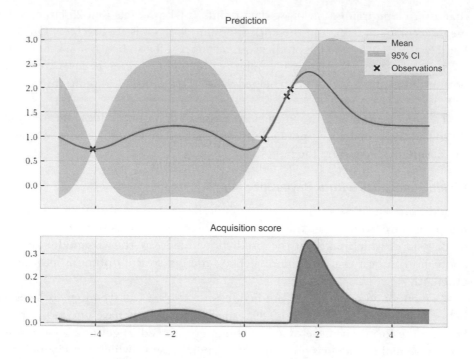

Figure 1.4   A BayesOpt policy scores each individual data point by its usefulness in locating the global optimum. The policy prefers high predictive values (where the payoff is more likely) as well as high uncertainty (where the payoff may be large).

location, add the new point to our training data, and repeat the entire procedure until we reach some condition for terminating. Things might be getting a bit confusing, so it is time for us to take a step back and look at the bigger picture of BayesOpt.

Connection to design of experiments

The description of BayesOpt at this point might remind you of the concept of *design of experiments* (DoE) in statistics, which sets out to solve the same problem of optimizing an objective function by tweaking the controllable settings. Many connections exist between these two techniques, but BayesOpt can be seen as a more general approach than DoE that is powered by the ML model GP.

1.2.3   Combining the GP and the optimization policy to form the optimization loop

In this subsection, we tie in everything we have described so far and make the procedure more concrete. We see the BayesOpt workflow as a whole and better understand how the various components work with each other.

We start with an initial dataset, like those in tables 1.1, 1.2, and 1.3. Then, the BayesOpt workflow is visualized in figure 1.5, which is summarized as follows:

1. We train a GP model on this set, which gives us a belief about what our objective looks like everywhere based on what we have observed from the training data. This belief is represented by the solid curve and shaded region, like those in figures 1.3 and 1.4.
2. A BayesOpt policy then takes in this GP and scores each point in the domain in terms of how valuable the point is in helping us locate the global optimum. This is indicated by the bottom curve, as in figure 1.4.
3. The point that maximizes this score is the point we will choose to evaluate the objective at next and is then added to our training dataset.
4. The process repeats until we cannot afford to evaluate the objective anymore.

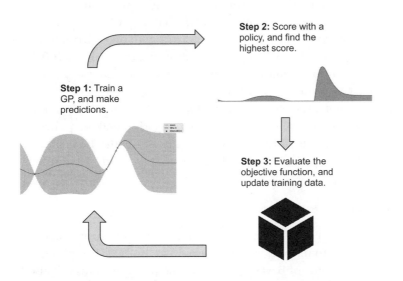

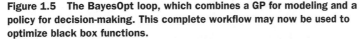

Figure 1.5 The BayesOpt loop, which combines a GP for modeling and a policy for decision-making. This complete workflow may now be used to optimize black box functions.

Unlike a supervised learning task in which we just fit a predictive model on a training dataset and make predictions on a test set (which only encapsulates steps 1 and 2), a BayesOpt workflow is what is typically called *active learning*. Active learning is a subfield in ML in which we get to decide which data points our model learns from, and that decision-making process is, in turn, informed by the model itself.

As we have said, the GP and the policy are the two main components of this BayesOpt procedure. If the GP does not model the objective well, then we will not be able to do a good job of informing the policy of the information contained in the training data. On the other hand, if the policy is not good at assigning high scores to "good" points and low scores to "bad" points (where *good* means helpful at locating the global optimum), then our subsequent decisions will be misguided and will most likely achieve bad results.

In other words, without a good predictive model, such as a GP, we won't be able to make good predictions with calibrated uncertainty. Without a policy, we can make good *predictions*, but we won't make good *decisions*.

An example we consider multiple times throughout this book is weather forecasting. Imagine a scenario in which you are trying to decide whether to bring an umbrella with you before leaving the house to go to work, and you look at the weather forecasting app on your phone.

Needless to say, the predictions made by the app need to be accurate and reliable so you can confidently base your decisions on them. An app that always predicts sunny weather just won't do. Further, you need a sensible way to make decisions based on these predictions. Never bringing an umbrella, regardless of how likely rainy weather is, is a bad decision-making policy and will get you in trouble when it does rain. On the other hand, always bringing an umbrella, even with a 100% chance of sunny weather, is also not a smart decision. You want to *adaptively* decide to bring your umbrella, based on the weather forecast.

Adaptively making decisions is what BayesOpt is all about, and to do it effectively, we need both a good predictive model and a good decision-making policy. Care needs to go into both components of the framework; this is why the two main parts of the book following this chapter cover modeling with GPs and decision-making with BayesOpt policies, respectively.

1.2.4   *BayesOpt in action*

At this point, you might be wondering whether all of this heavy machinery really works—or works better than some simple strategy like random sampling. To find out, let's take a look at a "demo" of BayesOpt on a simple function. This will also be a good way for us to move away from the abstract to the concrete and tease out what we are able to do in future chapters.

Let's say the black box objective function we are trying to optimize (specifically, in this case, maximize) is the one-dimensional function in figure 1.6, defined from −5 to 5. Again, this picture is only for our reference; in black box optimization, we, in fact, do not know the shape of the objective. We see the objective has a couple of local maxima around −5 (roughly, −2.4 and 1.5) but the global maximum is on the right at approximately 4.3. Let's also assume we are allowed to evaluate the objective function a maximum of 10 times.

Before we see how BayesOpt solves this optimization problem, let's look at two baseline strategies. The first is a random search, where we uniformly sample between −5 and 5; whatever points we end up with are the locations we will evaluate the objective

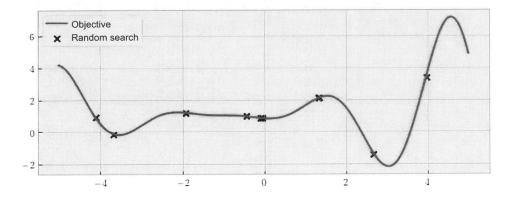

Figure 1.6 The objective function that is to be maximized, where random search wastes resources on unpromising regions

at. Figure 1.6 is the result of one such scheme. The point with the highest value found here is at roughly $x = 4$, having the value of $f(x) = 3.38$.

How random search works

Random search involves choosing points uniformly at random within the domain of our objective function. That is, the probability that we end up at a point within the domain is equal to the probability that we end up at any other point. Instead of uniform sampling, we can draw these random samples from a non-uniform distribution if we believe there are important regions in the search space we should give more focus to. However, this non-uniform strategy requires knowing which regions are important before starting the search.

Something you might find unsatisfactory about these randomly sampled points is that many of them happen to fall into the region around 0. Of course, it's only by chance that many random samples cluster around 0, and in another instance of the search, we might find many samples in another area. However, the possibility remains that we could waste valuable resources inspecting a small region of the function with many evaluations. Intuitively, it is more beneficial to spread out our evaluations so we learn more about the objective function.

This idea of *spreading out* evaluations leads us to the second baseline: grid search. Here, we divide our search space into evenly spaced segments and evaluate at the endpoints of those segments, as in figure 1.7.

The best point from this search is the very last point on the right at 5, evaluating at roughly 4.86. This is better than random search but is still missing the actual global optimum.

Now, we are ready to look at BayesOpt in action! BayesOpt starts off with a randomly sampled point, just like random search, shown in figure 1.8.

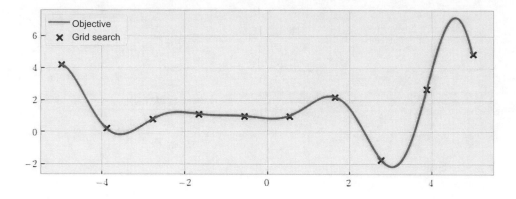

Figure 1.7   Grid search is still inefficient at narrowing down a good region.

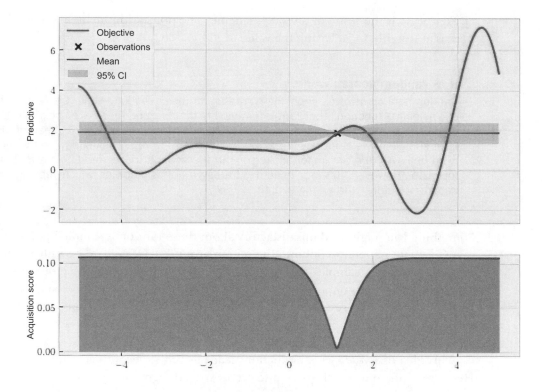

Figure 1.8   The start of BayesOpt is similar to random search.

The top panel of figure 1.8 represents the GP trained on the evaluated point, while the bottom panel shows the score computed by the Expected Improvement policy. Remember, this score tells us how much we should value each location in our search space, and we should pick the one that gives the highest score to evaluate next. Interestingly enough, our policy at this point tells us that almost the entire range between −5 and 5 we're searching within is promising (except for the region around 1, where we have made a query). This should make intuitive sense, as we have only seen one data point, and we don't yet know how the rest of the objective function looks in other areas. Our policy tells us we should explore more! Let's now look at the state of our model from this first query to the fourth query in figure 1.9.

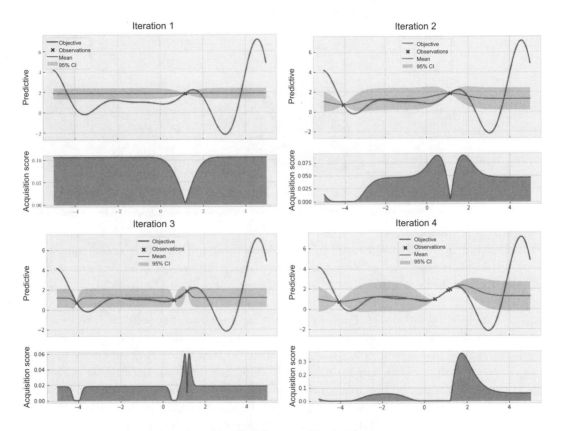

Figure 1.9 After four queries, we have identified the second-best optimum.

Three out of four queries are concentrating around the point 1, where there is a local optimum, and we also see that our policy is suggesting we query yet another point in this area next. At this point, you might be worried that we will get stuck in this locally optimal area and fail to break out to find the true optimum, but we will see that this is not the case. Let's fast-forward to the next two iterations in figure 1.10.

After having five queries to scope out this locally optimal region, our policy decides there are other, more promising regions to explore—namely, the one to the

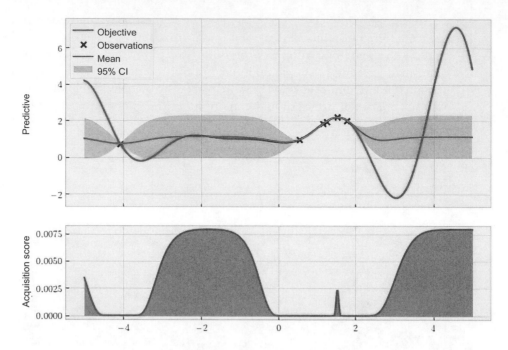

Figure 1.10   After exploring a local optimum sufficiently, we are encouraged to look at other areas.

left around –2 and the one to the right around 4. This is very reassuring, as it shows that once we have explored a region enough, BayesOpt does not get stuck in that region. Let's now see what happens after eight queries in figure 1.11.

Here, we have observed two more points on the right, which update both our GP model and our policy. Looking at the mean function (the solid line, representing the most likely prediction), we see that it almost matches the true objective function from 4 to 5. Further, our policy (the bottom curve) is now pointing very close to the global optimum and basically no other area. This is interesting because we have not thoroughly inspected the area on the left (we only have one observation to the left of 0), but our model believes that regardless of what the function looks like in that area, it is not worth investigating compared to the current region. This is, in fact, true in our case.

Finally, at the end of the search with 10 queries, our workflow is now visualized in figure 1.12. There is now little doubt that we have identified the global optimum around 4.3.

This example has clearly shown us that BayesOpt can work a lot better than random search and grid search. This should be a very encouraging sign for us considering that the latter two strategies are what many ML practitioners use when faced with a hyperparameter tuning problem.

For example, scikit-learn is one of the most popular ML libraries in Python, and it offers the `model_selection` module for various model selection tasks, including

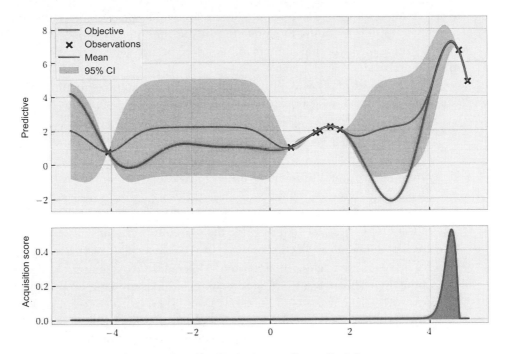

Figure 1.11   BayesOpt successfully ignores the large region on the left.

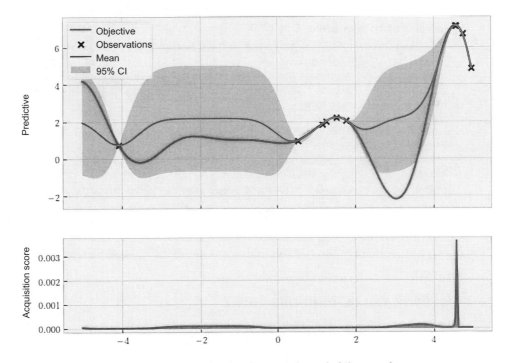

Figure 1.12   BayesOpt has found the global optimum at the end of the search.

hyperparameter tuning. However, random search and grid search are the only hyper-parameter tuning methods implemented in the module. In other words, if we are indeed tuning our hyperparameters with random or grid search, there is a lot of head-room to do better.

Overall, employing BayesOpt may result in a drastic improvement in optimization performance. We can take a quick look at a few real-world examples:

- A 2020 research paper entitled "Bayesian Optimization is Superior to Random Search for Machine Learning Hyperparameter Tuning" (https://arxiv.org/pdf/2104.10201.pdf), which was the result of a joint study by Facebook, Twitter, Intel, and others, found that BayesOpt was extremely successful across many hyperparameter tuning tasks.
- Frances Arnold, Nobel Prize winner in 2018 and professor at Caltech, uses BayesOpt in her research to guide the search for enzymes efficient at catalyzing desirable chemical reactions.
- A study entitled "Design of Efficient Molecular Organic Light-Emitting Diodes by a High-Throughput Virtual Screening and Experimental Approach" (https://www.nature.com/articles/nmat4717) published in *Nature* applied BayesOpt to the problem of screening for molecular organic light-emitting diodes (an important type of molecules) and observed a large improvement in efficiency.

And there are many more of these examples out there.

When not to use BayesOpt

It's also important to know when the problem setting isn't appropriate and when *not* to use BayesOpt. As we have said, BayesOpt is useful when our limited resources prevent us from evaluating the objective function many times. If this is not the case and evaluating the objective is cheap, we have no reason to be frugal with how we observe the objective function.

Here, if we can inspect the objective thoroughly across a dense grid, that will ensure the global optimum is located. Otherwise, other strategies, such as the DIRECT algorithm or evolutionary algorithms, which are algorithms that often excel at optimization when evaluations are cheap, may be used. Further, if information about the gradient of the objective is available, gradient-based algorithms will be better suited.

I hope this chapter was able to whet your appetite and get you excited for what's to come. In the next section, we summarize the key skills you will be learning throughout the book.

1.3   *What will you learn in this book?*

This book provides a deep understanding of the GP model and the BayesOpt task. You will learn how to implement a BayesOpt pipeline in Python using state-of-the-art tools and libraries. You will also be exposed to a wide range of modeling and optimization strategies when approaching a BayesOpt task. By the end of the book, you will be able to do the following:

- Implement high-performance GP models using GPyTorch, the premiere GP modeling tool in Python; visualize and evaluate their predictions; choose appropriate parameters for these models; and implement extensions, such as variational GPs and Bayesian neural networks, to scale to big data
- Implement a wide range of BayesOpt policies using the state-of-the-art BayesOpt library BoTorch, which integrates nicely with GPyTorch, and inspect as well as understand their decision-making strategies
- Approach different specialized settings, such as batch, constrained, and multi-objective optimization, using the BayesOpt framework
- Apply BayesOpt to a real-life task, such as tuning the hyperparameters of an ML model

Further, we use real-world examples and data in the exercises to consolidate what we learn in each chapter. Throughout the book, we run our algorithms on the same dataset in many different settings so we can compare and analyze the different approaches taken.

Summary

- Many problems in the real world may be cast as expensive black box optimization problems. In these problems, we only observe the function values without any additional information. Further, observing one function value is expensive, rendering many cost-blind optimization algorithms unusable.
- BayesOpt is an ML technique that solves this black box optimization problem by designing intelligent evaluations of the objective function so the optimum may be found as quickly as possible.
- In BayesOpt, a GP acts as a predictive model, predicting what the value of the objective function is at a given location. A GP produces not only a mean prediction but also a 95% CI, representing uncertainty via normal distributions.
- To optimize a black box function, a BayesOpt policy iteratively makes decisions about where to evaluate the objective function. The policy does this by quantifying how helpful each data point is in terms of optimization.
- A GP and a policy go hand in hand in BayesOpt. The former is needed to make good predictions, and the latter is needed to make good decisions.
- By making decisions in an adaptive manner, BayesOpt is better at optimization than random search or grid search, which are often used as the default strategies in black box optimization problems.
- BayesOpt has seen significant success in hyperparameter tuning in ML and other scientific applications, such as drug discovery.

Part 1

Modeling with Gaussian processes

The predictive model plays a crucial role in BayesOpt by guiding decision-making with accurate predictions. As we saw in section 1.2.1 and see again and again in this part, GPs offer calibrated quantification of uncertainty, which is a key component in any decision-making task and a feature that many ML models lack.

We begin with chapter 2, which explains the intuition behind a GP as a distribution over functions as well as a generalization of a multivariate normal distribution in infinite dimensions. We explore how via Bayes' theorem, a GP can be updated to reflect our belief about a function's value in light of new data.

Chapter 3 showcases the mathematical flexibility of GPs. This flexibility allows us, the users, to incorporate prior information into the predictions via the global trend and the variability of the GP's predictions. By combining different components of the GP, we gain the ability to mathematically model a wide range of functions.

Our discussions in this part are accompanied by code implementation, using the state-of-the-art Python GP library GPyTorch. As you go through this part's materials, you will gain hands-on experience designing and training GP models using GPyTorch.

2

Gaussian processes as distributions over functions

This chapter covers

- A crash course on multivariate Gaussian distributions and their properties
- Understanding GPs as multivariate Gaussian distributions in infinite dimensions
- Implementing GPs in Python

Having seen what BayesOpt can help us do, we are now ready to embark on our journey toward mastering BayesOpt. As we saw in chapter 1, a BayesOpt workflow consists of two main parts: a Gaussian process (GP) as a predictive, or surrogate, model and a policy for decision-making. With a GP, we don't obtain only point estimates as predictions for a test data point, but instead, we have an entire *probability distribution* representing our belief about the prediction.

With a GP, we produce similar predictions from similar data points. For example, in weather forecasting, when estimating today's temperature, a GP will look at the climatic data of days that are similar to today, either the last few days or this exact day a year ago. Days in another season wouldn't inform the GP when making this prediction. Similarly, when predicting the price of a house, a GP will say that similar houses in the same neighborhood as the prediction target are more informative than houses in another state.

How similar a data point is to another is encoded using the covariance function of a GP, which, in addition, models the uncertainty in the GP's predictions. Remember from chapter 1 our comparison of a ridge regression model and a GP, shown again in figure 2.1. Here, while the ridge regressor only produces single-valued predictions, the GP outputs a normal distribution at each test point. Uncertainty quantification is what sets the GP apart from other ML models, specifically in the context of decision-making under uncertainty.

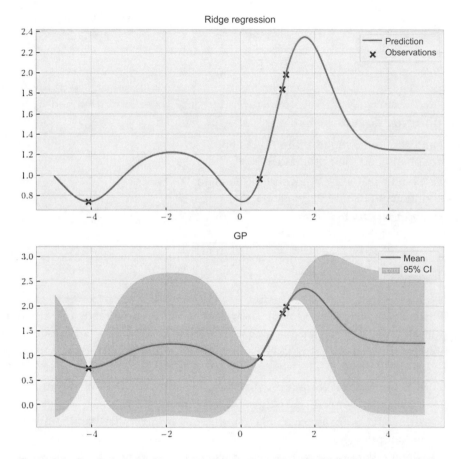

Figure 2.1   Predictions by ridge regression vs. those by a GP. While the mean prediction of the GP is the same as the prediction of ridge, the GP also offers CIs indicating the predictive level of uncertainty.

We will see how correlation modeling and uncertainty quantification are mathematically realized with Gaussian distributions and learn to actually implement a GP in GPyTorch, the premiere GP modeling tool in Python. Being able to model a function with a GP is the first step toward BayesOpt—a step we will take in this chapter.

Why GPyTorch?

There are other GP modeling libraries in Python, such as GPy or GPflow, but we have chosen GPyTorch for this book. Built on top of PyTorch and actively maintained, GPyTorch offers a streamlined workflow from array manipulation to GP modeling and, eventually, to BayesOpt with BoTorch, which we start using in chapter 4.

The library is also actively maintained and has many state-of-the-art methods implemented. For example, chapter 12 covers using GPyTorch to scale a GP to large datasets, and in chapter 13, we learn to integrate a neural network into a GP model.

2.1 How to sell your house the Bayesian way

Before we jump right into GPs, let's consider an example scenario in the domain of housing price modeling and how the price of a house is determined in relation to other houses. This discussion serves as an example of how correlation works in a multivariate Gaussian distribution, which is a central part of a GP.

Say you are a homeowner in Missouri who is looking to sell your house. You are trying to set an appropriate asking price and are talking to a friend about how to do this:

You: I'm not sure what to do. I just don't know exactly how much my house is worth.

Friend: Do you have a rough estimate?

You: Somewhere between 150k and 300k would be my guess.

Friend: That's a pretty big range.

You: Yeah, I wish I knew people who have sold their houses. I need some references.

Friend: I heard Alice sold her house for 250k.

You: Alix who's in California? That's really surprising! Also, I don't think a house in California will help me make a better estimate for my own house. It could still be anything between 150k and 300k.

Friend: No, it's Alice who lives right next to you.

You: Oh, I see. That's very useful actually, since her house is really similar to mine! Now, I would guess that my house will be valued at somewhere between 230k and 270k. Time to talk to my realtor!

Friend: Glad I could help.

In this conversation, you said that using your neighbor Alice's house as a reference is a good strategy for estimating your own price. This is because the two houses are similar in attributes and physically close to each other, so you expect them to sell for similar amounts. Alix's house, on the other hand, is in California and is entirely irrelevant to our house, so even if you know how much she sold her house for, you won't be able to gain any new information about what you're interested in: how much your own house is worth.

The calculation we just went through is a Bayesian update to our belief about the price of our house. You might be familiar with Bayes' theorem, which is shown in figure 2.2. For an excellent introduction to Bayes' theorem and Bayesian learning, check out chapter 8 of Luis Serrano's *Grokking Machine Learning* (Manning, 2021).

Bayes' theorem gives us a way of updating our belief about a quantity we're interested in, which, in this case, is the appropriate price for our house. When applying Bayes' theorem, we go from our prior belief, which is our first guess, to a posterior belief about the quantity in question. This posterior belief combines the prior belief and the likelihood of any data we observe.

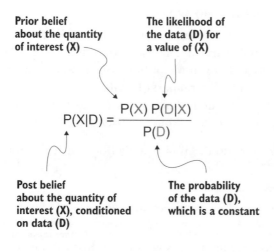

Figure 2.2   Bayes' theorem, which gives a method of updating a belief about a quantity of interest, represented as a probability distribution of a random variable. Before observing any data, we have the prior belief about X. After being updated with data, we obtain the posterior belief about X.

In our example, we start out with a prior belief that the price is between 150k and 300k. The range from 150k to 300k, like your friend remarked, is quite big, so there's not much information contained in this initial prior belief—anything between 150k and 300k is possible for this price. Now, an interesting thing happens when we *update* this range to a posterior belief, considering new information about either of the two houses' price.

First, assuming that Alix's house in California is valued at 250k, our posterior belief about our own house remains unchanged: from 150k to 300k. Again, this is because Alix's house is not relevant to ours, and the price of her house doesn't inform us about the quantity we're interested in.

Second, if the new information is that Alice's house, which is right next to our own, is valued at 250k, then our posterior belief significantly changes from the prior: to the 230k–270k range. Having Alice's house as a reference, we have updated our belief to be around the observed value, 250k, while narrowing down the range of our belief (going from a 150k difference to a 40k difference). This is a very reasonable thing to do, as the price of Alice's house is very informative with respect to the price of our house. Figure 2.3 visualizes this entire process.

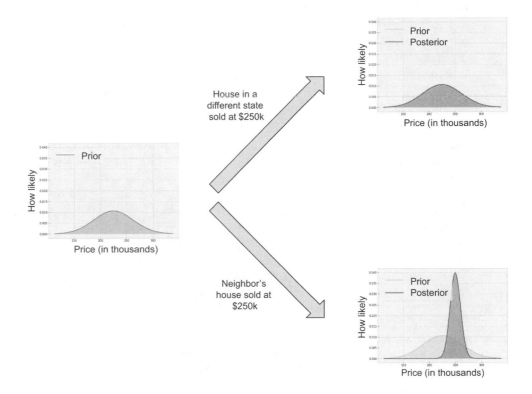

Figure 2.3   **Updating the belief about the price of our house in a Bayesian way. Depending on how similar the house whose price was observed is to our house, the posterior belief either stays the same or is drastically updated.**

Note that the numbers in the example are not exact and are only used so that the example makes intuitive sense. However, we will see that by using a multivariate Gaussian distribution to model our belief, we can realize this intuitive update procedure in a quantifiable way. Further, with such a Gaussian distribution, we can determine whether a variable (someone's house) is similar enough to the variable we're interested in (our own house) to influence our posterior belief and to what extent.

2.2   *Modeling correlations with multivariate Gaussian distributions and Bayesian updates*

In this section, we learn about multivariate Gaussian distributions (or multivariate Gaussians—or simply Gaussians) and see how they facilitate the update rule we saw previously. This serves as the basis for our subsequent discussion on GPs.

2.2.1 *Using multivariate Gaussian distributions to jointly model multiple variables*

Here, we first cover what multivariate Gaussians are and what they can model. We will see that with a covariance matrix, a multivariate Gaussian (MVN) describes not only the behavior of the individual random variables but also the correlation of these variables.

First, let's consider normal distributions—aka the bell curve. Normal distributions are highly common in the real world and are used to model a wide range of quantities; examples include height, IQ, income, and weight at birth.

An MVN distribution is what we would use when we want to model more than one quantity. To do this, we aggregate these quantities into a vector of random variables, and this vector is then said to follow an MVN distribution. This aggregation is depicted in figure 2.4.

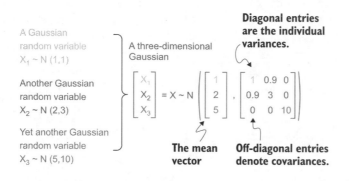

Figure 2.4   An MVN distribution groups multiple normally distributed random variables together. While the mean vector of the MVN concatenates the mean values, the covariance matrix models the correlations between the individual variables.

> **DEFINITION**   Consider a random vector $X = [X_1 X_2 \dots X_n]$ that follows a Gaussian distribution denoted by $N(\mu, \Sigma)$, where μ is a vector of length n and Σ is an n-by-n matrix. Here, μ is called the mean vector, whose individual elements denote the expected values of corresponding random variables in X, and Σ is the covariance matrix, which describes the variance of individual variables as well as correlations between variables.

Let's take a moment to parse the definition of an MVN distribution:

- First, due to the convenient properties of an MVN, each random variable in the vector X follows a normal distribution. Specifically, the i-th variable X_i has the mean value of μ_i, which is the i-th element of the mean vector μ of the MVN.
- Further, the variance of X_i is the i-th *diagonal* entry of the covariance matrix Σ.

- If we have a vector of random variables following an MVN, then each individual variable corresponds to a known normal distribution.

If the diagonal entries in the covariance matrix Σ are the variances of the individual variables, what about the off-diagonal entries? The entry in the i-th row and j-th column of this matrix denotes the covariance between X_i and X_j, which is related to the correlation between the two random variables. Assuming the correlation is positive, the following is true:

- If this correlation is high, then the two random variables X_i and X_j are said to be correlated. This means that if the value of one increases, the value of the other also tends to increase, and if the value of one decreases, the value of the other will decrease. Your neighbor Alice's house and your own are examples of correlated variables.
- On the other hand, if this correlation is low and close to zero, then no matter what the value of X_i is, what we know about the value of X_j most likely does not change much. This is because there is no correlation between the two variables. Alix's house in California and our house fall into this category.

Negative correlations

The previous description is for positive correlations. A correlation can also be negative, indicating that the variables move in opposite directions: if one variable increases, the other will decrease, and vice versa. Positive correlations illustrate the important concepts we aim to learn here, so we won't worry about the negative correlation case.

To make our discussion more concrete, let's define an MVN distribution that jointly models three random variables: the price of our house, A; the price of our neighbor Alice's house, B; and the price of Alix's house in California, C. This three-dimensional Gaussian also has a covariance matrix described in figure 2.4.

NOTE It's usually convenient to assume that the mean vector of this Gaussian is normalized to be the zero vector. This normalization is usually done, in practice, to simplify a lot of mathematical details.

Once again, the diagonal cells tell us the variances of individual random variables. B has a slightly larger variance (3) than A (1), meaning we are more uncertain about the value of B because we don't know everything about our neighbor's house, so a more accurate estimate cannot be done. The third variable, C, on the other hand, has the largest variance to denote the fact that houses in California have an overall wider price range.

NOTE   The values being used here (1, 3, 10) are example values to make the point that the larger a variance of a random variable, the more uncertain we are about the value of the variable (before learning what its value is).

Further, the covariance between our house, A, and our neighbor's, B, is 0.9, which indicates the prices of the two houses are correlated in a non-negligible way. This makes sense because if we know the price of our neighbor's house, we will be able to obtain a better estimate for our own house that is on the same street. Also notice that neither A nor B has any correlation with the price of the house in California, since location-wise, C has nothing in common with A or B. Another way to say this is that even if we know how much the house in California costs, we won't learn anything about the price of our own house. Let's now visualize this three-dimensional Gaussian using a parallel coordinates plot in figure 2.5.

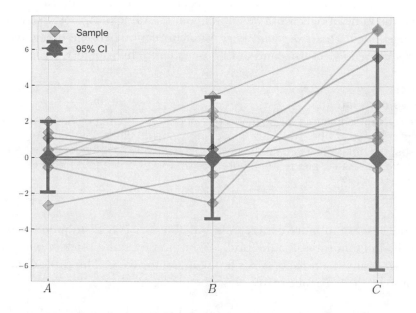

Figure 2.5   Parallel coordinates plot visualizing a mean-normalized MVN from the housing price example. The error bars indicate 95% CIs of corresponding normal distributions, while the faded lines show samples drawn from the multivariate Gaussian.

Note the bold diamonds and corresponding error bars in the figure:

- The bold diamonds represent the mean vector of our Gaussian, which is simply the zero vector.
- The error bars denote the 95% credible intervals (CIs) of the three individual variables. Going from A to B to C, we observe larger and larger CIs, corresponding to the increasing values of the respective variances.

Credible intervals

A $(1 - \alpha)$ CI of a normal distribution of a random variable x is a range in which the probability that x falls inside this range is exactly $(1 - \alpha)$. Statisticians typically use 95% CIs for normal distributions. There is nothing really special about the number 95% here, except for the fact that 95% is the threshold many statistical procedures use to determine whether something is meaningful or not. For example, a t test typically uses a confidence level of $1 - \alpha = 0.95$, corresponding to the fact that a p-value less than $\alpha = 0.05$ indicates significant results. A convenient fact about normal distributions is that $\mu \pm 1.96\sigma$ is a 95% CI (some even use $\mu \pm 2\sigma$), where μ and σ are the mean and standard deviation of the variable x, which is an easy-to-compute quantity.

Figure 2.5 represents our *prior belief* about the normalized prices of the three houses. Starting from this prior, we guess that all three have a normalized price of zero, and we have varying levels of uncertainty regarding our guesses. Further, as we are working with a random distribution, we could draw samples from this MVN. These samples are shown as connected faded diamonds.

2.2.2   Updating MVN distributions

With an MVN distribution in hand, we will see how we can update this distribution given some data we observe in this subsection. Specifically, following our example at the beginning of the chapter, we'd like to derive the *posterior belief* about these prices upon observing the value of either B or C. This is an important task as it is how an MVN, as well as a GP, learns from data.

> **DEFINITION**   This update process is sometimes called *conditioning*: deriving the *conditional distribution* of a variable, given that we know the value of some other variable. More specifically, we are conditioning our belief—which is a joint trivariate Gaussian—on the value of either B or C, obtaining the joint posterior distribution for these three variables.

Here, using the Bayes' theorem in figure 2.2, we can derive this posterior distribution in closed form. However, the derivation is rather math-heavy, so we won't go into it here. We just need to know that we have a formula in which we can plug the value of B or C that we'd like to condition on, and the formula will tell us what the posterior distributions of A, B, and C are. Surprisingly, the posterior distribution of a Gaussian is conditioned on data that is also Gaussian, and we can obtain the exact posterior means and variances that specify the posterior Gaussians. (Later in the chapter, we see that when we implement a GP in Python, GPyTorch takes care of this math-heavy update for us.)

NOTE   For the interested reader, this formula and its derivation can be found in chapter 2, section 2 of the book *Gaussian Processes for Machine Learning* by Carl Edward Rasmussen and Christopher K. I. Williams (MIT Press, 2006), which is often considered the bible of GPs.

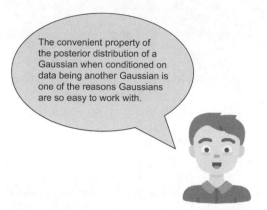

Let's now regenerate the parallel coordinates plot, conditioning the MVN on B = 4 as an example value for B. The result is shown in figure 2.6.

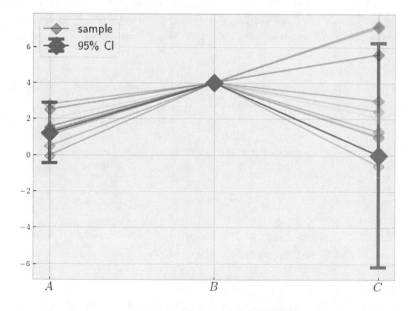

Figure 2.6   Parallel coordinates plot visualizing the MVN from figure 2.5, conditioned on B = 4. Here, the distribution of A is updated, and all drawn samples interpolate B = 4.

Upon updating our belief with an observation about B, a few things have changed in our posterior belief:

- The distribution of A changes, taking on a slightly larger mean value due to the positive correlation between A and B. Further, its error bars now have a smaller range.
- The posterior distribution of B simply becomes a special normal distribution with zero variance since we know for sure what its value is in the posterior. In other words, there is no uncertainty about the value of B anymore.
- Meanwhile, the distribution of C stays the same after the update as it has no correlation with B.

All of this makes sense and corresponds with our intuition from the housing price example. Specifically, when we find out about our neighbor's house, the belief about our own house is updated to be similar to the observed price, and our uncertainty also decreases.

What happens when we condition on C? As you might have guessed, for the same reason that C stays the same after conditioning on a value of B, both the posterior distribution of A and that of B remain unchanged when we condition on C. Figure 2.7 shows this for C = 4.

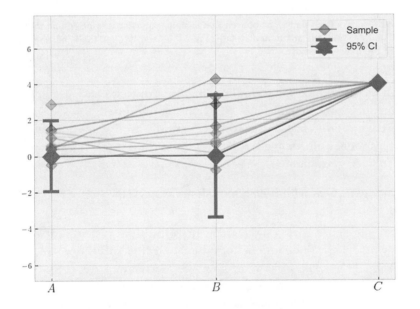

Figure 2.7 Parallel coordinates plot visualizing the MVN from figure 2.5, conditioned on C = 4. Here, no other marginal distribution changes. All drawn samples interpolate C = 4.

This is when we find out that a house in California was sold. As this house has nothing to do with our own house in Missouri, the belief about the price of our house stays the same.

There is another interesting thing about figures 2.6 and 2.7. Notice that when we condition on B = 2 in figure 2.6, all the samples we draw of the posterior MVN pass through the point (B, 2). This is because in our posterior belief, we don't have any uncertainty about what value B takes anymore, and any sample drawn from the posterior distribution needs to satisfy the constraints from this condition. The same thing goes for the point (C, 2) in figure 2.7.

Visually, you could think of this as meaning that when we condition on a variable, we "tie" the samples drawn from the prior distribution (in figure 2.5) into a knot at the same point corresponding to the variable we condition on, as shown in figure 2.8.

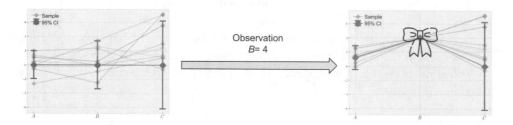

Figure 2.8   Conditioning a Gaussian on an observation is similar to tying a knot around that observation. All samples from the posterior distribution need to pass through the knot, and there's no uncertainty at the observed point.

Finally, we can picture the Bayesian conditioning procedure we have just gone through with a diagram analogous to figure 2.3. This is shown in figure 2.9.

Again, if we condition our Gaussian on C, the posterior distributions of the uncorrelated variables remain unchanged. If we condition on B, however, the variable that is correlated to it, A, gets updated.

2.2.3   *Modeling many variables with high-dimensional Gaussian distributions*

An MVN distribution need not only contain three random variables; it can, in fact, simultaneously model any finite number of variables. In this subsection, we learn that a higher-dimensional Gaussian works in the same way as what we have seen so far. So, let's say that instead of a 3-dimensional Gaussian representing three houses, we have a 20-dimensional Gaussian encoding information about an array of houses on a street. An even higher-dimensional Gaussian would model houses in a city or country.

Further, with these parallel coordinates plots, we can visualize all individual variables of a high-dimensional Gaussian at the same time. This is because each variable corresponds to a single error bar, occupying only one slot on the *x*-axis.

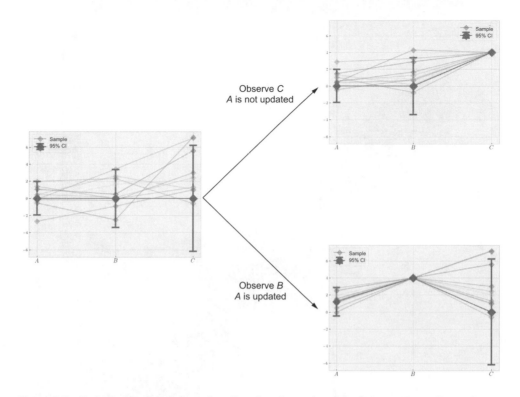

Figure 2.9   Updating the belief about the price of our house in a Bayesian way. Depending on how similar the house whose price was observed in relation to our house is, the posterior belief either stays the same or is drastically updated.

We once again normalize its mean vector to be the zero vector, and while it's not convenient to show its 20-by-20 covariance matrix, we could plot a heat map visualizing this matrix, as in figure 2.10.

The diagonal entries, or the variance of individual variables, are all 1s, in this case. Further, variables are ordered so that those that are close to each other are correlated; that is, their covariance takes a larger value. Variables that are far away from each other are, on the other hand, less correlated, and their covariances are close to zero. For example, any pair of consecutive variables in this Gaussian (the first and the second, the second and the third, etc.) have a covariance of roughly 0.87. That is, any two houses that are next to each other have a covariance of 0.87. If we consider the 1st and the 20th variable—that is, the house at one end of the street and the house at the other end—their covariance is effectively zero.

This is very intuitive as we expect houses that are close by to have similar prices, so once we know the price of a house, we gain more information about the prices of those that are around that area than about the prices of those that are far away.

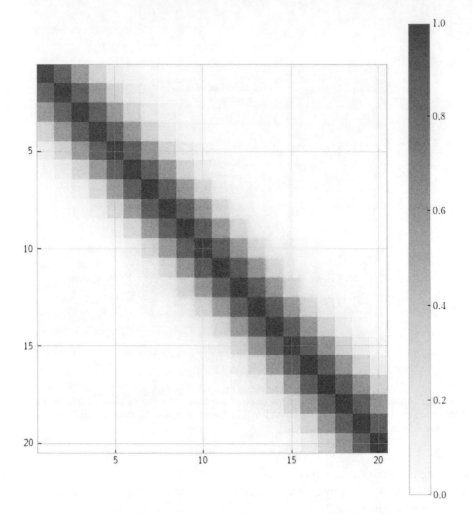

Figure 2.10   Heat map showing the covariance matrix of a 20-dimensional Gaussian distribution. Neighboring variables are more correlated than those that are far away, as indicated by a darker shade.

How does this play out in a parallel coordinates plot? Figure 2.11 shows our prior Gaussian on the left and the posterior Gaussian conditioned on the 10th variable having a value of 2 on the right. Basically, we are simulating the event in which we find out that the price of the 10th house is 2 (whose exact unit is omitted):

- First, we once again see this phenomenon in which the error bars and samples are tied into a knot around the observation we condition on in the posterior distribution.
- Second, due to the correlation structure imposed by the covariance matrix, variables close to the 10th have their mean values "dragged up" so that the mean vector now smoothly interpolates the point (10, 2). This means we have

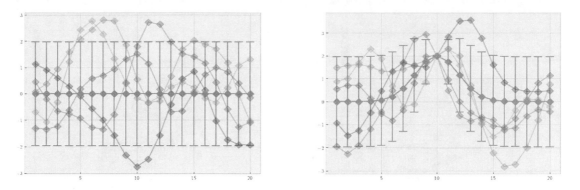

Figure 2.11 Error bars and samples drawn from a prior (left) and a posterior (right) Gaussian distribution, conditioned on the 10th variable having a value of 2. Uncertainty in variables close to the 10th reduces in the posterior, and their mean values are updated to be close to 2.

updated our belief, as the surrounding houses now have their prices increased to reflect the information we have learned.

- Finally, the uncertainty (denoted by the error bars) around this point (10, 2) decreases after the conditioning. This is a very good property to have, as intuitively, if we know the value of a variable, we should become more certain about the values of other variables correlated with the variable we know. That is, if we know the price of a house, we become more certain about the prices of nearby houses. This property is the basis of the calibrated quantification of uncertainty that GPs offer, which we see in the next section of this chapter.

2.3 Going from a finite to an infinite Gaussian

We are now ready to discuss what a GP is. In the same manner as when we have three variables, A, B, and C, or 20, as in the previous section, let's say we now have an infinite number of variables, all belonging to an MVN. This *infinite-dimensional* Gaussian is called a *Gaussian process*.

Imagine predicting housing prices across a very large, densely populated area. The scale of the entire area is so large that if we move away from a house by a very small amount, we will arrive at a different house. Given the high density of the variables (houses) in this Gaussian, we can treat this whole area as having infinitely many houses; that is, the Gaussian distribution has infinitely many variables.

This is illustrated in figure 2.12 using a dataset containing 5,000 house prices in California. In the top-left panel, we show the individual data points in a scatter plot. In the remaining panels, we model the data using various numbers of variables, where each variable corresponds to a region inside the map of California. As the number of variables increases, our model becomes more fine-grained. When this number is infinite—that is, when we can make a prediction in any region on this map, however small—our model exists in an infinite-dimensional space.

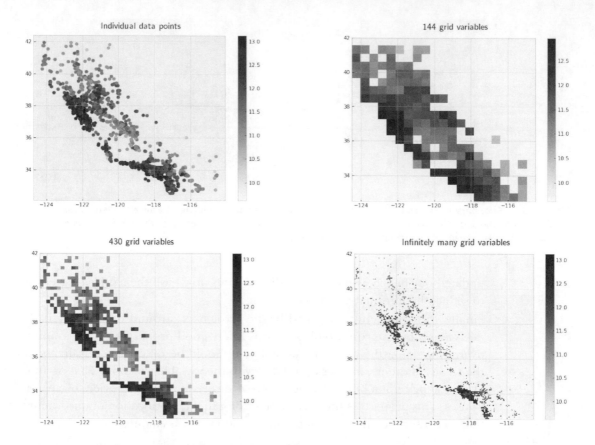

Figure 2.12   Modeling housing prices in California using different numbers of variables. The more variables we have, the smoother our model becomes and the closer we approach an infinite-dimensional model.

This is exactly what a Gaussian process is: a Gaussian distribution in an infinite-dimensional space. The ability to make a prediction in any region helps us move away from a finite-dimensional MVN and obtain an ML model. Strictly speaking, the concept of a Gaussian distribution doesn't apply when there are infinitely many variables, so the technical definition is the following.

> **DEFINITION**   A Gaussian process is a collection of random variables such that the joint distribution of every finite subset of those variables is an MVN.

This definition means that if we have a GP model to describe a function f, then the function values at *any* set of points are modeled by an MVN distribution. For example, the vector of variables $[f(1)\ f(2)\ f(3)]$ follows a three-dimensional Gaussian; $[f(1)\ f(0)\ f(10)\ f(5)\ f(3)]$ follows a different, five-dimensional Gaussian; and $[f(0.1)\ f(0.2)\ ...\ f(9.9)\ f(10)]$ follows yet another Gaussian.

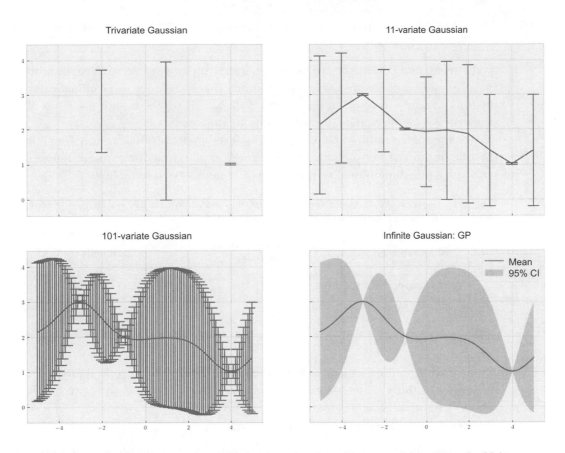

Figure 2.13   Parallel coordinates plots of different Gaussian distributions. Any finite subset of a GP is an MVN. As the number of variables approaches infinity, we obtain a GP and can make predictions everywhere in the domain.

This is illustrated in figure 2.13. The first three panels show, in parallel coordinates plots, a trivariate Gaussian for $[f(-2)\ f(1)\ f(4)]$, an 11-variate Gaussian for $[f(-4.5)\ f(-4)\ \ldots\ f(4)\ f(4.5)]$, and a 101-variate Gaussian across a denser grid. Finally, in the last panel, we have infinitely many variables, which gives us a GP.

Since we are now in infinite dimensions, it doesn't make sense to talk about the mean vector and covariance matrix anymore. Instead, what we have with a GP is a mean *function* and a covariance *function*, but the respective roles of these two objects are still the same as with an MVN:

- First, the mean function, which takes in one input, x, computes the expectation of the function value $f(x)$.
- Second, the covariance function takes in two inputs, x_1 and x_2, and computes the covariance between the two variables, $f(x_1)$ and $f(x_2)$. If x_1 is the same as x_1, then this covariance value is simply the variance of the normal distribution of

$f(x)$. If x_1 is different from x_2, the covariance denotes the correlation between the two variables.

As the mean and covariance are functions, we are no longer tied to a fixed number of variables—instead, we effectively have infinitely many variables and can make our predictions *anywhere*, as illustrated in figure 2.13. This is why although a GP has all the properties of an MVN, the GP exists in infinite dimensions.

For the same reason, a GP can be considered as a distribution over functions, as the title of this chapter suggests. The progression we have gone through in this chapter, from a one-dimensional normal to a GP, is summarized in table 2.1.

Table 2.1 Gaussian distribution objects and what they model. With a GP, we operate under infinite dimensions, modeling functions instead of numbers or vectors.

Distribution type	Number of modeled variables	Description
A one-dimensional normal distribution	One	A distribution over numbers
An MVN distribution	Finitely many	A distribution over vectors of finite length
A GP	Infinitely many	A distribution over functions

To see a GP in action, let's reexamine the curve-fitting procedure in figure 2.1 at the beginning of this chapter, where we limit our domain to between −5 and 5. This is shown in figure 2.14.

In each of the panels, the following is true:

- The solid line in the middle is the mean function, which is analogous to the solid line connecting the diamonds in figure 2.11.
- The shaded region, on the other hand, is the 95% CI across the domain, corresponding to the error bars in figure 2.11.
- The various wiggly lines are samples drawn from the corresponding GP.

Before observing any data, we start out with the *prior GP* in the top-left panel. Just like a prior MVN, our prior GP produces constant mean prediction and uncertainty in the absence of training data. This is a reasonable behavior to have.

The interesting part comes when we condition our GP on various data points. This is visualized in the remaining panels of figure 2.14. Exactly like the discrete case of an MVN, with a GP working in a continuous domain, the mean prediction as well as samples drawn from the posterior distribution smoothly interpolate data points in the training set, while our uncertainty about the function value, quantified by the CI, smoothly decreases in the areas around these observations. This is what we call a *calibrated quantification of uncertainty*, which is one of the biggest selling points of a GP.

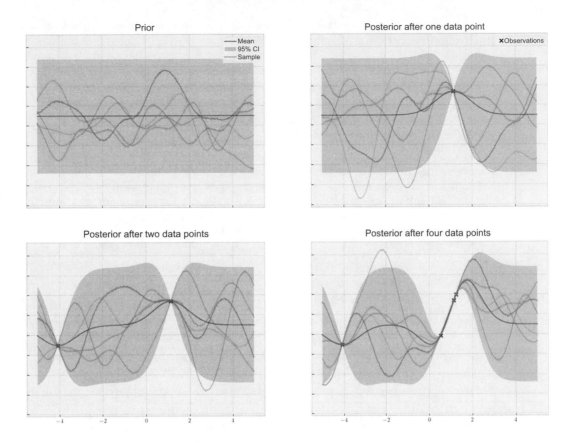

Figure 2.14   Predictions made by a GP conditioned on zero, one, two, and four observations

Smoothness of a GP

The *smoothness* property refers to the constraint that requires similar points to be correlated with each other. In other words, points that are similar should result in similar function values. This is, again, why when we condition on the data point at 3 in the top-right panel, the mean predictions at 2.9 and 3.1 are updated to take on larger values than their prior means. These points, 2.9 and 3.1, are similar to 3 because they are close to each other. This smoothness is set using the covariance function of the GP, which is the topic of chapter 3. While the examples we have seen so far are in one dimension, this smoothness is preserved when our search space is higher-dimensional, as we see later.

Overall, we have seen that a GP is an MVN, distribution when extended to infinite dimensions, and thanks to many convenient mathematical properties of Gaussian distributions, a GP not only produces a mean prediction but also quantifies our uncertainty about the function values in a principled way via its predictive covariances.

The mean prediction goes exactly through the training data points, and the uncertainty collapses at these data points.

> **Modeling non-Gaussian data**
>
> In real life, not all data follows Gaussian distributions. For example, for values that are limited within a numerical range or variables that don't follow bell-shaped distributions, Gaussian distributions are inappropriate and might lead to low-quality predictions.
>
> In these cases, we can apply various data processing techniques to "convert" our data points to follow Gaussian distribution. For example, the Box–Muller transform is an algorithm that generates pairs of normally distributed random numbers from uniformly distributed random numbers. The interested reader can find more details about this algorithm on Wolfram's MathWorld (https://mathworld.wolfram.com/Box -MullerTransformation.html).

2.4   *Implementing GPs in Python*

In this final section of the chapter, we take our first step toward implementing GPs in Python. Our goal is to become familiar with the syntax and API of the libraries we will be using for this task and learn how to recreate the visualizations we have seen thus far. This hands-on section will also help us understand GPs more deeply.

First, make sure you have downloaded the accompanying code for the book and installed the necessary libraries. Detailed instructions on how to do this are included in the front matter. We use the code included in the Jupyter notebook CH02/01 - Gaussian processes.ipynb.

2.4.1   *Setting up the training data*

Before we start implementing the code for our GP model, let's first spend some time creating an objective function we'd like to model and a training dataset. To do this, we need to import PyTorch for calculating and manipulating tensors and Matplotlib for data visualization:

```
import torch
import matplotlib.pyplot as plt
```

Our objective function in this example is the one-dimensional Forrester function. The Forrester function is multimodal with one global maximum and one local maximum (https://www.sfu.ca/~ssurjano/forretal08.html), making fitting and finding the maximum of the function a nontrivial task. The function has the following formula:

$$f(x) = -\frac{1}{5}(x + 1)^2 \sin(2x + 2) + 1$$

This is implemented as follows:

```
def forrester_1d(x):
    y = -((x + 1) ** 2) * torch.sin(2 * x + 2) / 5 + 1
    return y.squeeze(-1)
```

Let us quickly plot this function in a graph. Here, we restrict ourselves to the domain between −3 and 3 and compute this Forrester function on a dense grid of 100 points in this range. We also need some sample points for training, which we generate by randomly sampling with `torch.rand()` and store in `train_x`; `train_y` contains the labels of these training points, which can be obtained by evaluating `forrester_1d(train_x)`. This plot is generated by the following code, which produces figure 2.15:

```
xs = torch.linspace(-3, 3, 101).unsqueeze(1)
ys = forrester_1d(xs)

torch.manual_seed(0)
train_x = torch.rand(size=(3, 1)) * 6 - 3
train_y = forrester_1d(train_x)

plt.figure(figsize=(8, 6))

plt.plot(xs, ys, label="objective", c="r")
plt.scatter(train_x, train_y, marker="x", c="k", label="observations")

plt.legend(fontsize=15);
```

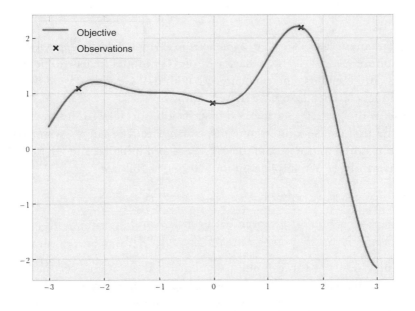

Figure 2.15 **The objective function that is used in the current example, as shown by the solid line. The markers indicate points in the training dataset.**

The three markers we see are points that we randomly select to include in our training dataset. The locations of these training data points are stored in `train_x`, and their labels (the values of the Forrester function at these locations) are stored in `train_y`. This sets up our regression task: implementing and training a GP on these three data points and visualizing its predictions on the range between –3 and 3. Here, we have also created `xs`, which is a dense grid over this range.

2.4.2 *Implementing a GP class*

In this subsection, we learn how to implement a GP model in Python. We use the GPy-Torch library, a state-of-the-art tool for modern GP modeling.

> **IMPORTANT**   The design philosophy of GPyTorch is to follow the DL library PyTorch and have all of its model classes extend a base model class. If you are familiar with implementing neural networks in PyTorch, you might know that this base is `torch.nn.Module`. With GPyTorch, we typically extend the `gpy-torch.models.ExactGP` class.

To implement our model class, we use the following structure:

```
import gpytorch


class BaseGPModel(gpytorch.models.ExactGP):
    def __init__(self, train_x, train_y, likelihood):
        ...

    def forward(self, x):
        ...
```

Here, we implement a class called `BaseGPModel`, which has two specific methods: `__init__()` and `forward()`. The behavior of our GP model heavily depends on how we write these two methods, and no matter what kind of GP model we'd like to implement, our model class needs to have these methods.

Let's discuss the `__init__()` method first. Its job is to take in the training dataset defined by the first and second arguments, `train_x` and `train_y`, as well as a likelihood function, stored in the variable `likelihood`, and initialize the GP model, which is a `BaseGPModel` object. We implement the method as follows:

```
def __init__(self, train_x, train_y, likelihood):
        super().__init__(train_x, train_y, likelihood)
        self.mean_module = gpytorch.means.ZeroMean()
        self.covar_module = gpytorch.kernels.RBFKernel()
```

Here, we simply pass the three input arguments to the `__init__()` method of our super class, and the built-in implementation of `gpytorch.models.ExactGP` takes care of the heavy lifting for us. What remains is the definition of the mean and the covariance functions, which, as we have said, are the two main components of a GP.

In GPyTorch, there is a wide range of choices for both the mean and the covariance function, which we explore in chapter 3. For now, we use the most common options for a GP:

- `gpytorch.means.ZeroMean()` for the mean function, which outputs zero mean predictions in prior mode
- `gpytorch.kernels.RBFKernel()` for the covariance functions, which implements the *radial basis function* (RBF) kernel—one of the most commonly used covariance function for GPs, which implements the idea that data points close to each other are correlated to each other

We store these objects in the `mean_module` and `covar_module` class attributes, respectively. That's all we need to do for the `__init__()` method. Now, let's turn our attention to the `forward()` method.

The `forward()` method is very important as it defines how the model should process its input. If you have worked with neural networks in PyTorch, you know that the `forward()` method of a network class sequentially passes its input through the layers of the network, and the output of the final layer is what the neural network produces. In PyTorch, each layer is implemented as a *module*, which is a term to denote the basic building block of any object in PyTorch that processes data.

The `forward()` method of a GP in GPyTorch works in a similar way: the GP's mean and covariance functions are implemented as modules, and the input of the method is passed to these modules. Instead of sequentially passing the result through different modules, we pass the input to the mean and the covariance functions simultaneously. The output of these modules is then combined to create an MVN distribution. This difference between PyTorch and GPyTorch is illustrated in figure 2.16.

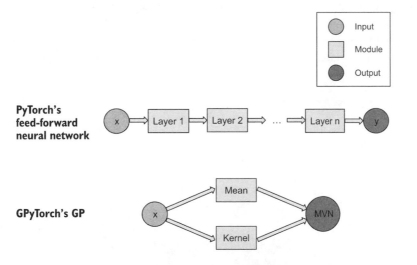

Figure 2.16 **How PyTorch and GPyTorch process data in their respective `forward()` methods. The input is processed by different modules to produce the final output, either a number for a feed-forward neural network or an MVN distribution for a GP.**

The `forward()` method is implemented in the following code:

```
def forward(self, x):
        mean_x = self.mean_module(x)
        covar_x = self.covar_module(x)
        return gpytorch.distributions.MultivariateNormal(mean_x, covar_x)
```

The logic here is pretty straightforward: As we have a mean function and a covariance function, we simply call them on the input x to compute the mean and covariance predictions. Finally, what we need to return is an MVN distribution, implemented by the `gpytorch.distributions.MultivariateNormal` class, with corresponding mean and covariance. In other words, we are doing nothing more than creating an MVN distribution with a mean vector and a covariance matrix computed from the `mean_module` and `covar_module` attributes of our model class.

And that is all there is to it! It's quite surprising how easy it is to implement a GP model with GPyTorch. The biggest takeaway for us is that we need to implement a mean and covariance function in the `__init__()` method. In the `forward()` method, when we need to make a prediction, we simply call these two functions on the input passed in.

2.4.3 *Making predictions with a GP*

With the `BaseGPModel` class in hand, we are ready to make predictions with a GP! Recall that in the `__init__()` method, we need to pass in a likelihood function, `likelihood`, in addition to our training data. In many regression tasks, a `gpytorch.likelihoods.GaussianLikelihood` object suffices. We create this object like so:

```
likelihood = gpytorch.likelihoods.GaussianLikelihood()
```

Now, we can initialize our `BaseGPModel` object. But before we initialize it with our three-entry training data, we would like to first make predictions with the prior GP.

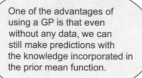

One of the advantages of using a GP is that even without any data, we can still make predictions with the knowledge incorporated in the prior mean function.

To initialize a GP object without any training data, we pass `None` as both the training features (`train_x`) and labels (`train_y`). So our prior GP is created as follows:

```
model = BaseGPModel(None, None, likelihood)
```

Finally, some bookkeeping is necessary before we can make any predictions. First, we set the hyperparameters of the GP:

```
lengthscale = 1
noise = 1e-4

model.covar_module.lengthscale = lengthscale
model.likelihood.noise = noise

model.eval()
likelihood.eval()
```

We discuss what each of these hyperparameters controls in chapter 3. For now, we just use the values that I personally like to use as the default: 1 for the length scale and 0.0001 for the noise variance. The very last detail is to enable prediction mode in both the GP model and its likelihood by calling the `eval()` method from the corresponding objects.

With these bookkeeping tasks out of the way, we can now finally call this GP model on our test data to make predictions. We do this like so:

```
with torch.no_grad():
    predictive_distribution = likelihood(model(xs))
```

Remember, in the `forward()` method of the model class, we return the MVN distribution, so that is the output when we pass some test data through our model using `model(xs)`. (In the syntax of PyTorch, calling `model(xs)` is a shorthand for calling the `forward()` method on the test data `xs`.) We also pass that same output through the likelihood function `likelihood`, which incorporates the noise variance into our predictions. In short, what we store in `predictive_distribution` is an MVN distribution that represents our prediction for the test points `xs`. Moreover, we compute this object within a `torch.no_grad()` context, which is good practice when we don't want PyTorch to keep track of the gradients of these computations.

> **NOTE**   We only want to compute the gradients of operations when we'd like to optimize some parameters of our model using gradient descent. But when we want to make predictions, we should keep our model completely fixed, so disabling gradient checking is appropriate.

2.4.4   *Visualizing predictions of a GP*

With this predictive Gaussian distribution in hand, we can now recreate the GP plots we have seen so far. Each of these plots consists of a mean function, μ, which we could obtain from the MVN with

```
predictive_mean = predictive_distribution.mean
```

Additionally, we want to show the 95% CI. Mathematically, this can be done by extracting the diagonal elements of the predictive covariance matrix, Σ (remember that these elements denote the individual variances σ^2), taking the square roots of these values to compute the standard deviations, σ, and computing the CI range of $\mu \pm 1.96\sigma$.

Fortunately for us, computing the 95% CI is a common operation when working with a GP, so GPyTorch offers a convenient helper method called `confidence_region()` that we may call directly from an MVN distribution object:

```
predictive_lower, predictive_upper =
        predictive_distribution.confidence_region()
```

This method returns a tuple of two Torch tensors, which store the lower and upper endpoints of the CI, respectively.

Finally, we may want samples drawn for our plot from our current GP model. We can do this directly by calling the method `sample()` from the Gaussian object `predictive_distribution`. If we don't pass in any input argument, the method will return a single sample. Here, we want to sample from our GP five times, which is done as follows:

```
torch.manual_seed(0)
    samples = predictive_distribution.sample(torch.Size([5]))
```

We pass in a `torch.Size()` object to denote that we want five samples to be returned. Setting the random seed before sampling is a good practice to ensure reproducibility of our code. And with that, we are ready to make some plots!

The first thing to do is simply plot the mean function:

```
plt.plot(xs, predictive_mean.detach(), label="mean")
```

As for the 95% CI, we typically use a shaded region like what we have seen so far, which can be done using Matplotlib's `fill_between()` function:

```
plt.fill_between(
    xs.flatten(),
    predictive_upper,
    predictive_lower,
    alpha=0.3,
    label="95% CI"
)
```

Finally, we plot the individual samples:

```
for i in range(samples.shape[0]):
    plt.plot(xs, samples[i, :], alpha=0.5)
```

This code will produce the plot in figure 2.17.

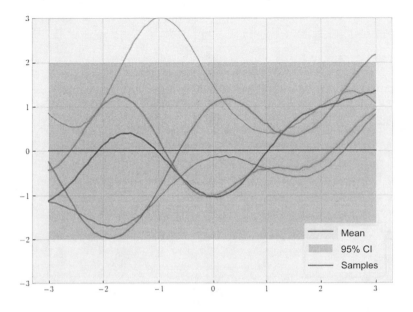

Figure 2.17   Predictions made by a prior GP with a zero mean and RBF kernel. While the mean and CI are constant, individual samples exhibit complex, nonlinear behaviors.

We see that across the domain, our prior GP produces a mean function that is constant at zero, and our 95% CI is constant. This is to be expected as we used a `gpytorch.means.ZeroMean()` object to implement the mean function, and without any training data, our prior predictions default to this 0 value.

With that said, the mean and CI are only measurements of expectation: they denote the average behavior of our predictions across many, many different realizations of what could be. When we draw individual samples, however, we see that each of these samples has a very complex shape that is not at all constant. All of this is to say that while the expected value of our prediction at any point is zero, there is a wide range of values it could take. This demonstrates that a GP can model complex, nonlinear behaviors in a flexible manner.

So far, we have learned to make and visualize predictions from a prior GP without any training data. Now, let's actually train a GP model on the training set we randomly generated and see how the predictions change. The nice thing about what we have coded so far is that everything may be repeated exactly, except we now initialize our GP with our training data (remember that we used None for the first and second arguments before):

```
model = BaseGPModel(train_x, train_y, likelihood)
```

Rerunning the code will give us figure 2.18.

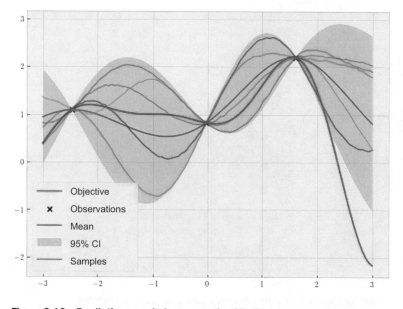

Figure 2.18   Predictions made by a posterior GP. The mean function and randomly drawn samples smoothly interpolate the training data points, while uncertainty vanishes in the regions surrounding these data points.

This is exactly the type of prediction we'd like to see: the mean line and samples nicely interpolate our observed data points, and our uncertainty (measured by the CI) also reduces around those data points.

We can already see how this uncertainty quantification is useful in terms of modeling the objective function. After only observing three data points, our GP has obtained a rather good approximation of the true objective function. In fact, almost all of the objective lies inside the 95% CI, indicating our GP is successfully accounting for how the objective function might behave, even in regions where we don't have any data from the function yet. This calibrated quantification is especially beneficial when we actually need to make decisions based on our GP model—that is, when we decide at which points we should observe the function value to find the optimum—but let's save that for the next part of the book.

2.4.5   *Going beyond one-dimensional objective functions*

So far, we have only seen examples of GPs trained on one-dimensional objective functions. However, there is nothing inherent about a GP that confines us to just one dimension. In fact, as long as our mean and covariance function can handle high-dimensional inputs, a GP can operate in high dimensions without difficulty. In this subsection, we learn how to train a GP on a two-dimensional dataset.

We follow the procedure in the previous section. First, we need a training dataset. Here, I'm artificially creating a dummy set with points at $(0, 0)$, $(1, 2)$, and $(-1, 1)$ with respective labels of 0, −1, and 0.5. In other words, the objective function we're learning from has a value of 0 at $(0, 0)$, −1 at $(1, 2)$, and 0.5 at $(-1, 1)$. We'd like to make predictions within the $[-3, 3]$-by-$[-3, 3]$ square.

This is set up in Python as follows:

```
# training data
train_x = torch.tensor(
    [
        [0., 0.],
        [1., 2.],
        [-1., 1.]
    ]
)

train_y = torch.tensor([0., -1., 0.5])

# test data
grid_x = torch.linspace(-3, 3, 101)          One-dimensional grid

grid_x1, grid_x2 = torch.meshgrid(grid_x, grid_x,    Two-dimensional grid
    indexing="ij")
xs = torch.vstack([grid_x1.flatten(), grid_x2.flatten()]).transpose(-1, -2)
```

The variable xs is a 10,201-by-2 matrix that contains the lattices of a grid over the square we'd like to predict on.

> **IMPORTANT**   There are 10,201 points because we are taking a 101-endpoint grid in each of the two dimensions. Now, we simply rerun the GP code we previously ran to train a GP and make predictions on this two-dimensional dataset. Note that no modification to our BaseGPModel class or any of the prediction code is needed, which is quite amazing!

One thing we do need to change, though, is how we visualize our predictions. As we are operating in two dimensions, plotting the predictive mean and CI in a single plot becomes more difficult. Here, a typical solution is to draw a heat map for the predictive mean and another heat map for the predictive standard deviation. While the standard deviation is not exactly the 95% CI, these two objects, in essence, do quantify the same thing: our uncertainty about the function values.

So, instead of calling `predictive_distribution.confidence_region()`, as we did before, we now extract the predictive standard deviation like so:

```
predictive_stddev = predictive_distribution.stddev
```

Now, to draw the heat maps, we use the `imshow()` function from Matplotlib. We need to be careful with the shape of our predictions in `predictive_mean` and `predictive_stddev` here. Each of them is a tensor of length 10,000, so it will need to be reshaped into a square matrix before being passed to the `imshow()` function. This can be done as follows:

```
fig, ax = plt.subplots(1, 2)

ax[0].imshow(
    predictive_mean.detach().reshape(101, 101).transpose(-1, -2),
    origin="lower",
    extent=[-3, 3, -3, 3]          The first heat map
)                                  for the predictive
                                   mean
ax[1].imshow(
    predictive_stddev.detach().reshape(101, 101).transpose(-1, -2),
    origin="lower",
    extent=[-3, 3, -3, 3]          The second heat map
)                                  for the predictive
                                   standard deviation
```

This code produces the two heat maps in figure 2.19.

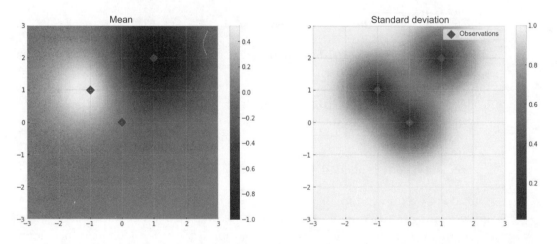

Figure 2.19   Predictions made by a two-dimensional GP. The mean function still agrees with the training data, and uncertainty once again vanishes in the regions surrounding these data points.

We see that what we have in the one-dimensional case extends to this example too:

- The left panel shows that our mean prediction agrees with our training data: the bright blob on the left corresponds to (–1, 1), which has a value of 0.5, while the dark blob on the right corresponds to (1, 2), which has a value of –1 (our observation at (0, 0) has a value of 0, which is also the prior mean, so it is not as obvious to point out in the left panel as the other two).
- Our uncertainty (measured by the predictive standard deviation) is close to zero around the three points in our training data, as demonstrated by the right panel. Going away from these data points, the standard deviation smoothly increases to the normalized maximum uncertainty of 1.

This means all of the nice properties of a GP, such as smooth interpolation and uncertainty quantification, are preserved when we go to higher dimensions.

This marks the end of chapter 2. We have gained a conceptual understanding of what a GP is and learned how to implement a base GP model in Python using GPyTorch. As mentioned, we dive deeper into the mean and covariance functions of a GP in chapter 3, including their hyperparameters, and see how each of these components controls the behavior of our GP model.

2.5   Exercise

In this exercise, we train a GP on a real-world dataset we saw in chapter 1, which is shown again in table 2.2. Each data point (row) corresponds to an alloy (a kind of metal) created by mixing lead (Pb), tin (Sn), germanium (Ge), and manganese (Mn)—these are called the *parent compounds*—at different ratios. The features are contained in the first four columns, which are the percentages of the parent compounds. The prediction target, mixing temperature, is in the last column, denoting the lowest temperature at which an alloy can form. The task is to predict mixing temperature given the compositional percentages of an alloy.

Table 2.2   Data from a materials discovery task. The features are the structure of a material expressed in percentages of parent compounds, and the prediction target is the mixing temperature.

% of Pb	% of Sn	% of Ge	% of Mn	Mixing temp. (°F)
0.50	0.50	0.00	0.00	192.08
0.33	0.33	0.33	0.00	258.30
0.00	0.50	0.50	0.00	187.24
0.00	0.33	0.33	0.33	188.54

There are multiple steps:

1. Create the four-dimensional dataset included in table 2.2.
2. Normalize the fifth column by subtracting the mean from all values and dividing the results by their standard deviation.

3   Treat the first four columns as features and the fifth as labels. Train a GP on this data. You can reuse the GP model class we implemented in the chapter.

4   Create a test dataset containing compositions with zero percent germanium and manganese. In other words, the test set is a grid over the unit square whose axes are percentages of lead and tin.

The test set should look like the following PyTorch tensor:

```
tensor([[0.0000, 0.0000, 0.0000, 0.0000],
        [0.0000, 0.0100, 0.0000, 0.0000],
        [0.0000, 0.0200, 0.0000, 0.0000],
        ...,
        [1.0000, 0.9800, 0.0000, 0.0000],
        [1.0000, 0.9900, 0.0000, 0.0000],
        [1.0000, 1.0000, 0.0000, 0.0000]])
```

Notice that the third and fourth columns are all zeros.

5   Predict the mixing temperature on this test set. That is, compute the posterior mean and standard deviation of the normalized mixing temperature for every point in the test set.

6   Visualize the predictions. This involves showing the mean and standard deviation as heat maps in the same way as in figure 2.19. The solution is included in CH02/02 - Exercise.ipynb.

Summary

- A multivariate Gaussian (MVN) distribution models the joint distribution of many random variables. The mean vector denotes the expected values of the variables, while the covariance matrix models both the variances and the covariances among these variables.

- By applying Bayes' theorem, we can compute the posterior distribution of an MVN. Through this Bayesian update, variables that are similar to the observed variable are updated to reflect this similarity. Overall, similar variables produce similar predictions.

- A GP extends an MVN distribution to infinite dimensions, making it a distribution over functions. However, the behavior of a GP is still similar to that of an MVN distribution.

- Even without any training data, a GP may still produce predictions specified by the prior GP.

- Once trained on a dataset, the mean prediction of a GP smoothly interpolates the training data points.

- One of the biggest advantages of using a GP is the calibrated quantification of uncertainty the model offers: predictions around observed data points are more confident; predictions far away from training data, on the other hand, are more uncertain.

- Conditioning with an MVN distribution or a GP is visually similar to tying a knot at an observation. This forces the model to exactly go through the observation and reduces the uncertainty to zero.

- When using GPyTorch to implement GPs, we can write a model class that extends the base class in a modular way. Specifically, we implement two specific methods: `__init__()`, which declares the mean and covariance functions of the GP, and `forward()`, which constructs an MVN distribution for a given input.

Customizing a Gaussian process with the mean and covariance functions

This chapter covers

- Controlling the expected behavior of a GP using mean functions
- Controlling the smoothness of a GP using covariance functions
- Learning the optimal hyperparameters of a GP using gradient descent

In chapter 2, we saw that the mean and covariance functions are the two core components of a Gaussian process (GP). Even though we used the zero mean and the RBF covariance function when implementing our GP, you can choose from many options when it comes to these two components.

By going with a specific choice for either the mean or the covariance function, we are effectively specifying prior knowledge for our GP. Incorporating prior knowledge into prediction is something we need to do with any Bayesian model, including GPs. Although I say we need to do it, being able to incorporate prior knowledge into a model is always a good thing, especially under settings in which data acquisition is expensive, like BayesOpt.

For example, in weather forecasting, if we'd like to estimate the temperature of a typical day in January in Missouri, we won't have to do any complex calculations to be able to guess that the temperature will be fairly low. At the other end of the spectrum, we can make a good guess that a summer day in California will be relatively hot. These rough estimates may be used as initial first guesses in a Bayesian model, which are, in essence, the model's prior knowledge. If we didn't have these first guesses, we would have to do more involved modeling to produce predictions.

As we learn in this chapter, incorporating prior knowledge into a GP can drastically change the model's behavior, which can lead to better predictive performance (and, eventually, more effective decision-making). We should only use no prior knowledge when we have absolutely no good guess about the behavior of the function; otherwise, this equates to wasting information.

In this chapter, we discuss the different options when it comes to the mean and covariance functions and how they affect the resulting GP model. Unlike in chapter 2, we take a hands-on approach here and revolve our discussions around code implementation in Python. By the end of this chapter, we develop a pipeline for selecting appropriate mean and covariance functions as well as optimizing their hyperparameters.

3.1 The importance of priors in Bayesian models

Question: Why can't you seem to change some people's mind? Answer: because of their priors. To show how important priors are in a Bayesian model, consider the following scenario.

Let's say you are hanging out with your friends, Bob and Alice, at a carnival, and you are talking to someone who claims they are a psychic. The way they allow you to test this claim is via the following procedure: you and your friends each think of a number between 0 and 9, and the "psychic" will tell you what number each of you is thinking of. You can repeat this process however many times you'd like.

Now, all three of you are curious about this supposed psychic, and you decide to conduct this test 100 times. Amazingly, after these 100 tests, the supposed psychic at the carnival correctly guesses the numbers you each think of. However, after you are done, you each have different reactions, as seen in figure 3.1.

Figure 3.1 Reaction among your group of friends after seeing a person correctly guess a secret number 100 times. Each person reached a different conclusion due to their prior belief.

Further reading on Bayes' theorem

If you need to refresh your memory, feel free to return to figure 2.2, in which we studied Bayes' theorem. We only sketch this out on a high level in this book, but I recommend chapters 1 and 2 of Will Kurt's *Bayesian Statistics the Fun Way* (No Starch Press, 2019) if you'd like to examine this process in greater depth.

How can all three of you observe the same event (the person at the carnival guessing correctly 100 times) but arrive at different conclusions? To answer this question, consider the process of updating one's belief using Bayes' theorem:

1 Each person starts out with a specific prior probability that the person is a psychic.

2 Then, you each observe the event that they guess your number correctly once.

3 You each then compute the likelihood terms. First, the likelihood their guess is correct, given that they're indeed a psychic, is exactly 1, since a true psychic can always pass this test. Second, the likelihood their guess is correct, given that they're *not* a psychic, is 1 out of 10. This is because each time, you are randomly choosing a number between 0 and 9, so any guess among these 10 options has an equal chance of being correct: 1 out of 10.

4 Finally, you update your belief by computing the posterior probability that this person is not a psychic by combining your prior with these likelihood terms. Specifically, this posterior will be proportional to the prior and the first likelihood term *multiplied* together.

5 You then repeat this process 100 times, each time using the posterior probability of the previous iteration as your prior for the current iteration.

What is important on a high level here is that after each test, you and your friends' posterior belief that this person is a psychic *never decreases,* since that statement doesn't agree with the data you observe. Specifically, figure 3.2 shows the progressive posterior probability of each person in your group as a function of how many tests the "psychic" at the carnival has passed.

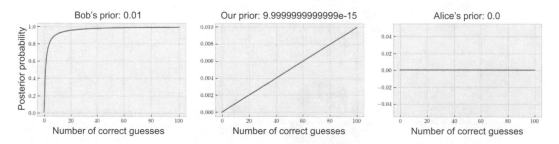

Figure 3.2   Progressive posterior probability that the woman at the carnival is a psychic as a function of the number of successful guesses. This posterior never decreases but behaves differently depending on the initial prior.

As we can see, each of the three curves either increases or stays flat—none of them actually decreases, since a decreasing probability of being a psychic doesn't match the 100 successful guesses in a row. But why do the three curves look so different? As you might have already guessed, the starting position of the curve—that is, each person's prior probability that the woman is a psychic—is the cause.

In Bob's case, in the left panel, he started out with a relatively high prior that the person is a psychic: 1%. Bob is a believer. As he observes more and more data that agrees with this belief, his posterior probability increases more and more.

In your own case, in the middle, being a skeptic, you started with a much lower prior: 1 in 10 raised to the 14th power. However, since your observations do suggest the woman is a psychic, your posterior probability also increases as more data comes in, reaching 1% at the end.

Alice's case, on the right, on the other hand, is different. From the start, she didn't believe psychics are real, so she assigned exactly zero probability to her prior. Now, remember that according to Bayes' theorem, the posterior probability is proportional to the prior multiplied by the likelihood. Since Alice's prior is exactly zero, this multiplication in the Bayesian update will always produce another zero.

Since Alice started out with zero probability, even after a successful test, this probability stays the same. After one correct guess, Alice's posterior is zero. After two guesses, it's still zero. After all 100 correct guesses, this number is still zero. Everything is consistent with the Bayesian update rule, but because Alice's prior doesn't allow for the possibility that psychics exist, no amount of data could convince her otherwise.

This highlights an important aspect of Bayesian learning—our prior determines how learning is done (see figure 3.3):

- Bob's prior is fairly high, so by the end of the 100 tests, he's completely convinced the person is psychic.
- You, on the other hand, are more skeptical, in that your initial prior is much lower than Bob's. This means it would take more evidence for you to arrive at a high posterior.
- Alice's complete disregard of the possibility, denoted by her zero prior, prevents her posterior probability from changing from zero.

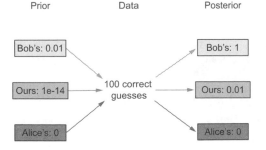

Figure 3.3 How each person's prior belief is updated by the same data. Compared to Bob's, your prior is much lower and increases more slowly. Alice's prior is 0 and stays at 0 throughout.

Although the claim in our example is about the event that someone is a psychic, the same Bayesian update procedure applies to all situations in which we have a probabilistic belief about some event and frequently update it in light of data. In fact, this is actually the reason we can't seem to be able to change someone's mind sometimes, even in the face of overwhelming evidence: because they start out with zero prior probability, and nothing will update the posterior to anything other than zero.

This discussion is philosophically interesting, in that it shows that to be able to convince someone of something, they need to at least entertain the idea by assigning nonzero prior probability to that event. More relevant to our topic, the example shows the importance of having good prior knowledge for a Bayesian model. As we have said, we specify a GP's prior knowledge with the mean and covariance functions. Each choice leads to a different behavior in the GP's prediction.

3.2   *Incorporating what you already know into a GP*

In this section, we identify situations in which specifying prior knowledge in a GP is important. This discussion motivates our discussions in the remaining portion of this chapter.

A prior GP may start out having a constant mean and CI everywhere. This GP then gets updated to smoothly interpolate the observed data points, as figure 3.4 denotes. That is, the mean prediction exactly goes through the data points, and the 95% CI vanishes in those regions.

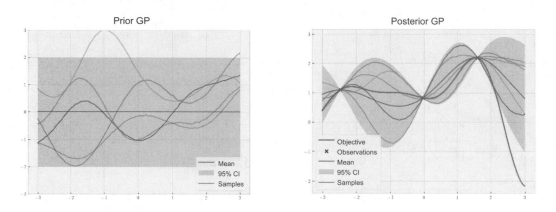

Figure 3.4   Comparison between a prior and a posterior GP. The prior GP contains prior information about the objective function, while the posterior GP combines that information with actual observations.

The prior GP in figure 3.4 assumes nothing about the objective function we are modeling. That's why this GP's mean prediction is zero everywhere. In many cases, however, even though we don't know the exact form of our objective function, there are aspects of the objective that we *do* know.

Take the following, for example:

- When modeling the accuracy of a model in a hyperparameter tuning application, we know that the range of the objective function is between 0 and 1.
- In our housing price example from section 2.1, the function values (the prices) are strictly positive and should increase when a desirable property of the house, such as living area, increases.
- Again, in the housing example, the function value is more sensitive to some features than others. For instance, the price of a house increases more quickly as a function of the number of stories than as a function of living area—one extra story increases the price of a house more than one extra square foot of living area.

This kind of information is exactly the prior knowledge that we'd like to represent with a GP, and one of the biggest advantages of using a GP is that we have many ways to incorporate prior knowledge. Doing so helps close the gap between the GP surrogate and the actual objective function it models, which will also more effectively guide optimization down the line.

> **Incorporating prior knowledge with a GP**
>
> We incorporate prior knowledge by selecting appropriate mean and covariance functions for our GP and setting their parameters' values. Specifically
>
> - The mean function defines the expected behavior of the objective function.
> - The covariance function defines the structure of the objective, or, more specifically, the relationship between any pair of data points and how quickly and smoothly the objective function changes across its domain.

Each of the preceding choices leads to drastically different behavior in the resulting GP. For example, a linear mean function will lead to a linear behavior in the GP's predictions, while a quadratic mean function will lead to a quadratic behavior. By using different parameters in the covariance function, we can also control for the variability of our GP.

3.3 *Defining the functional behavior with the mean function*

First, we cover the mean function of a GP, which defines the expected behavior of the GP, or what we believe the function looks like on average, across all possible scenarios of the function. This, as we will see, helps us specify any prior knowledge related to the function's general behavior and shape. The code we use throughout this section is included in CH03/01 - Mean functions.ipynb. To make our discussions concrete, we use a housing price dataset with five data points in table 3.1.

Table 3.1   Example training dataset. The prediction target (price) increases as a function of the feature (living area).

Living area (in squared feet times 1000)	Price (in dollars times 100,000)
0.5	0.0625
1	0.25
1.5	0.375
3	2.25
4	4

In this dataset, the function values we model are the housing prices, which are strictly positive and increase with larger values of living area. These properties make intuitive sense, and even without knowing the prices of unobserved houses, we know for sure that those unseen prices also have these properties.

Our goal here is to incorporate these properties into our mean function, as they describe how we expect the function to behave. Before we jump right to modeling, we first write a helper function that takes in a GP model (along with its likelihood function) and visualizes its predictions in the range from 0 to 10 (that is, a 10,000-square-foot living area). This is implemented as follows:

```
def visualize_gp_belief(model, likelihood):
    with torch.no_grad():
        predictive_distribution = likelihood(model(xs))       Computes
        predictive_mean = predictive_distribution.mean        predictions
        predictive_upper, predictive_lower =
            predictive_distribution .confidence_region()

    plt.figure(figsize=(8, 6))

    plt.plot(xs, ys, label="objective", c="r")
    plt.scatter(train_x, train_y, marker="x", c="k", label="observations")

    plt.plot(xs, predictive_mean, label="mean")              Plots the
    plt.fill_between(                                         mean line
        xs.flatten(), predictive_upper, predictive_lower, alpha=0.3,
        label="95% CI"
    )                                                         Plots the 95%
                                                              CI region
    plt.legend(fontsize=15);
```

We saw how this code works in section 2.4.3, and now we are putting it into a convenient function. And with that, we are ready to implement our GP models and see how our choices affect the predictions being produced.

3.3.1 Using the zero mean function as the base strategy

The simplest form of the mean is a constant function at zero. In the absence of data, this function will produce zero as its default prediction. The zero mean function is used when there is no extra information about the objective function that we may incorporate into the GP as prior knowledge.

A GP with a zero mean function is implemented as follows:

```
class ConstantMeanGPModel(gpytorch.models.ExactGP):
    def __init__(self, train_x, train_y, likelihood):
        super().__init__(train_x, train_y, likelihood)
        self.mean_module = gpytorch.means.ConstantMean()
        self.covar_module = gpytorch.kernels.RBFKernel()

    def forward(self, x):
        mean_x = self.mean_module(x)
        covar_x = self.covar_module(x)
        return gpytorch.distributions.MultivariateNormal(mean_x, covar_x)
```

Constant mean function with a default value of zero

Remember from section 2.4.2 that to build a GP model with GPyTorch, we implement the `__init__()` and `forward()` methods. In the first method, we initialize our mean and covariance functions; in the second, we push the input x through these functions and return the corresponding multivariate Gaussian distribution.

> **NOTE** Instead of the `gpytorch.means.ZeroMean` class in our implementation from section 2.4.2, we are using the `gpytorch.means.ConstantMean` class to initialize our mean function. However, this constant mean function has a default value of zero, so effectively, we are still implementing the same GP model. While these two choices lead to identical models for now, in this chapter, we show how `gpytorch.means.ConstantMean` allows us to adjust the constant mean value to obtain a better model shortly.

Let's now initialize an object of this class, train it on our training data, and visualize its predictions. We do this with the following code:

```
lengthscale = 1
noise = 1e-4

likelihood = gpytorch.likelihoods.GaussianLikelihood()
model = ConstantMeanGPModel(train_x, train_y, likelihood)

model.covar_module.lengthscale = lengthscale
model.likelihood.noise = noise

model.eval()
likelihood.eval()

visualize_gp_belief(model, likelihood)
```

Declares the GP

Fixes the hyperparameters

Here, we initialize the GP model and set its hyperparameters—the length scale and noise variance—to 1 and 0.0001, respectively. We will see how to set the values of these hyperparameters appropriately later in this chapter; for now, let's just stick with these values. Finally, we call the helper function we just wrote, `visualize_gp_belief()`, on our GP model, which produces figure 3.5.

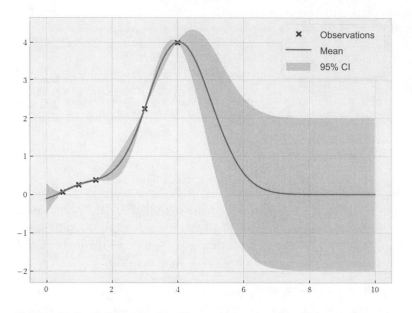

Figure 3.5   Predictions by a GP with a zero mean function. The posterior mean function interpolates the observed data points and reverts back to zero in regions that are far away from these observations.

All the nice properties of the GP that we pointed out in section 2.4.4 are still here:

- The posterior mean function smoothly interpolates the xs that are our training data points.
- The 95% CI vanishes around these data points, denoting a well-calibrated quantification of uncertainty.

We also notice from this plot that once we have gone sufficiently far away from our training data points (the right side of the plot), our posterior mean function *reverts* back to the prior mean, which is zero. This is, in fact, an important feature of a GP: in the absence of data (in regions without observations), the prior mean function is the main driving force of the inference procedure. This makes intuitive sense, as without actual observations, the best thing that a predictive model can do is simply appeal to the prior knowledge encoded in its mean function.

> **NOTE**   At this point, we see why having well-defined prior knowledge encoded into the prior GP is so important: in the absence of data, the only thing that drives predictions is the prior GP.

A natural question then arises: Is it possible to use a nonzero mean function to induce a different behavior for our GP in these unexplored regions, and if so, what are our options? The remaining portion of this section aims to answer this question. We start by using a constant mean function that is not zero.

3.3.2 *Using the constant function with gradient descent*

A constant mean function that is not zero is appropriate when we expect the objective function we are modeling to take on some range of values that we know *a priori*. As we are modeling housing prices, using a constant mean function with a constant greater than zero makes sense, as we indeed expect the prices to be positive.

Of course, it's not possible to know what value the objective function takes, on average, in many cases. How, then, should we find an appropriate value for our mean function? The strategy we use is to appeal to a specific quantity: how likely the training dataset is, given the value for our mean function. Roughly speaking, this quantity measures how well our model explains its training data. We show how to use this quantity to select the best mean function for our GP in this subsection.

If the likelihood of the training data given some value c_1 is higher than that given another value c_2, then we prefer using c_1 to using c_2. This quantifies our previous intuition about using nonzero mean functions to model positive functions: a constant mean function whose value is positive explains observations from an exclusively positive function better than a function whose value is zero (or negative) does.

How can we compute this likelihood? GPyTorch offers a convenient class, `gpytorch.mlls.ExactMarginalLogLikelihood`, that takes in a GP model and computes the marginal log likelihood of its training data, given the hyperparameters of the model.

To see that this likelihood quantity is effective at quantifying data fit, consider figure 3.6. This figure visualizes the predictions made by two separate GP models: a zero mean GP we saw in the previous subsection, on the left, and the GP with a mean function whose value is 2, on the right. Notice how in the second panel, the mean function reverts to 2 instead of 0 on the right side of the plot. Here, the second GP has a higher (log) likelihood than the first, which means the value 2 explains our training data better than the value 0.

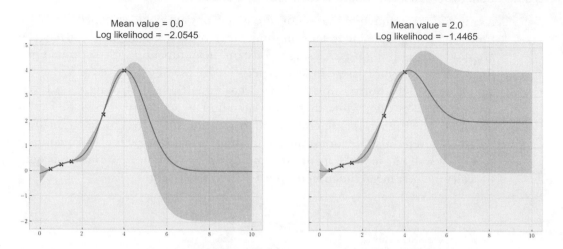

Figure 3.6   GP predictions, given two different constant mean functions. The value 2 gives a higher likelihood value than the value 0, indicating the former mean function is a better fit than the latter.

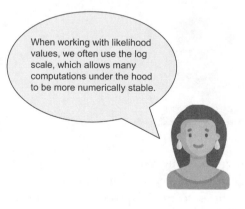

When working with likelihood values, we often use the log scale, which allows many computations under the hood to be more numerically stable.

With this log likelihood computation in hand, our last step is to simply find the value for our mean function such that the log likelihood is maximized. In other words, we aim to seek the mean value that explains our training data the best. Since we have access to the log likelihood computation, we can use gradient-based optimization algorithms, such as gradient descent, to iteratively refine the mean value we have. Upon convergence, we will have arrived at a good mean value that gives high data likelihood. If you need a refresher on how gradient descent works, I recommend appendix B of Luis Serrano's *Grokking Machine Learning* (Manning, 2021), which does a good job of explaining the concept.

Now, let's see how we can implement this process with code. Since we implemented our GP model with the `gpytorch.means.ConstantMean` class for our mean function, we don't need to change anything here. So, for now, let's initialize our GP model again:

```
# declare the GP
lengthscale = 1
noise = 1e-4

likelihood = gpytorch.likelihoods.GaussianLikelihood()
model = ConstantMeanGPModel(train_x, train_y, likelihood)

# fix the hyperparameters
model.covar_module.lengthscale = lengthscale
model.likelihood.noise = noise
```

The central step of this procedure is to define the log likelihood function as well as a gradient descent algorithm. As mentioned previously, the former is an instance of the `gpytorch.mlls.ExactMarginalLogLikelihood` class, implemented like so:

```
mll = gpytorch.mlls.ExactMarginalLogLikelihood(likelihood, model)
```

For the gradient descent algorithm, we use Adam, which is a state-of-the-art algorithm that has enjoyed a lot of success in many ML tasks, especially DL. We declare it using PyTorch as follows:

```
optimizer = torch.optim.Adam([model.mean_module.constant], lr=0.01)
```

Note that we are passing to the `torch.optim.Adam` class `model.mean_module.constant`, which is the mean value we seek to optimize. When we run the gradient descent procedure, the Adam algorithm iteratively updates the value of `model.mean_module.constant` to improve the likelihood function.

The last thing we need to do now is to run gradient descent, which is implemented as follows:

```
model.train()                      Enables the
likelihood.train()                 training mode

losses = []
constants = []
for i in tqdm(range(500)):
    optimizer.zero_grad()
                                              Loss as the
    output = model(train_x)                   negative marginal
    loss = -mll(output, train_y)   ◁──────    log likelihood
```

**Gradient
descent on
the loss**

```
loss.backward()

losses.append(loss.item())
constants.append(model.mean_module.constant.item())

optimizer.step()
```

```
model.eval()          Enables the
likelihood.eval()     prediction mode
```

The calls to `train()` at the beginning and `eval()` at the end are the bookkeeping steps we always need to take, enabling the training mode and prediction mode of our GP model, respectively. Resetting the gradients at each step with `optimizer.zero_grad()` is another bookkeeping task to make sure we don't incorrectly compute the gradients.

In the middle, we have a 500-step gradient descent procedure in which we iteratively compute the loss (which is the negative of our log likelihood) and descend on this loss based on its gradients. During this `for` loop, we keep track of the negative log likelihood values that we obtain as well as the mean value, adjusted in each step. This is so that after training, we can visually inspect these values to determine whether they have converged.

Figure 3.7 includes this visualization, showing the running values for the negative log likelihood (which we aim to minimize) and the value for the mean function of the GP. Our loss consistently decreases (which is a good thing!) with increasing values of the mean constant, showing that a positive constant does give a higher likelihood than zero. Both curves plateau after 500 iterations, indicating we have converged at an optimal value for the mean constant.

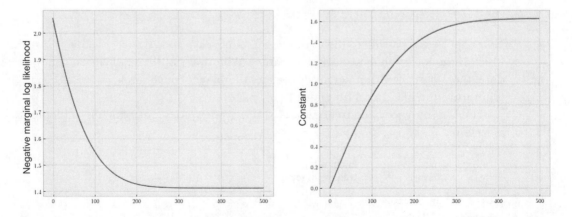

Figure 3.7 Running negative log likelihood (lower is better) and mean value during gradient descent. In both panels, the values have converged, indicating we have arrived at an optimum.

NOTE   I recommend that you *always* plot out the progressive loss, like we just did here, when using gradient descent to see whether you have converged at

an optimal value. Stopping before convergence might lead to poor performance for your model. While we won't be showing these progressive loss plots
again throughout this chapter, the accompanying code does include them.

So far, we have learned how to use a zero mean function as the default for our GP
model as well as optimize the mean constant value with respect to the data likelihood.
However, in many use cases, you might have prior knowledge about how the objective
function is expected to behave and, thus, prefer to incorporate more structure into
your mean function.

For example, how can we implement the idea that the price of a house increases
with a larger living area? Moving forward, we learn to do this with a GP by using a linear or quadratic mean function.

3.3.3   *Using the linear function with gradient descent*

We proceed with the linear mean function, which is in the form of $\mu = \boldsymbol{w}^T\boldsymbol{x} + b$. Here, μ
is the predictive mean value at the test point $\boldsymbol{x}$, while $\boldsymbol{w}$ is the weight vector that concatenates the coefficients for each of the features in $\boldsymbol{x}$, and b is a constant bias term.

By using the linear mean function, we are encoding the assumption that the
expected behavior of our objective function is equal to a linear combination of the
features of the data point $\boldsymbol{x}$. For our housing price example, we only have one feature,
the living area, and we expect it to have a positive weight, so by increasing the living
area, our model will predict a higher price.

Another way to think about this linear mean model is that we have a linear regression model (which also assumes the target label to be a linear combination of the features) and we put a probabilistic belief, a GP model, on top of our predictions. This
gives us the power offered by a linear regression model, while maintaining all the benefits of modeling with a GP—namely, uncertainty quantification.

> **NOTE**   Under a constant mean function, the weight vector $\boldsymbol{w}$ is fixed at the
> zero vector, and the bias b is the mean value that we learned to optimize in
> the previous subsection. In other words, the linear function is a more general
> model than the constant mean function.

Regarding implementation, building a GP model with a linear mean function is quite
straightforward. We simply swap out our constant mean and replace it with a `gpy-`
`torch.means.LinearMean` instance, as follows (our `forward()` method remains
unchanged):

```
class LinearMeanGPModel(gpytorch.models.ExactGP):
    def __init__(self, train_x, train_y, likelihood):
        super().__init__(train_x, train_y, likelihood)
        self.mean_module = gpytorch.means.LinearMean(1)        ← Linear mean
        self.covar_module = gpytorch.kernels.RBFKernel()
```

Here, we use `1` to initialize our mean module, indicating we are working with a one-
dimensional objective function. When working with a higher-dimensional function,

you can simply pass in the dimensionality of that function here. Aside from this, everything else about our model is similar to what we had before. Fitting and training this new model on our three-point dataset, we obtain the predictions in figure 3.8.

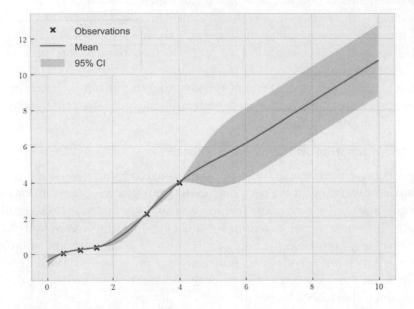

Figure 3.8   Predictions by a GP with a linear mean function. The GP has an upward trend, which is a direct result of the positive slope of the linear mean function.

Unlike what we have seen so far with the constant mean, the linear mean function we're using here drives the entire GP model to have an upward trend. This is because the best-fit line of the five data points in our training data is one with a positive slope, which is exactly what we wanted to model as a relationship between living area and price.

3.3.4   *Using the quadratic function by implementing a custom mean function*

Our linear mean function here successfully captures the increasing trend of the price, but it assumes the rate of price increase is constant. That is, adding an extra square foot to the living area leads, in expectation, to a constant increase in price.

In many cases, however, we might have prior knowledge that our objective function increases at a non-constant rate, which a linear mean cannot model. In fact, the data points we've been using were generated so that the price is a quadratic function of the living area. This is why we see the larger houses become more expensive faster than the smaller houses. In this subsection, we implement our GP mean as a quadratic function.

At the time of this writing, GPyTorch only provides implementations for the constant and linear mean functions. But the beauty of this package, as we will see again and again in the book, is its modularity: all components of a GP model, such as the mean function, the covariance function, the prediction strategy, and even the marginal log likelihood function, are implemented as modules, and therefore, they can be modified, reimplemented, and extended in an object-oriented manner. We see this first-hand when implementing our own quadratic mean function.

The first thing for us to do is define a mean function class:

```python
class QuadraticMean(gpytorch.means.Mean):
    def __init__(self, batch_shape=torch.Size(), bias=True):
        ...

    def forward(self, x):
        ...
```

This class extends the `gpytorch.means.Mean` class, which is the base for all GPyTorch mean function implementations. To implement our custom logic, we need to rewrite two methods: `__init__()` and `forward()`, which are exactly the same as when we implement a GP model!

In `__init__()`, we need to declare what parameters our mean function contains. This process is called *parameter registration.*

While a linear function has two parameters, a slope and an intercept, a quadratic function has three: a coefficient for the second-order term x^2; a coefficient for the first-order term x; and a coefficient for the zeroth-order term, which is typically called the bias. This is illustrated in figure 3.9.

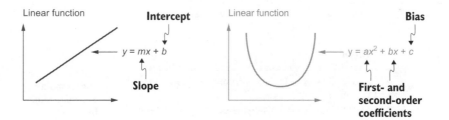

Figure 3.9   The functional forms of a linear function and a quadratic function. The linear function has two parameters, while the quadratic function has three. When these functions are used as a GP's mean function, the corresponding parameters are the GP's hyperparameters.

With that in mind, we implement the `__init__()` method like so:

```python
class QuadraticMean(gpytorch.means.Mean):
    def __init__(self, batch_shape=torch.Size(), bias=True):
        super().__init__()
        self.register_parameter(
```

```
                      name="second",
                      parameter=torch.nn.Parameter(torch.randn(*batch_shape, 1, 1))
```
Second-order
coefficient ⊳ `)`

```
          self.register_parameter(
              name="first",
```
First-order
coefficient ⊳ `          parameter=torch.nn.Parameter(torch.randn(*batch_shape, 1, 1))`
```
          )

          if bias:
              self.register_parameter(
                  name="bias",
                  parameter=torch.nn.Parameter(torch.randn(*batch_shape, 1))
```
Bias ⟶⊳ `              )`
```
          else:
              self.bias = None
```

We sequentially call `register_parameter()` to register the second-order coefficient, the first-order coefficient, and the bias. As we don't have a good idea of what values these coefficients should take, we simply initialize them randomly using `torch.randn()`.

> **NOTE** We need to register these parameters as instances of the `torch.nn` `.Parameter` class, which allows their values to be adjusted (trained) during gradient descent.

For the `forward()` method, we need to define how our mean function should process an input. As we have said, a quadratic function is in the form of $ax^2 + bx + c$, where a, b, and c are the second-order coefficient, first-order coefficient, and the bias, respectively. So we only need to implement that logic, as follows:

```
class QuadraticMean(gpytorch.means.Mean):
    def __init__(self, train_x, train_y, likelihood):
```
Omitted ⟶⊳ `        ...`
```

    def forward(self, x):
        res = x.pow(2).matmul(self.second).squeeze(-1) \
            + x.matmul(self.first).squeeze(-1)        ⟵  The formula
        if self.bias is not None:                          of a quadratic
            res = res + self.bias                          function
        return res
```

With this quadratic mean function in hand, we can now write a GP model that initializes its mean module using the custom `QuadraticMean` class we just implemented:

```
class QuadraticMeanGPModel(gpytorch.models.ExactGP):
    def __init__(self, train_x, train_y, likelihood):
        super().__init__(train_x, train_y, likelihood)
        self.mean_module = QuadraticMean()
        self.covar_module = gpytorch.kernels.RBFKernel()

    def forward(self, x):
        ...              ⟵——⊐ Omitted
```

Rerunning our entire training procedure with gradient descent gives us the predictions in figure 3.10.

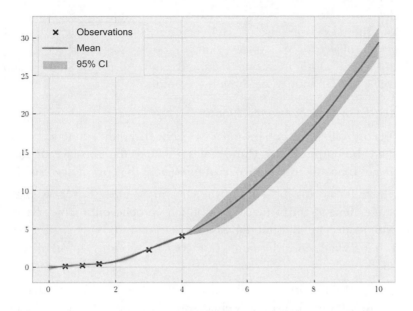

Figure 3.10   Predictions by a GP with a quadratic mean function. This GP predicts that with a larger living area, the price increases at a faster rate.

Here, we successfully model the non-constant rate of increase in housing prices with respect to living area. Our predictions increase much more quickly on the right side of the plot than on the left.

We can do this for any functional form we want to assume about the objective, such as a higher-degree polynomial or a sublinear function. All we need to do is implement a mean function class with appropriate parameters and use gradient descent to assign values to these parameters that will give us a good fit for our training data.

Our discussion so far demonstrates the mathematical flexibility of GP models, in that they can make use of a mean function of any structure and still produce probabilistic predictions. This flexibility motivates and drives the design of GPyTorch, whose emphasis on modularity helps us extend and implement our own custom mean function effortlessly. We see the same flexibility and modularity in GPyTorch's covariance functions, which we discuss next.

3.4   *Defining variability and smoothness with the covariance function*

While the mean function defines our expectation of the overall behavior of the objective function, the covariance function, or the kernel, of a GP plays a more complex role: defining the relationship between data points within the domain and controlling for the structure and smoothness of the GP. In this section, we compare how the predictions by a GP change as we change different components of our model. From there, we gain practical insights into how to select an appropriate covariance function for a GP model. The code that we use is in CH03/02 - Covariance functions.ipynb.

Throughout these examples, we use the Forrester function, which we saw in section 2.4.1, as our objective. We, once again, randomly sample three data points between -3 and 3 and use them as our training dataset. All predictions visualized in this section are from a GP trained on these three points.

3.4.1   *Setting the scales of the covariance function*

The first way of controlling the behavior of a GP via its covariance function is to set the length scale and the output scale. These scales, just like the constant or the coefficients in the mean function, are the hyperparameters of the covariance function:

- A length scale controls the scale of the GP's input and, thus, how fast the GP can change along an axis—that is, how much we believe the objective function varies with respect to an input dimension.
- The output scale defines the range of the GP's output or, in other words, the range of its predictions.

By setting these scales to different values, we can either increase or decrease the uncertainty in our GP's predictions as well as scale the range of our predictions. We use the following implementation:

```
class ScaleGPModel(gpytorch.models.ExactGP):
    def __init__(self, train_x, train_y, likelihood):
        super().__init__(train_x, train_y, likelihood)
        self.mean_module = gpytorch.means.ZeroMean()
        self.covar_module =
        ➥ gpytorch.kernels.ScaleKernel(
          gpytorch.kernels.RBFKernel())          ◁──┐  gpytorch.kernels.ScaleKernel
                                                      implements the output scale.
    def forward(self, x):
        ...          ◁──────  Omitted
```

Notice that our code for the `covar_module` attribute here is different from before: we are placing a `gpytorch.kernels.ScaleKernel` object outside of our usual RBF kernel. This effectively implements the output scale that scales the output of the RBF kernel by some constant factor. The length scale, on the other hand, is already included within `gpytorch.kernels.RBFKernel`.

```
gpytorch.kernels.ScaleKernel(gpytorch.kernels.RBFKernel())
```

A Scale kernel
multiplies its input
by an output scale.

An RBF kernel
already has a length
scale implemented.

In the code we have been using thus far, there is one line where we set the length scale of our kernel with `model.covar_module.base_kernel.lengthscale = lengthscale`. This is where the value of the length scale is stored. Using a similar API, we can set the output scale of our kernel with `model.covar_module.outputscale = outputscale`. Now, to see that the length scale effectively controls how fast the function varies, we compare the predictions made by two GPs—one with a length scale of 1 and the other with a length scale of 0.3, shown in figure 3.11.

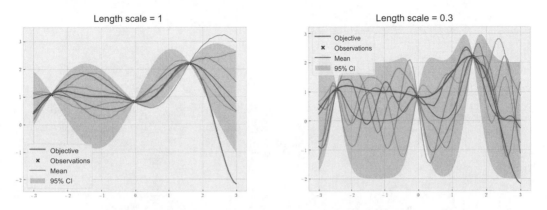

Figure 3.11 The GP's predictions with the length scale set to 1 (left) and to 0.3 (right). With a small length scale, the GP predictions have more variability, leading to more uncertainty.

The stark difference between the two panels makes clear the effect of our length scale:

- A shorter length scale corresponds with more variability in the objective function, given a constant change in the input.
- A longer length scale, on the other hand, forces the function to be smoother, in the sense that it varies less, given the same input change.

For instance, going one unit along the *x*-axis, the samples in the left panel in figure 3.11 vary less than those in the right panel.

More variability means more uncertainty, which means a shorter length scale, leading to a wider credible interval. This is because we are less certain about the behavior of the function.

What about the output scale, then? We said earlier that this parameter scales the output of the covariance function to a different range. This is done by simply multiplying the covariance output with this parameter. Hence, a large output scale leads to the range of the GP's predictions being wider, while a small output scale shrinks this prediction range. To see that this is true, let's once again run our code and regenerate the predictions, this time setting the output scale to 3. The produced output is shown in figure 3.12.

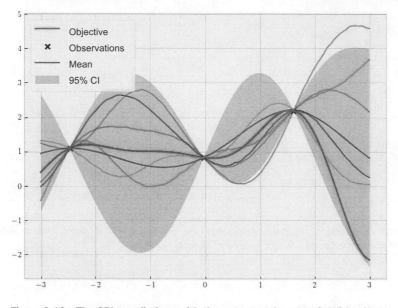

Figure 3.12   The GP's predictions with the output scale set to 3. With a large output scale, the GP models the function to have a wider range, also allowing more uncertainty in the predictions.

While the left panel of figures 3.11 and 3.12 may look the same in that the GP and its samples have the same shape across the two plots, we notice that figure 3.12 has a larger *y*-axis, as both its predictions and its samples take on larger values (both negative and positive). This is the direct result of scaling the covariance values from the RBF kernel with a large output scale.

With just two hyperparameters for our covariance function, we have seen that we can account for a wide range of functional behaviors that are modeled by our GP, which we summarize in table 3.2. I invite you to rerun this code with different values for the length and output scales to see their effects and verify the table for yourself!

Table 3.2   Summary of the roles that the length and output scales of a GP play

Parameter	With a large value	With a small value
Length scale	Smoother predictions, less uncertainty	More variability, more uncertainty
Output scale	Larger output values, more uncertainty	Narrower output range, less uncertainty

NOTE This flexibility in modeling gives rise to a natural question: How should you appropriately set the values for these hyperparameters? Luckily, we already know a good way of setting the hyperparameters of a GP model. We can do this by choosing the values that explain our data the best or, in other words, maximizing the marginal log likelihood, specifically via gradient descent.

Just like when we wanted to optimize the hyperparameters of the mean function, we now do this by simply passing the variables we'd like to optimize—the parameters of the covariance function—to Adam:

```
optimizer = torch.optim.Adam(model.covar_module.parameters(), lr=0.01)
```

By running gradient descent, we can arrive at good values for these parameters. Specifically, I obtained a length scale of roughly 1.3 and an output scale of roughly 2.1. That is, to fit the three-point training dataset well, we want the GP to be slightly smoother (with a length scale greater than 1), and we also want the range of our predictions to be larger (with a larger output scale). This is certainly a reassuring result, as our objective function does have a wide range of values—at input 3, it takes on a value of –2, which is well outside of the CI with an output scale of 1.

3.4.2 *Controlling smoothness with different covariance functions*

Thus far, we have exclusively used the RBF kernel as our covariance function. It is, however, entirely possible to use a different kernel for our GP if RBF is not appropriate. In this subsection, we learn to use another family of kernels, the Matérn kernel, and see what effect this kernel would have on our GP.

NOTE By using a Matérn kernel, we are specifying the smoothness of the function of our GP models. *Smoothness* is a technical term here that refers to the differentiability of the function; the more times a function is differentiable, the smoother it is. We can roughly think of this as how much the function values "jump" up and down in a jagged manner.

The RBF kernel models functions that are *infinitely* differentiable, which is a property that not many functions in the real world have. Meanwhile, a Matérn kernel produces functions that are finitely differentiable, and exactly how many times these functions may be differentiated (that is, how smooth these functions are) is controlled by a settable parameter, as we discuss shortly.

To see the Matérn kernel in action, we first reimplement our GP model class:

```
class MaternGPModel(gpytorch.models.ExactGP):
    def __init__(self, train_x, train_y, likelihood, nu):
        super().__init__(train_x, train_y, likelihood)
        self.mean_module = gpytorch.means.ZeroMean()
        self.covar_module = gpytorch.kernels.MaternKernel(nu)

    def forward(self, x):
        ...            ◁——— Omitted
```

Here, our `covar_module` attribute is initialized as an instance of the `gpytorch.kernels.MaternKernel` class. This initialization takes in a parameter `nu` that defines the level of smoothness our GP will have, which is also a parameter of our `__init__()` method.

> **IMPORTANT** At the time of this writing, three values for `nu` are supported by GPyTorch, $1/2$, $3/2$, and $5/2$, corresponding to functions being non-, once-, and twice-differentiable. In other words, the larger this `nu` parameter, the smoother our GP.

Let's try `nu = 0.5` first by setting that value when we initialize the GP:

```
likelihood = gpytorch.likelihoods.GaussianLikelihood()
model = MaternGPModel(train_x, train_y, likelihood, 0.5)

...          ◁─────  Fixes hyperparameters and
                     enables the prediction mode

visualize_gp_belief(model, likelihood)
```

This code produces figure 3.13.

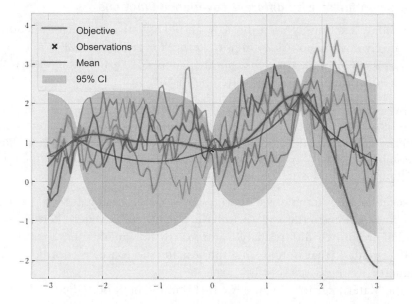

Figure 3.13 The GP's predictions with the Matérn 1/2 kernel, which induces the belief that the objective function is not differentiable, corresponding to very rough samples

Unlike what we have seen before with RBF, the samples from this Matérn kernel are all very jagged. In fact, none of them are differentiable. `nu = 0.5` is a good value for the Matérn kernel when modeling time-series data, such as stock prices.

However, this value is typically not used in BayesOpt, as jagged functions like those in figure 3.13 are highly volatile (they can jump up and down in an unpredictable way) and are usually not the target for automated optimization techniques. We need a certain level of smoothness from our objective function that is to be optimized; otherwise, effective optimization is an unrealistic goal.

The Matérn 5/2 kernel is commonly preferred. Its predictions, along with those generated by Matérn 3/2, are visualized in figure 3.14.

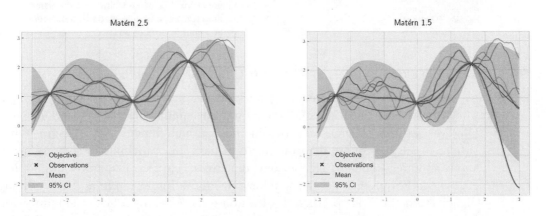

Figure 3.14 The GP's predictions with the Matérn 5/2 (left) and Matérn 3/2 (right) kernel. The samples here are smooth enough for the GP to effectively learn from data but are also jagged enough to realistically model real-life processes.

We see that the samples from this 5/2 kernel are much smoother, which leads to more effective learning by the GP. However, these samples are also rough enough that they resemble functions we might see in the real world. For this reason, most efforts, both research and applied, in BayesOpt utilize this Matérn 5/2 kernel. In future chapters, when we discuss decision-making for BayesOpt, we default to this kernel, accordingly.

> **NOTE** While we do not include the corresponding details here, a Matérn kernel has its own length scale and output scale, which may be specified to further customize the behavior of the resulting GP in the same manner as in the previous subsection.

By pairing a mean function with a kernel, we can induce complex behavior in the predictions of the GP. Just like our prior affects the conclusion each person in our group of friends reaches after seeing someone correctly guess a secret number 100 times, our choice of the mean function and the kernel determines the predictions made by a GP. Figure 3.15 shows three examples in which each combination of a mean function and a kernel leads to a drastically different behavior.

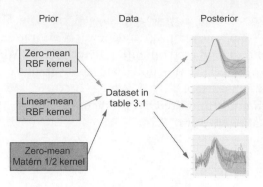

Figure 3.15   Three different choices for the mean function and kernel and the predictions made by their respective posterior GPs when trained on the same dataset. Each choice leads to a different behavior in prediction.

3.4.3   *Modeling different levels of variability with multiple length scales*

As we have only been considering one-dimensional objective functions (functions whose inputs have one feature), there is only one length scale that we need to consider. However, we can imagine scenarios in which a high-dimensional objective function (whose inputs have more than one feature) has more variability in some dimensions and is smoother in others. That is, some dimensions have small-length scales, while others have large-length scales. Remember our motivating example at the beginning of this chapter: the price prediction of a house increases by a larger amount with an extra story than with an extra square foot of living area. We explore how to maintain multiple length scales in a GP to model these functions in this subsection.

If we were to only use a single length scale for all dimensions, we wouldn't be able to faithfully model the objective function. This situation calls for the GP model to maintain a separate length scale for each dimension to fully capture the variability in each of them. In this final section of the chapter, we learn how to do this with GPyTorch.

To aid our discussion, we use a concrete two-dimensional objective function called Ackley, which can be modified to have various levels of variability in different dimensions. We implement the function as follows:

```
def ackley(x):
    # a modification of https://www.sfu.ca/~ssurjano/ackley.html
    return -20 * torch.exp(
        -0.2 * torch.sqrt((x[:, 0] ** 2 + x[:, 1] ** 2) / 2)
    )
    ➥ - torch.exp(torch.cos(2 * pi * x[:, 0] / 3)
    ➥ + torch.cos(2 * pi * x[:, 1]))
```

We specifically restrict the domain of this function to the square region between –3 and 3 in both dimensions, which is typically denoted as $[-3, 3]^2$. To visualize this objective function, we use the heat map in figure 3.16.

Each dark blob in the heat map can be thought of as a valley that has a low value across the surface of the objective function. Here, there are many more valleys across the *y*-axis than across the *x*-axis, indicating that the second dimension has more variability

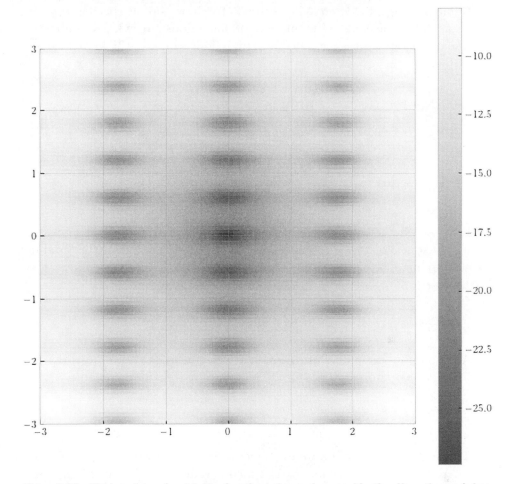

Figure 3.16   **The two-dimensional Ackley function to be used as our objective. Here, the *x*-axis has less variability (it changes less) than the *y*-axis, requiring different length scales.**

than the first—that is, the objective function goes up and down many times across the *y*-axis, more often than across the *x*-axis.

Once again, this means that using only one length scale for both dimensions is not a good choice. Instead, we should have a length scale for *each* dimension (two, in this case). Each length scale can then be independently optimized using gradient descent.

IMPORTANT   Using a kernel with a length scale for each dimension is called *automatic relevance determination* (ARD). This term denotes the fact that after using gradient descent to optimize these length scales, we can infer how relevant each dimension of the objective function is with respect to the function values. A dimension with a large length scale has low variability and is, therefore, less relevant in modeling the objective function values than a dimension with a small length scale.

Implementing ARD is very easy with GPyTorch: we simply specify the `ard_num_dims` parameter to be equal to the number of dimensions our objective function has when initializing our covariance function. This is done with the RBF kernel like so:

```
class ARDGPModel(gpytorch.models.ExactGP):
    def __init__(self, train_x, train_y, likelihood):
        super().__init__(train_x, train_y, likelihood)
        self.mean_module = gpytorch.means.ZeroMean()
        self.covar_module = gpytorch.kernels.ScaleKernel(
            gpytorch.kernels.RBFKernel(ard_num_dims=2)
        )

    def forward(self, x):
        ...                   ⟵————|  Omitted
```

Let's see whether, when trained on our Ackley function, this model gives us different length scales for the two dimensions. To do this, we first construct a randomly sampled training dataset consisting of 100 points:

```
torch.manual_seed(0)
train_x = torch.rand(size=(100, 2)) * 6 - 3
train_y = ackley(train_x)
```

After training the model using gradient descent, like we have been doing, we could inspect the optimized values for the length scales by printing out

```
>>> model.covar_module.base_kernel.lengthscale
tensor([[0.7175, 0.4117]])
```

This is, indeed, the result we expected: a larger length scale for the first dimension, where there is less variability in the function values, and a smaller length scale for the second dimension, where there is more variability.

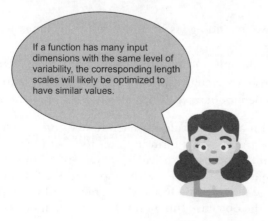

If a function has many input dimensions with the same level of variability, the corresponding length scales will likely be optimized to have similar values.

> **More reading on kernels**
>
> Kernels, in and of themselves, have enjoyed a lot of interest from the ML community. One thing to note, in addition to what we have covered so far, is that kernels can also encode complex structures, such as periodicity, linearity, and noise. For a more thorough and technical discussion on kernels and their roles in ML, the interested reader may refer to David Duvenaud's *The Kernel Cookbook* (https://www.cs.toronto.edu/~duvenaud/cookbook/).

This discussion marks the end of chapter 3. Throughout this chapter, we have extensively investigated how our GP model is influenced by the mean and covariance functions, specifically by their various parameters. We use this as a way to incorporate what we know about the objective function—that is, prior information—into our GP models. We have also learned to use gradient descent to estimate the values for these parameters to obtain the GP model that explains our data the best.

This also marks the end of the first part of the book, where we focus on GPs. Starting from the next chapter, we begin learning about the second component of the BayesOpt framework: decision-making. We begin with two of the most commonly used BayesOpt policies that seek to improve from the best point seen: Probability of Improvement and Expected Improvement.

3.5 *Exercise*

This exercise provides practice for implementing a GP model with ARD. To do this, we create an objective function that varies along one axis more than it does along another axis. We then train a GP model, with and without ARD, on data points from this function and compare the learned length scale values. The solution is included in CH03/03 - Exercise.ipynb.

There are multiple steps to this process:

1 Implement the following two-dimensional function in Python using PyTorch:

$$f(x_1, x_2) = \sin\left(\frac{5x_1 - 5}{2}\right)\cos(2.5 - 5x_2) + \frac{1}{10}\left(\frac{5x_2 + 1}{2}\right)^2$$

This function simulates the accuracy surface of a support-vector machine (SVM) model in a hyperparameter tuning task. The *x*-axis denotes the value of the penalty parameter *c*, while the *y*-axis denotes the value for the RBF kernel parameter γ. (We use this function as our objective in future chapters as well.)

2 Visualize the function over the domain [0, 2]^2. The heat map should look like figure 3.17.

3 Randomly draw 100 data points from the domain [0, 2]^2. This will be used as our training data.

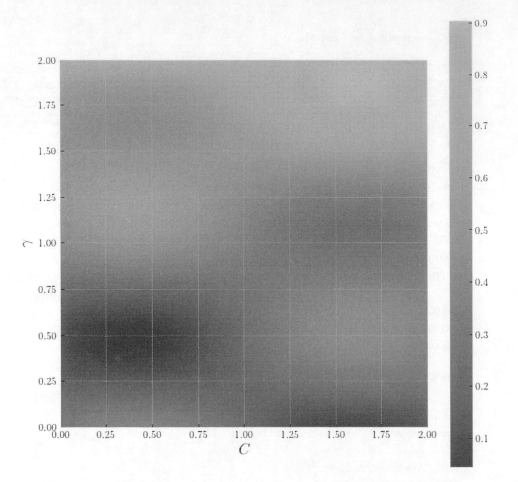

Figure 3.17   The accuracy of an SVM model on a test dataset as a function of the penalty parameter c and the RBF kernel parameter γ. The function changes more quickly with respect to γ than to c.

4   Implement a GP model with a constant mean function and a Matérn 5/2 kernel with an output scale implemented as a `gpytorch.kernels.ScaleKernel` object.

5   Don't specify the `ard_num_dims` parameter when initializing the kernel object or set the parameter to `None`. This will create a GP model without ARD.

6   Train the hyperparameters of the GP model using gradient descent, and inspect the length scale after training.

7   Redefine the GP model class, this time setting `ard_num_dims = 2`. Retrain the GP model with gradient descent, and verify that the two length scales have significantly different values.

Summary

- Prior knowledge plays an important role in a Bayesian model and can heavily influence the posterior predictions of the model.
- With a GP, prior knowledge can be specified using the mean and the covariance functions.
- The mean function describes the expected behavior of the GP model. In the absence of data, a GP's posterior mean prediction reverts to the prior mean.
- A GP's mean function can take on any functional form, including a constant, a linear function, and a quadratic function, which can be implemented with GPyTorch.
- A GP's covariance function controls the smoothness of the GP model.
- The length scale specifies the level of variability of the output with respect to the function input. A large length scale leads to more smoothness and, thus, less uncertainty in predictions.
- Each dimension in a GP can have its own length scale. This is called automatic relevance determination (ARD) and is used to model objective functions that have different levels of variability in different dimensions.
- The output scale specifies the range of the function output. A large output scale leads to a larger output range and, thus, more uncertainty in the predictions.
- The Matérn kernel class is a generalization of the RBF kernel class. By specifying its parameter nu, we can model various levels of smoothness in the GP's predictions.
- The hyperparameters of a GP can be optimized by maximizing the marginal likelihood of the data using gradient descent.

Part 2

Making decisions with Bayesian optimization

The GP is only one part of the equation. To fully realize the BayesOpt technique, we need the second part of the equation: decision-making policies that dictate how function evaluations should be carried out to optimize the objective function as quickly as possible. This part enumerates the most popular BayesOpt policies, including their motivations, mathematical intuitions, and implementations. While different policies are motivated by different objectives, they all aim to balance the tradeoff between exploration and exploitation—a core challenge in BayesOpt, specifically, and decision-making under uncertainty problems, more generally.

Chapter 4 kicks things off by introducing the idea of an acquisition score as a way to quantify the value of making a function evaluation. The chapter also describes the heuristic of seeking to improve from the best point we have seen so far, which leads to two popular BayesOpt policies: Probability of Improvement and Expected Improvement.

Chapter 5 connects BayesOpt with a closely related problem: multi-armed bandits. We explore the popular Upper Confidence Bound policy, which uses the optimism under uncertainty heuristic, and the Thompson sampling policy, which uses the probabilistic nature of the GP to aid decision-making.

Chapter 6 introduces us to information theory, a subfield of mathematics that has many applications in decision-making problems. Using a central concept of information theory called entropy, we design a BayesOpt policy that seeks to gain the most information about our search target.

Throughout this part, we learn about the different ways to address the exploration–exploitation tradeoff and build a diverse tool set of optimization methods. While we have learned to use GPyTorch to implement GPs in the previous part, the premiere BayesOpt library, BoTorch, is our focus in this part. We learn how to declare BayesOpt policies, use them to facilitate an optimization loop, and compare their performance across a wide range of tasks. By the end of this part, you will obtain hands-on knowledge regarding implementing and running BayesOpt policies.

Refining
the best result with
improvement-based policies

This chapter covers

- The BayesOpt loop
- The tradeoff between exploitation and exploration in a BayesOpt policy
- Improvement as a criterion for finding new data points
- BayesOpt policies that use improvement

In this chapter, we first remind ourselves of the iterative nature of BayesOpt: we alternate between training a Gaussian process (GP) on the collected data and finding the next data point to label using a BayesOpt policy. This forms a virtuous cycle in which our past data inform future decisions. We then talk about what we look for in a BayesOpt policy: a decision-making algorithm that decides which data point to label. A good BayesOpt policy needs to balance sufficiently exploring the search space and zeroing in on the high-performing regions.

Finally, we learn about two policies that seek to improve upon the best-seen data point in the BayesOpt loop so far: Probability of Improvement, and one of the most commonly used BayesOpt policies, Expected Improvement. For example, if we have a hyperparameter tuning application where we want to identify the neural network that gives the highest validation accuracy on a dataset, and the highest accuracy we have seen so far is at 90%, we will likely want to improve upon this 90% threshold. The policies we learn in this chapter attempt to create this improvement. In the material discovery task we saw in table 1.2, where we'd like to search for metal alloys that mix at a low temperature (corresponding to high stability) and 187.24 is the lowest temperature we have found, the two aforementioned policies will seek to find values lower than this 187.24 benchmark.

Amazingly, thanks to the Gaussianity of our belief about the objective function, how much we can expect to improve from the best-seen point may be computed in closed form. This is to say that while we don't know what the objective function looks like at unseen locations, computing improvement-based quantities can still be done easily under a GP. By the end of the chapter, we gain a thorough understanding of what a BayesOpt policy needs to do and how this is done with the two improvement-based policies. We also learn how to integrate BoTorch, the BayesOpt library in Python (https://botorch.org/docs/introduction) that we use from this chapter through the end of the book, to implement BayesOpt policies.

4.1   *Navigating the search space in BayesOpt*

How can we make sure we are using our past data to inform future decisions correctly? What are we looking for in a BayesOpt policy as an automated decision-making procedure? This section answers these questions and gives us a clear idea of how BayesOpt works when using a GP.

Specifically, in the following subsection, we reinspect the BayesOpt loop that was briefly introduced in section 1.2.2 to see how decision-making via BayesOpt policies is done in tandem with training a GP. Then, we discuss the main challenge BayesOpt policies need to address: the balance between exploring regions with high uncertainty and exploiting good regions in the search space.

Take, as an example, figure 4.1, which shows a GP trained on two data points at 1 and 2. Here, a BayesOpt policy needs to decide at which point between –5 and 5 we

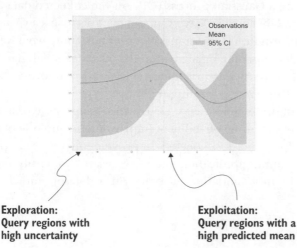

Figure 4.1   The exploration–exploitation tradeoff in BayesOpt. Each policy needs to decide whether to query regions with high uncertainty (exploration) or to query regions with a high predicted mean (exploitation).

Exploration: Query regions with high uncertainty

Exploitation: Query regions with a high predicted mean

should evaluate the objective function next. The exploration–exploitation tradeoff is clear: we need to decide whether to inspect the objective function at the left and right extremes of our search space (around –5 and 5), where there's considerable uncertainty in our predictions, or stay within the region around 0, where the mean prediction is at the highest. The exploration–exploitation tradeoff will set the stage for the different BayesOpt policies that we discuss in this and following chapters.

4.1.1   The BayesOpt loop and policies

First, let's remind ourselves of what the BayesOpt loop looks like and the role BayesOpt policies play in this process. In this chapter, we also implement a scaffold of this loop, which we use to inspect BayesOpt policies in future chapters. Review figure 4.2, which is a repeat of figure 1.6 and shows how BayesOpt works on a high level.

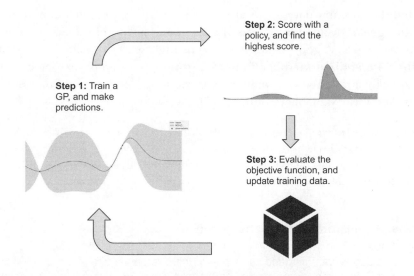

Figure 4.2   The BayesOpt loop, which combines a GP for modeling and a policy for decision making. This complete workflow may now be used to optimize black box functions.

Specifically, BayesOpt is done via a loop that alternates between the following:

- Training a GP on the current training set. We have thoroughly covered how to do this in previous chapters.
- Using the trained GP to score data points in the search space by how valuable they are at helping us identify the optimum of the objective function (step 2 in figure 4.2). The point that maximizes this score is selected to be labeled and added to the training data (step 3 in figure 4.2). How this scoring is done is determined by the BayesOpt policy used. We learn more about different policies in this chapter and chapters 5 and 6.

We repeat this loop until we reach a termination condition, most often once we have evaluated the objective function for a target number of loop iterations. This procedure is end to end, as we don't just use a GP to make predictions for the sake of making predictions—these predictions inform the decisions we make about which data points to collect next, which, in turn, drive how future predictions are generated.

> **DEFINITION**   The BayesOpt loop is a virtuous cycle of model training (the GP) and data collection (the policy), each of which helps and benefits from the other, with the goal of locating the optimum of the objective function. The virtuous cycle of BayesOpt is a feedback loop that iterates toward an equilibrium with desired properties; its components act in concert to achieve the desired result, rather than aggravating one another in a vicious cycle that results in an undesirable outcome.

The rule that dictates how data points are scored according to their value in helping us achieve this goal is decided by a BayesOpt policy and is, therefore, essential to optimization performance. A good policy that assigns high scores to data points that are truly valuable to optimization will point us toward the optimum of the objective function more quickly and efficiently, while a badly designed policy might misguide our experiments and waste valuable resources.

> **DEFINITION**   A *BayesOpt policy* scores each potential query according to its value and thus decides where we should query the objective function next (where the score is maximized). This score computed by the policy is called the *acquisition score* as we are using it as a method of data acquisition.

Connection to reinforcement learning policies

If you have had experience with reinforcement learning (RL), you might notice a connection between a BayesOpt policy and an RL policy. In both techniques, the policy tells us which action to take in a decision-making problem. While in RL, a policy might assign a score to each action and we, in turn, pick the one with the highest score, or the policy might simply output the action we should take. In BayesOpt, it's always the former, where the policy outputs a score quantifying the value of each possible query, so it's our job to identify the query maximizing this score.

Unfortunately, there's no perfect solution to the problem of designing a good BayesOpt policy. That is, there's no single BayesOpt policy that consistently excels across all objective functions. Different policies, as we see in this and following chapters, use different focuses and heuristics. While some heuristics work well on one type of objective function, others might prove effective on different types of functions. This means we need to expose ourselves to a wide range of BayesOpt policies and understand what they aim to do to be able to apply them to appropriate situations—which is exactly what we will be doing in chapters 4 to 6.

> ## What is a policy?
> Each BayesOpt policy is a decision rule that scores data points in terms of useful-
> ness in optimization according to a given criterion or heuristic. Different criteria
> and heuristics give rise to different policies, and there is no predetermined set of
> BayesOpt policies. In fact, BayesOpt researchers still publish papers proposing new
> policies. In this book, we only discuss the most popular and commonly used policies
> in practice.

Let us now take a moment to implement a placeholder BayesOpt loop, which we will
be using from now on to inspect various BayesOpt policies. This code is implemented
in CH04/01 - BayesOpt loop.ipynb. The first component we need is an objective
function that we'd like to optimize using BayesOpt. Here, we use the familiar one-
dimensional Forrester function, which is defined to be between –5 and 5, as the objective function to be maximized. We also compute the value of the Forrester function
inside its domain [–5, 5], with xs and ys as the ground truth:

```
def forrester_1d(x):
    y = -((x + 1) ** 2) * torch.sin(2 * x + 2) / 5 + 1
    return y.squeeze(-1)
```
Form of the objective function, assumed to be unknown

```
bound = 5

xs = torch.linspace(-bound, bound, bound * 100 + 1).unsqueeze(1)
ys = forrester_1d(xs)
```
Test data computed over a grid between –5 and 5

Another thing we need to do is modify how GP models are implemented so that they
can be used with BayesOpt policies in BoTorch. Implementing the GP makes up the
first step of our BayesOpt loop.

Since BoTorch is built right on top of GPyTorch, only minimal modifications are
required. Specifically, we use the following GP implementation, in which we inherit
from the `botorch.models.gpytorch.GPyTorchModel` class in addition to our usual
`gpytorch.models.ExactGP` class. Further, we declare the class-specific attribute
`num_outputs` and set it to 1. These are the minimal modifications we need to make to
use our GPyTorch model with BoTorch, which implements the BayesOpt policies we
use later in this chapter:

```
class GPModel(gpytorch.models.ExactGP,
  botorch.models.gpytorch.GPyTorchModel):
    num_outputs = 1

    def __init__(self, train_x, train_y, likelihood):
        super().__init__(train_x, train_y, likelihood)
        self.mean_module = gpytorch.means.ConstantMean()
        self.covar_module = gpytorch.kernels.ScaleKernel(
            gpytorch.kernels.RBFKernel()
        )
```
Modifications for BoTorch integration

```
def forward(self, x):
    mean_x = self.mean_module(x)
    covar_x = self.covar_module(x)
    return gpytorch.distributions.MultivariateNormal(mean_x, covar_x)
```

Aside from these, everything else in our GP implementation remains the same. We now write a helper function that trains the GP on our training data:

```
def fit_gp_model(train_x, train_y, num_train_iters=500):
    noise = 1e-4                                          ◁─┐  Trains the GP using
                                                            │  gradient descent

    likelihood = gpytorch.likelihoods
    ➥.GaussianLikelihood()
    model = GPModel(train_x, train_y, likelihood)            Declares the GP
    model.likelihood.noise = noise

    optimizer = torch.optim.Adam(model.parameters(),
    ➥lr=0.01)                                             ┐
    mll = gpytorch.mlls.ExactMarginalLogLikelihood         │
    ➥(likelihood, model)                                   │

    model.train()                                           │  Trains the GP
    likelihood.train()                                      │  using gradient
                                                            │  descent
    for i in tqdm(range(num_train_iters)):                  │
        optimizer.zero_grad()                               │

        output = model(train_x)                             │
        loss = -mll(output, train_y)                        │

        loss.backward()                                     │
        optimizer.step()                                    │

    model.eval()                                            │
    likelihood.eval()                                       ┘

    return model, likelihood
```

NOTE We have used all the preceding code in previous chapters. If you are having trouble understanding a piece of code, refer to section 3.3.2 for more details.

This covers step 1 of figure 4.2. For now, we are skipping step 2, in which we implement BayesOpt policies, and saving it for the next section and future chapters. The next component to be implemented is the visualization of the data that has been collected so far, the current GP belief, and how a BayesOpt policy scores the rest of the data points. The target of this visualization is shown in figure 4.3, which we saw in chapter 1. Specifically, the top panel of the plot shows the predictions made by a GP model against the true objective function, while the bottom panel shows the acquisition scores as computed by a BayesOpt policy.

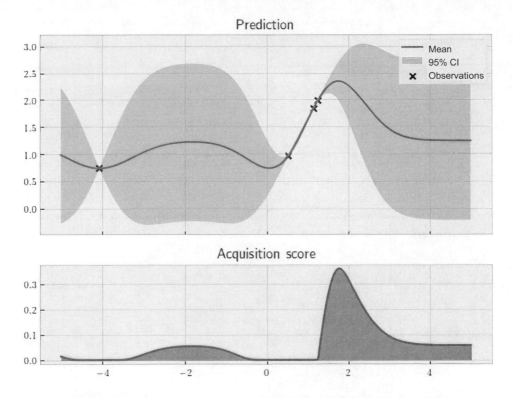

Figure 4.3 A typical visualization of progress in BayesOpt. The top panel shows the GP predictions and the ground truth objective function, while the bottom panel shows the acquisition scores made by a BayesOpt policy named Expected Improvement, which we learn about in section 4.3.

We are already familiar with how to generate the top panel, and generating the bottom panel is just as simple. This will be done using a helper function similar to the one we used in section 3.3. The function takes in a GP model and its likelihood function as well as two optional inputs:

1 `policy` refers to a BayesOpt policy object, which can be called in a way similar to any PyTorch module. Here, we are calling it on the grid `xs` that represents our search space to obtain the acquisition scores across the space. We discuss how to implement these policy objects with BoTorch in the next section, but we don't need to know more about these objects right now.

2 `next_x` is the location of the data point that maximizes the acquisition score, which is to be added to the running training data:

```
def visualize_gp_belief_and_policy(
    model, likelihood, policy=None, next_x=None
):
    with torch.no_grad():
```

```
                   predictive_distribution = likelihood(model(xs))
   GP predictions  predictive_mean = predictive_distribution.mean
                   predictive_upper, predictive_lower =
                      ➥predictive_distribution.confidence_region()

                   if policy is not None:
                       acquisition_score = policy(xs.unsqueeze(1))
```
GP predictions (label for first block)

Acquisition score (label for `if policy is not None:` block)

```
       ...        ◄──── Omitted
```

Here, we are generating the predictions from the GP and the acquisition scores on the test data xs. Note that we don't compute the acquisition scores if `policy` is not passed in, in which case we also visualize the GP predictions in the way we're already familiar with—scattered points to indicate the training data, a solid line for the mean predictions, and shaded regions for the 95% CIs:

```
       if policy is None:
           plt.figure(figsize=(8, 3))

           plt.plot(xs, ys, label="objective", c="r")         ◄─┐ Ground
           plt.scatter(train_x, train_y, marker="x", c="k",      │ truth
               label="observations")
           plt.plot(xs, predictive_mean, label="mean")
           plt.fill_between(
               xs.flatten(),
               predictive_upper,
               predictive_lower,
               alpha=0.3,
               label="95% CI",
           )

           plt.legend()
           plt.show()
```
Training data (label pointing to `plt.scatter`)

Mean predictions and 95% CIs (label for `plt.plot(xs, predictive_mean...` through `fill_between` block)

NOTE   Refer to section 2.4.4 for a refresher on this visualization.

If, on the other hand, a policy object is passed in, we create another subplot to show the acquisition scores across the search space:

```
       else:
           fig, ax = plt.subplots(
               2,
               1,
               figsize=(8, 6),
               sharex=True,
               gridspec_kw={"height_ratios": [2, 1]}
           )

           ...        ◄──┤ GP predictions
                         │ (the same as before)
```

```
        if next_x is not None:
            ax[0].axvline(next_x, linestyle="dotted", c="k")
```

Acquisition scores
```
    ax[1].plot(xs, acquisition_score, c="g")
    ax[1].fill_between(
      xs.flatten(),
      acquisition_score,
      0,
      color="g",
      alpha=0.5
    )
```

The point maximizing the acquisition score, visualized using a dotted vertical line

```
        if next_x is not None:
            ax[1].axvline(next_x, linestyle="dotted", c="k")

        ax[1].set_ylabel("acquisition score")

        plt.show()
```

This function, when `policy` and `next_x` are passed in, will create a lower panel showing the acquisition score according to the BayesOpt policy. Finally, we need to implement step 3 of the BayesOpt loop in figure 4.2, which (1) finds the point with the highest acquisition score and (2) adds it to the training data and updates the GP. For the first task of identifying the point giving the highest acquisition score, while it's possible in our Forrester example to scan over a one-dimensional search space, an exhaustive search becomes more and more expensive as the number of dimensions of the objective function increases.

NOTE We can use BoTorch's helper function `botorch.optim.optimize.optimize_acqf()`, which finds the point that maximizes the score of any BayesOpt policy. The helper function uses L-BFGS, a quasi-Newton optimization method that generally works better than gradient descent.

We do this as follows:

- `policy` is the BayesOpt policy object, which we learn about shortly.
- `bounds` stores the boundary of our search space, which is –5 and 5 in this case.
- `q = 1` specifies the number of points we'd like the helper function to return, which is one. (In chapter 7, we learn about the setting where we are allowed to make multiple queries to the objective functions at the same time.)
- `num_restarts` and `raw_samples` denote the number of repeats and initial data points L-BFGS uses when searching for the optimal candidate that gives the highest acquisition score. Generally, I recommend using 20 times and 50 times the number of dimensions for these parameters, respectively.
- The returned values, `next_x` and `acq_val`, are the location of the point giving the highest acquisition score and the corresponding maximized acquisition score, respectively:

```
next_x, acq_val = botorch.optim.optimize_acqf(
    policy,
    bounds=torch.tensor([[-bound * 1.0], [bound * 1.0]]),
    q=1,
    num_restarts=20,
    raw_samples=50,
)
```

Setting the number of restarts and raw samples

The higher the values of `num_restarts` and `raw_samples` are, the more exhaustive L-BFGS will be when searching for the optimal candidate maximizing the acquisition score. This also means the L-BFGS algorithm will take longer to run. You can increase these two numbers if you see that L-BFGS is failing at maximizing the acquisition score or decrease them if the algorithm is taking too long to run.

As the last step, we put together what we have implemented so far in a BayesOpt loop. We do the following at each iteration of this loop:

1 We first print out the best value we have seen so far (`train_y.max()`), which shows how optimization is progressing.
2 Then, we retrain the GP on the current training data and redeclare the BayesOpt policy.
3 Using the helper function `botorch.optim.optimize_acqf()` from BoTorch, we identify the point in the search space that maximizes the acquisition score.
4 We call the helper function `visualize_gp_belief_and_policy()`, which visualizes our current GP belief and optimization progress.
5 Finally, we query the function value at the identified point (`next_x`) and update our observed data.

This entire procedure is summarized in figure 4.4, which shows the steps in the BayesOpt loop and the corresponding code that implements them. Each step is implemented by modular code from our helper functions or BoTorch, making the entire procedure easy to follow.

The actual code implementation is as follows:

```
num_queries = 10                              ◁──── The number of evaluations of the
                                                     objective function that can be made
for i in range(num_queries):
    print("iteration", i)
    print("incumbent", train_x[train_y.argmax()], train_y.max())

    model, likelihood = fit_gp_model(train_x, train_y)    ◁──── Updates the
                                                                 model on the
    policy = ...       ◁──── Initializes the                     current data
                             BayesOpt policy, to
                             be discussed later
```

```
next_x, acq_val = botorch.optim.optimize_acqf(
    policy,
    bounds=torch.tensor([[-bound * 1.0],
    ➥[bound * 1.0]]),
    q=1,
    num_restarts=20,
    raw_samples=50,
)
```
Finds the point that gives the highest acquisition score

Visualizes the current GP model and acquisition scores
```
visualize_gp_belief_and_policy(model, likelihood, policy,
    next_x-next_x)
```

```
next_y = forrester_1d(next_x)

train_x = torch.cat([train_x, next_x])
train_y = torch.cat([train_y, next_y])
```
Makes an observation at the identified point and updates the training data

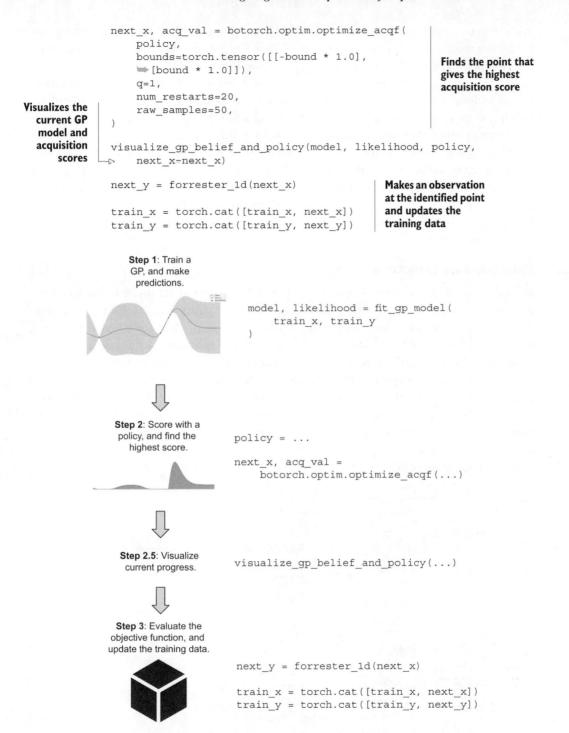

Step 1: Train a GP, and make predictions.

```
model, likelihood = fit_gp_model(
    train_x, train_y
)
```

Step 2: Score with a policy, and find the highest score.

```
policy = ...

next_x, acq_val =
    botorch.optim.optimize_acqf(...)
```

Step 2.5: Visualize current progress.

```
visualize_gp_belief_and_policy(...)
```

Step 3: Evaluate the objective function, and update the training data.

```
next_y = forrester_1d(next_x)

train_x = torch.cat([train_x, next_x])
train_y = torch.cat([train_y, next_y])
```

Figure 4.4   Steps in the BayesOpt loop and the corresponding code. The code for each step is modular, which makes the entire loop easy to follow.

With that, we have implemented a skeleton of a BayesOpt loop. All that's left to do is fill in the initialization of `policy` with an actual BayesOpt policy we would like to use, and the notebook will be able to run BayesOpt on the Forrester function. Note that while calling `visualize_gp_belief_and_policy()` isn't necessary (that is, the previous BayesOpt loop will still be able to run without that line of code), the function is useful in helping us observe the behavior and characteristics of BayesOpt policies as well as diagnosing any potential problems, as we discuss later in this chapter.

One of the most important characteristics of a BayesOpt policy is the balance between exploration and exploitation, a classical tradeoff in many AI and ML problems. Here, the possibility of discovering a high-performance region we currently don't know about (exploration) is traded off against the chance of zeroing in on a known good region (exploitation). We discuss this tradeoff in greater detail in the next subsection.

4.1.2   *Balancing exploration and exploitation*

In this subsection, we discuss one of the problems inherent in any decision-making procedure, including BayesOpt: the balance between sufficient exploration of the entire search space and timely exploitation of regions that yield good results. This discussion will help us form an idea of what a good BayesOpt policy should do and make us aware of how each of the policies we learn about addresses this tradeoff.

To illustrate the exploration–exploitation tradeoff, imagine you are dining at a restaurant you have only been to a few times before (see figure 4.5). You know that this restaurant has great burgers, but you're not sure if their fish and steaks are any good. Here, you are faced with a exploration–exploitation problem, where you need to choose between ordering something new that might be an excellent dish (exploration) and ordering your usual but reliable meal (exploitation).

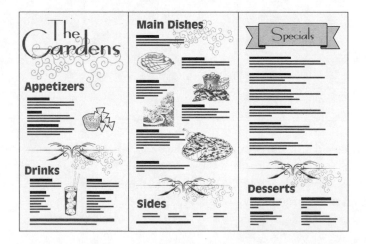

Figure 4.5   Ordering from a menu at a restaurant has an inherent exploration (trying something new) vs. exploitation (ordering the usual) tradeoff.

Excessive exploration might cause you to order something you don't like, while constant exploitation runs the risk of causing you to miss out on a dish you will really like. Therefore, a reasonable balance between the two is crucial.

This ubiquitous problem is found not only in ordering food but in common problems in AI, such as reinforcement learning, product recommendation, and scientific discovery. In BayesOpt, we face the same tradeoff: we need to sufficiently explore the search space so we don't miss out on a good region, but we should also focus on regions with high objective values to ensure we are making progress in terms of optimization.

> **NOTE** By "regions with high objective values," we mean the regions that comprise inputs x that yield high values of outputs $f(x)$, which are the target of our optimization (specifically maximization) task.

Let's return to our code example and assume that when we first start out, our training dataset contains two observations from the Forrester objective function, at $x = 1$ and at $x = 2$:

```
train_x = torch.tensor([
    [1.],
    [2.]
])
train_y = forrester_1d(train_x)

model, likelihood = fit_gp_model(train_x, train_y)

print(torch.hstack([train_x, train_y.unsqueeze(1)]))
```

This gives the output

```
tensor([[1.0000, 1.6054],
        [2.0000, 1.5029]])
```

This indicates that the point at 1 evaluates at roughly 1.6, while the point at 2 evaluates at 1.5. Visualizing the predictions made by the trained GP, we obtain the familiar-looking plot in figure 4.6. This figure shows the exploration–exploitation tradeoff we face: Should we evaluate the objective function where uncertainty is high, or should we stay within the region where the mean prediction is high?

Each BayesOpt policy has a different way of addressing the tradeoff and, therefore, offers different advice on how to best explore the search space. In figure 4.6, some policies might lead us to further explore unknown regions, while others might suggest zeroing in on what we know to give high values. Again, there's usually no one-size-fits-all approach (that is, no policy that always works well).

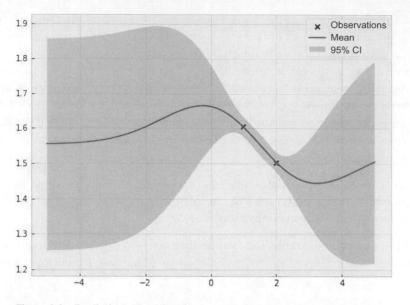

Figure 4.6   Predictions by a GP trained on two data points from the Forrester function

4.2   *Finding improvement in BayesOpt*

We have almost everything ready to run BayesOpt on a given objective function. We now need a policy with a scoring rule about how valuable each data point we could potentially label is in our search for the optimum of the objective. Again, each policy we will see gives a different scoring rule, motivated by different heuristics for optimization.

In this section, we learn about one such heuristic that makes intuitive sense when the goal is optimization. It comes in the form of seeking to improve from the best point we have seen so far throughout optimization. In the upcoming subsection, we learn that GPs are amenable to facilitating the computation of this measure of improvement. Then, we cover how different ways to define improvement give rise to two of the most common BayesOpt policies: Probability of Improvement and Expected Improvement.

4.2.1   *Measuring improvement with a GP*

In this subsection, we examine how improvement in BayesOpt is defined, how it constitutes a good measure of utility, and that working with improvement-related quantities is straightforward with normal distributions. As our final goal in BayesOpt is to identify the global optimum of the objective function—the point that gives the highest objective value—the higher the values are that we observe while making evaluations of the objective function, the higher our utility should be. Suppose that as we make an evaluation of the objective function at some point x_1, we observe the value 2. In another situation in which we evaluate another point x_2, we observe the value 10. Intuitively, we should value the second point more, as it gives us a higher function value.

However, what if before observing x_1 and x_2, we have already seen a point x_0 that yields a value of 20? In this case, it's natural to think that even though x_2 is better than x_1, neither point results in any additional utility, as we already have a much better observation in x_0. On the other hand, if we were to have a point x_3 that yields a value of 21, then we would be happier, as we would have found a better value than that of x_0. This is illustrated in figure 4.7.

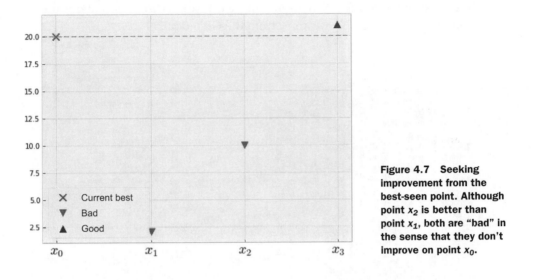

Figure 4.7   Seeking improvement from the best-seen point. Although point x_2 is better than point x_1, both are "bad" in the sense that they don't improve on point x_0.

These comparisons point to the idea that in BayesOpt, we care about not only the raw values of our observations but also whether the newly found observations are better than our observations. In this case, since x_0 sets a very high bar in terms of function values, neither x_1 nor x_2 constitute improvement—at least the kind of improvement we care about in optimization. In other words, a reasonable goal in optimization is to seek to *improve* from the best point that we have seen so far because as long as we improve from the best-seen point, we are making progress.

> **DEFINITION**   The best-seen point, or the point that yields the highest function value we have found so far, is often called *the incumbent*. This term denotes the fact that this point currently holds the highest value among all points queried during our search.

Given that we have a GP belief about the objective function, inspecting how much we can expect to improve from the best-seen point may be easily accomplished. Let's start from our running example of the Forrester function, where our current GP is shown in figure 4.6.

Out of the two data points in our training set, ($x = 1$, $y = 1.6$) is the better one, as it has a higher function value. This is our current incumbent. Again, we are focusing on improving from this 1.6 threshold; that is, we'd like to find data points that will yield function values higher than 1.6.

Visually, we can imagine this improvement-based idea as cutting off the GP horizontally at the incumbent, as shown in figure 4.8. The portion highlighted in the darker color corresponds to "improving from the incumbent" (at 1.6). Anything below this line does not constitute improvement and, therefore, won't give us any additional optimization utility. Whether a point—for instance, $x = 0$—will yield a higher function value is unknown, but we can still try to reason about the probability that it is true using what we know from the GP model.

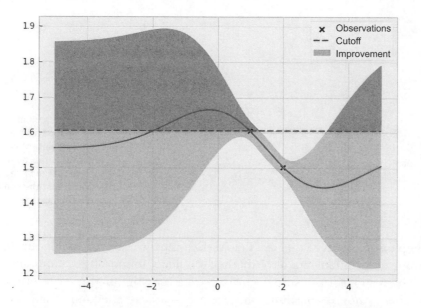

Figure 4.8   Improvement from the incumbent from the perspective of a GP. The portion of the GP's predictions that corresponds to improvement from the incumbent is highlighted in a darker shade.

Reasoning about the probability that $x = 0$ will yield a higher function value is easy to do, as by querying point $x = 0$, the improvement from the incumbent that we may observe exactly corresponds to a *normal distribution* that is partially truncated, as shown in figure 4.9.

The left panel of figure 4.9 contains the same GP in figure 4.8 that is cut off at the incumbent, with an addition showing the CI of the normal distribution prediction at $x = 0$. Slicing the GP vertically at this point 0, we obtain the right panel of figure 4.9, where the CIs in the two panels are the same. We see that only the highlighted portion of the normal distribution in the right panel represents the improvement we may observe from the incumbent, which is what we care about. This highlighted portion is part of a normal distribution, which, as we cover in the upcoming subsections, leads to many mathematical conveniences.

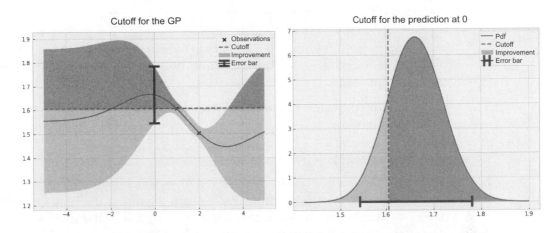

Figure 4.9 Improvement from the incumbent at 0, highlighted in a darker shade. The left panel shows the entire GP, while the right panel only shows the normal distribution corresponding to the prediction at 0 (the error bars are the same across the two panels). Here, improvement from the incumbent follows a truncated normal distribution.

These conveniences don't only apply to $x = 0$. Since the prediction made by the GP at any given point is a normal distribution, the improvement at any point also follows a normal distribution that is cut off, as shown in figure 4.10.

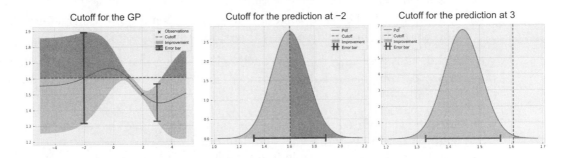

Figure 4.10 Improvement from the incumbent at −2 and 3, highlighted in a darker shade. The left panel shows the entire GP, the center panel shows the prediction at −2, and the right panel shows the prediction at 3. The highlighted portions show possible improvements, which depend on the normal distribution at a given point.

We see that compared with figure 4.9, where a large portion of the normal distribution at 0 is highlighted as possible improvements, the following is true:

- The prediction at –2 (center panel) is worse in the sense that only half of it shows possible improvements. This is because the mean prediction at –2 is roughly equal to the incumbent, so there's a 50–50 chance that the function value at –2 will improve from 1.6.
- As another example, the right panel shows the prediction at 3, where it is almost impossible (according to our GP belief about the objective) to improve from the incumbent, as almost the entire normal distribution at 3 lies below the incumbent threshold.

This shows that different points will lead to different possible improvements, depending on the GP's predictions.

4.2.2   *Computing the Probability of Improvement*

Having isolated what we aim to achieve in BayesOpt—namely, improving from the current incumbent—we are now ready to finally begin discussing the BayesOpt policies that seek to achieve this goal. In this subsection, we learn about *Probability of Improvement* (PoI), which is a policy that measures how likely a candidate point is to be able to improve.

The idea of measuring how likely it is that a candidate point improves from the incumbent corresponds to the probability that a point is a "good" one, according to figure 4.7. This was also hinted at in section 4.2.1 with the GP, where we said the following:

1. The point at 0 (figure 4.9) has a large portion of its normal distribution highlighted as possible improvements. In other words, it has a high probability of improving.
2. The point at –2 (the center panel of figure 4.10) has a 0.5 probability of improving, as only half of its normal distribution exceeds the incumbent.
3. The point at 3 (the right panel of figure 4.10) has most of its normal distribution below the threshold, so it has a very low probability of improving.

We can make this computation more concrete by noticing that the probability that a point improves from the incumbent is equal to the area of the highlighted portion in figures 4.9 and 4.10.

DEFINITION   The entire area under any normal curve is 1, so the area of the highlighted portion in figures 4.9 and 4.10 exactly measures how likely it is that the normal random variable in question (the function value at a given point) exceeds the incumbent.

The quantity corresponding to the area of the highlighted region is related to the *cumulative density function* (CDF), which is defined as the probability that a random variable will take a value less than or equal to a target. In other words, the CDF measures the area of the region *not* highlighted, which is 1 minus the area of the high-lighted region.

Thanks to how mathematically convenient normal distributions and GPs are, we can easily compute the area of this highlighted region using the CDF, which requires the mean and the standard deviation of the normal distribution in question. Computationally, we can make use of PyTorch's `torch.distributions.Normal` class, which implements normal distributions and offers the useful `cdf()` method. Specifically, suppose we are interested in calculating how likely the point at 0 is to be able to improve from the incumbent. We will follow the procedure describe in figure 4.11:

1   First, we use the GP to compute the mean and standard deviation predictions at the point at 0.
2   We then compute the area under the normal curve defined by the previous mean and standard deviation, with the incumbent being the cutoff. We use the CDF for this computation.
3   Finally, we subtract the CDF value from 1 to obtain the PoI for the candidate point.

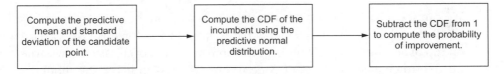

Figure 4.11   Flowchart of how the PoI score is computed. By following this procedure, we can compute how likely any candidate point is to be able to improve from the incumbent.

NOTE   Technically, the CDF computes the area of the portion of a normal distribution to the left of a threshold, so we need to subtract from 1 the output of the CDF to get the area of the portion to the right of the threshold, which corresponds to possible improvements.

We first generate the GP's prediction at this point:

```
with torch.no_grad():
    predictive_distribution = likelihood(model(torch.tensor([[0.]])))
    predictive_mean = predictive_distribution.mean
    predictive_sd = predictive_distribution.stddev
```

The predictive mean at 0

The predictive standard deviation at 0

Then, we initialize a one-dimensional normal distribution with the corresponding mean and standard deviation:

```
normal = torch.distributions.Normal(predictive_mean, predictive_sd)
```

This normal distribution is the one visualized in the right panel of figure 4.9. Finally, to compute the area of the highlighted portion, we call the `cdf()` method with the incumbent as its input (which is `train_y.max()`, the maximum value of our training data) and subtract the result from 1:

```
>>> 1 - normal.cdf(train_y.max())
tensor([0.8305])
```

Here, our code shows that at point 0, we have a greater than 80% chance of improving from the incumbent, which agrees with the fact that a large portion of the normal distribution in figure 4.9 is highlighted. Using the same computation, we can find out that there is a 0.4948 PoI at –2 and 0.0036 at 3. Looking at figure 4.10, we see that these numbers make sense. Beyond these three points (0, –2, and 3), we can also compute how likely a given point is to be able to improve—that is, the PoI of a given point—across our search space, using the same formula.

> **DEFINITION** The procedure in figure 4.11 gives us the scoring rule for the PoI policy, where the score of each point in the search space is equal to how likely it is that the point can improve from the incumbent. Again, this score is also called the *acquisition score*, as we are using it as a method of data acquisition.

We can see that this PoI policy uses the `cdf()` method, but it's cleaner to use *BoTorch*, the Python library that implements BayesOpt policies, for this task. BoTorch is built on top of and works seamlessly with PyTorch and GPyTorch. As we saw earlier, we only needed to change two lines of code in our GP class to make the model compatible with BoTorch. Further, BoTorch implements its policies as *modules*, allowing us to swap different policies in and out of a BayesOpt loop in a modular manner.

> ### The modularity of BoTorch's policies
> By *modular*, we mean that we can replace the policy currently in use with another policy in a BayesOpt loop by only changing the initialization of the policy. The rest of the BayesOpt loop (training the GP model, visualizing optimization progress, and updating the training data) doesn't have to change. We have seen a similar modularity with GPyTorch's mean functions and kernels in sections 3.3 and 3.4.2.

To implement the PoI policy with BoTorch, we do the following:

```
policy = botorch.acquisition.analytic.ProbabilityOfImprovement(    # Declares the PoI policy
    model, best_f=train_y.max()
)

with torch.no_grad():       # Computes the score
    scores = policy(xs.unsqueeze(1))
```

The BoTorch class `ProbabilityOfImprovement` implements the PoI as a PyTorch module, taking in a GP as the first argument and the incumbent value as the second. The variable `scores` now stores the PoI scores of the points in `xs`, which is a dense grid between –5 and 5.

Again, the acquisition score of each point equals the probability that the point will improve from the incumbent, according to our GP belief. Figure 4.12 shows this score across our search space, together with our GP.

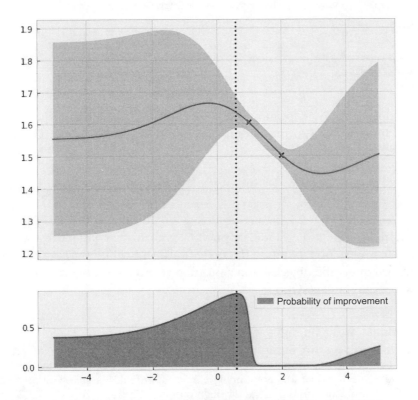

Figure 4.12 GP predictions (top) and PoI (bottom), where the dotted line indicates the point that maximizes the PoI score. This point is where we query the objective function at the next iteration of optimization.

We observe some interesting behavior in the PoI scores:

- The region to the left of the incumbent (from 0 to 1) has relatively high PoI scores. This corresponds to the high mean predictions in this area.
- The region on the left of the plot has slightly lower scores. This is because the mean predictions are not as high, but there is enough uncertainty in this region that there's still a considerable probability of improving.
- The region around 2 has a PoI close to 0. As we saw, the predictive normal distributions of the points here mostly lie below the incumbent threshold.

Now, all that's left for us to do is identify the point between −5 and 5 that has the highest PoI score—that is, the point that maximizes the probability of improving from the incumbent. As mentioned, we take advantage of BoTorch's helper function `botorch.optim.optimize.optimize_acqf()`, which finds the point that maximizes the score of any BayesOpt policy. We do this using the following code, which is a part of the code that implements the BayesOpt loop:

```
next_x, acq_val = botorch.optim.optimize.optimize_acqf(
    policy,
    bounds=torch.tensor([[-bound], [bound]], dtype=torch.float),
    q=1,
    num_restarts=10,
    raw_samples=20,
)
```

The returned values are the location of the point giving the highest acquisition score that L-BFGS finds and the corresponding maximized acquisition score. Upon inspection, we have the following:

```
>>> next_x, acq_val

(tensor([[0.5985]]), tensor(0.9129))
```

This output indicates that the candidate point maximizing the PoI score at 0.91 PoI is at roughly 0.6, which corresponds to the dotted vertical line in figure 4.12. This point is where we will query the objective function (that is, evaluate the function) to collect the next data point in BayesOpt.

> **The candidate with the highest predictive mean**
>
> Interestingly, the point we select to query (roughly at 0.6) is *not* the point with the highest predictive mean (which is around –0.5). The latter has a slightly lower PoI because our uncertainty at this point is high, so it is, in fact, less likely to be able to improve from the incumbent, despite the high predictive mean.

And that's all there is to deciding which point to query using the PoI policy at a single iteration of BayesOpt. But remember the BayesOpt loop in figure 4.2, where we alternate between finding the next data point to query using a policy (step 2) and updating our GP with that new data (steps 1 and 3). We will do this in section 4.2.3.

4.2.3   *Running the PoI policy*

In this subsection, we finally run the PoI policy and analyze its behavior. Once again, we repeat the entire process—training the model, declaring the PoI policy, and using `optimize_acqf()` to find the best point—multiple times until we reach a termination condition. As we saw, this loop is implemented in the CH04/01 - BayesOpt loop.ipynb notebook. Now, we need to initialize the PoI policy within the appropriate `for` loop.

This code produces a series of plots generated by the helper function `visualize_gp_belief_and_policy()`, each showing the current state of our BayesOpt loop throughout

the 10 queries we make. These plots look similar to figure 4.12, with the addition of
the objective function for our reference:

```
num_queries = 10

for i in range(num_queries):
    print("iteration", i)
    print("incumbent", train_x[train_y.argmax()], train_y.max())

    model, likelihood = fit_gp_model(train_x, train_y)

    policy = botorch.acquisition.analytic.ProbabilityOfImprovement(
        model, best_f=train_y.max()
    )

    next_x, acq_val = botorch.optim.optimize_acqf(
    ...
```

Our PoI policy

Omitted

> ### The number of function evaluations in BayesOpt
>
> The number of queries we use in BayesOpt entirely depends on how many function
> evaluations we can afford to make. Section 1.1 defines the problem of expensive
> black box optimization, which assumes that the number of queries we can make is
> relatively low due to the cost of function evaluation.
>
> There are other criteria that could be used to determine when to terminate the
> BayesOpt loop. For example, we can stop when we have achieved a targeted objective
> value or when there hasn't been significant improvement among the last 5 or 10 que-
> ries. Throughout the book, we stick with the assumption that we have a predeter-
> mined number of function evaluations that can be made.

We use 10 queries as the default to run the BayesOpt policies for the one-dimensional
Forrester function and inspect the behavior of the policies. Exercise 2 of this chapter
deals with a two-dimensional function and uses 20 queries.

Figure 4.13 shows these plots at the first, fifth, and final iterations. We see that the
PoI policy stays inside the region between 0 and 2, and at the 10th and final iteration,

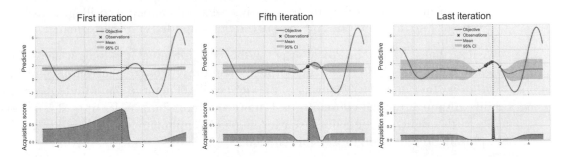

**Figure 4.13   Progress made by the PoI policy. As the policy seeks to pursue improvement of any magnitude,
progress gets stuck at the local optimum near 2, and we fail to explore other regions of the search space.**

we have converged at a local optimum. This means we are failing to adequately explore the search space and, therefore, missing out on the global optimum of the objective function in the right area, around 4.

The BoTorch warning when using the helper function optimize_acqf()

When running the code for the BayesOpt with the PoI on the previous page, you might receive the following warning from BoTorch:

```
RuntimeWarning: Optimization failed in
`gen_candidates_scipy` with the following warning(s):
[OptimizationWarning('Optimization failed within `scipy.optimize.minimize`
with status 2 and message ABNORMAL_TERMINATION_IN_LNSRCH.')]
Trying again with a new set of initial conditions.
  warnings.warn(first_warn_msg, RuntimeWarning)
```

This warning is displayed when the helper function `optimize_acqf()` (specifically, the line search subroutine) fails to successfully optimize the acquisition score (the PoI score, in this case). This failure often happens when the acquisition score function is highly non-smooth (e.g., in the last panel of figure 4.13, where there's a sharp peak around $x = 1.5$), making numerical optimization unstable.

Without going into the details of the optimization routine, we can resort to increasing the number of restarts (the `num_restarts` argument) and the number of raw samples (the `raw_samples` argument) when using `optimize_acqf()`, which increases our chance of finding the data point with the highest acquisition score.

For ease of exposition, from this point onward, we turn off this warning when running the helper function `optimize_acqf()` in our code, using a context manager with the `warnings` module as follows:

```
with warnings.catch_warnings():
    warnings.filterwarnings('ignore', category=RuntimeWarning)
    next_x, acq_val = botorch.optim.optimize_acqf(...)
```

NOTE Although the performance of the PoI in figure 4.13 might be disappointing (after all, we have spent a lot of time building up to this PoI policy that seems overly exploitative), analyzing what is happening will give us insights into how to refine and *improve* (no pun intended) our performance.

We note that although the PoI gets stuck at the local optimum, it is doing what it's supposed to do. Specifically, since the PoI seeks to improve from the current incumbent, the policy finds that slowly moving to the right of 1 will achieve that with high probability. Although the PoI constantly finds more and more improvement by slowly moving to the right, we view this behavior as overly exploitative, as the policy is not exploring other regions thoroughly enough.

IMPORTANT In other words, even though what the PoI is doing is consistent with what we initially wanted to achieve—namely, improving from the incumbent—the resulting behavior isn't what we want. This means that simply pursuing improvement of any kind from the incumbent shouldn't be what we care about.

There are two ways to fix this overly exploitative behavior. The first is to restrict what we mean by *improvement*. Our experiment with the PoI shows that at each iteration, the policy only finds marginal improvement from the incumbent by slowly moving in the direction that the GP believes the function moves upward in.

If we were to redefine what we mean by *improvement* by saying that an improvement from the incumbent is only valid if it is at least ε greater than the current incumbent value and modifying the PoI accordingly, then the policy will be more likely to explore the search space more effectively. This is because the GP will know that staying at a local optimum won't lead to significant improvement from the incumbent. Figure 4.14 illustrates this idea.

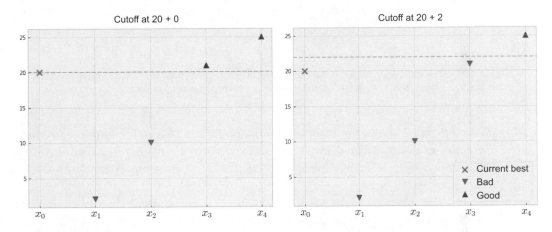

Figure 4.14   **Defining a stricter definition of *improvement* by requiring an improvement of at least ε = 0 (left) and ε = 2 (right). The larger the requirement, the more explorative the PoI policy becomes. See exercise 1 for more details.**

We won't go into more detail here, but exercise 1 explores this approach. Interestingly, we will observe that the more improvement we require the PoI to observe, the more explorative the policy becomes.

4.3   *Optimizing the expected value of improvement*

As we saw in the previous section, naïvely seeking to improve from the incumbent leads to over-exploitation from the PoI. This is because simply moving away from the incumbent by a small amount in the appropriate direction can achieve a high PoI. Therefore, optimizing this PoI is *not* what we want to do. In this section, we learn to further account for the *magnitude* of the possible improvements we may observe. In other words, we also care about how much improvement we can make from the incumbent. This leads us to one of the most popular BayesOpt policies: *Expected Improvement* (EI).

The motivation for seeking to account for the magnitude of the improvement is clear. Consider the example in figure 4.15.

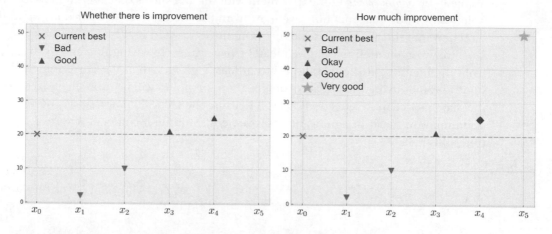

Figure 4.15   **The difference between PoI (left) and EI (right). The former only cares whether we improve from the incumbent, while the latter considers how much improvement is made.**

The left panel shows the computation made by the PoI policy, which considers only whether each candidate data point improves from the incumbent. Therefore, a point that improves by a small amount and one that significantly improves from the incumbent are treated equally.

On the other hand, the right panel shows what happens if we also consider the magnitude of the possible improvements. Here, although points x_1 and x_2 are still treated as undesirable (since they don't improve from the incumbent x_0), x_4 is considered better than x_3, as the former offers a larger improvement. Similarly, x_5 is considered the best out of the five candidate points.

Of course, this doesn't mean we can now simply design the policy that picks out the data point that offers the largest improvement from the incumbent. We still need to know how much (if any) improvement we will observe, which we only discover once we actually query the objective function.

NOTE   Despite not knowing the exact value of the improvement we will observe, we can reason about the magnitude of the improvement of each candidate point in a probabilistic manner.

Recall that in figures 4.9 and 4.10, we have a truncated normal distribution representing the improvement we will observe at a given point. By computing the area of the highlighted region, we obtain the probability that a point will improve from the incumbent, giving us the PoI policy. However, we can perform other computations as well.

DEFINITION   In addition to the PoI, we may compute the *expected value* of the random variable corresponding to the highlighted region. The fact that we are dealing with truncated normal distributions enables us to compute this expected value in closed form. The BayesOpt policy that scores data points using this measure is called *Expected Improvement* (EI).

While the closed-form formula for the EI score isn't as simple as the CDF like for PoI, EI's scoring formula is still just as easy to calculate. Intuitively, using the expected value of improvement may allow us to better balance exploration and exploitation than PoI. After all, points around the current incumbent may improve with high probability, but their improvements are likely to be minimal (which is what we empirically observed in our experiment).

A point that is far away, which we don't know much about, might give a lower improvement probability, but because there's a chance that this point will give a large improvement, EI might assign a higher score to it. In other words, while PoI might be considered a *risk-averse* BayesOpt policy that cares about improving from the incumbent, however small the improvement is, EI balances between the risk and reward to find the point that best balances the tradeoff. This is illustrated in figure 4.16, which compares PoI and EI using the same dataset and trained GP.

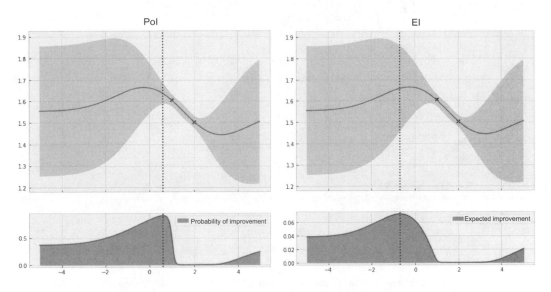

Figure 4.16   The difference between PoI (left) and EI (right). EI balances exploration and exploitation better.

We see that the candidate data point chosen by PoI (around 0.6) is different from one chosen by EI (around −0.7). The former is close to the current incumbent, so it's likely that querying it will help us improve. However, EI sees that there's more uncertainty in other regions far away from the incumbent, which may lead to greater improvement. Thanks to this reasoning, EI favors data points that provide a better balance between exploration and exploitation.

Another nice property of EI that showcases this balance is the way it assigns the acquisition scores to data points with the same predictive mean or standard deviation. Specifically, it does this in the following ways:

- If two data points have the same predictive mean but different predictive standard deviations, then the one with the higher uncertainty will have a higher score. The policy, therefore, rewards exploration.
- If two data points have the same predictive standard deviations but different predictive means, then the one with the higher mean will have a higher score. The policy, therefore, rewards exploitation.

This is a desideratum of a BayesOpt policy, as it expresses our preference for exploration when all else is equal (that is, when the predictive means are equal) but also for exploitation when all else is equal (that is, when uncertainties are equal). We see this property again in chapter 5 with another BayesOpt policy called *upper confidence bound*.

Computationally, we can initialize EI as a BayesOpt policy object using code that is almost identical to the code for PoI:

```
policy = botorch.acquisition.analytic.ExpectedImprovement(
    model, best_f=train_y.max()
)
```

Now, let's rerun our entire BayesOpt loop with the EI policy, making sure we are starting with the same initial dataset. This generates figure 4.17, which is to be compared to figure 4.13 of PoI.

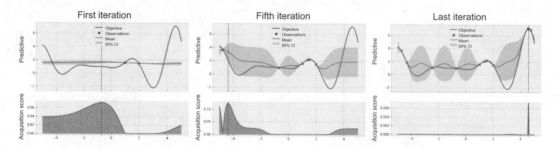

Figure 4.17   Progress made by the EI policy. The policy balances exploration and exploitation better than PoI and finds the global optimum at the end.

Here, we see that while EI still focuses on the local optimal region around 2 initially, the policy quickly explores other regions in the search space to look for larger improvements from the incumbent. At the fifth iteration, we see that we are now inspecting the region on the left. Finally, after spending all 10 queries, EI has successfully identified the global optimum of the objective function, outperforming PoI in the previous section.

NOTE Due to its simplicity and natural balance between exploration and exploitation, EI is one of the most, if not the most, commonly used policies in BayesOpt. The policy is a good default option if there's no reason to prefer other policies.

4.4 Exercises

There are two exercises in this chapter:

1 The first covers using PoI for exploration by changing our definition of improvement.
2 The second covers hyperparameter tuning using BayesOpt in an objective function that simulates the accuracy surface of an SVM model.

4.4.1 Exercise 1: Encouraging exploration with PoI

One way to address the PoI's tendency to over-exploit is to set a higher bar for what constitutes *improvement*. Specifically, we saw that naïvely finding points that maximize the probability of improving from the incumbent prevents us from escaping local optima.

As a solution to this, we can modify the policy to specify that we only accept improvements by at least ε. This would guide the PoI to look for improvement in other regions in the search space once a local region has been sufficiently covered. This exercise, implemented in CH04/02 - Exercise 1.ipynb, walks us through this modification and showcases the positive effect it has on the PoI. Its steps are as follows:

1 Recreate the BayesOpt loop in CH04/01 - BayesOpt loop.ipynb, which uses the one-dimensional Forrester function as the optimization objective.
2 Before the `for` loop that implements BayesOpt, declare a variable named `epsilon`. This variable will act as the minimum improvement threshold to encourage exploration. Set this variable to 0.1 for now.
3 Inside the `for` loop, initialize the PoI policy as before, but this time, specify that the incumbent threshold, set by the `best_f` argument, is the incumbent value *plus* the value stored in `epsilon`.
4 Rerun the notebook, and observe whether this modification leads to better optimization performance than the original PoI policy by encouraging more exploration.
5 How much more explorative PoI becomes heavily depends on the minimum improvement threshold stored in `epsilon`. Set this variable to 0.001 to observe that an improvement threshold that is not sufficiently large may not necessarily encourage exploration successfully. What happens when this value is set to 0.5?
6 In the previous step, we saw that setting the improvement threshold to an appropriate value is crucial for PoI. However, it's not obvious how to do this across multiple applications and objective functions. A reasonable heuristic is to dynamically set it to some α percentage of the incumbent value, specifying that we would like to see $1 + \alpha$ increase in the incumbent value. Implement this in the code with a 110% improvement requirement.

4.4.2   *Exercise 2: BayesOpt for hyperparameter tuning*

This exercise, implemented in CH04/03 - Exercise 2.ipynb, applies BayesOpt to an objective function that simulates the accuracy surface of an SVM model in a hyperparameter tuning task. The x-axis denotes the value of the penalty parameter C, while the y-axis denotes the value for the RBF kernel parameter γ. See the exercise in chapter 3 for more detail. The steps are as follows:

1   Recreate the BayesOpt (BayesOpt) loop in CH04/01 - BayesOpt loop.ipynb:

   a   We don't need the Forrester function anymore; instead, copy the code for the two-dimensional function described in the exercise in chapter 3, and use it as the objective function.

   b   Note that the domain for this function is $[0, 2]^2$.

2   Declare the corresponding test data with xs for a two-dimensional grid representing the domain and ys for the function values of xs.

3   Modify the helper function that visualizes optimization progress. For one-dimensional objective functions, it's easy to visualize the GP predictions along with the acquisition scores. For this two-dimensional objective, the helper function should generate a plot of two panels: one showing the ground truth and the other showing the acquisition scores. Both panels should also show the labeled data. The plot should look similar to figure 4.18.

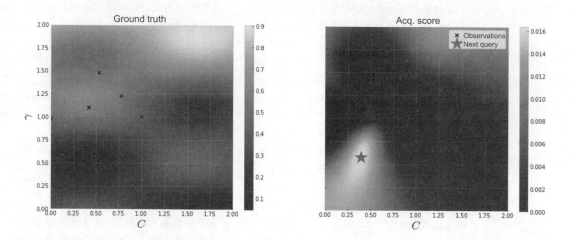

Figure 4.18   A reference showing what the helper function that visualizes BayesOpt progress should look like. The left panel shows the true objective function, while the right panel shows the acquisition scores.

4   Copy the GP class from the exercise in chapter 3, which implements a Matérn 2.5 kernel with ARD. Further modify this class to make it integratable with BoTorch.

5 Reuse the helper function `fit_gp_model()` and the `for` loop that implements BayesOpt:

  a The initial training dataset should contain the point in the middle of the domain: $(1, 1)$.

  b As our search space is two-dimensional, make the search for the point maximizing the acquisition score more exhaustive by setting `num_restarts = 40` and `raw_samples = 100` in `botorch.optim.optimize_acqf()`.

  c Set the number of queries we can make (the number of times we can evaluate the objective function) to 20.

6 Run the PoI policy on this objective function. Observe that the policy, once again, gets stuck at a local optimum.

7 Run the modified version of PoI, where the minimum improvement threshold is set at 0.1:

  a See Exercise 1 for more detail about setting the minimum improvement threshold for PoI.

  b Observe that this modification, again, leads to better optimization performance.

  c What is the first iteration where we reach an accuracy of at least 90%? What are the model's parameters achieving this accuracy?

8 Run the EI policy on this objective function:

  a Observe that the policy outperforms PoI.

  b What is the first iteration where we reach an accuracy of at least 90%? What are the model's parameters achieving this accuracy?

9 Inspecting the performance of a policy based on a single run of BayesOpt can be misleading. It's better for a BayesOpt experiment to be repeated multiple times with different starting data:

  a Implement this idea of repeated experiments, and visualize the average incumbent values and error bars across 10 experiments.

  b Each experiment should start with a single data point uniformly sampled from the search space.

  c Run the policies we have listed, and compare their performance.

This marks the end of our chapter on improvement-based BayesOpt policies. It's important to keep the code that implements the BayesOpt loop for the Forrester function we used here in mind, as we use it again to benchmark other policies in future chapters. Specifically, in chapter 5, we learn about BayesOpt policies inspired by the multi-armed bandit problem.

Summary

- A BayesOpt policy uses the trained GP to score how valuable each data point is in our quest to find the optimum of the objective function. The score computed by the policy is called the acquisition score.

- In each iteration of a BayesOpt loop, a GP is trained on the observed data, a policy suggests a new data point to query, and the label of this point is added to the training set. This repeats until we cannot make any more function evaluations.

- A GPyTorch model only needs minimal modifications to be integrated into BoTorch, which implements BayesOpt policies.

- BoTorch provides a helper function named `optimize_acqf()` from the `optim.optimize` module that takes in a policy object and returns the datapoint that maximizes the acquisition score.

- A good BayesOpt policy needs to balance exploration (learning about regions with high uncertainty) and exploitation (narrowing down high-performing regions).

- Different BayesOpt policies address the exploration–exploitation tradeoff differently. It is important to inspect optimization progress to analyze and adjust the performance of the policy in use.

- One heuristic that could be used in BayesOpt is to find points that improve upon the best-seen value.

- Finding the point that gives the best chance of improving from the best-seen value results in the PoI policy.

- Finding the point that gives the highest expected improvement from the best-seen value results in the EI policy.

- PoI may be considered an overly exploitative and risk-averse policy as the policy only aims to improve from the best-seen value, however small the improvement is. Without any further modification, EI tends to balance exploration and exploitation better than PoI.

- Thanks to the Gaussian belief about the function values, computing scores by PoI and EI may be done in closed form. We, therefore, can compute and optimize the scores defined by these policies easily.

5
Exploring the search space with bandit-style policies

This chapter covers

- The multi-armed bandit problem and how it's related to BayesOpt
- The Upper Confidence Bound policy in BayesOpt
- The Thompson sampling policy in BayesOpt

Which slot machine should you play at a casino to maximize your winnings? How can you develop a strategy to intelligently try out multiple slot machines and narrow down the most profitable machine? What does this problem have to do with BayesOpt? These are the questions this chapter will help us answer.

Chapter 4 was our introduction to BayesOpt policies, which decide how the search space should be explored and inspected. The exploration strategy of a BayesOpt policy should guide us toward the optimum of the objective function we'd like to optimize. The two particular policies we learned about were Probability of Improvement (PoI) and Expected Improvement (EI), which use the idea that we'd like to improve from the best objective value we have seen so far. This improvement-based mindset is only a heuristic and, therefore, doesn't constitute the only approach to BayesOpt.

In this chapter, we learn about two more BayesOpt policies that are directly taken from the heavily related decision-making problem called the *multi-armed bandit* (MAB). Posed as a question of which is the most profitable slot machine to play at a casino, the MAB problem sets the stage for many decision-making-under-uncertainty problems. MAB has enjoyed a long history and extensive research, and many good solutions have been developed for this problem. As we learn in this chapter, MAB and BayesOpt are very similar problems—both deal with decision-making under uncertainty for optimization—so the expectation is that solutions to the MAB problem will work well on BayesOpt too.

First, we briefly talk about the MAB problem and how it is related to BayesOpt. This discussion provides some background on the problem and puts into perspective how BayesOpt is related to other problems in AI. Then, we learn about the two most popular policies in MAB and apply them to BayesOpt. The first is the *Upper Confidence Bound* policy, which uses the *optimism in the face of uncertainty* principle to reason about its decisions. The second policy is called *Thompson sampling*, which is a randomized solution that actively uses the probabilistic nature of our predictive models. We then implement and run these policies on our running examples and analyze their performance.

By the end of this chapter, we gain an understanding of the MAB problem and its relationship with BayesOpt. More importantly, we add two more items to our portfolio of BayesOpt policies, exposing ourselves to more ways of exploring the search space in a black box optimization problem.

5.1 Introduction to the MAB problem

In this section, we learn about the MAB problem on a high level. We start by discussing its problem statement and setting in the first subsection.

> **IMPORTANT**   In a MAB problem, we need to choose an action to take at each step over a long horizon. Each action yields a reward according to an unknown reward rate, and our goal is to maximize the total reward we receive at the end of the long horizon.

We also explore its connections to BayesOpt, as well as other problems in AI and ML. This provides us with context, relating MAB to the rest of the text.

5.1.1 Finding the best slot machine at a casino

While *multi-armed bandit* may evoke a mysterious image in your mind, the term actually refers to a gambler's problem of choosing which slot machines to play at a casino to obtain the largest amount of reward. Imagine you're at a casino and there's a slot machine with an "arm" you can pull.

Upon pulling the arm of the slot machine, you may receive coins as a reward; however, there's randomness in this process. Specifically, programmed within the inner-workings of this slot machine is a reward probability p. Each time the arm of the machine is pulled, the machine returns coins according to that probability. This slot machine is visualized in figure 5.1. If $p = 0.5$, then the machine rewards its players half of the time. If $p = 0.01$, then roughly only 1 in 100 pulls will result in coins being returned. Since this probability is programmed inside the machine—and therefore hidden away from us—there's no way for us to know for sure what that probability is.

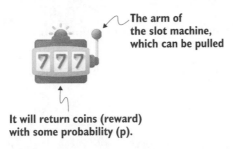

**The arm of
the slot machine,
which can be pulled**

**It will return coins (reward)
with some probability (p).**

Figure 5.1   A slot machine with an arm
that can be pulled. The machine may
return coins according to its reward
probability when its arm is pulled.

In this hypothetical setting, the casino programs its slot machines so that the rate at which these machines reward players with coins is lower than that of the machines being played and receiving coins. In other words, even if there are occasional winners who receive rewards from these slot machines, on average, it's the casino that makes a profit.

> **DEFINITION**   A particularly unsuccessful player who is losing coins faster than winning them might begrudgingly call the slot machine they have been playing "a bandit," thinking the machine is stealing their money. Since the machine has an arm that may be pulled, it can be called a *one-armed bandit*.

Now, imagine there's not just one slot machine but a *row* of machines we may choose to play, each with its own reward probability p, as visualized in figure 5.2.

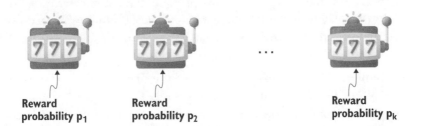

**Reward
probability p_1**   **Reward
probability p_2**   **Reward
probability p_k**

Figure 5.2   A slot machine with an arm that can be pulled. The machine may
return coins according to its reward probability when its arm is pulled.

With this row of slot machines, a strategic player may turn this setting into a decision-making challenge and aim to try out the slot machines in some intelligent manner so they can most quickly identify the machine that has the highest reward probability. Their intent here is to maximize the amount of reward they receive given that they can only pull the arms of these machines a specific number of times.

> **DEFINITION**   This decision-making problem is called the *multi-armed bandit* (or MAB), as there are multiple arms we may pull. The goal is to design a policy of deciding which machine's arm we should pull next to maximize the total reward we obtain at the end.

We see that MAB possesses many characteristics of an optimization-under-uncertainty problem, like BayesOpt:

- *We can take specific actions.* Each action corresponds to pulling the arm of a specific slot machine.
- *We have a limited budget.* We can only pull these arms for a specific number of times until we have to stop.
- *There's uncertainty in the outcomes of the actions that may be taken.* We don't know what the reward probability of each slot machine is, and we can't even estimate it until we have pulled its arm multiple times. Further, upon pulling an arm, we can't know for sure whether we will receive coins, as there's randomness in the reward.
- *We'd like to optimize for an objective.* We aim to maximize the *cumulative reward*, which is the total number of coins we receive while pulling the arms of these machines until we stop.

Perhaps most importantly, in MAB, we face the same exploration–exploitation tradeoff we discussed in section 4.1.2. In particular, each time we decide to pull the arm of a machine, we need to choose between the machine that has been giving us a good success rate so far (exploitation) and others with a reward probability we don't know much about (exploration).

The problem we face is a tradeoff because by exploring, we run the risk of wasting our pulls on machines that have low reward probability, but excessive exploitation means we might completely miss out on a machine that has a higher reward rate than what we currently observe. Figure 5.3 shows an example of this where the following is true:

1 We have collected 70 coins over 100 pulls of the first machine. That is, the first machine offers the highest empirical success rate so far, at 70%.
2 We have more data from the second machine, so we have the least uncertainty about its reward rate, which is around 50%.
3 Although the empirical success rate of the third machine is the lowest (0%), we may need to try pulling its arm more times to be more certain of its reward rate.

It is the job of a MAB policy, similar to that of a BayesOpt policy, to look at the data on past rewards and decide which arm we should pull next, while balancing this tradeoff

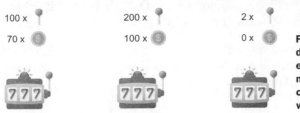

Figure 5.3 An example of an MAB dataset showing the exploration–exploitation dilemma. An MAB policy must choose between a machine with a consistently high success rate and one with a reward rate that is uncertain.

between exploration and exploitation. The MAB problem models a wide range of applications you might see in the real world:

- In product recommendation, an engine needs to pick from a number of products in a store to suggest one to a user. Each product can be seen as the arm of a slot machine, and pulling the arm means the engine picks that product to present to the user. If the user clicks on the advertisement for the product, we may see it as receiving a reward, as the user's click is something we want to achieve.
- Many resource management problems may be framed as MAB, where we need to consider how to best allocate different resources to different organizations to best optimize some high-level objective (e.g., profit or productivity) without knowing in advance how well each organization will operate. Portfolio management can also be framed as an MAB problem in the same way.
- MAB also has seen application in the design of clinical trials, where each patient needs to be assigned to a specific treatment. We wish to optimize the treatment outcome across all patients but need to contend with limited resources and determining how likely each patient is to benefit from a given treatment.

In each of these applications, we can take a set of actions—that is, a set of arms we can pull—to optimize an objective under uncertainty.

5.1.2 From MAB to BayesOpt

We have seen that MAB and BayesOpt have many shared characteristics. In both problems, we need to reason about what decision we should take so that we can maximize a quantity we care about. Further, the outcome of each action is not deterministic. This means we don't know whether an action will yield a good result until we actually take it.

However, these two problems are not equivalent. In MAB, we aim to maximize the *cumulative reward* over time—that is, the total number of coins one receives. With BayesOpt, we seek to simply find an input of a function that leads to a high value; so as long as among the dataset we collect there is a good objective value, we will succeed at optimization. This single-valued objective is sometimes called the *simple reward*. This difference means we need to make sure we are frequently receiving rewards in MAB to maintain a good cumulative reward, while in BayesOpt, we could afford to be more explorative to potentially find a good objective value.

> **DEFINITION**   The term *simple reward* doesn't mean the objective is easier or simpler to optimize, but rather that the objective is a single number as opposed to a sum that is the cumulative reward.

Further, there are only a finite number of actions to take in MAB (a finite number of arms we could pull). In BayesOpt, as we are attempting to optimize an objective function in a continuous domain, there are infinitely many actions. Since we assume with a GP that function values at nearby points are similar to one another, we can think of this as actions close to each other yielding similar reward rates. This is illustrated in figure 5.4, where each infinitesimal point is a slot machine whose arm we could pull (that is, query the objective function value at), and machines that are close to each other have similar colors.

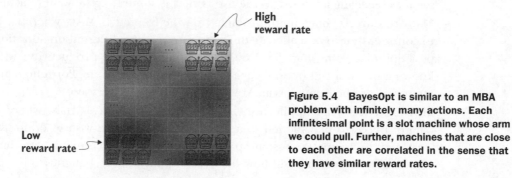

Figure 5.4   BayesOpt is similar to an MBA problem with infinitely many actions. Each infinitesimal point is a slot machine whose arm we could pull. Further, machines that are close to each other are correlated in the sense that they have similar reward rates.

Most formalizations of the MAB problem consider the binary setting where a slot machine, when pulled, either returns a coin or doesn't return anything. The function value we may observe in BayesOpt, on the other hand, could take on any real value.

The main differences between MAB and BayesOpt are summarized in table 5.1. Although these are fundamental differences, the tradeoff between exploration and exploitation in decision-making is present in both problems, so it's reasonable to aim to repurpose MAB policies to BayesOpt.

Table 5.1   The differences between the MAB and BayesOpt

Criterion	MAB	BayesOpt
Objective to be maximized	Cumulative reward	Simple reward
Type of observation/reward	Binary	Real-valued
Number of actions	Finite	Infinite
Correlation between actions	No	Yes for similar actions

In the rest of this chapter, we learn about two such policies, the motivations behind them, and how to implement them with BoTorch. We start with the Upper Confidence Bound policy in the next section.

5.2   Being optimistic under uncertainty with the Upper Confidence Bound policy

How should we account for the infinitely many possibilities for the value we may observe when we evaluate the objective function at a particular location? Further, how should we reason about these possibilities in a simple, efficient way that is conducive to decision-making? In this section, we explore the *Upper Confidence Bound* (UCB) policy from MAB, which results in a BayesOpt policy of the same name.

UCB operates under the *optimism in the face of uncertainty* principle. In MAB, the idea is to use an upper bound of our estimate for each slot machine's reward rate as a substitute for the true, unknown reward rate. That is, we optimistically estimate the reward rate of each machine using an upper bound of what we believe it to be and, finally, choose the one with the highest upper bound.

We first discuss this principle and how it aids our decision-making reasoning. Afterwards, we learn how to implement the UCB policy using BoTorch and analyze its behavior.

5.2.1   Optimism under uncertainty

Let's consider a simple example to make this idea concrete. Say you wake up one day and observe that even though it's sunny outside, there are dark clouds on the horizon. You check the weather app on your phone to see if it will stay sunny throughout the day and whether you should bring an umbrella to work in case it rains later. Unfortunately, the app can't tell you with absolute certainty whether it will stay sunny. Instead, you only see an estimate that the probability of sunny weather is between 30% and 60%.

You think to yourself that if the probability that it will stay sunny is less than 50%, then you will bring an umbrella. However, you don't have a single-valued estimate here, but instead, a range between 30% and 60%. How, then, should you decide whether an umbrella is necessary?

A pessimist might say that since the probability of sunny weather could be as low as 30%, you should be on the safe side and prepare for the worst. Someone who considers the average case might look further into the app to see what the mean estimate is for the probability it will stay sunny and make their decision accordingly. From the perspective of an optimist, on the other hand, a 60% chance is reason enough to think that it will stay sunny, so this person wouldn't bother bringing an umbrella with them to work. These ways of thinking are shown in figure 5.5.

In figure 5.5, the third person's reasoning corresponds to the idea behind the UCB policy: being optimistic about the outcome of an unknown event and making decisions based on this belief. In the MAB problem, the UCB would construct an upper bound of the reward rate of each slot machine and proceed to pick the machine with the highest bound.

Figure 5.5   **Different ways of thinking about the future and making decisions. The last person corresponds to the UCB policy, which reasons about an unknown quantity in an optimistic manner.**

NOTE   The way this policy is realized in BayesOpt is particularly simple since with a GP as our predictive model of the objective function, we already have an upper bound of the reward rate of each action. That is, we have an upper bound of the objective value at any given input location.

Specifically, we know that the objective value at a given location follows a normal distribution, and a commonly used measure to quantify uncertainty of a normal distribution is the 95% CI, which contains 95% of the probability mass of the distribution. With a GP, we visualize this 95% CI across the input space as the thick line in figure 5.6. The upper bound of this 95% CI, which is the upper boundary of the shaded region highlighted in figure 5.6, is exactly what the UCB policy uses as the acquisition scores for the data points in the search space, and the point that gives the highest score is the one at which we will evaluate the objective function next, which, in this case, is the location indicated by the dotted line around −1.3.

DEFINITION   *Acquisition scores* quantify how valuable a data point is in guiding us towards the optimum of the objective function. We first learned about acquisition scores in section 4.1.1.

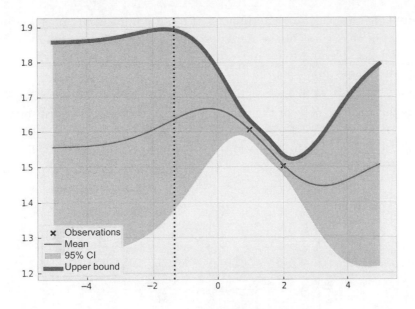

Figure 5.6   The UCB of a GP that corresponds to the 95% CI. This bound can be used as the acquisition score of the UCB policy.

You might think that this form of decision-making might not be appropriate, especially in high-stakes situations where the cost of a bad decision is high. In our umbrella example, by optimistically underestimating the probability of rain, you might run the risk of getting caught in the rain without an umbrella.

However, it is a particularly computationally efficient way of reasoning, as we simply need to extract an upper bound of our estimate of a quantity of interest and use that bound for decision-making. Moreover, as we see in the next subsection, by choosing which CI we'd like to use (as opposed to sticking with the 95% CI), we have complete control over how optimistic the UCB is. This control also allows the policy to balance exploration and exploitation, which is the core question that needs to be addressed by any BayesOpt policy.

5.2.2   *Balancing exploration and exploitation*

In this subsection, we talk further about how the UCB policy may be adjusted by us, the BayesOpt users. This offers a level of control that balances between regions with high uncertainty (exploration) and regions with high predictive mean (exploitation). This discussion aims to provide a deeper understanding of UCB before moving ahead with BoTorch implementation in the next subsection.

Remember that with a normal distribution, going two standard deviations away from the mean (that is, mean μ plus/minus 2 times standard deviation σ) gives us the 95% CI. The upper bound of this interval ($\mu + 2\sigma$) is the acquisition score of UCB we saw in the previous subsection.

However, the 95% CI is not the only CI of a normal distribution. By setting the multiplier, denoted as β, for the standard deviation σ in the formula $\mu + \beta\sigma$, we obtain other CIs. For example, the following is true in a one-dimensional normal distribution, as shown in figure 5.7:

- Going one standard deviation above the mean ($\mu + \sigma$)—that is, setting β = 1— gives the 68% CI: 68% of the probability mass of the normal distribution lies between $\mu - \sigma$ and $\mu + \sigma$.

- Similarly, three standard deviations away from the mean (β = 3) gives us the 99.7% CI.

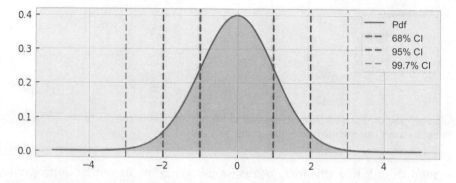

Figure 5.7   Different CIs of standard normal distributions. Going away from the mean to one, two, and three standard deviations, we obtain the 68%, 95%, and 99.7% CIs. The upper bounds of these intervals are used by the UCB policy.

In fact, any value of β would give us a unique CI for the normal distribution. Since the UCB only dictates that we should use an upper bound from our predictive model to make decisions, any value of the form $\mu + \beta\sigma$ can serve as the upper bound used in UCB. By setting this parameter β, we can control for the behavior of the UCB policy.

Figure 5.8 shows three different upper bounds corresponding to β = 1, 2, 3, while the mean function, in fact, corresponds to setting β = 0. We see that although the upper bounds are of roughly the same shape, these bounds go up and down at different rates. Further, since the data point maximizing this bound is the point the UCB selects to query for optimization, different bounds, that is, different values of β will induce different optimization behaviors.

> **IMPORTANT**   The smaller β is, the more exploitative UCB becomes. Conversely, the larger β is, the more explorative UCB becomes.

We can see that the value of β controls the behavior of UCB by inspecting the formula for the acquisition score: $\mu + \beta\sigma$. When β is small, the mean μ contributes the most to the acquisition score. So, the data point with the highest predictive mean will maximize

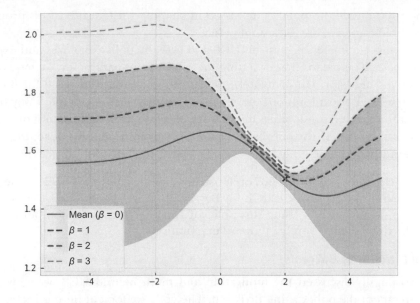

Figure 5.8 Different upper bounds of a GP, corresponding to different CIs and
β values. The larger β is, the more explorative the UCB policy becomes.

this score. This selection corresponds to pure exploitation, as we are simply picking out the point with the largest predicted value. When β is large, on the other hand, the standard deviation σ, which quantifies our uncertainty, becomes more important in the UCB score, emphasizing the need for exploration.

We see this distinction in figure 5.8 where around 0 is where we achieve the highest predictive mean, indicating it is the region of exploitation. As β increases, the point at which the different upper bounds peak gradually moves to the left where there is more uncertainty in our prediction.

> **NOTE** Interestingly, in the limit where $\beta \rightarrow \infty$, the point that maximizes UCB's acquisition score is where the standard deviation σ is maximized—that is, where our uncertainty is at its highest. This behavior corresponds to pure exploration, as we are selecting data points with high uncertainty.

Finally, UCB correctly assigns higher scores to data points that offer better balance between exploration and exploitation:

- If two data points have the same predictive mean but different predictive standard deviations, then the one with the higher uncertainty will have a higher score. The policy, therefore, rewards exploration.
- If two data points have the same predictive standard deviations but different predictive means, then the one with the higher mean will have a higher score. The policy, therefore, rewards exploitation.

Remember that one of the policies discussed in chapter 4, EI, also has this property, which is a desideratum of any BayesOpt policy.

All in all, this parameter, β, controls UCB and how the policy explores and exploits the search space. This means that by setting the value of this parameter, we have direct control over its behavior. Unfortunately, beyond the fact that the value for β corresponds to the level of exploration, there's no straightforward, principled way of setting this parameter, and some values might work on some problems but not on others. Exercise 1 of this chapter further discusses a more-involved method of setting β that might generally work sufficiently well.

> **NOTE** The documentation of BoTorch usually shows UCB with $\beta = 0.1$, while many research papers that use UCB for BayesOpt opt for $\beta = 3$. So, 0.1 could be your go-to value when using this policy if you prefer exploitation, and 3 should be the default if you lean toward exploration.

5.2.3 *Implementation with BoTorch*

Having thoroughly discussed the motivation and math behind UCB, we now learn how to implement the policy using BoTorch. The code we look at here is included in CH05/01 - BayesOpt loop.ipynb. Remember from section 4.2.2 that although we could manually implement the PoI policy ourselves, declaring the BoTorch policy object, using it with the GP model, and optimizing the acquisition score using BoTorch's helper function `optimize_acqf()` make it easier to implement our BayesOpt loop.

For this reason, we do the same thing here and use the built-in UCB policy class, even though we could simply compute the quantity $\mu + \beta\sigma$ ourselves. This can be done with

```
policy = botorch.acquisition.analytic.UpperConfidenceBound(
    model, beta=1
)
```

Here, the UCB class implementation in BoTorch takes in the GP model as its first input and a positive value for its second input `beta`. As you might expect, this second input denotes the value for the UCB parameter β in the score formula $\mu + \beta\sigma$, which trades off between exploration and exploitation. Here, we set it to 1 for now.

> **NOTE** Believe it or not, this is all we need to change from our BayesOpt code from the previous chapter to run the UCB policy on the objective functions we have. This demonstrates the benefit of BoTorch's modularity, which allows us to plug and play any policy we'd like to use into our BayesOpt pipeline.

Running our UCB policy with $\beta = 1$ on our familiar Forrester objective function generates figure 5.9, which shows optimization progress throughout 10 function evaluations. We see that like what happened to the PoI policy, UCB with $\beta = 1$ fails to sufficiently explore the search space and is stuck at a local optimum in the case of the Forrester function. This means the value for β is too small.

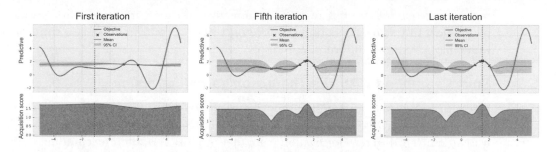

Figure 5.9   Progress made by the UCB policy with the tradeoff parameter β = 1. The value of the parameter is not sufficiently large to encourage exploration, causing progress to be stuck at a local optimum.

NOTE   We learn about the Probability of Improvement policy in section 4.2.

Let us try again, this time setting this tradeoff parameter to a larger value:

```
policy = botorch.acquisition.analytic.UpperConfidenceBound(
    model, beta=2
)
```

The progress of this version of the UCB policy is shown in figure 5.10. This time, UCB is able to find the global optimum thanks to the higher level of exploration induced by the larger value of β. However, if β is so large that UCB only spends its budget exploring the search space, then our optimization performance might also suffer. (We see an example of this in this chapter's exercises later on.)

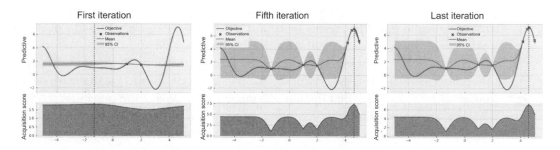

Figure 5.10   Progress made by the UCB policy with the tradeoff parameter β = 2. The policy successfully finds the global optimum.

Overall, the importance of using a good value for this tradeoff parameter while using the UCB policy is clear. However, again, it's difficult to say what value will work well for a given objective function. Exercise 1 of this chapter explores a certain strategy to adjust the value of this parameter as we progress through the search.

This marks the end of our discussion on UCB. We have seen that by adopting the *optimism in the face of uncertainty* mindset from the MAB problem, we obtain a BayesOpt policy whose explorative behavior can be directly controlled and tuned with a tradeoff parameter. In the next section, we move on to the second policy taken from MAB, which has an entirely different motivation and strategy.

5.3   *Smart sampling with the Thompson sampling policy*

In this section, we learn about another heuristic in MAB that directly translates to a widely used BayesOpt policy called *Thompson sampling* (TS). As we will see, this policy uses an entirely different motivation from that of UCB and, therefore, induces different optimization behavior. Similar to section 5.2 with UCB, we learn the general idea behind this BayesOpt policy first and then move on to its code implementation later.

5.3.1   *One sample to represent the unknown*

With UCB, we make decisions based on an optimistic estimate of the unknown quantity we care about. This offers a simple way to reason about the consequences of the actions we take and the rewards we receive that trades off exploration and exploitation. What about TS?

> **DEFINITION**   The idea of Thompson sampling is to first maintain a probabilistic belief about the quantity we care about and then *sample* from that belief and treat that sample as a replacement of the true unknown quantity in question. This sampled replacement is then used to pick out the best decision we should make.

Let's come back to our weather forecast example to see how this works. Again, we are interested in the problem of deciding whether we should bring an umbrella to work in which we are given an estimate of the probability that the weather will stay sunny throughout the day. Remember that the UCB relies on an upper bound of this estimate to inform its decisions, but what will the TS policy do?

The TS first draws a sample from the probability distribution we use to model the unknown quantity—whether it will stay sunny, in this case—and make decisions based on this sample. Let's say that instead of a range like we saw in the previous section, the weather app on our phone now announces there's a 66% (roughly two out of three) chance the weather will say sunny. This means that when following the TS policy, we first flip a coin with a two-thirds bias for heads:

- If the coin lands on heads (with a 66% chance), then we treat it as if the weather will stay clear throughout the day and conclude we won't need an umbrella.
- If the coin lands on tails (with 34% chance), then we treat it as if it will rain and conclude we should bring an umbrella to work.

This process of TS is visualized in figure 5.11 as a decision tree, where at the beginning, we flip a biased coin to obtain a sample from the probability distribution of sunny weather. Based on whether the coin lands on heads (representing a sample of sunny weather) or tails (a sample of rain), we decide whether or not we should bring an umbrella to work.

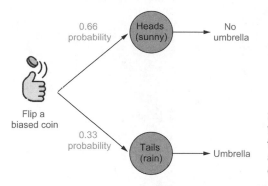

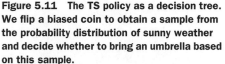

Figure 5.11   The TS policy as a decision tree. We flip a biased coin to obtain a sample from the probability distribution of sunny weather and decide whether to bring an umbrella based on this sample.

While this might seem like an arbitrary method of decision-making at first, TS is particularly effective in both MAB and BayesOpt. First of all, given a probability distribution representing a quantity of interest, a sample of that distribution is a possible realization of that quantity, so that sample may be used as a representation of the distribution. In optimization under uncertainty problems, TS offers the same benefit as UCB in that sampling from a probability distribution is often easy to do. Just as UCB's optimistic estimates of the reward rates may be generated in an efficient manner, sampling may be done just as efficiently.

Let's consider how TS works in BayesOpt. From a GP trained on the current observed data, we draw one sample. Remember from chapter 3 that a sample from a GP is a function representing a particular realization of the objective function according to our GP belief. However, unlike the true objective function, which is unknown in regions without observed data, a sample drawn from a GP is entirely known. This means we can find the location at which this sample is maximized.

Figure 5.12 shows the GP we trained on the Forrester function and three samples drawn from it as dashed lines. Further, along each of the samples, we use a diamond to indicate the location at which the sample is maximized. As we can see, one sample is maximized around –3.2, another around –1.2, and the third at 5.

When using the TS policy, it's entirely up to chance to determine which of these three samples (or a completely different sample) we draw from the GP. However, whichever sample we draw, the data point that maximizes the sample is the one we will query next. That is, if we draw the sample maximized at –3.2, then –3.2 is where we will evaluate the objective function next. If we draw the sample maximized at 5, then we will query the point $x = 5$ next.

DEFINITION   The acquisition scores that TS computes are the values of a random sample drawn from the GP. The data point that maximizes this sample is the one we will query next.

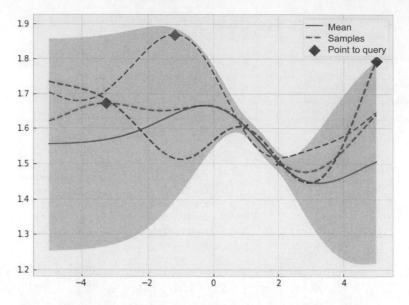

Figure 5.12   Samples drawn from a GP and data points that maximize the corresponding samples. Whichever sample is drawn, TS selects the data point that maximizes that sample as the next point at which to evaluate the objective function.

Unlike other policies we have seen so far, TS is a *randomized* policy, which means that when faced with the same training data and GP, it's not guaranteed that the policy will make the same decision (unless we computationally set the random seed). However, this randomness is in no way a disadvantage. We have said that drawing a sample from a GP is easy, so computing the TS acquisition score may be done efficiently. Further, maximization of a random sample inherently balances between exploration and exploitation, which, as we know, is the main concern in BayesOpt:

- If a data point has a high predictive mean, then the value of a random sample at that data point is likely to be high, making it more likely to be the one maximizing the sample.
- If a data point has a high predictive standard deviation (that is, uncertainty), then a random sample at that data point will also have a higher variability and, thus, a higher chance of having a high value. This higher variability, therefore, also makes the data point more likely to be chosen as the next point to query.

TS is likely to exploit with a random sample that is maximized in a region with a high predictive mean, but the policy is just as likely to explore with another sample given the same situation. We see this in figure 5.12, where one sample is maximized around –1.2, which has a relatively high predictive mean. If this is the sample we draw, then by evaluating the objective at –1.2, we will be exploiting the function. However, if we draw either of the other two samples, then we will be exploring, as the regions where the samples are maximized have high uncertainty.

This is quite an elegant tradeoff scheme. By using the randomness of the samples, TS directly uses the probabilistic nature of our predictive model, the GP, to explore and exploit the search space. The randomized nature of TS means that at any given iteration of the BayesOpt loop, the policy might not make the best decision to trade off exploration and exploitation, but over time, in the aggregation of its decisions, the policy will be able to explore the space sufficiently and narrow down high-performing regions.

5.3.2   *Implementation with BoTorch*

Let's now move on to implementing this TS policy in Python. Once again, the code is included in the CH05/01 - BayesOpt loop.ipynb notebook. Remember that for the BayesOpt policies we have seen, implementation comes down to declaring a BoTorch policy object and specifying the relevant information. Then, to find the data point we should query next, we optimize the acquisition score, as computed by the policy. This, however, is *not* the case with TS.

The main challenge of implementing TS as a generic PyTorch module that takes in a data point and scores it according to some criterion is that sampling from a GP can only be done with a finite number of points. In the past, we have represented a sample from a GP using a sample of a high-dimensional MVN distribution of a dense grid over the search space. When samples of this dense Gaussian are plotted, they appear to be actual functions with smooth curves, but in reality, they are defined over a grid.

All of this is to say that it is computationally impossible to draw a sample as a function from a GP since that would require an infinite number of bits. A typical solution is to draw the corresponding MVN over a large number of points that span the input space so that all regions in the search space are represented.

> **IMPORTANT**   This is exactly what we do to implement TS: generate a large number of points throughout the search space and draw a sample from the MVN distribution corresponding to predictions from a GP over these points.

The procedure for TS is summarized in figure 5.13, where we use a *Sobol sequence* as the points that span the search space. (We discuss why a Sobol sequence is preferred over other sampling strategies shortly.) We then draw a sample from the GP on these points and pick out the point that yields the highest value from the sample. This sample is then used to represent a sample from the GP itself, and we evaluate the objective function at the location where the sampled value is maximized next.

> **DEFINITION**   A *Sobol sequence* is an infinite list of points in a region in Euclidean space that aims to cover the region evenly.

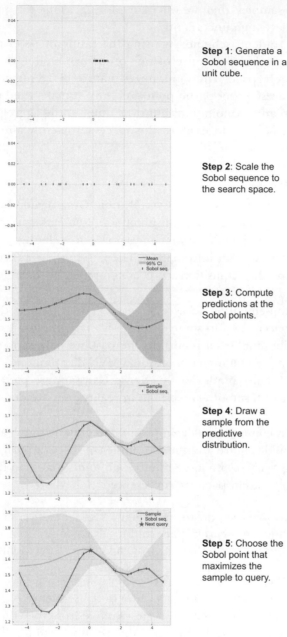

Step 1: Generate a Sobol sequence in a unit cube.

Step 2: Scale the Sobol sequence to the search space.

Step 3: Compute predictions at the Sobol points.

Step 4: Draw a sample from the predictive distribution.

Step 5: Choose the Sobol point that maximizes the sample to query.

Figure 5.13   **Flowchart of the implementation of TS in BoTorch. We use a Sobol sequence to populate the search space, draw a sample from the GP on the sequence, and choose the point in the sequence that maximizes the sample to evaluate the objective function at.**

Let's first discuss why we need to use a Sobol sequence to generate points that span our search space. A simpler solution is to use a dense grid. However, generating a dense grid quickly becomes intractable as the number of dimensions of our search space grows, so this strategy is out of the question. Another potential solution is to uniformly sample from that space, but statistical theory shows that uniform sampling is, in fact, not the best way to generate points that cover a space evenly, and a Sobol sequence does a better job.

Figure 5.14 shows the comparison between a Sobol sequence of 100 points and the same number of points uniformly sampled within the two-dimensional unit square. We see that the Sobol sequence covers the square more evenly, which is what we'd like to achieve with TS. This contrast is even more glaring in higher dimensions, giving us more reason to prefer Sobol sequences than uniformly sampled data points. We don't discuss Sobol sequences in detail here; what is important for us to know is that a Sobol sequence is the go-to method of sample generation if our goal is to cover a space evenly.

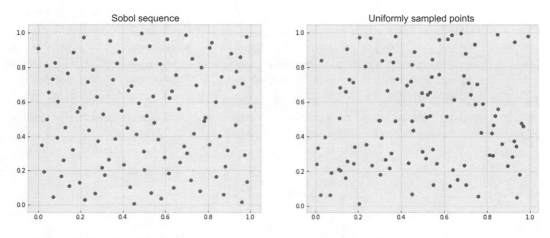

Figure 5.14   Points from a Sobol sequence vs. uniformly sampled points in the two-dimensional unit square. The Sobol sequence covers the square more evenly and, therefore, should be used by TS.

PyTorch provides an implementation of Sobol sequences, which can be used as follows:

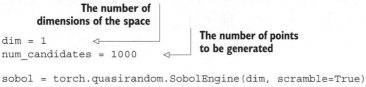

```
dim = 1
num_candidates = 1000

sobol = torch.quasirandom.SobolEngine(dim, scramble=True)
candidate_x = sobol.draw(num_candidates)
```

Here, `sobol` is an instance of the `SobolEngine` class, which implements the sampling logic of Sobol sequences in the unit cube, and `candidate_x` is a PyTorch tensor of the shape `(num_candidates, dim)` that contains the generated points with the correct dimensionality.

> **NOTE**   It's important to remember that `SobolEngine` generates points that cover the unit cube. To get `candidate_x` to cover the space we want, we need to resize this tensor accordingly.

How many points the Sobol sequence should contain (that is, the value of `num_candidates`) is up to us (the users) to decide; the preceding example shows that we are using 1,000. In a typical case, you would want a value large enough so that the search space could be sufficiently covered. However, a value that is too large will make sampling from the posterior GP numerically unstable.

> **Numerical instability when drawing GP samples**
>
> The numerical instability when drawing GP samples could, at times, lead to the following warning when we run TS:
>
> ```
> NumericalWarning: A not p.d., added jitter of 1.0e-06 to the diagonal
>     warnings.warn(
> ```
>
> This warning indicates that the code has encountered a numerical problem due to the fact that the covariance matrix of the GP is not positive definite (`p.d.`) when it should be. However, this code also applies an automatic fix where we add a "jitter" of 1e–6 to this covariance matrix, making the matrix positive definite, so we, the users, don't have to do anything further.
>
> Just as we did in section 4.2.3, we use the `warnings` module to disable this warning to make the output of our code cleaner as follows:
>
> ```
> with warnings.catch_warnings():
>     warnings.filterwarnings('ignore', category=RuntimeWarning)
>     ...              ◁─── Code for TS
> ```

You could play around with multiple thousands of points to find the number that works best for your use case, objective function, and trained GP. However, you should always use at least 1,000 points.

Next, we move on to the second component of TS, which is the process of sampling an MVN from our posterior GP and maximizing it. First, the sampler object that implements the sampling may be declared as

```
ts = botorch.generation.MaxPosteriorSampling(model, replacement=False)
```

The `MaxPosteriorSampling` class in BoTorch implements the logic of TS: sampling from the posterior of a GP and maximizing that sample. Here, `model` refers to the GP trained on observed data. It is important to set `replacement` to `False`, making sure we are sampling without replacement (sampling with replacement isn't appropriate for TS). Finally, to obtain the data point that gives the highest sampled value among `candidate_x`, we pass it to the sampler object:

```
next_x = ts(candidate_x, num_samples=1)
```

The returned value is, indeed, the point that maximizes the sample, which is the point we query next. And with that, our implementation of the TS policy is complete. We may plug this into the code we have been using so far for the BayesOpt loop on the Forrester function with the following:

```
for i in range(num_queries):
  print("iteration", i)
  print("incumbent", train_x[train_y.argmax()], train_y.max())

  sobol = torch.quasirandom.SobolEngine(1, scramble=True)      Generates points
  candidate_x = sobol.draw(num_candidates)                     from a Sobol engine
  candidate_x = 10 * candidate_x - 5    ◁──────────
                                                          Resizes the generated points
  model, likelihood = fit_gp_model(train_x, train_y)      to be between −5 and 5,
                                                          which is our search space
  ts = botorch.generation.MaxPosteriorSampling(model,
  ➥replacement=False)                                    Generates the TS candidate
  next_x = ts(candidate_x, num_samples=1)                 to be queried next

  visualize_gp_belief_and_policy(model, likelihood, next_x=next_x)   ◁──
                                                          Visualizes our current
  next_y = forrester_1d(next_x)                           progress without the
                                                          acquisition function
  train_x = torch.cat([train_x, next_x])
  train_y = torch.cat([train_y, next_y])
```

Note that the overall structure of our BayesOpt loop remains the same. What's different is that instead of a BoTorch policy object, we now have a Sobol sequence to generate the set of points that cover our search space, which are then fed into a `MaxPosterior-Sampling` object that implements the TS policy. The variable `next_x`, like before, contains the data point we will query next.

> **NOTE** Since we don't have a BoTorch policy object when visualizing our progress using the `visualize_gp_belief_and_policy()` helper function, we don't specify the `policy` argument anymore. This function, therefore, will only show the trained GP at each iteration, without the acquisition scores.

Optimization progress of TS is shown in figure 5.15, where we can observe that the policy successfully zeros in on the global optimum throughout the procedure—but not without spending a couple of queries exploring the space. This showcases the ability to trade off exploration and exploitation of TS in BayesOpt.

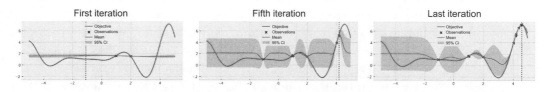

Figure 5.15 Progress made by the TS policy. The policy explores the search space for some iterations and then gradually zeros in on the global optimum.

Our discussion on BayesOpt policies inspired by policies under the MAB setting is thus concluded. We have seen that each of the two policies we learned, UCB and TS, uses natural heuristics to reason about unknown quantities in an efficient manner and make decisions accordingly. One challenge in BayesOpt, the balance between exploration and exploitation, is also addressed by both policies, allowing the policies to have good optimization performance. In the next and final chapter of the second part of the book, we learn about yet another commonly used heuristic to decision-making in BayesOpt, this time by using information theory.

5.4   *Exercises*

There are two exercises in this chapter:

1 The first exercise explores a potential method to set the tradeoff parameter for the UCB policy that considers how far along we are in optimization.
2 The second exercise applies the two policies we have learned in this chapter to the hyperparameter tuning problem seen in previous chapters.

5.4.1   *Exercise 1: Setting an exploration schedule for the UCB*

This exercise, implemented in CH05/02 - Exercise 1.ipynb, discusses a strategy of adaptively setting the value of the tradeoff parameter β of the UCB policy. As mentioned in the section on UCB, the performance of the policy heavily depends on this parameter, but it's not obvious how we should set its value. A value might work well on some objective functions but poorly on others.

BayesOpt practitioners have noticed that as we collect more and more data, UCB can become too exploitative. This is because as the size of our training dataset increases, we gain more knowledge about the objective function, and our uncertainty about the predictions made by the GP decreases. This means the CI produced by the GP will become tighter, moving the upper bound that makes up the acquisition score used by UCB closer to the mean prediction.

However, if the UCB acquisition score is similar to the mean prediction, then the policy is exploitative, as it will only query data points with high predictive means. This phenomenon shows that the more data we have observed, the more explorative we should be with UCB. Here, a natural way of gradually encouraging more exploration from UCB is to slowly increase the value of the tradeoff parameter β, which is what we learn to do in this exercise, following these steps:

1 Recreate the BayesOpt loop in CH04/02 - Exercise 1.ipynb, which uses the one-dimensional Forrester function as the optimization objective.
2 We aim to slowly increase the value of the tradeoff parameter β by multiplying it with a constant at each iteration of the loop. That is, at the end of each iteration, we need to update the parameter with `beta *= multiplier`.

   Say we want β to start out with a value of 1 and to have a value of 10 at the end of the search (the tenth iteration). What is the value that the multiplier for β needs to have?

3 Implement this scheduling logic, and observe the resulting optimization performance:

  a Specifically, even though this version of UCB starts out with $\beta = 1$, does it get stuck at a local optimum like the version for which the parameter is fixed at 1?

5.4.2 *Exercise 2: BayesOpt for hyperparameter tuning*

This exercise, implemented in CH05/03 - Exercise 2.ipynb, applies BayesOpt to an objective function that simulates the accuracy surface of a support-vector machine model in a hyperparameter tuning task. The x-axis denotes the value of the penalty parameter C, while the y-axis denotes the value for the RBF kernel parameter γ. See the exercises in chapters 3 and 4 for more detail. Follow these steps:

1 Recreate the BayesOpt loop in CH04/03 - Exercise 2.ipynb, including the outer loop that implements repeated experiments.

2 Run the UCB policy, setting the value of the tradeoff parameter to $\beta \in \{ 1, 3, 10, 30 \}$, and observe the values' aggregated performance:

  a Which value leads to over-exploitation, and which leads to over-exploration? Which value works best?

3 Run the adaptive version of UCB (see exercise 1):

  a The tradeoff parameter should start at 3 and end at 10.

  b Observe that changing the end value from 10 to 30 doesn't affect optimization performance too much. We, therefore, say that this strategy is robust against the value of this end value, which is a desideratum.

  c Compare the performance of this adaptive version and that of other versions with fixed β.

4 Run the TS policy, and observe its aggregated performance.

Summary

- The MAB problem consists of a set of actions that may be performed (arms of slot machines that may be pulled), each of which returns a reward according to its specific reward rate. The goal is to maximize the sum of the reward (cumulative reward) we receive given a number of iterations.
- An MAB policy selects which action to take next based on past data. A good policy needs to balance under-explored actions and high-performing actions.
- Unlike the MAB problem, where there are a finite set of sections, there are infinitely many actions that we can take in BayesOpt.
- The goal of BayesOpt is to maximize the largest observed reward, which is often called the *simple reward*.
- The rewards in BayesOpt are correlated: similar actions yield similar rewards. This is not necessarily true with the MAB.

- The UCB policy uses an optimistic estimate of the quantity of interest to make decisions. This *optimism in the face of uncertainty* heuristic can balance exploration and exploitation, with a tradeoff parameter that we, the users, can set.

- The smaller the tradeoff parameter of the UCB policy is, the more exploitative the policy becomes, tending to stay within regions known to give high rewards. The larger the tradeoff parameter is, the more explorative the policy becomes, tending to query regions far away from observed data.

- The TS policy draws a sample from a probabilistic model of the quantity of interest and uses this sample to make decisions.

- The random nature of TS allows the policy to explore and exploit the search space appropriately: both regions of high uncertainty and those of high predictive mean are likely to be chosen by TS.

- For computational reasons, more care is needed when implementing TS: we first generate a set of points to cover the search space evenly, and then a sample from the GP posterior is drawn for these points.

- To cover a space evenly, we can use a Sobol sequence to generate the points within the unit cube and scale them to the targeted space.

Using information theory with entropy-based policies

6

This chapter covers

- Entropy as an information-theoretic measure of uncertainty
- Information gain as a method of reducing entropy
- BayesOpt policies that use information theory for their search

We saw in chapter 4 that by aiming to improve from the best value achieved so far, we can design improvement-based BayesOpt policies, such as Probability of Improvement (POI) and Expected Improvement (EI). In chapter 5, we used multi-armed bandit (MAB) policies to obtain Upper Confidence Bound (UCB) and Thompson sampling (TS), each of which uses a unique heuristic to balance exploration and exploitation in the search for the global optimum of the objective function.

In this chapter, we learn about another heuristic to decision-making, this time using information theory to design BayesOpt policies we can use in our optimization pipeline. Unlike the heuristics we have seen (seeking improvement, optimism in the face of uncertainty, and random sampling), which might seem unique to optimization-related tasks, information theory is a major subfield of mathematics that has applications in a wide range of topics. As we discuss in this chapter, by appealing to information theory or, more specifically, *entropy*, a quantity that measures uncertainty in terms of information, we can design BayesOpt policies that seek to reduce our uncertainty about the objective function to be optimized in a principled and mathematically elegant manner.

The idea behind entropy-based search is quite simple: we look at places where our information about a quantity of interest will most increase. As we cover later in the chapter, this is similar to looking for a lost remote control in the living room, where the TV is, as opposed to in the bathroom.

The first part of this chapter is a high-level exposition on information theory, entropy, and ways to maximize the amount of information we receive upon performing an action. This is done by reinterpreting the familiar example of binary search. Armed with the fundamentals of information theory, we then move on to discussing BayesOpt policies that maximize information about the global optimum of an objective function. These policies are the result of applying information theory to the task of BayesOpt. As always, we also learn how to implement these policies in Python.

By the end of the chapter, you will gain a working understanding of what information theory is, how entropy as a measure of uncertainty is quantified, and how entropy is translated to BayesOpt. This chapter adds another policy to our BayesOpt toolkit and concludes the second part of the book on BayesOpt policies.

6.1 Measuring knowledge with information theory

Information theory is a subfield of mathematics that studies how to best represent, quantify, and reason about information in a principled, mathematical manner. In this section, we introduce information theory on a high level and discuss how it is related to decision-making under uncertainty. We do this by reexamining the idea behind binary search, a popular algorithm in computer science, from the perspective of information theory. This discussion subsequently allows us to connect information theory to BayesOpt and motivates an information-theoretic policy for optimization.

6.1.1 Measuring uncertainty with entropy

Information theory is especially prevalent in computer science, where digital information is represented as bits (0s and 1s). You might remember calculating how many bits are required to represent a given number of integers—for example, a single bit is enough to represent two numbers, 0 and 1, while five bits are necessary to represent 32 (2 raised to the fifth power) different numbers. These calculations are examples of information theory in practice.

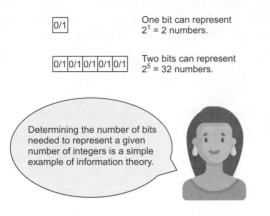

One bit can represent
$2^1 = 2$ numbers.

Two bits can represent
$2^5 = 32$ numbers.

Determining the number of bits
needed to represent a given
number of integers is a simple
example of information theory.

The information-theoretic concept of interest within the context of decision-making under uncertainty is *entropy*. Entropy measures the level of uncertainty we have in an unknown quantity. If this unknown quantity is modeled as a random variable, entropy measures the variability in the possible values of the random variable.

NOTE This uncertainty measure, entropy, is similar to but not quite the same as what we've been calling *uncertainty* in the predictions made by a GP thus far, which is simply the standard deviation of the predictive distribution.

In this subsection, we learn more about entropy as a concept and how it is computed for a simple Bernoulli distribution for binary events. We show how entropy successfully quantifies uncertainty in an unknown quantity.

Let's go back to the first example of any Introduction to Probability course: coin flipping. Say you are about to flip a biased coin that will land on heads with some probability p between 0 and 1, and you'd like to reason about the event that the coin will, indeed, land on heads. Denote X as the binary random variable that indicates whether the event happens (that is, $X = 1$ if the coin lands on heads and $X = 0$ otherwise). Then, we say that X follows a Bernoulli distribution with parameter p, and the probability that $X = 1$ is equal to p.

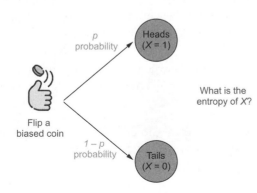

Here, the entropy of X is defined as $-p \log p - (1 - p) \log(1 - p)$, where *log* is the logarithmic function in base 2. We see that this is a function of the probability of heads p. Figure 6.1 shows the function of entropy for p in $(0, 1)$, from which we can gain some insights:

- The entropy is always nonnegative.
- The entropy increases when p increases before 0.5, reaches its highest at $p = 0.5$, and then decreases afterwards.

When the coin is fair, heads are just as likely as tails— hence, maximum entropy

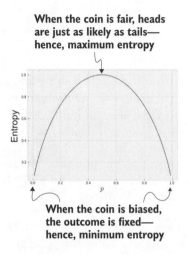

When the coin is biased, the outcome is fixed— hence, minimum entropy

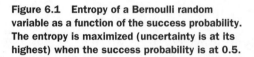

Figure 6.1 Entropy of a Bernoulli random variable as a function of the success probability. The entropy is maximized (uncertainty is at its highest) when the success probability is at 0.5.

Both insights are valuable when we study our uncertainty about whether or not the coin will land on heads. First, we shouldn't have negative uncertainty about something, so it makes sense that the entropy is never negative. More importantly, entropy is maximized right at the middle, when $p = 0.5$. This is quite reasonable: as p gets farther and farther away from 0.5, we become more certain about the outcome of the event—whether the coin will land on heads.

For instance, if $p = 0.7$, then we are more certain it will land on heads—our entropy is around 0.9 here. If $p = 0.1$, then we are even more certain about the outcome (this time that it will land on tails)—the entropy here is roughly 0.5. While entropy is not defined at the endpoints (due to the logarithmic function), entropy approaches zero as we get closer to either endpoint, indicating zero uncertainty. When $p = 0.5$, on the other hand, our uncertainty is at its maximum, as we are maximally unsure whether the coin will land on heads or tails. These calculations demonstrate that entropy is an appropriate measure of uncertainty.

DEFINITION   For a given probability distribution, the entropy is defined to be $-\Sigma_i\, p_i \log p_i$, where we sum over the different possible events indexed by i.

> **Entropy vs. standard deviation**
>
> When we used the term *uncertainty* in previous chapters, we were referring to the standard deviations of the predictive normal distributions produced by a GP. The *standard deviation* of a distribution, as the name suggests, measures how much the values within the distribution deviate from the mean and is, therefore, a valid measure of uncertainty.
>
> Entropy, on the other hand, is motivated by concepts of information theory, and it is also a valid measure of uncertainty. In fact, it is a more elegant and general approach to quantify uncertainty and could more accurately model uncertainty in edge cases of many situations.

We see that what we used for the preceding Bernoulli distribution is a special case of this formula. We also use this formula later in the chapter when we work with uniform distributions.

6.1.2 *Looking for a remote control using entropy*

As entropy measures how much uncertainty there is in our knowledge about a quantity or event of interest, it can inform our decisions, helping us most efficiently reduce our uncertainty about the quantity or event. We look at an example of this in this subsection, in which we decide where to best look for a lost remote control. Although simple, the example presents the information-theoretic reasoning we use in subsequent discussions, where entropy is used for more complex decision-making problems.

Imagine that while trying to turn on the TV in your living room one day, you realize you can't find the remote control on the table, which is where it usually is. You, therefore, decide to conduct a search for this remote. First, you reason that it should be in the living room somewhere, but you don't have any idea about where the remote is within the living room, so all locations are equally likely. In the language of probabilistic inference that we've been using, you can say that the *distribution of the location of the remote* is uniform over the living room.

Figure 6.2 visualizes this belief about the location of the remote control that you have, indicated by the shaded living room, which is where the remote is (according to your belief). Now, you might ask yourself this question: Where in this house should you look for the remote? It's reasonable to think that you should look in the living room, as opposed to, say, the bathroom, because that's where the TV is. But how does one quantifiably justify that choice?

Information theory, specifically entropy, offers a way of doing that by allowing us to reason about how much entropy remains after a search for a remote in the living room versus in the bathroom. That is, it allows us to determine how much uncertainty about the location of the remote we have left after looking in the living room as opposed to after looking in the bathroom.

Figure 6.2   A sample floor plan for the example of finding the remote control. The living room is uniformly shaded to indicate that the distribution of the location of the remote is uniform over the living room.

Figure 6.3 shows how entropy of the location of the remote decreases once the upper portion of the living room is searched. We can reason the following:

- If the remote is found within the searched region, then you will no longer have any uncertainty about its location. In other words, the entropy will be zero.
- If the remote is not found, then our posterior belief about the location of the remote is updated to the shaded region in the lower-right section. This distribution spans a smaller region than the one in figure 6.2, so there is less uncertainty (entropy).

Either way, the entropy is reduced by looking in the specified portion of the living room. What would happen, then, if you decided to search for the remote in the bathroom? Figure 6.4 shows the corresponding reasoning:

- If the remote is found in the bathroom, then entropy will still drop to zero. However, this is unlikely to happen, according to your belief about the location of the remote.
- If the remote is not found in the bathroom, then your posterior belief about the location of the remote doesn't change from figure 6.2, and the resulting entropy remains the same.

Searching for and not finding the remote in the bathroom doesn't reduce the entropy of the location of the remote. In other words, looking in the bathroom doesn't provide any extra information about the location of the remote, so it is the suboptimal decision according to information theory.

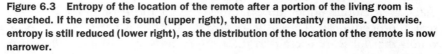

Figure 6.3   Entropy of the location of the remote after a portion of the living room is searched. If the remote is found (upper right), then no uncertainty remains. Otherwise, entropy is still reduced (lower right), as the distribution of the location of the remote is now narrower.

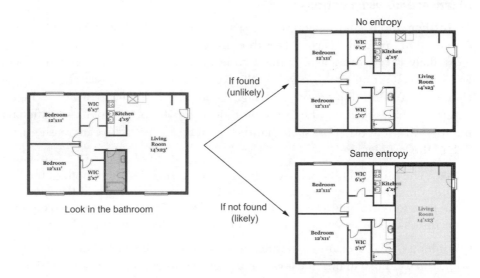

Figure 6.4   Entropy of the location of the remote after the bathroom is searched. As the remote cannot be found in the bathroom, the entropy in the posterior distribution of the location of the remote is unchanged.

This comparison would not be as cut and dried if the prior distribution of the location of the remote (your initial guess about where it is) was over the entire house, not just the living room. After all, there is always a small probability that the remote got misplaced outside the living room. However, the procedure of determining where to look—that is, the portion of the house that will give you maximal information about the location of the remote—is still the same:

1. Consider the posterior distribution of the location of the remote if it is found, and compute the entropy of that distribution.
2. Compute the same entropy if the remote is not found.
3. Compute the average entropy over the two cases.
4. Repeat this computation for all locations you are considering looking in, and pick the one that gives the lowest entropy.

Entropy gives us a way to quantify our uncertainty about a quantity of interest, using its probabilistic distribution in an information-theoretic manner. This procedure uses entropy to identify the action that maximally reduces entropy.

> **NOTE** This is a mathematically elegant procedure applicable to many decision-making situations under uncertainty. We can think of this entropy-based search procedure as a kind of search for the truth in which we aim to take the action that takes us as close to the truth as possible by maximally reducing uncertainty.

6.1.3   *Binary search using entropy*

To further understand entropy-based search, we now see how this procedure manifests itself in one of the classic algorithms in computer science: binary search. You are most likely already familiar with this algorithm, so we don't go into much detail here. For an excellent and beginner-friendly explanation of binary search, I recommend chapter 1 of Aditya Bhargava's *Grokking Algorithms* (Manning, 2016). On a high level, we employ binary search when we want to look for the position of a specific targeted number within a sorted list such that the elements in the list are increasing from the first to the last element.

> **TIP** The idea behind binary search is to look at the middle element of the list and compare it to the target. If the target is smaller than the middle element, then we know to only look at the first half of the list; otherwise, we look at the second half. We repeat this process of halving the list until we find the target.

Consider a concrete example in which we have a sorted list of 100 elements $[x_1, x_2, \ldots, x_{100}]$, and we'd like to find the location of a given target z, assuming z is, indeed, in the sorted list.

As illustrated by figure 6.5, binary search works by dividing the list into two halves: the first 50 elements and the last 50 elements. Since we know the list is sorted, we know the following:

- If our target z is less than the 50th element x_{50}, then we only need to consider the first 50 elements, since the last 50 elements are all greater than target z.
- If our target is greater than x_{50}, then we only need to look at the second half of the list.

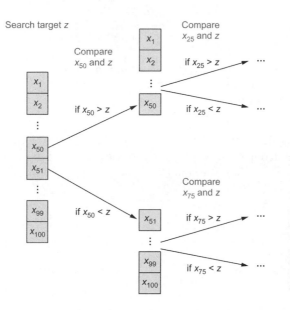

Figure 6.5 **An illustration of binary search on a 100-element list. At each iteration of the search, the target is compared against the middle element of the current list. Depending on the result of this comparison, we remove either the first or second half of the list from the search space.**

Terminating the search

For each comparison in figure 6.5, we omit the situation where z is equal to the number it's being compared to, in which case we can simply terminate the search.

On average, this procedure helps us find the location of z within the list much more quickly than sequentially searching through the list from one end to the other. Binary search is a realization of the goal of making the optimal decision based on information theory in this game of searching for the location of a number within a sorted list, if we were to tackle the problem from a probabilistic angle.

NOTE Binary search strategy is the optimal solution for finding z, allowing us to locate it more quickly than any other strategy, on average.

First, let's use the random variable L to denote the location of our target z within the sorted list. Here, we would like to use a distribution to describe our belief about the variable. Since from our perspective, any location within the list is equally likely to contain the value of z, we use a uniform distribution for modeling.

Figure 6.6 visualizes this distribution, which, again, represents our belief about the location of z. Since each location is equally as likely as any other, the probability that a given location contains z is uniformly 1 ÷ 100, or 1%.

Probability that z is at a given location

Figure 6.6   Prior distribution of the location of the target z within the 100-element list. Since each location is as equally likely as any other, the probability that a given location contains z is 1%.

NOTE   Let's try computing the entropy of this uniform distribution. Remember, the formula for the entropy is $-\Sigma_i\, p_i \log p_i$, where we sum over the different possible events indexed by i. This is equal to

$$-\sum_{i=1}^{100} 0.01 \log 0.01 \approx 6.64$$

So, the amount of uncertainty we have in our prior distribution of L is roughly 6.64.

Next, we tackle the same question: How should we search over this 100-element list to locate z as quickly as possible? We do this by following the entropy search procedure described in section 6.1.2, where we aim to minimize the entropy in the posterior distribution of the quantity that we care about—in this case, the location L.

How do we compute the entropy of the posterior distribution of L after inspecting a given location? This calculation requires us to reason about what we can conclude about L upon inspecting a given location, which is quite easy to do. Say we decide to inspect the first location x_1. According to our belief about L, there is a 1% chance that L is at this location and a 99% chance that L is in one of the remaining slots:

- If L is, indeed, at this location, then our posterior entropy about L drops to 0, as there's no more uncertainty about this quantity.
- Otherwise, the distribution of L is updated to reflect this observation that z is not the first number of the list.

Figure 6.7 shows this process as a diagram in which we need to update the distribution for L so that each of the 99 locations has a 1 ÷ 99, or roughly 1.01%, probability of containing z. Each of the 99 locations is still equally likely, but the probability of each location has gone up a bit since we have ruled out the first location in this hypothetical scenario.

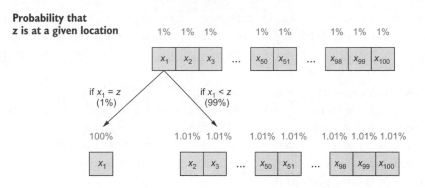

Figure 6.7 Posterior distributions of the location of target *z* within the 100-element list upon inspecting the first element. In each scenario, the probability that *z* is at a given location is updated accordingly.

NOTE Again, we're only considering the case where *z* exists in the list, so either the smallest element in the list x_1 is equal to *z*, or the former is less than the latter.

Following the same calculation, we can obtain the entropy for this new distribution as

$$-\sum_{i=2}^{100} 0.0101(\log 0.0101) = 6.63$$

Again, this is the posterior entropy of *L* in the second case, where *z* is not present in the first location. The last step we need to take to compute the overall posterior entropy after inspecting the first location is to take the average of the two cases:

- If *z* is in the first slot, which is 1% likely, then the posterior entropy is 0.
- If *z* is not in the first slot, which is 99% likely, then the posterior entropy is 6.63.

Taking the average, we have 0.01 (0) + 0.99 (6.63) = 6.56. So, on average, we expect to see a posterior entropy of 6.56 when we choose to look into the first element of the array. Now, to determine whether looking at the first element is the optimal decision or there's a better location for obtaining more information about *L*, we need to repeat this procedure for the other locations in the list. Specifically, for a given location, we need to

1 Iterate over each of the potential scenarios while inspecting the location
2 Compute the posterior entropy of the distribution of *L* for each scenario
3 Compute the average posterior entropy across the scenarios based on how likely each of them is

Let's do this one more time for, say, the 10th location x_{10}; the corresponding diagram is shown in figure 6.8. While this scenario is slightly different from what we just went over, the underlying idea is still the same. First, there are various scenarios that can take place when we look at x_{10}:

1 The 10th element x_{10} can be greater than z, in which case we can rule out the last 91 elements in the list and focus our search on the first 9 elements. Here, each of the 9 locations has an 11% chance of containing z, and the posterior entropy, by using the same formula, can be computed to be roughly 3.17.
2 The tenth element x_{10} can be exactly equal to z, in which case our posterior entropy is once again zero.
3 The tenth element x_{10} can be less than z, in which case we narrow our search to the last 90 elements. The posterior entropy in this case is around 6.49.

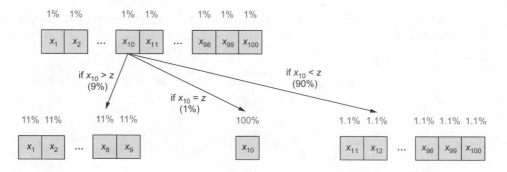

Figure 6.8   Posterior distributions of the location of target z within the 100-element list upon inspecting the 10th element. In each scenario, the probability that z is at a given location is updated accordingly.

> **NOTE**   Make sure you attempt the entropy computations yourself to understand how we are getting these numbers.

Finally, we take the weighted average of these entropies using the corresponding probabilities: $0.09 (3.17) + 0.01 (0) + 0.9 (6.49) = 6.13$. This number presents the expected posterior entropy—that is, the expected posterior uncertainty we have about L, the location of z, after inspecting the 10th element x_{10}.

Compared to the same number for the first element x_1, 6.56, we conclude that looking at x_{10} on average gives us more information about L than looking at x_1. In other words, inspecting x_{10} is the better decision in terms of information theory.

But what is the *optimal* decision in terms of information theory—the one that gives us the most information about L? To determine this, we simply repeat the computation we just performed on x_1 and x_{10} for the other locations in the list and pick out the one with the lowest expected posterior entropy.

Figure 6.9 shows this quantity, the expected posterior entropy in the location of our target, as a function of the location we choose to inspect. The first thing we notice is the symmetry of the curve: looking at the last location gives us the same expected posterior entropy (uncertainty) as looking at the first; similarly, the 10th and the 90th locations give the same amount of information, and so on.

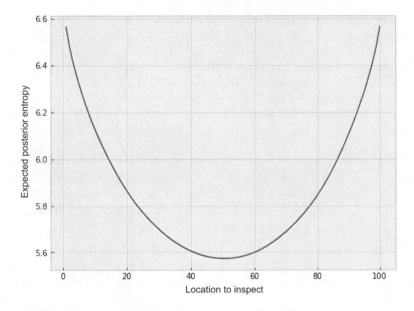

Figure 6.9   Expected posterior entropy in the location of the target as a function of the location within the list to inspect. The middle location is optimal, minimizing the expected entropy.

More importantly, we see that inspecting the locations in the middle, either the 50th or 51st number in the list, gives us the maximal amount of information. This is because once we do, we are guaranteed to rule out *half* of the list, regardless of whether our target number is greater or less than the number in the middle. This is not the case for other locations. As we saw earlier, we may be able to rule out 90 numbers in the list when looking at the 10th number, but this only happens with 0.1 probability. When looking at the first number, there's a 99% probability that we will only be able to rule out one number.

NOTE   All in all, inspecting the numbers in the middle maximizes the amount of information we gain, on average.

The rest of the search for the target follows the same procedure: computing the expected posterior entropy that will result from each decision and then choosing the decision that minimizes that entropy. As the probability distribution we work with is always a uniform distribution after each update, the optimal number to inspect is always the one in the middle of the array that hasn't been ruled out.

This is exactly the strategy of binary search! From the perspective of information theory, binary search is the optimal solution to the problem of search for a number in a sorted list.

> **Justifying binary search with information theory**
>
> When I first learned about this algorithm, I remember thinking that the strategy of searching in the middle of an array seemed, although reasonable, quite unique and "out of nowhere." However, we have just learned to derive the same solution from an information-theoretic perspective, which concretely quantifies the idea of ruling out half of our search space in the service of gaining as much information as possible or reducing as much entropy as possible.

The application of information theory and entropy doesn't stop at binary search. As we saw, the procedure we went through is generalizable to other decision-making problems: if we can model the problem of interest in terms of probability distributions for unknown quantities, actions we can take, and how the distributions can be updated when an action is taken, then we can once again choose the optimal action in terms of information theory, which is the action that reduces our uncertainty about the quantity of interest the most. For the remainder of this chapter, we learn to apply this idea to BayesOpt and implement the resulting entropy search policy with BoTorch.

6.2   *Entropy search in BayesOpt*

Taking the same approach presented in the previous section, we obtain entropy search policies in BayesOpt. The main idea is to choose our actions, our experiments, so that we can reduce the most amount of entropy in the posterior distribution of what we care about. In this section, we first discuss how to do this on a high level and then move on to implementation in BoTorch.

6.2.1   *Searching for the optimum using information theory*

In our remote control example, we aim to search for the remote within an apartment and, thus, want to reduce the entropy of the distribution of the location of the remote. In binary search, the process is similar: our target is the location of a specific number we'd like to search for within a list, and we want to reduce the entropy of the distribution of that number. Now, to design an entropy search policy, we must determine what to use as our target in BayesOpt and how to use information theory to aid the search process, which we learn how to do here.

Recall our ultimate goal in using BayesOpt: to search within the domain D of a black box function at the location where the function is maximized. This means a natural search target for us is the location x^* that maximizes the objective value of the function f. That is, $f^* = f(x^*) \geq f(x)$, for all x in D.

DEFINITION The optimal location x^* is often called the *optimizer* of the objective function f.

Given a GP belief about the objective function f, there is a corresponding probabilistic belief about the optimizer x^*, which is treated as a random variable. Figure 6.10 shows an example of a trained GP and the distribution of the objective optimizer x^* induced from the GP. It's important to keep a few interesting characteristics of this distribution in mind:

- The distribution is complicated and multimodal (having several local optima).
- The most likely location for the optimizer x^* is a bit to the left of zero. This is where the predictive mean of the GP is maximized.
- There is non-negligible probability that the optimizer x^* is at an end point -5 or 5.
- The probability that x^* is around 2 is almost zero, corresponding to the fact that we already observed a higher objective value than $f(2)$.

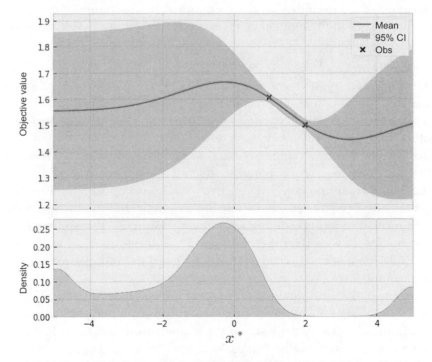

Figure 6.10 **GP belief (top) and the distribution of the function optimizer x^* (bottom). The distribution of the optimizer is non-Gaussian and fairly complicated, posing a challenge for modeling and decision-making.**

These characteristics make modeling this distribution of x^* very challenging. The most simple method of gauging how this quantity x^* is distributed is to simply draw many samples from the GP and record the location at which each sample is maximized. This is, in fact, how figure 6.10 is generated.

Making matters worse is the fact that we need exponentially more samples to estimate the distribution of x^* when the dimensionality of the objective function (the length of the input vector x or the number of features each x has) increases.

> **DEFINITION**   This is an instance of the *curse of dimensionality*, which, in ML, is often used to refer to the exponential cost of many procedures with respect to the dimensionality of an object of interest.

To use entropy search in BayesOpt, we need to model our belief about the location of the optimum x^* using a probability distribution. However, we can't exactly model the distribution of the optimizer x^*; instead, we must approximate it using samples drawn from a GP. Unfortunately, this process quickly becomes computationally expensive as the number of dimensions in the objective function (the length of x) increases.

> **NOTE**   There are, in fact, research papers in BayesOpt that seek to search for the location of the optimizer x^* using entropy. The resulting policies, however, often prove too computationally expensive to run and are not implemented in BoTorch.

But that doesn't mean we need to abandon the effort of using information theory in BayesOpt altogether. It just means we need to modify our search procedure to make it more amenable to computational methodologies. One easy way to achieve this is to target a quantity other than the optimizer x^* that is, on the one hand, connected to the search for x^* and, on the other, easier to reason about.

A quantity of interest in optimization, other than the optimizer x^*, is the optimal value $f^* = f(x^*)$, achieved at the optimizer, which is also a random variable, according to our GP belief about the objective function f. As one can imagine, learning about the optimal value f^* might tell us a lot about the optimizer x^*; that is, the two quantities are connected in terms of information theory. However, the optimal value f^* is much easier to work with than the optimizer x^*, as the former is just a real-valued number, while the latter is a vector of length equal to the number of dimensions of the objective function.

An example of the distribution of the optimal value f^* induced by a GP is shown in figure 6.11, on the right panel. We see that that this distribution is roughly truncated around 1.6, which is exactly the value of the incumbent in our training dataset; this makes sense, as the optimal value f^* must be at least the incumbent value 1.6.

> **NOTE**   The main advantage of focusing our effort on this distribution of f^* is the fact that the distribution is always one-dimensional, regardless of the dimensionality of the objective function.

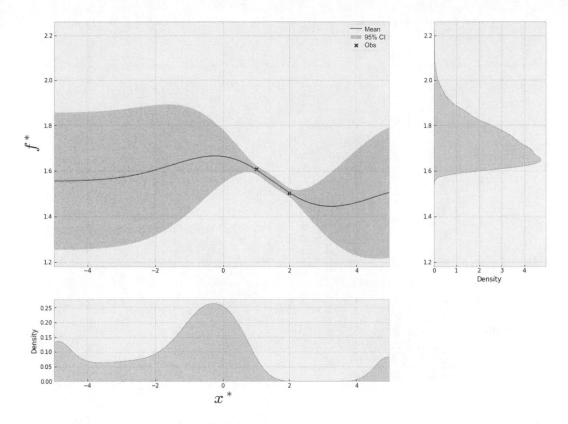

Figure 6.11   The GP belief (top left), the distribution of the function optimizer *x** (bottom), and the distribution of the optimal value *f** (right). The distribution of the optimal value is always one-dimensional and, therefore, easier to work with than that of the optimizer.

Specifically, we can draw samples from this one-dimensional distribution to approximate the expected posterior entropy upon making a query. From this point, we follow the same idea behind entropy search: choosing the query that (approximately) minimizes the expected posterior entropy or, in other words, maximizes the expected *reduction* in entropy.

> **DEFINITION**   By using this expected-reduction-in-entropy quantity as the acquisition score, we obtain the *Max-value Entropy Search* (MES) policy. The term *max-value* denotes the fact that we are using information theory to search for the max value, or the optimal value *f**, of the objective function.

Figure 6.12 shows the MES acquisition score in our running example in the bottom panel, where the point around –2 is where we should query next, according to this information-theory–based criterion. The MES policy prefers this location because it has both a relatively high mean and a high CI, thus balancing exploration and exploitation.

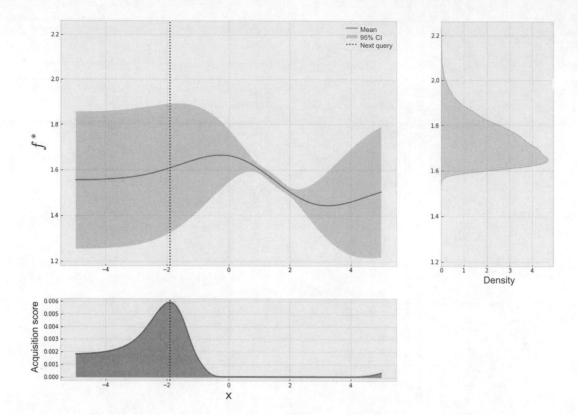

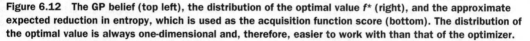

Figure 6.12   The GP belief (top left), the distribution of the optimal value f^* (right), and the approximate expected reduction in entropy, which is used as the acquisition function score (bottom). The distribution of the optimal value is always one-dimensional and, therefore, easier to work with than that of the optimizer.

Interestingly, the acquisition landscape here looks somewhat similar to the distribution of the optimizer x^* itself, which is shown in figure 6.11, where we see that the curve

1 Reaches its zenith somewhere in the middle
2 Achieves a non-negligible value at the end points
3 Bottoms out at 0 around 2, where we know for certain the location is not optimal

This is an indication that the optimal value f^* is intimately linked to the optimizer x^*, and while we lose some information by altering our objective, searching for f^* is a good proxy for searching for x^* and is much more computationally tractable.

6.2.2   *Implementing entropy search with BoTorch*

Having discussed the high-level idea behind MES, we are now ready to implement it using BoTorch and plug it into our optimization pipeline. The MES policy is implemented by the `qMaxValueEntropy` class in `botorch.acquisition.max_value_entropy_search` as a PyTorch module, similar to most BayesOpt policies we have seen. When initialized, this class takes in two arguments: a GPyTorch GP model and a set of points that will be used as samples in the approximation procedure described in the previous section.

While there are many ways that these sample points can be generated, one particular way we have learned from section 5.3.2 is using a Sobol sequence, which does a better job of covering the targeted space. Overall, the MES policy is implemented as follows:

```
num_candidates = 1000                                        Generates the samples
sobol = torch.quasirandom.SobolEngine(1, scramble=True)      between 0 and 1 using
candidate_x = sobol.draw(num_candidates)                     a Sobol sequence

candidate_x = 10 * candidate_x - 5            ◁─────────      Rescales the samples
                                                             to be inside the
policy = botorch.acquisition.max_value_entropy_search        domain
➥.qMaxValueEntropy(                          Declares the MES
    model, candidate_x                       policy object
)

with torch.no_grad():                                        Computes the
    acquisition_score = policy(xs.unsqueeze(1))              acquisition scores
```

Here, `num_candidates` is a tunable parameter that sets the number of samples you'd like to use in the MES computation. A larger value would mean an approximation with higher fidelity, but it would come at a higher computational cost.

Let's now apply this code to our running problem of optimizing the one-dimensional Forrester function, as implemented in the CH06/01 - BayesOpt loop.ipynb notebook. We are already familiar with most of this code, so we don't go into the details here.

Figure 6.13 shows the progress made by MES for 10 queries, in which the policy quickly finds the global optimum of the Forrester after five queries. Interestingly, as optimization progresses, we become more and more certain that looking at other regions in the search space will not result in any substantial reduction in entropy, which helps us stay close to the optimal location.

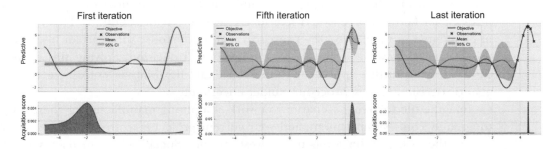

Figure 6.13   Progress made by the MES policy. The policy quickly finds the global optimum after five queries.

We have seen that information theory gives us a principled, mathematically elegant framework for decision-making that revolves around trying to learn as much as possible about a quantity of interest. This comes down to reducing the expected posterior entropy in the distribution that models the quantity we care about.

Within BayesOpt, we saw that a direct translation of this procedure poses computational challenges in modeling the location of the optimal value of the objective function, our primary search target. Instead, we shift our focus to the optimal value of the objective function itself, making the computation more tractable. Fortunately, all of this math is nicely abstracted away by BoTorch, leaving us with a convenient, modular interface we can plug into any optimization problem.

This is also where the second part of the book on BayesOpt policies comes to an end. The last three chapters covered some of the most commonly used heuristics to decision-making in BayesOpt and the corresponding policies, ranging from seeking improvement from the incumbent to borrowing multi-armed bandit methods and, in this chapter, using information theory.

The remainder of the book takes our discussion to the next level by introducing special optimization settings that differ from what we have seen so far, where we sequentially observe a single data point at each step of the optimization. These chapters show that the methods we have learned can be translated to practical settings in the real world to accelerate optimization.

6.3   Exercises

There are two exercises in this chapter:

1   The first exercise covers a variant of binary search in which prior information can be taken into account when making decisions.
2   The second walks us through the process of implementing MES in the hyperparameter tuning problem seen in previous chapters.

6.3.1   *Exercise 1: Incorporating prior knowledge into entropy search*

We saw in section 6.1.3 that by placing a uniform prior distribution on the location of the target within the array, the optimal information-theoretical search decision is to cut the array in half. What happens if a uniform distribution doesn't represent your prior belief faithfully and you'd like to use a different distribution? This exercise, implemented in the CH06/02 - Exercise 1.ipynb notebook, shows us an instance of this as well as how to derive the resulting optimal decision. Solving this exercise should help us further appreciate the elegance and flexibility of entropy search as a generic decision-making procedure under uncertainty.

Imagine the following scenario: you work at a phone manufacturing company in the quality control department, and your current project is to stress test the robustness of the casing of the company's newest product. Specifically, your team wants to find out from which floor of a 10-story building one can drop the phone to the ground and not break it. A few rules apply:

- The engineers who made the phone are sure it won't break if dropped from the first floor.
- If the phone breaks when dropped from a given floor, then it will also break when dropped from a higher floor.

You are tasked with finding the highest floor from which one can drop the phone without it breaking—we denote this unknown floor as X—by conducting trials. That is, you must drop actual phones from specific floors to determine X. The question is the following: How should you choose which floors to drop the phones from to find X? Since the phones are expensive, you need to conduct as few trials as possible and would like to use information theory to aid the search:

1 Assume that by taking into account physics and the materials and construction of the phone, the engineers have an initial guess regarding which floors might be possible.

Specifically, the prior distribution of X is exponential in that the probability that X is equal to a number is inversely exponential with respect to that number: $Pr(X = n) = 1 / 2^n$, for $n = 1, 2, ..., 9$; the probability corresponding to the highest (tenth) floor is $Pr(X = 10) = 1 / 2^9$. So the probability that $X = 1$ is 50%, and this probability is cut in half as the number increases. This probability distribution is visualized in figure 6.14.

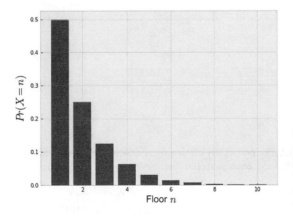

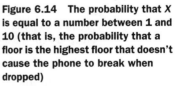

Figure 6.14 The probability that X is equal to a number between 1 and 10 (that is, the probability that a floor is the highest floor that doesn't cause the phone to break when dropped)

Verify that this is a valid probability distribution by proving that the probabilities sum to one. That is, prove that $Pr(X = 1) + Pr(X = 2) + ... + Pr(X = 10) = 1$.

2 Calculate the entropy of this prior distribution using the formula given at the end of section 6.1.1.

3 Given the prior distribution defined between 1 and 10, what is the probability that the phone will break when dropped from the second floor? What is this probability for the fifth floor? How about the first floor?

4   Assume that after observing the result of any trial, the posterior distribution for
    X is once again exponential and is defined between the lowest and highest possible floors.

    For example, if you observe that the phone doesn't break when dropped
    from the fifth floor, then we know that X is at least 5 and the posterior distribution of X is such that $Pr(X = 5) = 1 / 2$, $Pr(X = 6) = 1 / 4$, ..., $Pr(X = 9) = 1 / 32$,
    $Pr(X = 10) = 1 / 32$. If, on the other hand, the phone breaks when dropped
    from the fifth floor, then we know that X is at most 4 and the posterior distribution is such that $Pr(X = 1) = 1 / 2$, $Pr(X = 2) = 1 / 4$, $Pr(X = 3) = 1 / 8$, $Pr(X = 4)$
    $= 1 / 8$. Figure 6.15 shows these two scenarios.

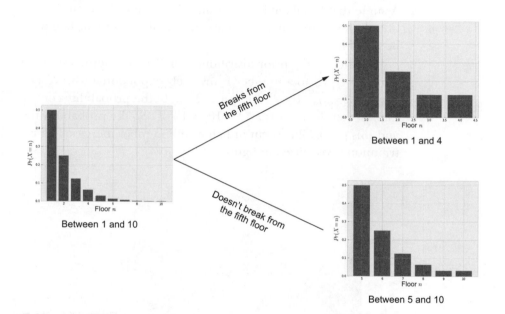

**Figure 6.15 The posterior probability distributions of X in two scenarios when the phone is
dropped from the fifth floor. Each posterior distribution is still exponential.**

    Compute the entropy of this fictitious posterior distribution in the two cases.

5   Given the prior distribution, compute the expected posterior entropy after you
    conduct a trial on the fifth floor (that is, after you drop the phone from the
    fifth floor and observe whether it breaks).

6   Compute this expected posterior entropy for other floors. Which floor gives the
    highest reduction in entropy? Is this still the same result as binary search? If
    not, what has changed?

6.3.2 *Exercise 2: Bayesian optimization for hyperparameter tuning*

This exercise, implemented in the CH06/03 - Exercise 2.ipynb notebook, applies BayesOpt to an objective function that simulates the accuracy surface of a support-vector machine model in a hyperparameter tuning task. The *x*-axis denotes the value of the penalty parameter *C*, while the *y*-axis denotes the value of the RBF kernel parameter γ. See the exercises in chapters 3 and 4 for more detail. Complete the exercise using the following steps:

1. Recreate the BayesOpt loop in the CH05/03 - Exercise 2.ipynb notebook, including the outer loop that implements repeated experiments.
2. Run the MES policy. Since our objective function is two-dimensional, we should increase the size of the Sobol sequence used by MES. For example, you can set it at 2,000. Observe its aggregated performance.

> **Repeated experiments in BayesOpt**
> Refer to step 9 of exercise 2 from chapter 4 to see how we can run repeated experiments in BayesOpt.

Summary

- Information theory studies the representation, quantification, and transfer of information. One of the core concepts in this field is entropy, which quantifies our uncertainty about a random variable from the variable's probability distribution.
- An entropy search procedure considers the expected reduction in entropy (and therefore in uncertainty) of a quantity of interest by taking an action, choosing the action that maximizes this reduction. We can apply this generic procedure to many decision-making problems under uncertainty.
- Binary search may be obtained as the result of entropy search applied to the problem of finding the location of a specific number in a sorted array.
- The curse of dimensionality refers to the exponential cost of many procedures in ML with respect to the dimensionality of an object of interest. As the number of dimensions increases, exponentially more time is needed to finish the procedure.
- In BayesOpt, while entropy search may be applied to the problem of finding the location of the function optimizer, it is computationally expensive due to the curse of dimensionality.
- To overcome the curse of dimensionality, we modify our goal of finding the function's optimized value, making it a one-dimensional search problem. The resulting BayesOpt policy is called Max-value Entropy Search (MES).
- Due to the complex behavior of the global optimum of a function modeled by a GP, it is infeasible to compute the acquisition scores of MES in closed form.

However, we can draw samples from probability distributions to approximate the acquisition scores.

- Implementing MES in BoTorch follows the same procedure as implementing other BayesOpt policies. To facilitate the sampling procedure in the acquisition score approximation, we use a Sobol sequence when initializing the policy object.

Part 3

Extending Bayesian optimization to specialized settings

The BayesOpt loop we have learned represents a wide range of optimization problems. However, real-life scenarios often don't follow this highly idealized model. What if you can run multiple function evaluations at the same time, which is common in hyperparameter tuning applications where multiple GPUs are available? What if you have multiple, competing objectives you'd like to optimize for? This part presents some of the most common optimization scenarios you might encounter in the real world and discusses how to extend BayesOpt to these settings.

To increase throughput, many settings allow experiments to run in parallel. Chapter 7 introduces the batch BayesOpt framework, in which function evaluations are made in batches. We learn how to extend the decision-making policies we have learned in part 2 to this setting, while ensuring we fully take advantage of the parallelism of the system.

In safety-critical use cases, we cannot explore the search space freely, as some function evaluations may have detrimental effects. This motivates the setting where there are constraints on how the function in question should behave and there is a need to factor in these constraints in the design of optimization policies. Chapter 8 deals with this setting, called constrained optimization, and develops the necessary machinery to apply BayesOpt.

Chapter 9 explores the setting in which we have access to multiple ways of observing the function's values at different levels of cost and accuracy; this is commonly known as multifidelity BayesOpt. We discuss the natural extension of entropy to quantify the value of making an evaluation at various levels of fidelity and apply the algorithm to balance information and cost.

Pairwise comparisons have been shown to reflect one's preference more accurately than number evaluations or ratings, as they are simpler and pose a lighter cognitive load on the labeler. Chapter 10 applies BayesOpt to this setting, first by using a special GP model and then by modifying existing policies to fit into this pairwise comparison workflow.

Multiobjective optimization is a common use case in which we aim to optimize multiple potentially conflicting objectives at the same time. We study this problem of multiobjective optimization and develop a BayesOpt solution that jointly optimizes the multiple objectives we have.

Across this diverse set of special optimization settings is a common theme: trading off exploration and exploitation when accounting for the structures of the problem. By seeing how BayesOpt is applied to a wide range of settings in this part, we not only solidify our understanding of this technique but also make the technique more applicable in practical scenarios. The code developed in these chapters will help you hit the ground running right away with any optimization problem you might have in real life.

Maximizing throughput with batch optimization

This chapter covers

- Making function evaluations in batches
- Extending BayesOpt to the batch setting
- Optimizing hard-to-compute acquisition scores

The BayesOpt loop we have been working with thus far takes in one query at a time and returns the function evaluation for the query before the next query is made. We use this loop in settings where function evaluations can only be made sequentially. However, many real-world scenarios of black box optimization allow the user to evaluate the objective functions in batches. For example, when tuning the hyperparameters of an ML model, we can try out different hyperparameter combinations in parallel if we have access to multiple processing units or computers, instead of running individual combinations one by one. By taking advantage of all the resources available to us, we can increase the number of experiments we conduct and maximize throughput during the function evaluation step of the BayesOpt loop.

We call this variant of BayesOpt in which multiple queries can be made in parallel *batch Bayesian optimization*. Examples of batch BayesOpt other than hyperparameter tuning include drug discovery, where a scientist uses each of multiple machines in their laboratory to synthesize an individual drug prototype, and product recommendation, where the recommendation engine presents multiple products to a customer at the same time. Overall, any black box optimization setting in which more than one experiment can be run simultaneously calls for batch BayesOpt.

Given that computational and physical resources are often parallelizable, batch BayesOpt is one of the most common settings of BayesOpt in the real world. In this chapter, we are introduced to batch BayesOpt and see how the policies we have learned about in previous chapters can be extended to this setting. We discuss why extending a BayesOpt policy to the batch setting is not a trivial endeavor and why it requires careful consideration. We then learn about various strategies that facilitate extending to the batch setting and how to implement BayesOpt policies in Python using BoTorch.

By the end of the chapter, you will understand what batch BayesOpt is, when the batch setting is applicable, and how to implement BayesOpt policies in this setting. With the knowledge of how to parallelize BayesOpt in the batch setting, we can make BayesOpt more practical and applicable in the real world.

7.1   *Making multiple function evaluations simultaneously*

The ability to make multiple function evaluations at the same time in a black box problem is common in many real-world scenarios, and batch BayesOpt is the setting of BayesOpt in which this parallelism of function evaluations is taken into account. In this section, we cover the exact setting of batch BayesOpt and what challenges we might face when using BayesOpt policies to make multiple queries to the objective function. This section will motivate the various strategies to extend BayesOpt policies to the batch setting. We cover these strategies later in the chapter, starting in section 7.2.

7.1.1   *Making use of all available resources in parallel*

One of the defining characteristics of an expensive black box optimization problem is that making function evaluations can be cost prohibitive. In section 1.1, we examined the high cost of making function evaluations in many applications; hyperparameter tuning a neural network takes a lot of time and computational resources, and the cost of creating new drugs has been exponentially increasing in recent years, to name two examples. This cost of querying the objective function in black box optimization gives rise to the need to make the process of querying the objective function more efficient. One way we can achieve this is via *parallelism*.

> **DEFINITION**   *Parallelism* refers to the act of running independent processes at the same time so that the total time taken to complete these processes is cut short.

The benefits of parallelism are summarized in figure 7.1, where three processes (which can be programs to run, computations to complete, and so on) run either sequentially or in parallel. When run in parallel, the three processes only take one third of the total time required if run sequentially.

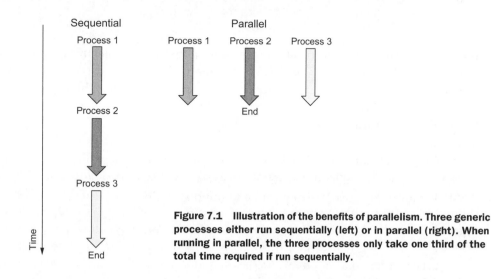

Figure 7.1   Illustration of the benefits of parallelism. Three generic processes either run sequentially (left) or in parallel (right). When running in parallel, the three processes only take one third of the total time required if run sequentially.

Parallelism is particularly common in computer science, where a computer may use multiple processing units in parallel to process multiple programs at the same time. If these programs are independent from each other (they don't use each other's data or write to the same files), they can run in parallel without any issue.

The same idea applies to optimization settings that employ BayesOpt. For example, an ML engineer tuning a neural network may take advantage of the multiple GPUs to which they have access to train multiple models at the same time. A scientist attempting to discover new drugs can experiment with more than one recipe using the equipment in the lab to synthesize the multiple recipes simultaneously. Making multiple queries at the same time allows us to obtain more information given the same amount of time spent learning about the objective function.

What are GPUs?
GPUs, or graphics processing units, are the hardware that is optimized to perform parallel matrix multiplications. Therefore, they are commonly used for training neural networks.

Take the example of baking a batch of cookies. You *could* bake one cookie at a time if you wanted to, but doing so would waste resources such as power for the oven and time. Instead, you're much more likely to bake multiple cookies simultaneously in a batch.

BayesOpt for baking cookies

On the topic of baking, there is, in fact, a research paper on batch BayesOpt (https://static.googleusercontent.com/media/research.google.com/en//pubs/archive/46507.pdf) that tackles optimizing cookie recipes by finding the optimal amount of eggs, sugar, and cinnamon to use when making the cookie dough.

In BayesOpt, the batch setting allows multiple inputs of the objective function to be evaluated at the same time. That is, we can send multiple queries, x_1, x_2, ..., x_k, to the black box that evaluates the objective all at once and receive the corresponding objective values $f(x_1)$, $f(x_2)$, ..., $f(x_k)$ in a batch. In contrast, in the classic sequential BayesOpt setting, only after observing $f(x_1)$ can we proceed to query at another location x_2.

At each iteration of the batch BayesOpt loop, we pick out multiple input locations to evaluate the objective function at, as opposed to a single location like we've been doing thus far. This batch BayesOpt loop is illustrated in figure 7.2. The requirement for multiple queries at a time means we need new BayesOpt policies to score the usefulness of these input locations. We talk more about why the BayesOpt policies we have learned cannot be easily extended to the batch setting in the next section. The other component of the BayesOpt loop, the GP, remains unchanged, as we still need an ML model that produces probabilistic predictions. In other words, it's the decision-making component of BayesOpt that needs to be modified for us to adopt the batch setting.

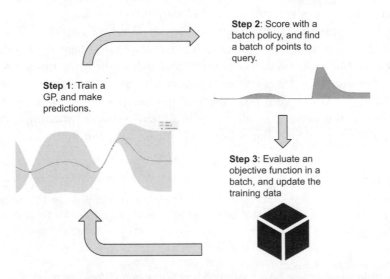

Figure 7.2   The batch BayesOpt loop. Compared to sequential BayesOpt, batch BayesOpt requires multiple query points to be identified at step 2 and evaluates the objective function at these points simultaneously at step 3.

> **Acquisition scores of a policy**
>
> A BayesOpt policy assigns a score, called the *acquisition score*, to each input location in the search space that quantifies how useful the input is in our search for the global optimum of the objective function. Each policy uses a different heuristic to compute this score, as detailed in chapters 4 to 6.

The number of queries that could be made simultaneously—that is, the size of the batch—is application dependent. For example, how many cookies you could bake at the same time depends on the size of your oven and baking trays. The computing resources you have available (the number of CPUs and GPUs) dictate how many neural networks you can train in parallel when tuning the model's hyperparameters. Figure 7.1 shows three processes running at the same time as an example, so the batch size is 3.

7.1.2 Why can't we use regular BayesOpt policies in the batch setting?

We said in the previous section that the BayesOpt policies we have learned under the sequential setting (where queries to the objective function are made sequentially, one after another) cannot be repurposed and used in the batch setting without modifications. In this section, we discuss in more detail why this is the case and why we need specialized policies for the batch setting.

Remember from section 4.1 that a BayesOpt policy assigns a score to each point in the search space that quantifies how useful the point is in our search for the global optimum of the objective function. We then look for the point that gives the highest score and choose it as the next query of the objective function. Figure 7.3 shows the score computed by the Expected Improvement (EI) policy (introduced in section 4.3) as the curve in the bottom panel, where 1.75, as indicated by the vertical mark on the lower curve, maximizes the score and is our next query.

What would happen if we were to use the same EI score, the lower curve in figure 7.3, to pick out not one but multiple points to query the objective function with? We would need to identify the many points that give the highest EI scores. However, these points that give high EI scores would simply cluster around the point picked under the sequential setting. This is because along the lower curve, if we were to move an infinitesimal distance from 1.75, we would still receive a high EI score. That is, the points close to the one giving the highest acquisition score also give high acquisition scores.

If we were to simply pick out the points with the highest acquisition scores, our queries would cluster around a single region in the search space, essentially putting all our eggs in one basket. This is illustrated in figure 7.4, where the queries giving the highest EI scores cluster around 1.75. This clustering effect is undesirable because we are wasting our valuable resources evaluating the objective function at essentially a single input location. These clustered points are less useful than points that are more spread out.

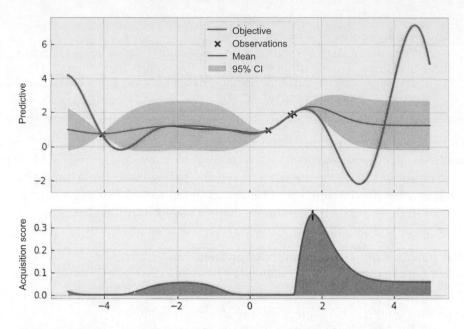

Figure 7.3 An example of BayesOpt. The top panel shows the GP predictions and the ground truth objective function, while the bottom panel shows the acquisition scores made by EI, discussed in section 4.3. The vertical tick on the lower curve at 1.75 indicates the next query.

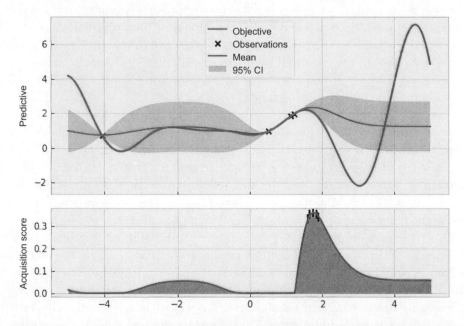

Figure 7.4 Queries made in the batch setting if we were to simply pick out the points with the highest acquisition scores, denoted by the vertical ticks on the lower curve. These queries are close to each other and are less useful than if they were more spread out.

Choosing all of our queries to be points clustered around one location prevents us from benefiting from the parallelism inherent in the batch setting. Our discussion so far shows that designing a batch of queries is not as simple as choosing the top points giving the highest acquisition scores of a BayesOpt policy. In the remainder of this chapter, we discuss BayesOpt policies that are specifically designed for the batch setting. Conveniently for us, these policies are extensions of the BayesOpt policies we have learned in chapters 4 through 6, so we only need to learn about extending the optimization heuristics we have learned to the batch setting.

7.2 Computing the improvement and upper confidence bound of a batch of points

The first policies we will extend to the batch setting are the improvement-based policies, which are the topic of chapter 4, and the UCB policy, discussed in section 5.2. The heuristics used by these policies allow for the policies to be modified to work in the batch setting, as we see shortly.

In the next section, we introduce the mathematical modification of those heuristics and discuss how resulting batch policies work. Afterwards, we learn how to declare and run these batch policies with BoTorch.

7.2.1 Extending optimization heuristics to the batch setting

The discussion in section 7.1.2 shows that choosing a batch of points to evaluate the objective function with is not as simple as finding the top points that maximize the acquisition score of a sequential policy. Instead, we need to redefine the mathematical formulations of these sequential policies to repurpose them to the batch setting.

One strategy applies for three BayesOpt policies that we have learned, PoI, EI, and UCB, which formulate their acquisition scores as averages over normal distributions. That is, the score each of the three policies assigns to a given point can be written as the average of a quantity of interest over a normal distribution in the sequential setting. For PoI, this quantity is whether we will observe an improvement; for EI, the quantity of interest is the magnitude of the improvement.

As shown in the top portion of figure 7.5, a sequential BayesOpt policy scores a candidate query x using the average of some quantity $G(f(x))$ over the normal distribution that is our belief about the value of the objective function $f(x)$. This quantity G depends on the heuristic that the BayesOpt policy uses to balance between exploration and exploitation. With a batch of queries x_1, x_2, ..., x_k, we instead compute the average of the maximum value of the quantity G across the points in the batch, as shown in the bottom portion of figure 7.5. This average is computed across the multivariate Gaussian distribution corresponding to the objective values $f(x_1)$, $f(x_2)$, ..., $f(x_k)$.

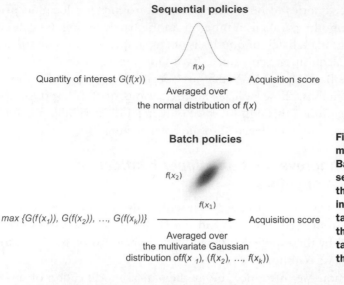

Figure 7.5   Extending the mathematical formulation of a BayesOpt policy to the batch setting. In both cases, we use the average of a quantity of interest. In the batch setting, we take the maximum value across the points in a batch before taking the average to represent the utility of the whole batch.

The balance between exploration and exploitation

All BayesOpt policies need to address the tradeoff between zeroing in on a high-performing region in the search space (exploitation) and inspecting unexplored regions (exploration). Refer to section 4.1.2 for a more thorough discussion of this tradeoff.

This strategy of using the maximum of the quantity of interest G to represent the utility of the whole batch makes intuitive sense in the context of optimization, which is our goal. The higher the maximum G, the more valuable the whole batch of queries. With a way to quantify the value of any given batch of queries, we can now proceed to find the batch maximizing that quantity. The heuristic we use is similar to what we do in sports competitions like the Olympics: each country might train many athletes throughout the year, but when the time comes, only the best individuals are chosen to take part in the competition. Figure 7.6 visualizes this process.

Figure 7.6   The batch BayesOpt heuristic picks out the best element with the highest G value to represent the whole batch (bottom). This strategy is similar to team selection in the Olympics, where only the best athletes are selected to represent a country.

How is this strategy realized with the three aforementioned policies? Let's first discuss the first two: improvement-based policies. Remember from chapter 4 that PoI uses the probability that the next query will improve from the best-seen point (the incumbent) as the acquisition score. The more likely that a point will yield a better result than the incumbent, the higher the score that PoI assigns to that point. The EI policy, on the other hand, takes into account the magnitude of the improvement, assigning a high acquisition score to points that are likely to both improve from the incumbent and improve by a large amount.

The difference between these two policies is visualized in figure 7.7, where different outcomes lie on the *x*-axis, and the *y*-axis shows the objective value that is to be optimized. PoI treats all points on the *x*-axis that yield higher values than the incumbent equally, while EI considers how much each point improves.

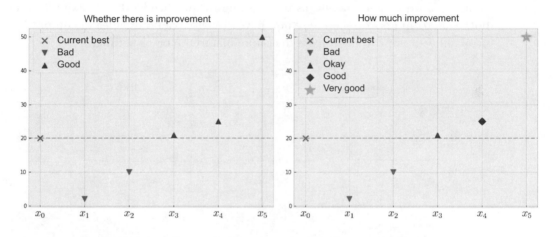

Figure 7.7 **The difference between PoI (left) and EI (right). The former only considers whether we improve from the incumbent or not, while the latter considers how much improvement is made.**

In the batch setting, we can reason about the improvement we observe after the current iteration of the BayesOpt loop in a similar manner. Instead of reasoning about the multiple points within a batch of queries, we can single out the maximum value among the function evaluations at these points. That is, if our batch of queries to the objective function were at x_1, x_2, ..., x_k, we wouldn't need to use all function evaluations $f(x_1)$, $f(x_2)$, ..., $f(x_k)$ to reason about the improvement we observe. We'd need just the maximum value $\max \{f(x_1), f(x_2), ..., f(x_k)\}$ since this maximum value defines the improvement we observe.

Following the example in figure 7.7, assume our incumbent has an objective value of 20, and consider the following scenarios visualized in the right panel of figure 7.8:

- If our batch of queries, with the batch size of 3, returned values that are all lower than 20 (corresponding to X_1 in the right panel), then we would observe no improvement. The highest function evaluation in X_1 is 3, meaning no function evaluation from this batch improved from the incumbent.

- If all returned values exceeded the incumbent (corresponding to X_2), then we would observe an improvement from the incumbent. In particular, the maximum of this batch X_2 is 30, leading to an improvement of 10.
- More importantly, if only some but not all returned function evaluations were better than the incumbent (X_3, as an example), then we would still observe an improvement. The maximum of X_3 is 22, which is, indeed, an improvement from the incumbent 20.

By focusing on the maximum evaluated value returned from a batch of queries, we can determine right away whether this batch has resulted in an improvement from the incumbent. Figure 7.8 shows this improvement-based reasoning of PoI, where batches X_2 and X_3 are treated equally, as they (or, more specifically, their maximum values) both lead to an improvement. We now have a way to extend the idea of computing the probability of improvement from the sequential to the batch setting.

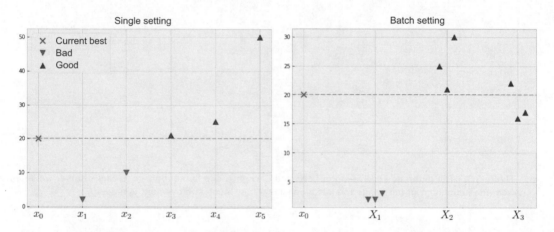

Figure 7.8 Whether a query (left) or a batch of queries (right) leads to an improvement from the incumbent. In the batch setting on the right, we only consider the maximum value within each batch to determine whether there is an improvement.

DEFINITION   The *acquisition score* PoI assigns to a given batch of candidate queries is equal to the probability that the maximum among the returned function evaluations will exceed the incumbent.

Mathematically, we go from computing the probability that the function evaluation $f(x)$ will exceed the incumbent f^*, denoted as $Pr(f(x) > f^*)$, in the sequential setting, to computing the probability that the maximum function evaluation will exceed the incumbent, $Pr(\max \{f(x_1), f(x_2), ..., f(x_k)\} > f^*)$. This probability $Pr(\max$

$\{f(x_1), f(x_2), ..., f(x_k)\} > f^*)$ is then used as the PoI acquisition score for the batch of queries $x_1, x_2, ..., x_k$.

As mentioned earlier in this section, these probabilities, $Pr(f(x) > f^*)$ and $Pr(\max \{f(x_1), f(x_2), ..., f(x_k)\} > f^*)$, can be viewed as averages of quantities that are important to our optimization progress over Gaussian distributions. Specifically, the probabilities are averages of the binary random variable indicating whether $f(x) > f^*$ and $\max \{f(x_1), f(x_2), ..., f(x_k)\} > f^*$ are true, respectively. This comparison is visualized in figure 7.9.

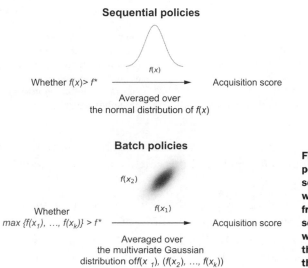

Figure 7.9 Extending the POI policy to the batch setting. In the sequential case (top), we consider whether the next query improves from the incumbent. In the batch setting (bottom), we reason about whether the maximum value across the points in a batch improves from the incumbent.

To complete the batch BayesOpt loop with this PoI policy, we then find the batch x_1, $x_2, ..., x_k$ that maximizes the acquisition score $Pr(\max \{f(x_1), f(x_2), ..., f(x_k)\} > f^*)$. As we learned in section 4.1.1, we can use the helper function `optimize_acqf()` from BoTorch's `optim.optimize` module to facilitate this search for the batch $x_1, x_2, ..., x_k$ that optimizes the acquisition score, as we will see in section 7.2.2.

We now move on to the EI policy, which computes the expected value of the improvement from the incumbent we will observe from querying a particular point. Since we already have a way to reason about improvement from the incumbent upon observing a batch of function evaluations, the batch extension of EI presents itself. That is, we only compute the expected value of the improvement from the incumbent that results from the maximum function evaluation within the returned batch, max $\{f(x_1), f(x_2), ..., f(x_k)\}$. Just as PoI computes the probability that this maximum value exceeds the incumbent, EI considers how much the maximum exceeds the improvement. The difference between EI and its batch variant is visualized in figure 7.10.

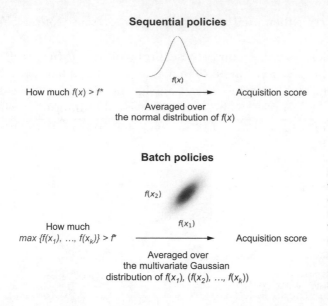

Figure 7.10   Extending the EI policy to the batch setting. In the sequential case (top), we use the average of how much the next query improves from the incumbent. In the batch setting (bottom), we take the average of how much the maximum value across the points in a batch improves from the incumbent.

To illustrate this reasoning, figure 7.11 shows the distinction in how EI scores different outcomes in the sequential (left panel) and the batch setting (right panel). The following is true in the right panel:

- A batch that doesn't possess any point that improves from the incumbent at 20 (X_1, as an example) will constitute zero improvement.
- The maximum value from batch X_2 is 22, so we observe an improvement of 2, even though there are values in this batch that fall below the incumbent.

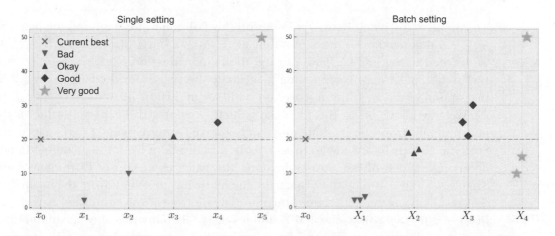

Figure 7.11   Whether a query (left) or a batch of queries (right) leads to an improvement from the incumbent. In the batch setting on the right, we only consider the maximum value within each batch to determine whether there is an improvement.

- Although the values in batch X_3 are all higher than the incumbent, the improvement we observe is once again completely determined by the maximum value 30.
- Finally, even if most of batch X_4 is lower than the incumbent 20, the maximum value of X_4 is 50, making this batch a very good outcome.

To proceed with batch EI, we compute the expected value of how much higher the maximum value within a batch is than the incumbent. This expected value of the improvement or expected improvement is the acquisition score batch that EI uses to rank how valuable a given batch x_1, x_2, ..., x_k is. The helper function `optimize_acqf()` can once again be used to find the batch that gives the highest expected improvement.

The discussions so far help us extend the two improvement-based policies, PoI and EI, to the batch setting. We are now left with the UCB policy. Fortunately, the strategy of picking out the maximum value from a batch of queries to compute the improvement also applies to UCB. To apply the same strategy of picking out the maximum value (with respect to a function G of interest) from a batch of queries to UCB, we need to reframe the UCB acquisition score as an average across a normal distribution.

> **The mathematical details of the UCB policy**
>
> In section 5.2.2, we discussed that the UCB acquisition score is $\mu + \beta\sigma$. Here, the terms μ and σ are the predictive mean and standard deviations of $f(x)$, and β is an adjustable parameter that trades off exploration and exploitation. We now need to rewrite $\mu + \beta\sigma$ as an average of some quantity over the normal distribution $N(\mu, \sigma^2)$ to extend UCB to the batch setting. While this reformulation can be done, we don't go into the math here. The interested reader can refer to appendix A of this paper (https://arxiv.org/pdf/1712.00424.pdf), which lays out the mathematical details.

The rest of extending UCB to the batch setting follows the same procedure:

1 We take the average of the maximum of the quantity that is the rewritten $\mu + \beta\sigma$ across the whole batch and use it as the batch UCB acquisition score.

2 We then use the helper function `optimize_acqf()` to find the batch that give us the highest score.

That's all we need to know about extending these three BayesOpt policies to the batch setting. We learn how to implement these policies in BoTorch in the next section.

7.2.2   *Implementing batch improvement and UCB policies*

Similar to what we saw in chapters 4 through 6, BoTorch makes it straightforward to implement and use BayesOpt policies in Python, and the batch variants of the three policies discussed in the previous section, PoI, EI, and UCB, are no exceptions. While it's important for us to learn about the mathematical formulations of these three policies, we will see that with BoTorch, we can simply replace a single line of code in our Python program to run these policies. The code we use in this section can be found in the Jupyter notebook named CH07/01 - Batch BayesOpt loop.ipynb.

You might think that as we are now working under a new setting where queries to the objective function are done in batches, we need to modify the code that implements the BayesOpt loop (obtaining multiple function evaluations at the same time, appending multiple points to the training set, training the GP model). Amazingly, however, the necessary modifications are minimal, thanks to BoTorch's ability to seamlessly support batch mode. In particular, when using the helper function `optimize_acqf()` to find the next queries maximizing the acquisition score, we only need to specify the parameter `q = k` to be the batch size (that is, the number of function evaluations that can be run in parallel).

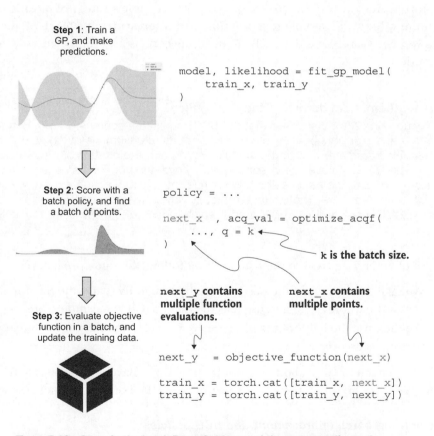

Figure 7.12   Steps in the batch BayesOpt loop and the corresponding code. Compared to the sequential setting, we need minimum modifications to our code when moving to the batch setting.

The entire batch BayesOpt loop is summarized in figure 7.12, which closely resembles figure 4.4. The few changes are annotated:

- We specify q = k to be the batch size *k* when using the helper function `optimize_acqf()`.
- This helper function returns `next_x`, which contains *k* points. The variable `next_x` is a *k*-by-*d* PyTorch tensor, where *d* is the number of dimensions in our search space (that is, the number of features in our data set).
- We then query the objective function at the locations specified in `next_x` and obtain `next_y`, which contains the function evaluations. Unlike the sequential setting, where `next_y` is a scalar or a one-element tensor, `next_y` here is a tensor that contains *k* elements, corresponding to the function evaluations of `next_x`.

NOTE For step 1 in figure 7.12, we still need a class implementation of a GP model and the helper function `fit_gp_model()` that trains the GP on the training data. Fortunately, the same code we use in the sequential setting can be reused without any modification. Refer to section 4.1.1 for the complete discussion of this code.

To facilitate our code demonstration, we use the two-dimensional synthetic objective function that simulates the model accuracy of a hyperparameter tuning application. This function is first introduced in chapter 3's exercise and is implemented as follows, where we specify that the function domain, our search space, is between 0 and 2 in each of the two dimensions:

```
def f(x):
  return (
    torch.sin(5 * x[..., 0] / 2 - 2.5) * torch
    ➥.cos(2.5 - 5 * x[..., 1])
    + (5 * x[..., 1] / 2 + 0.5) ** 2 / 10
  ) / 5 + 0.2
```
Function definition

```
lb = 0
ub = 2
bounds = torch.tensor([[lb, lb], [ub, ub]], dtype=torch.float)
```
Function domain, which is between 0 and 2 in each dimension

This objective function is visualized in figure 7.13, where we see the global optimum is achieved near the top right corner of the space, giving an accuracy of 90%.

To set up our batch optimization problem, we assume we can train the model in four different processes at the same time. In other words, our batch size is 4. Further, we can only retrain the model five times, so the number of iterations of our batch BayesOpt loop is 5, and the total number of queries we can make is $4 \times 5 = 20$:

```
num_queries = 20
batch_size = 4
num_iters = num_queries // batch_size
```
This variable equals 5.

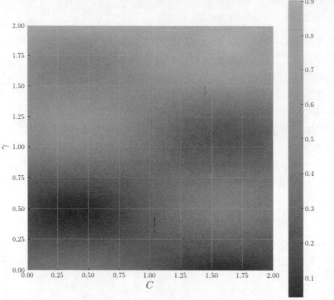
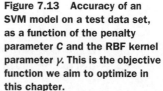

Figure 7.13   Accuracy of an SVM model on a test data set, as a function of the penalty parameter *C* and the RBF kernel parameter γ. This is the objective function we aim to optimize in this chapter.

Now, all that's left to do is run a batch BayesOpt policy. We do this with the following code that first randomly picks out a point in the search space as the training set:

Randomly picks a point in the search space

```
torch.manual_seed(0)
train_x = bounds[0] + (bounds[1] - bounds[0]) * torch.rand(1, 2)
train_y = f(train_x)
```

Evaluates the objective function at the randomly picked point

We then do the following for each of the five iterations:

1 Keep track of the best accuracy seen so far
2 Retrain the GP model with the current training set
3 Initialize a batch BayesOpt policy
4 Use the helper function `optimize_acqf()` to find the best batch of queries
5 Evaluate the objective function at the locations specified by the batch of queries
6 Append the new observations to the training set and repeat:

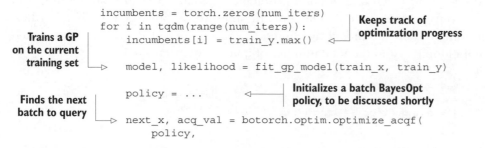

```
incumbents = torch.zeros(num_iters)
for i in tqdm(range(num_iters)):
    incumbents[i] = train_y.max()

    model, likelihood = fit_gp_model(train_x, train_y)

    policy = ...

    next_x, acq_val = botorch.optim.optimize_acqf(
        policy,
```

Keeps track of optimization progress

Trains a GP on the current training set

Finds the next batch to query

Initializes a batch BayesOpt policy, to be discussed shortly

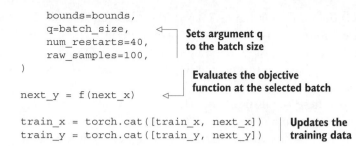

```
        bounds=bounds,
        q=batch_size,        ◁──  Sets argument q
        num_restarts=40,          to the batch size
        raw_samples=100,
    )
                             ┌── Evaluates the objective
                             │   function at the selected batch
    next_y = f(next_x)   ◁───┘

    train_x = torch.cat([train_x, next_x])   │  Updates the
    train_y = torch.cat([train_y, next_y])   │  training data
```

Again, this code is almost identical to the code we use in section 4.1.1 of chapter 4 that implements the sequential setting of BayesOpt. All we need to be careful of is setting argument `q` of the helper function `optimize_acqf()` to the correct batch size.

To run a batch BayesOpt policy, we then initialize it using BoTorch's class implementation of the policy. For the PoI policy, we use

```
policy = botorch.acquisition.monte_carlo.qProbabilityOfImprovement(
    model, best_f=train_y.max()
)
```

Similarly, for the EI policy, we use

```
policy = botorch.acquisition.monte_carlo.qExpectedImprovement(
    model, best_f=train_y.max()
)
```

Note the `q` in front of the class names, which indicates these classes implement batch BayesOpt policies. Similar to argument `best_f` that sequential PoI and EI take in, this argument `best_f` here specifies the current incumbent value, which we set at `train_y.max()`.

For UCB, we use an equivalent API, where the argument `beta` sets the tradeoff parameter β in the acquisition score $\mu + \beta\sigma$, where μ and σ are the mean and standard deviation of our prediction at a given point:

```
policy = botorch.acquisition.monte_carlo.qUpperConfidenceBound(
    model, beta=2
)
```

Arguments BayesOpt policies take

We learn about the implementation of sequential POI, EI, and UCB in sections 4.2.2, 4.3, and 5.2.3, respectively. The arguments each of these policies take in are identical to their batch counterparts, which makes transitioning to the batch setting in BoTorch straightforward.

Since we can now run the batch version of PoI, EI, and UCB, let's take a moment to inspect the behavior of these policies. In particular, assume our current BayesOpt progress is the same as in figure 7.3 with the one-dimensional objective function. This figure also shows the acquisition scores computed by EI for a single point in the bottom panel. We're interested in seeing what EI's acquisition scores look like for a batch of two points—that is, the expected improvement from the incumbent of a given pair of queries.

We show these acquisition scores with a heatmap in figure 7.14, where the brightness of each location on the square denotes the expected improvement of a given pair of queries, and the locations that give the highest acquisition scores are denoted as stars. (The top and right panels show the observed data and the current GP belief about the objective function along the axes of the heatmap.) We observe a few interesting trends:

- There are two straight bands on the heatmap denoting high acquisition scores. These bands are close to the data point $x = 2$, meaning any batch of queries (of size 2) that has a member close to $x = 2$ will give a high score. This makes sense because around $x = 2$ is where the posterior mean of the GP is maximized.

- The diagonal of the heatmap is dark, meaning that querying a batch x_1 and x_2, where x_1 is roughly equal to x_2, is likely to yield a low improvement. This observation verifies what we said in section 7.1.2: choosing the queries in a batch to cluster around each other is a bad strategy that essentially puts all our eggs in one basket.

- Finally, the two optimal batches of queries, denoted by the stars, are the same batch, since the locations are symmetric to each other. This batch contains 1.68 and 2.12, which are still in the neighborhood of $x = 2$, where the GP tells us the objective function yields high values. Further, the two selected queries 1.68 and 2.12 are far away from each other and, thus, help us escape the trap of clustering our queries around each other.

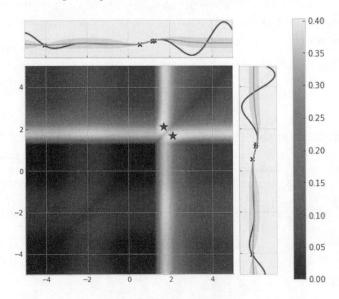

Figure 7.14 A heatmap showing the acquisition scores of the batch EI policy for batches of size 2 with a one-dimensional objective function. The top and right panels show the observed data and the current GP belief about the objective function along the axes of the heatmap. The two optimal pairs of queries, denoted as the two stars, contain 1.68 and 2.12, which are relatively far away from each other.

Figure 7.14 shows that the batch version of EI evaluates a given batch of queries in a reasonable manner, prioritizing batches that are both likely to yield high objective values and sufficiently spread out.

> **Batch versus sequential EI**
>
> Interestingly, the two points selected by batch EI, 1.68 and 2.12, are different from the point maximizing the sequential EI's acquisition score, 1.75. This difference between sequential EI and batch EI demonstrates that the optimal decision in the sequential setting isn't necessarily the optimal decision in the batch setting.

Returning to our hyperparameter tuning example, we are ready to use these initializations to run the batch policies. After saving the running incumbent values each policy achieves and plotting them against each other, we can generate figure 7.15, which shows the optimization progress each policy makes in our example. We first observe that this progress is being plotted in batches of four, which makes sense, since 4 is the batch size we use. In terms of performance, we see that EI and UCB are able to progress faster than PoI in the beginning, but all three converge to roughly the same accuracy at the end.

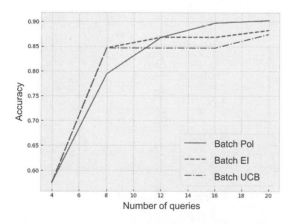

Figure 7.15   Progress made by various batch BayesOpt policies in the hyperparameter tuning example. Progress is made in batches of four, which is the batch size used.

> **Repeated experiments in BayesOpt**
>
> To accurately compare the performance of these policies in this hyperparameter tuning application, we need to repeat this experiment using different initial training sets that are randomly generated. Refer to step 9 of exercise 2 from chapter 4 to see how we can run repeated experiments in BayesOpt.

We have now learned how to implement the batch versions of PoI, EI, and UCB in BoTorch and have seen that the transition from the sequential to the batch setting requires minimum modifications to our code. Let's now move on to the remaining BayesOpt policies, TS and MES, which require different strategies to be extended to the batch setting.

7.3 *Exercise 1: Extending TS to the batch setting via resampling*

Unlike the other BayesOpt policies, Thompson sampling (TS) can be easily extended to the batch setting, thanks to its sampling strategy. We explore how this extension is done in this exercise. Remember that TS in the sequential setting, which, as we learned in section 5.3, draws one sample from the current GP belief about the objective function and queries the data point that maximizes that sample.

In the batch setting, we simply repeat this process of sampling from the GP and maximizing the sample multiple times to assemble a batch of queries of the desired size. For example, if the batch size of our batch BayesOpt problem is 3, then we draw three samples from the GP, and the batch of queries we end up with contains the maximizers of the three samples (one maximizer for each sample). This logic is illustrated in figure 7.16, where we keep sampling from the GP and adding the point that maximizes the latest sample to the running batch until the batch is full—that is, until we have reached the appropriate batch size.

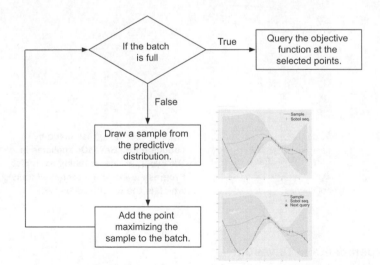

Figure 7.16   A flowchart of the implementation of the batch version of TS. We keep sampling from the GP and adding the point that maximizes the latest sample to the running batch until the batch is full.

Every time we draw a sample from the GP, we obtain a different realization of what the objective function could be. By optimizing the multiple samples drawn from the GP, we have an easy way of selecting multiple points that could guide us to the global optimum of the objective function. To implement and run this policy on the hyperparameter tuning example, we take the following steps, as implemented in the CH07/02 - Exercise 1.ipynb notebook:

1   Recreate the batch BayesOpt loop in CH07/01 - Batch BayesOpt loop.ipynb.
2   Implement TS with a Sobol sampler, as described in section 5.3:
    a   Use 2,000 candidates for the Sobol sampler.
    b   When calling the TS object, specify that the number of samples is equal to the batch size:

```
ts = botorch.generation.MaxPosteriorSampling(model, replacement=False)
next_x = ts(candidate_x, num_samples=batch_size)
```

3   Run this TS policy on the hyperparameter tuning objective function, and observe its performance.

Sobol sequences

A Sobol sampler generates a Sobol sequence, which can cover a space better than a uniformly sampled sequence. More discussion on Sobol sequences can be found in section 5.3.2.

7.4 Computing the value of a batch of points using information theory

We now learn how to extend the final BayesOpt policy in our toolkit, Max-value Entropy Search (MES), to the batch setting. Unlike the improvement-based and bandit policies, MES requires more careful consideration to run efficiently in the batch setting. We discuss the batch version of MES and the problems we run into when extending it to the batch setting in the next section and, finally, how to implement the policy in BoTorch afterwards.

> **NOTE**   MES is the topic of chapter 6, where we learn about the basics of information theory and how to implement the MES policy with BoTorch.

7.4.1 Finding the most informative batch of points with cyclic refinement

In the sequential setting, MES scores each candidate query according to how much information about the objective function's maximum value f^* we will gain after querying that candidate point. The more information about the maximum value a candidate point offers, the more likely it is that the point will guide us toward the objective function's global optimum x^*.

We'd like to use the same strategy for the batch setting. That is, we want to compute how much information about the maximum objective value f^* we will gain after querying a batch of candidate points. This information-theoretic value of a batch of points is a well-defined mathematical quantity, and we can theoretically compute and use it as the acquisition score in the batch setting. However, computing this information-theoretic quantity is quite expensive to do in practice.

The main bottleneck comes from the fact that we have to consider all possible function evaluations in the batch to know how much information about f^* we will gain. Although these function evaluations follow a multivariate Gaussian distribution, which offers many mathematical conveniences, computing the information gain about f^* is one of the tasks that aren't simplified by Gaussianity. This computational cost means that although we can compute the acquisition score for a batch of points, this computation is expensive to do and not amenable to optimization. That is, finding the batch of points that maximizes information about f^* is very hard to do.

NOTE   The search for the query maximizing the acquisition score is done by L-BFGS, a quasi-Newton optimization method that generally works better than gradient descent, in the helper function `optimize_acqf()`. However, due to the way the batch version of the information-theoretic acquisition score is computed, neither L-BFGS nor gradient descent can effectively optimize the score.

Acquisition scores in BayesOpt
Remember that the acquisition score quantifies the value of a query or a batch of queries in helping us locate the global optimum of the objective function, so at every iteration of the BayesOpt loop, we need to identify the query or the batch of queries that maximizes the acquisition score. See section 4.1 for a discussion on maximizing the acquisition score.

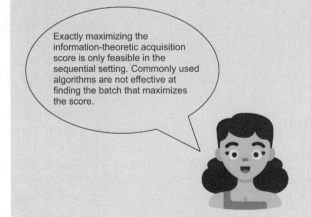

Exactly maximizing the information-theoretic acquisition score is only feasible in the sequential setting. Commonly used algorithms are not effective at finding the batch that maximizes the score.

If the method we usually use to find the next optimal query in terms of information theory, L-BFGS, only works in the sequential setting for one candidate point, how can we still use it in the batch setting? Our strategy here is to use the method to find individual members of the batch, one member at a time, in a cyclic manner, until convergence. Specifically, we do the following:

1   We start out with a starting batch x_1, x_2, ..., x_k. This batch can be randomly selected from the search space.

2   Since L-BFGS cannot run on all members of x_1, x_2, ..., x_k simultaneously, we only run it on x_1 while keeping the other members of the batch x_2, x_3, ..., x_k fixed. L-BFGS can, indeed, optimize x_1 individually, since this task is similar to maximizing the acquisition score in the sequential setting.

3   Once L-BFGS returns a value for x_1, we run L-BFGS on x_2 while keeping x_1 and the other members, x_3, x_4, ..., x_k, fixed.

4   We repeat these individual routines until we have finished processing the last member of the batch x_k, at which point we return to x_1 and repeat the entire procedure.

5   We run these cycles of optimization until convergence—that is, until the acquisition score we obtain doesn't increase anymore. These steps are summarized in figure 7.17.

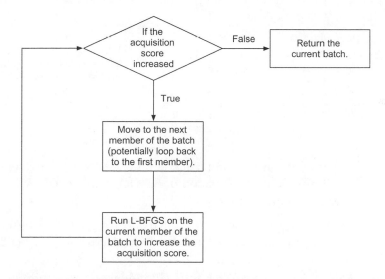

Figure 7.17   Flowchart of cyclic optimization used in finding the batch that maximizes information about the maximum objective value in batch MES. The procedure is cyclic in that we sequentially refine each member of the batch in a cycle until we converge on a good acquisition score.

DEFINITION   The entire procedure is called *cyclic optimization* as we sequentially refine each member of the batch in a cycle until we converge on a good acquisition score.

The cyclic optimization strategy allows us to bypass the challenge of running L-BFGS on a batch of multiple points, as we, instead, only run L-BFGS on individual points, making individual refinements to the acquisition score. With this optimization strategy, we can realize the MES policy in the batch setting.

> **NOTE** We can draw an analogy between cyclic optimization and how an artist might draw a painting. The artist might work on individual portions of the painting separately and switch around as they make progress. They might work on the foreground, move to the background for a bit, and then back to the foreground, each time making small refinements to each section.

7.4.2 *Implementing batch entropy search with BoTorch*

We now learn to declare the batch MES policy in BoTorch and hook it into our batch BayesOpt loop. Luckily, the details of cyclic optimization discussed in the previous section are abstracted away by BoTorch, and we can initialize batch MES in a straightforward manner. The following code is included in the CH07/03 - Max-value Entropy Search.ipynb notebook.

We still use the hyperparameter tuning example. First, we need to make a minor modification to our GP model. Specifically, to reason about the entropy of the posterior GP (that is, to "fantasize" about future observations), the class implementation of our GP model needs to inherit from the `FantasizeMixin` class from the `botorch.models.model` module:

```
class GPModel(
    gpytorch.models.ExactGP,
    botorch.models.gpytorch.GPyTorchModel,
    botorch.models.model.FantasizeMixin       ◁──┐  Inheriting from FantasizeMixin
):                                                   allows us to reason about the
    _num_outputs = 1                                 posterior GP more effectively.

    ...        ◁──  The remaining code
                    remains unchanged.
```

The rest of the code for this class implementation remains unchanged. Now, inside the `for` loop that implements the iteration of BayesOpt, we declare MES in the same way as we do in the sequential setting:

1 We draw samples from a Sobol sequence and use them as candidates for the MES policy. These samples are initially drawn within the unit cube and then resized to span our search space.

2 The MES policy is initialized with the GP model and the previously generated candidate set:

```
num_candidates = 2000              Our search space is two-dimensional.

sobol = torch.quasirandom.SobolEngine(2, scramble=True)   ◁──
candidate_x = sobol.draw(num_candidates)
candidate_x = (bounds[1] - bounds[0]) * candidate_x +      Resizes the candidates to
➥bounds[0]                                                 span the search space
```

```
policy = botorch.acquisition.max_value_entropy_search.qMaxValueEntropy(
    model, candidate_x
)
```

Sobol sequences

The Sobol sequence is first discussed in section 5.3.2 for the TS policy. The implementation of the MES policy also requires the Sobol sequence, which we learned about in section 6.2.2.

While the initialization of the batch MES policy is exactly the same as what we do in the sequential setting, we need a helper function other than `optimize_acqf()` for the cyclic optimization procedure described in the previous section to identify the batch that maximizes posterior information about *f**.

Specifically, we use the helper function `optimize_acqf_cyclic()`, which can be accessed from the same BoTorch module `botorch.optim`. Here, we only switch out `optimize_acqf()` for `optimize_acqf_cyclic()`; the rest of the arguments, such as the bounds and the batch size, remain the same:

```
next_x, acq_val = botorch.optim.optimize_acqf_cyclic(
    policy,
    bounds=bounds,
    q=batch_size,
    num_restarts=40,
    raw_samples=100,
)
```

BoTorch dimension warning

While running the code for batch MES, you might encounter a warning:

```
BotorchTensorDimensionWarning:

Non-strict enforcement of botorch tensor conventions. Ensure that target
tensors Y has an explicit output dimension.
```

This warning indicates that we are not formatting the tensor containing the observed values `train_y` according to BoTorch's convention. However, this is not a code-breaking error, so to be able to keep using the same GP implementation as with other policies, we simply ignore this warning using the `warnings` module.

NOTE Due to its algorithmic complexity, the batch MES policy can take quite some time to run. Feel free to skip the portion of the code that runs the optimization loop and proceed with the chapter.

And with that, we are now ready to run batch MES on our hyperparameter tuning example. Using the same initial training data, batch MES's progress is visualized in figure 7.18, which shows that the policy is comparable with the other policies in this run.

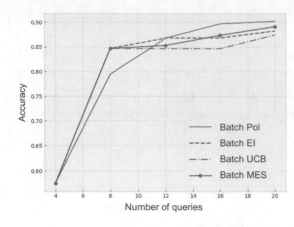

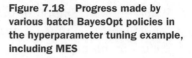

Figure 7.18   Progress made by various batch BayesOpt policies in the hyperparameter tuning example, including MES

We have now learned how to convert BayesOpt policies to the batch setting, where multiple queries are made in parallel. Depending on the policy, this conversion requires various levels of consideration. With the improvement-based policies and UCB, we use the heuristic that the best-performing member should represent the entire batch. In exercise 1, we see that TS can be extended to the batch setting by simply repeating the sampling process to assemble a batch of the desired size. MES, on the other hand, needs a modified routine that uses cyclic optimization to search for the batch that maximizes its acquisition score. In the next chapter, we learn about another specialized BayesOpt setting, in which constraints need to be taken into account when the objective function is being optimized.

7.5   *Exercise 2: Optimizing airplane designs*

In this exercise, we run the batch BayesOpt policies explored in this chapter on a simulated optimization problem in physics. This problem is the highest-dimensional problem we have encountered and will offer us an opportunity to see how BayesOpt tackles a generic black box optimization problem in high dimensions. More specific to this chapter, we will see how various batch BayesOpt policies perform on a real-world optimization problem.

We are interested in an aerostructural optimization problem that airplane engineers commonly deal with. In such an optimization problem, we have various tunable parameters (each making up a dimension in our search space) that control how an airplane works. These parameters could be the length and width of the plane, the shape and the angle of the wings with respect to the body of the plane, or the angle of the turbine blades and how fast they rotate. It's the job of an optimization engineer to tune the values of these parameters to get the plane to work or to optimize some performance metric, such as speed or energy efficiency.

While engineers might have a good idea about how some of these variables affect the performance of an airplane, a good way to test out an experimental plane design is to run various computer simulations and observe the simulated behavior of the airplane. From these simulations, we score the proposed plane design on how well it does on various performance metrics. With the simulation program in hand, we can treat this tuning process as a black box optimization problem. That is, we don't know how each tunable parameter affects the final performance of the simulated airplane, but we'd like to optimize these parameters to achieve the best result.

This exercise provides an objective function that simulates this process of benchmarking the performance of an airplane design. The code is provided in the CH07/04 - Exercise 2.ipynb notebook. There are multiple steps:

1 Implement the objective function that simulates performance benchmarking. This is a four-parameter function with the following code, which computes a score quantifying the utility of the airplane specified by the four input parameters. Since we treat this function as a black box, we assume that we don't know what goes on inside the function and how the output is produced:

```
def flight_utility(X):
  X_copy = X.detach().clone()
  X_copy[:, [2, 3]] = 1 - X_copy[:, [2, 3]]
  X_copy = X_copy * 10 - 5

  return -0.005 * (X_copy**4 - 16 * X_copy**2 + 5 * X_copy).sum(dim=-1) + 3
```

The four parameters are the various settings of the plane, scaled to be between 0 and 1. That is, our search space is the four-dimensional unit hypercube. Though not essential to our black box optimization approach, the names of these parameters are as follows:

```
labels = [
    "scaled body length",
    "scaled wing span",
    "scaled ?",
    "scaled ?"
]
```

While it's not easy to visualize an entire four-dimensional function, we can show how the function behaves in two-dimensional spaces. Figure 7.19 visualizes our objective function for various pairs of parameters we can tune, showing a complex nonlinear trend across these two-dimensional spaces.

Again, our goal is to find the maximum value of this function using BayesOpt.

2 Implement a GP model with a constant mean function and a Matérn 2.5 kernel with an output scale implemented as a `gpytorch.kernels.ScaleKernel` object:

a We need to specify the `ard_num_dims = 4` argument when initializing the kernel to account for the fact that our objective function is four-dimensional.

NOTE We learn how to work with Matérn kernels in section 3.4.2 as well as in the exercise in chapter 3.

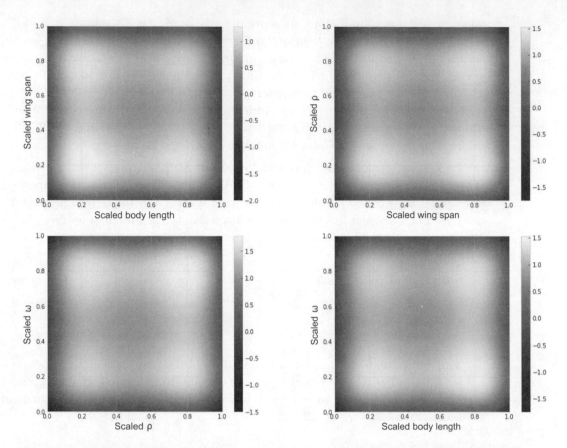

Figure 7.19 **The objective function of the simulated airplane design optimization problem in various two-dimensional subspaces, corresponding to pairs of tunable parameters, shown as axis labels. Bright spots indicate high objective values, which are our optimization goals; dark spots indicate low objective values.**

3 Implement a helper function that trains the GP on a given training dataset. This function should take in a training set, train a GP using gradient descent to minimize the negative log likelihood, and return that GP and its likelihood function. See section 4.1.1 for a refresher on how to implement this helper function.

4 Define the settings of our optimization problem:

   a The search space is the four-dimensional unit hypercube, so we should have a variable named `bounds` that stores the following tensor:

```
tensor([[0., 0., 0., 0.],
        [1., 1., 1., 1.]])
```

   We pass these bounds to the BayesOpt policies we run later in the exercise.

   b In each run, a BayesOpt policy can make in total 100 queries to the objective function (that is, 100 function evaluations) in batches of 5. We also repeat our experiments for each policy five times.

5 Run each batch BayesOpt policy we learn in this chapter on the objective function just implemented:

    a Each experiment should start with a randomly selected function evaluation
as the training set.

    b Record the best values found throughout the search.

    c Use a 5,000-point Sobol sequence for TS and MES.

    d Running MES in a high-dimensional problem is computationally expensive.
A common strategy to relieve this burden is to limit the number of cycles for
cyclic optimization. For example, to terminate the optimization of the MES
acquisition score after five cycles, we can pass `cyclic_options={"maxiter":
5}` to the helper function `optimize_acqf_cyclic()`. Run this more light-
weight version of MES in the experiments.

6 Plot the optimization progress of the BayesOpt policies we have run, and observe
their performance. Each policy should have a curve showing the average best-
seen point as a function of the number of queries used and the standard errors.
See the last step of chapter 4's exercise 2 for more details on how to make this
visualization.

Summary

- Many black box optimization settings in the real world allow multiple experiments (function evaluations) to be carried out at the same time in parallel. By
taking advantage of this parallelism, we can conduct more experiments in
BayesOpt and potentially achieve better performance.

- At each iteration of the batch BayesOpt setting, a batch of queries is selected,
and the objective function is evaluated at these queries. This setting requires
the BayesOpt policy used to be able to score a batch of queries in accordance
with the utility of the queries in helping us locate the global optimum.

- Extending BayesOpt policies to the batch setting isn't as simple as choosing the
top data points that score the highest acquisition value in the sequential setting.
Doing so leads to the selected queries being extremely close to one another,
defeating the purpose of parallelism.

- Three BayesOpt policies—PoI, EI, and UCB—can be extended to the batch setting using the same strategy. This strategy uses the maximum value within a
batch of queries to quantify the value of the whole batch. Mathematically, the
strategy of using the maximum value to represent an entire batch requires
rewriting the acquisition score as an average of some quantity of interest.

- Due to its random nature, the TS policy can be easily extended to the batch
setting. Instead of sampling from the GP and maximizing the sample only
once, batch TS repeats this sampling and maximizing process until we reach
the targeted batch size.

- Computing the information-theoretic value of multiple points is computationally challenging. This difficulty prevents the algorithm L-BFGS, used by the helper function `optimize_acqf()` to find the point or the batch of points that maximizes the acquisition score of a given policy, from being used with the MES policy in the batch setting.

- To circumvent the computational challenge of using L-BFGS with batch MES, we use cyclic optimization. This strategy involves refining individual members of our current batch of queries in a cyclic manner until the acquisition score converges. Cyclic optimization can be used in BoTorch with the helper function `optimize_acqf_cyclic()`.

- To maximize our optimization throughput, it's important to specify the correct batch size when using the helper functions `optimize_acqf()` and `optimize_acqf_cyclic()` when searching for the batch that maximizes the acquisition score of a given policy. We do this by setting the argument q to the desired batch size.

- The BoTorch implementation of most BayesOpt policies follows the same interface as the implementation in the sequential setting. This consistency allows the programmer to transition to the batch setting without having to significantly modify their code.

8

Satisfying extra constraints with constrained optimization

This chapter covers

- The problem of black box optimization with constraints
- Taking constraints into account when making decisions in BayesOpt
- Implementing constraint-aware BayesOpt policies

In previous chapters, we tackled black box optimization problems in which we aimed solely to maximize the objective function, without any other considerations. This is called an *unconstrained* optimization problem as we are free to explore the search space to look for the global optimum of the objective function. Many real-life situations do not follow this unconstrained formulation, however, and there might be a cost associated with the objective function's global optimum that makes the optimum infeasible to achieve in practice.

For example, when tuning the architecture of a neural network, you might find that increasing the number of layers in the network usually yields a higher accuracy, and a network with millions and billions of layers will perform the best. However, unless we have access to expensive, powerful computing resources, running such large neural networks isn't practical. That is, there's a cost associated with running a large neural network, which would otherwise correspond to the global optimum of the objective function in this hyperparameter tuning task. We, therefore, need to take this computational cost into account while tuning this neural network and only look for architectures that are actually feasible to implement in practice.

Another black-box optimization problem in which we need to consider additional constraints is scientific discovery, such as in chemistry and materials science. For instance, scientists aim to design chemicals and materials that optimize a desirable characteristic, such as drugs that are effective against a disease, glass that is resilient against pressure, or metals that are malleable and, thus, easy to manipulate. Unfortunately, the drugs that are the most effective against a disease might have many side effects that make them dangerous to use, or the most resilient type of glass might be too expensive to produce on a large scale.

These are examples of *constrained* optimization problems, where we need to optimize an objective function while satisfying other constraints. Seeking to optimize the objective function alone might lead us to solutions that violate important constraints, rendering the solutions we find useless in practice. Instead, we need to identify other regions in the search space that both yield high objective values and satisfy these important constraints.

In this chapter, we learn about the constrained optimization problem and see examples where having extra constraints may completely change the solution of an optimization problem. This need to account for these constraints gives rise to constraint-aware optimization policies in BayesOpt. We are introduced to a variant of the Expected Improvement (EI) policy that is constraint-aware and learn how to implement it in BoTorch. By the end of the chapter, you will understand the problem of constrained optimization, learn how it is solved using BayesOpt, and see that the constraint-aware policy we use performs much better than constraint-agnostic ones. What we learn in this chapter will help us tackle more practical BayesOpt problems in real life and, thus, make more effective decisions.

8.1 Accounting for constraints in a constrained optimization problem

As mentioned in the introduction, many constrained optimization problems exist in the real world: making drugs with high efficacy and minimal side effects, finding materials that maximize desirable characteristics and are cheap to produce, or hyperparameter tuning while keeping the computational cost low.

> **NOTE** We focus on *inequality constraints*, where we require a result y to be inside a predetermined numerical range $a \leq y \leq b$.

We first take a closer look at the constrained optimization problem in the next section and see why it's mathematically different from the unconstrained problem we see in previous chapters. We then redefine the BayesOpt framework we have been working with so far to account for extra constraints.

8.1.1   Constraints can change the solution of an optimization problem

How do constraints complicate the optimization of a black box function? In many cases, regions within the search space that give high objective values might violate the constraints that come with the optimization problem.

> **NOTE**   In an optimization problem, we aim to find regions that give high objective values since we want to maximize the value of the objective function.

If it is the case that regions with high objective values violate the given constraints, we need to rule out these regions that violate the constraints and only conduct our search within other regions that satisfy the constraints.

> **DEFINITION**   A data point that violates the predefined constraints in a constrained optimization problem is called an *infeasible* point, as it's infeasible to use the point as the solution to the optimization problem. On the other hand, a data point that satisfies the constraints is called a *feasible* point. Our goal is to find the feasible point that maximizes the value of the objective function.

Constraints can affect the quality of the optimal solution of the unconstrained optimization problem or change the optimal solution altogether. Consider the example in figure 8.1, where our objective function (the solid line) is the Forrester function we have used in previous chapters. In addition to this objective function, we have a cost function, shown as dashed line. Assume that in this constrained optimization problem, the constraint is that the cost needs to be a maximum of zero—that is, the cost $c \leq 0$. This constraint means only the feasible points in the shaded regions in the right panel of figure 8.1 can be used as the optimization result.

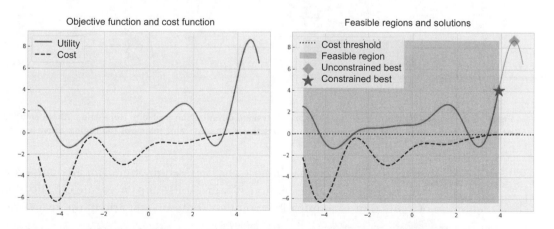

Figure 8.1   An example of a one-dimensional constrained optimization problem. The solid line is the objective function we aim to maximize, and the dashed line is the cost function that constrains the optimization problem. Only the shaded regions (right panel) that yield negative costs are feasible. Here, the constraint of nonpositive cost causes the highest objective value to decrease from more than 8 to 4.

NOTE   We first used the Forrester function as an example objective function in BayesOpt in section 2.4.1.

As a result, the region where $x > 4$, which contains the true global optimum of the objective value (denoted as the diamond marker in the right panel), is cut off. That is, the global optimum that yields an objective value of more than 8 is not feasible, and the constrained optimal solution (denoted as the star) only achieves an objective value of roughly 4. An example of this "cutoff" scenario is when an effective drug has too severe of a side effect, so the drug company decides to use a less effective variant of the same chemical to make the product safe.

Another example of the same objective function and a slightly different cost function is shown in figure 8.2, where having this extra cost constraint changes the optimal solution of our optimization problem. Without the constraint, the global optimum of the objective function is located at $x = 4.6$. This point, however, is an infeasible one that gives a positive cost and, thus, violates our constraint. The optimal solution of the constrained problem is at $x = 1.6$. This phenomenon can happen, for example, when the entire family of some highly effective drug is dangerous to patients and cannot be produced, so we need to look for other solutions that are chemically different from the dangerous drug.

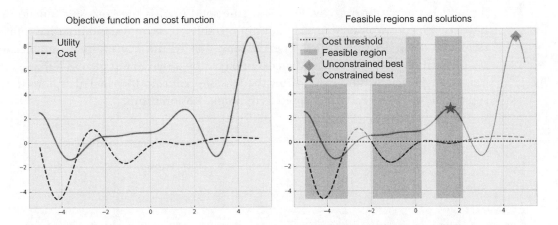

Figure 8.2   An example of a one-dimensional constrained optimization problem. Here, the optimal solution changes to a different local optimum, as the nonpositive cost constraint rules out the region where $x > 3$.

Overall, inequality constraints may impose complex requirements on an optimization problem and change its optimal solution. That is, constraints may rule out the global optimum of a function as an infeasible point—a common scenario in the real world:

- The prohibitively large neural networks tend to achieve good predictive performance but are infeasible to implement in practice.
- The most effective drugs are often too aggressive and dangerous to produce.
- The best materials are too expensive to use.

Instead of using the unconstrained optimal point that violates our constraints, we need to modify our optimization strategy to account for the constraints and find the optimal feasible solution. That is, we need to pursue two goals: optimizing the objective function and satisfying the given constraints. Solely optimizing the objective function without accounting for the constraints will lead to infeasible solutions that are not usable in practice. Instead, we need to find points that both yield high objective values and satisfy the constraints.

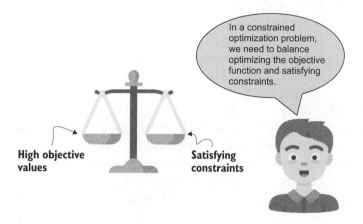

8.1.2 The constraint-aware BayesOpt framework

How should we approach this constrained optimization problem from the BayesOpt angle? In this section, we learn how to modify our BayesOpt framework to account for the constraints that are given in a constrained optimization problem.

Remember in BayesOpt that we use a Gaussian process (GP) to train on the data points we have observed from the objective function and make predictions on unseen data. In constrained optimization, we have, in addition, one or many functions that define the constraints we need to satisfy. For example, in section 8.1.1, the cost function shown as the dashed line in figures 8.1 and 8.2 defines the constraints that the solution needs to have a nonpositive cost.

> **NOTE** You can refer to sections 1.2.3 and 4.1.1 for a refresher on the BayesOpt framework.

We assume that, just like the objective function, we don't know what the true cost function looks like. In other words, the cost function is a black box. We only get to observe the cost values at the data points we query the objective function with, and from there, we determine whether those data points satisfy the constraints or not.

> **NOTE** If we did know what the functions that define our constraints look like, we could simply identify the feasible regions and restrict our search space to

be within those feasible regions. In our constrained optimization problem, we assume our constraints are also black boxes.

Since we only have black box access to the functions that define our constraints, we can also use a GP to model each of these functions. That is, in addition to the GP that models our objective function, we use more GPs, one for each function that defines a constraint, to inform our decisions about where to query the objective function next. We follow the same procedure to train each of these GPs—it's just a matter of using the appropriate training set for each GP:

- The GP that models the objective function trains on the observed objective values.
- A GP that models a constraint-defining function trains on the observed cost values.

Our constrained BayesOpt framework, which is a modified version of figure 1.6, is visualized in figure 8.3:

- At step 1, we train a GP on data from the objective function and another GP on data from each function that defines a constraint.
- At step 3, we use the point identified by a BayesOpt policy to query both the objective function and the constraint-defining functions.

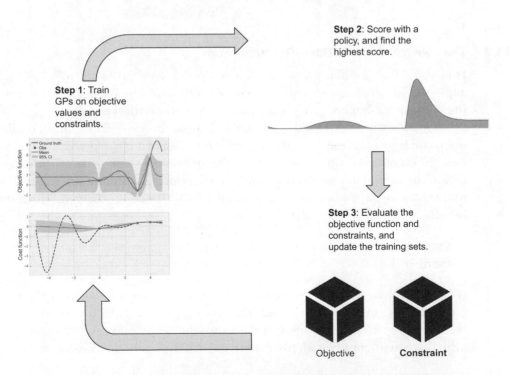

Figure 8.3   The constrained BayesOpt loop. A separate GP models either the objective function or a function that defines a constraint. A BayesOpt policy recommends the next point for us to query both the objective function and the constraint-defining functions.

Steps 1 and 3 of figure 8.3 are straightforward to implement: we only need to maintain multiple GPs at the same time, keep track of the corresponding datasets, and keep those datasets updated. The more interesting question comes in step 2: decision-making. That is, how should we design a BayesOpt policy that can guide us toward feasible regions that yield high objective values? This is the topic of our discussion in the next section.

8.2   *Constraint-aware decision-making in BayesOpt*

An effective constrained BayesOpt policy needs to pursue both optimization and satisfying the constraints. One straightforward way to design such a policy is to incorporate the constraints into the way an unconstrained BayesOpt policy makes its decisions. That is, we wish to modify a policy we already know to take into account constraints in a constrained optimization problem and derive a constraint-aware decision-making procedure.

   The policy we choose for this modification is EI, which we learned about in section 4.3. (We discuss other BayesOpt policies later in this section.) Remember that the EI policy scores each unseen data point with the expected value of how much improvement from the current incumbent we observe if we query the objective function at this unseen point.

> **DEFINITION**   The term *incumbent* refers to the point having the highest objective value within our training set, which is what we need to "beat" to make progress with optimization.

The acquisition score EI uses, which, again, computes the average value of the improvement of each potential query, ignores the inequality constraints in a constrained optimization problem, so we can't use EI "as is" when optimizing a constrained objective function. Fortunately, there's an easy way to account for these constraints: we can scale the EI acquisition score of each unseen point by how likely the data point is to satisfy the constraints—that is, the probability that the data point is a feasible point:

- If the data point is likely to satisfy the constraints, then its EI score will be multiplied by a large number (a high probability of feasibility), thus keeping the EI score high.
- If the data point is unlikely to satisfy the constraints, its EI score will be multiplied by a small number (a low probability of feasibility), thus de-prioritizing that data point.

> **TIP**   The acquisition score of the constrained variant of EI is the product of the regular EI score and the probability that a data point satisfies the constraints.

The formula for the acquisition score of this constraint-aware variant of EI is shown in figure 8.4. This acquisition score is the product of two terms: the EI score encourages optimization of the objective function, and the probability of feasibility encourages staying within the feasible regions. This balance between optimizing the objective function and satisfying the constraints is exactly what we want to achieve, as noted in section 8.1.1.

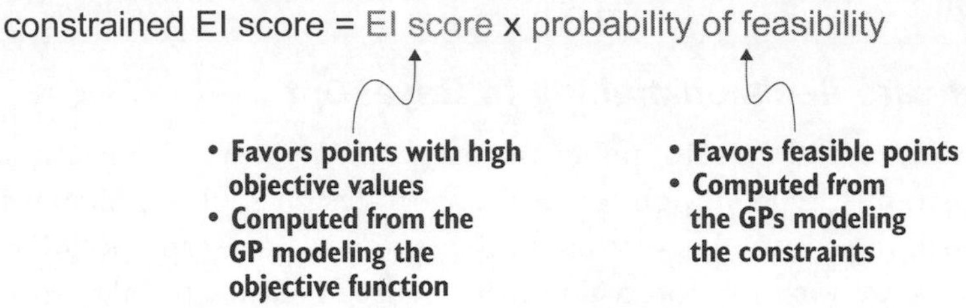

constrained EI score = EI score x probability of feasibility

- **Favors points with high objective values**
- **Computed from the GP modeling the objective function**

- **Favors feasible points**
- **Computed from the GPs modeling the constraints**

Figure 8.4   Formula for the acquisition score of constrained EI, which is the product of the regular EI score and the probability of feasibility. This policy aims to optimize the objective value and satisfy the constraints at the same time.

We already know how to compute the EI score, but how can we calculate the second term—the probability that a given data point is a feasible point? As noted in figure 8.4, we do this with the GPs modeling the constraints. Specifically, each GP provides a probabilistic belief about the shape of a function defining a constraint. From this probabilistic belief, we can calculate the probability that an unseen data point will satisfy the corresponding inequality constraint.

As an example, let's say when solving the constrained optimization problem defined in figure 8.2 that we have observed the objective function and the cost function at $x = 0$, $x = 3$, and $x = 4$. From this training set, we train two GPs, one for the objective function and the other for the cost function, and obtain the predictions visualized in figure 8.5.

Now, say we'd like to compute the constrained EI score for $x = 1$. We already have a way to compute the regular EI score for any data point, so all we need to do now is calculate the probability that $x = 1$ is a feasible data point. To do this, we look at the normal distribution representing our prediction about the cost value of $x = 1$, as illustrated in figure 8.6.

The left panel of figure 8.6 contains the same GP as in the bottom panel of figure 8.5 that is cut off at the constraint threshold 0, additionally showing the CI of the normal distribution prediction at $x = 1$. Slicing the GP vertically at this point $x = 1$, we obtain the right panel of figure 8.6, where the CIs in the two panels are the same. In other words, going from the left to the right panel of figure 8.6, we have zoomed in on the vertical scale, and instead of showing the cost function, we only keep the cost constraint (the dotted line) and the GP prediction at $x = 1$, which is a normal distribution. We see that only the highlighted portion of the normal distribution in the right panel represents the probability that $x = 1$ obeys the cost constraint, which is what we care about.

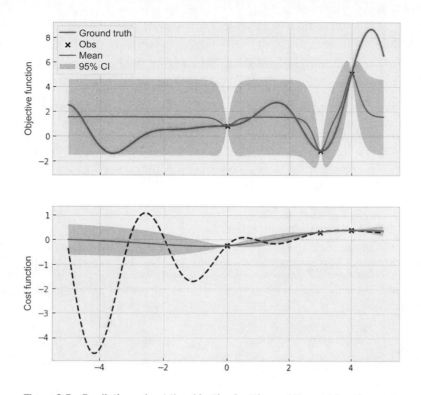

Figure 8.5 Predictions about the objective function and the cost function made by corresponding GPs. Each GP allows us to reason about the shape of the corresponding function in a probabilistic manner.

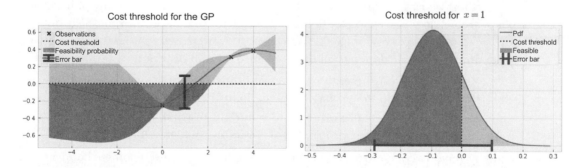

Figure 8.6 Probability of $x = 1$ being a feasible point, highlighted in a darker shade. The left panel shows the entire GP, while the right panel only shows the normal distribution corresponding to the prediction at $x = 1$ (the error bars are the same across the two panels). Here, feasibility follows a truncated normal distribution.

If figure 8.6 reminds you of figures 4.9 and 4.10, covering the PoI policy, that's because our thought process is the same in the two cases:

- With PoI, we compute the probability that a given data point yields an objective value *higher* than the incumbent. We, therefore, use the incumbent value as a *lower* bound, specifying that we only care about scenarios in which the objective value is *higher* than the incumbent.
- With the probability of feasibility, we compute the probability that a given data point yields a cost value *lower* than the cost threshold at 0. We use 0 as an *upper* bound to specify that we target scenarios in which the cost value is *lower* than the threshold (to obey our cost constraint).

Handling different inequality constraints

The constraint in our current example requires the cost to be less than 0. If we had a constraint requiring a function value to be higher than some threshold, then the probability of feasibility would be the probability that a given point yields a function value higher than some threshold, and the shaded region in figure 8.6 would be to the right of the cutoff.

If there was a constraint requiring the value to be inside a range ($a \leq y \leq b$), then the probability of feasibility would be the probability that the data point gives a value between the lower and upper bounds of the range.

In our case, we want to compute the probability that the cost value at $x = 1$ is lower than 0, which is the area of the shaded region under the curve in the right panel of figure 8.6. As we have seen in section 4.2.2 of chapter 4, the normal distribution allows us to compute this area under the curve using the cumulative density function (CDF). In figure 8.6, the probability that $x = 1$ is feasible is roughly 84%—this is the second term in figure 8.4 that we use to compute the constrained EI acquisition score.

Further, we can compute this probability-of-feasibility quantity at any point inside our search space. For example, figure 8.7 shows the truncated normal distributions for $x = -1$ (center panel) and $x = 2$ (right panel). As we can see, the probability that a given point is feasible depends on the predictive normal distribution at that point:

- At $x = -1$, almost the entire predictive normal distribution lies below the cost threshold at 0, so the probability of feasibility here is high, at almost 98%.
- At $x = 2$, only a small portion of the normal distribution falls below the cost threshold, causing the probability of feasibility to be much lower, roughly 6%.

With the ability to compute the probability of feasibility for any given point in hand, we can now compute the constrained EI acquisition score described in figure 8.4. Again, this score balances between a potentially high objective value, quantified by the regular EI score, and satisfying the inequality constraint(s), quantified by the probability of feasibility.

Figure 8.8 shows this score in the bottom right panel, along with the regular EI score and the current GPs. We see that constrained EI is aware of the cost constraint

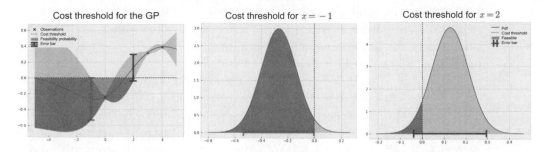

Figure 8.7   Probability of feasibility at *x* = –1 and *x* = 2, highlighted in a darker shade. The left panel shows the entire GP, the center panel shows the prediction at *x* = –1, and the right panel shows the prediction at *x* = 2. The highlighted portions show the probability of feasibility, which depends on the normal distribution at a given point.

we need to satisfy and assigns a roughly zero score to the region to the right of the space (where $x > 2$). This is because the cost GP (top right panel) thinks this is an infeasible region that should be avoided. Ultimately, the regular EI policy recommends the objective function with the infeasible point $x = 4$ as the next point to query. Constrained EI, on the other hand, recommends $x = -0.8$, which, indeed, satisfies our cost constraint.

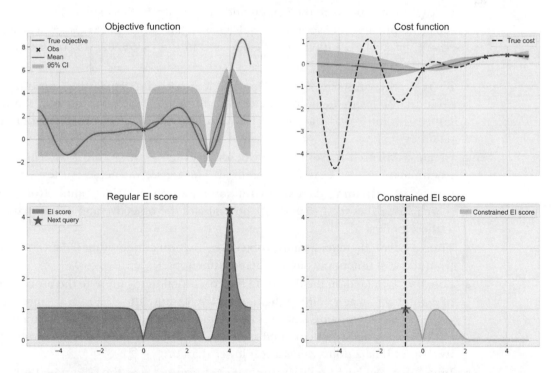

Figure 8.8   The acquisition score of EI (bottom left) and that of constrained EI (bottom right), along with our current belief about the objective function (top left) and about the cost function (top right). By being aware of the cost constraint, constrained EI can avoid the infeasible region and recommend an entirely different point to query from regular EI.

We have found a good heuristic of deriving a constraint-aware BayesOpt policy from a regular one: multiplying the acquisition score of the policy with the probability of feasibility to factor in the inequality constraints. Interestingly, adding the probability-of-feasibility factor to EI isn't simply a heuristic—the formula in figure 8.4 can be obtained from a heuristic-free, more mathematically rigorous procedure. The interested reader can refer to a research paper that defines the constrained EI policy for more details (http://proceedings.mlr.press/v32/gardner14.pdf).

While we can use the same heuristic on other BayesOpt policies we have learned, such as UCB, TS, and Entropy Search, the mathematically rigorous procedure won't apply anymore. Further, at the time of writing, BoTorch only supports constrained EI, which is also widely used to solve constrained optimization problems in practice. We, therefore, only focus on constrained EI and its optimization results for the rest of this chapter.

8.3   *Exercise 1: Manual computation of constrained EI*

We saw in figure 8.4 that the acquisition score of the constrained EI policy is the product of the EI score and the probability of feasibility. Although the `ConstrainedExpected-Improvement` class from BoTorch provides an implementation of the constrained EI score, we can, in fact, perform the computation manually. In this exercise, we explore this manual computation and verify our result against that of the `ConstrainedExpected-Improvement` class. The solution to this exercise is in the CH08/02 - Exercise 1.ipynb notebook:

1 Recreate the constrained BayesOpt problem used in CH08/01 - Constrained optimization.ipynb, including the objective function, the cost function, the GP implementation, and the helper function that trains a GP on some training data `fit_gp_model()`.

2 Create a PyTorch tensor that is a dense grid between -5 and 5 by using, for example, the `torch.linspace()` method. This tensor will act as our test set.

3 Create a toy training data set by randomly sampling 3 data points from our search space (between –5 and 5), and evaluate the objective and cost functions at these points.

4 Train a GP on the data from the objective function and another GP on the data from the cost function using the helper function `fit_gp_model()`.

5 Use the GP trained on the data from the cost function to compute the probability of feasibility for each point in the test set. You can use the `torch.distributions .Normal` class to initialize a normal distribution object and call the `cdf()` method of this object on 0 (implemented as `torch.zeros(1)`) to compute the probability that each data point yields a cost lower than 0.

6 Initialize a regular EI policy with the `model` argument as the GP trained on the data from the objective function and the `best_f` argument as the current feasible incumbent:

    a Compute the EI score for each point in the test set.

    b Refer to section 4.3 for more details on implementing the EI policy.

7 Initialize a constrained EI policy, and compute the constrained EI score for each point in the test set.

8 Compute the product of the EI scores and the probabilities of feasibility, and verify that this manual computation leads to the same results as those from BoTorch's implementation. You can use `torch.isclose(a, b, atol=1e-3)`, which performs element-wise comparisons between two tensors `a` and `b`, specifying `atol=1e-3` to account for numerical instability, to verify that all corresponding scores match up.

9 Plot the EI scores and the constrained EI scores in a graph, and visually verify that the former is always greater than or equal to the latter. Prove that this is the case using figure 8.4.

8.4   Implementing constrained EI with BoTorch

While we can manually multiply two quantities, the EI score and the probability of feasibility, to make a new acquisition score, BoTorch already takes care of the low-level bookkeeping. This means we can import the constrained EI policy from BoTorch and use it like any other BayesOpt policy, without much overhead. We learn how to do so in this section, and the code we use is included in the CH08/01 - Constrained optimization.ipynb notebook.

First, we need the objective function and the cost function that defines the constraint in figure 8.2. In the following code, the objective function is implemented as `objective()`, and the cost function is `cost()`. Our search space is between −5 and 5, and we make the variable `bounds` that contains these numbers, which will be passed to BayesOpt policies later:

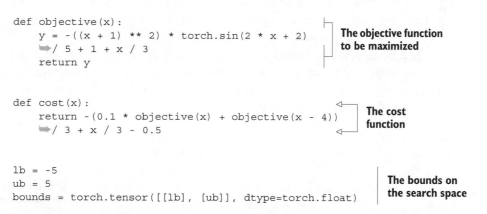

```
def objective(x):
    y = -((x + 1) ** 2) * torch.sin(2 * x + 2)
    / 5 + 1 + x / 3
    return y
```
The objective function to be maximized

```
def cost(x):
    return -(0.1 * objective(x) + objective(x - 4))
    / 3 + x / 3 - 0.5
```
The cost function

```
lb = -5
ub = 5
bounds = torch.tensor([[lb], [ub]], dtype=torch.float)
```
The bounds on the search space

We also need a class implementation of our GP model and a helper function `fit_gp_model()` that trains the GP given a training data set. As constrained optimization doesn't require any changes to the GP and how we train it, we can reuse the class implementation and the helper function we used in previous chapters. For a more in-depth discussion of this implementation, refer to section 4.1.1.

To benchmark the optimization performance of the policies we use, we specify that each BayesOpt run has 10 queries, and we have 10 runs in total:

```
num_queries = 10
num_repeats = 10
```

> **NOTE**   We run each BayesOpt policy multiple times to have a holistic view of the performance of the policy. Refer to exercise 2 of chapter 4 for the discussion on repeated experiments.

Finally, we need to modify our BayesOpt loop to account for the changes visualized in figure 8.3. At step 1 of figure 8.3—that is, at the beginning of each step in the BayesOpt loop—we need to retrain multiple GPs: one for the objective function and the other(s) for the constraint(s).

As we already have the helper function `fit_gp_model()` that trains a GP, this step comes down to passing appropriate datasets to this helper function. In our current example, we only have one cost function defining the constraint, so we have, in total, two GPs, which can be retrained with the following code:

```
utility_model, utility_likelihood = fit_gp_model(       │  Train a GP
    train_x, train_utility.squeeze(-1)                  │  on the objective
)                                                       │  function's data.

cost_model, cost_likelihood = fit_gp_model(             │  Train a GP on the cost
    train_x, train_cost.squeeze(-1)                     │  function's data.
)
```

Here, the variable `train_x` contains the locations at which we have evaluated the objective and cost functions; `train_utility` is the corresponding objective values, and `train_cost` is the cost values.

Step 2 of figure 8.3 refers to running a BayesOpt policy, which we learn to do shortly. For step 3 of figure 8.3, we evaluate the objective and cost functions at the data point recommended by the chosen BayesOpt policy, stored in the variable `next_x`. We do this by evaluating both the objective and cost functions at `next_x`:

```
next_utility = objective(next_x)    │  Evaluates the objective and cost
next_cost = cost(next_x)            │  functions at the recommended point

train_x = torch.cat([train_x, next_x])                       │  Updates the
train_utility = torch.cat([train_utility, next_utility])     │  various datasets
train_cost = torch.cat([train_cost, next_cost])
```

One more bookkeeping step we need to take is keeping track of our optimization progress. Unlike in an unconstrained optimization problem, where we simply record the incumbent value (highest objective value seen thus far) at every step, here we need to filter out the infeasible observations before taking the maximum. We do this by first creating a tensor with `num_repeats` rows (one for each repeated run) and `num_queries` columns (one for each time step). This tensor contains only one value by default, denoting our utility if no feasible points are found throughout BayesOpt.

Inspecting figure 8.2, we see that our objective function is greater than –2 everywhere within our search space (between –5_ and 5), so we use –2 as this default value:

```
default_value = -2
feasible_incumbents = torch.ones((num_repeats, num_queries)) * default_value
```

Checks whether a feasible point has been found ◁—┘ (pointing to `default_value = -2`)

Then, at each step of the BayesOpt loop, we only record the feasible incumbent by taking the maximum of the filtered observations:

```
feasible_flag = (train_cost <= 0).any()

if feasible_flag:
    feasible_incumbents[trial, i] = train_utility[train_cost <= 0].max()
```

Checks whether a feasible point has been found ◁—┤ (pointing to `feasible_flag = (train_cost <= 0).any()`)

The preceding code completes our constrained BayesOpt loop. All that's left for us to do is declare the BayesOpt policy we want to use to solve the constrained optimization problem. We use the constrained EI policy we discussed in section 8.2 by using the BoTorch class `ConstrainedExpectedImprovement`. This class takes in a number of important arguments:

- `model`—A list of GP models for the objective function (`utility_model` in our case) and the functions that define the constraints (`cost_model`, in our case). We create this list using the `model_list_gp_regression.ModelListGP` class from BoTorch's `models` module: `ModelListGP(utility_model, cost_model)`.
- `objective_index`—The index of the GP modeling the objective function in the model list `model`. Since `utility_model` is the first GP we pass to `ModelListGP`, this index is 0 in our case.
- `constraints`—A dictionary mapping the index of each function defining a constraint to a two-element list storing the lower and upper bounds for the constraint. If a constraint doesn't have a lower bound or an upper bound, we use `None` in lieu of an actual numerical value. Our example requires the cost corresponding to `cost_model`, which has an index of 1, to be a maximum of 0, so we set `constraints={1: [None, 0]}`.
- `best_f`—The current feasible incumbent, which is `train_utility[train_cost <= 0].max()`, if we have found at least one feasible point or the default value, –2, otherwise.

Overall, we initialize the constrained EI policy as follows:

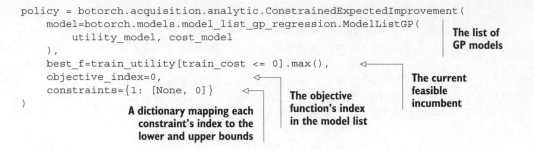

```
policy = botorch.acquisition.analytic.ConstrainedExpectedImprovement(
    model=botorch.models.model_list_gp_regression.ModelListGP(
        utility_model, cost_model
    ),
    best_f=train_utility[train_cost <= 0].max(),
    objective_index=0,
    constraints={1: [None, 0]}
)
```

The list of GP models

The current feasible incumbent

The objective function's index in the model list

A dictionary mapping each constraint's index to the lower and upper bounds

With the implementation of constrained EI in hand, let's now run this policy on our one-dimensional constrained optimization problem and observe its performance. As a baseline, we can also run the regular version of EI that is constraint agnostic.

Figure 8.9 shows the average feasible incumbent values found by these two policies and error bars as a function of time. We see that compared to the regular EI, the constrained variant finds a better feasible solution on average and almost always converges to the best possible solution. Figure 8.9 highlights the benefit of our constraint-aware optimization policy compared to a constraint-agnostic approach.

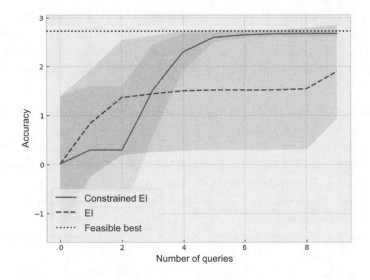

Figure 8.9   Optimization progress on a one-dimensional constrained optimization problem of constrained EI. Compared to the regular EI, the constrained variant finds a better feasible solution on average.

The EI policy, which is blind to the constraint placed on the optimization problem, tends to veer off toward the infeasible optimum. Inspecting the incumbent values found by this policy, we notice that in many runs, the policy fails to progress from its initial value:

```
torch.set_printoptions(precision=1)
print(ei_incumbents)

Output:
tensor([[ 0.8,   0.8,   0.8,   0.8,   0.8,   0.8,   0.8,   0.8,   0.8,   0.8],
        [-2.0,  -2.0,  -2.0,  -2.0,  -2.0,  -2.0,  -2.0,  -2.0,  -2.0,  -2.0],
        [ 2.2,   2.2,   2.7,   2.7,   2.7,   2.7,   2.7,   2.7,   2.7,   2.7],
        [ 2.5,   2.5,   2.5,   2.5,   2.5,   2.5,   2.5,   2.5,   2.5,   2.5],
        [-2.0,   0.2,   1.9,   2.3,   2.6,   2.7,   2.7,   2.7,   2.7,   2.7],
        [-2.0,   0.5,   2.1,   2.4,   2.5,   2.5,   2.5,   2.5,   2.7,   2.7],
        [-2.0,   1.5,   2.5,   2.5,   2.5,   2.5,   2.5,   2.5,   2.5,   2.5],
        [-2.0,  -2.0,  -2.0,  -2.0,  -2.0,  -2.0,  -2.0,  -2.0,  -2.0,  -2.0],
        [ 1.9,   1.9,   2.5,   2.5,   2.7,   2.7,   2.7,   2.7,   2.7,   2.7],
        [ 2.7,   2.7,   2.7,   2.7,   2.7,   2.7,   2.7,   2.7,   2.7,   2.7]])
```

In this chapter, we have learned about the problem of black box constrained optimization and how it is different from the classic black box optimization problem discussed in previous chapters. We learned that an effective optimization policy needs to pursue both optimizing the objective function and satisfying the constraints. We then designed one such policy, a variant of EI, by adding a factor equal to the probability of feasibility to the acquisition score. This new acquisition score biases our search strategy toward feasible regions, thus better guiding us toward the feasible optimum.

In the next chapter, we discuss a new BayesOpt setting, multifidelity optimization, with which there are different costs to querying the objective function. This setting requires us to balance finding a high objective value and preserving our querying budget.

8.5   Exercise 2: Constrained optimization of airplane design

In this exercise, we tackle a constrained optimization problem using the airplane-utility objective function in exercise 2 of chapter 7. This process allows us to run constrained BayesOpt on a higher-dimensional problem in which it's not obvious where the feasibility optimal solution is. The solution to this exercise is included in the CH08/03 - Exercise 2.ipynb notebook:

1   Recreate the BayesOpt problem used in the CH07/04 - Exercise 2.ipynb notebook, including the airplane-utility objective function named `flight_utility()`, the bounds of our search space (the four-dimensional unit hypercube), the GP implementation, and the helper function that trains a GP on some training data `fit_gp_model()`.

2   Implement the following cost function, which simulates the cost of making the airplane design specified by a four-dimensional input:

```
def flight_cost(X):
    X = X * 20 - 10

    part1 = (X[..., 0] - 1) ** 2
```

```
i = X.new(range(2, 5))
part2 = torch.sum(i * (2.0 * X[..., 1:] ** 2 - X[..., :-1]) ** 2, dim=-1)

return -(part1 + part2) / 100_000 + 2
```

Figure 8.10 visualizes this cost function for various pairs of parameters we can tune, showing a complex nonlinear trend across these two-dimensional spaces.

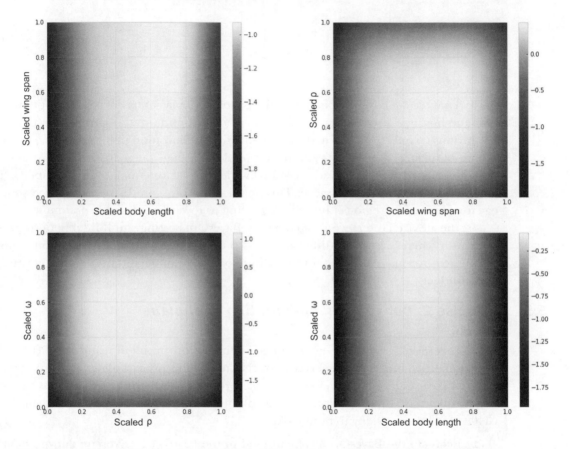

Figure 8.10   **The cost function of the simulated airplane design optimization problem in various two-dimensional subspaces, corresponding to pairs of tunable parameters, shown as axis labels.**

3   Our goal is to maximize the objective function `flight_utility()`, while following the constraint that the cost, as computed by `flight_cost()`, is less than or equal to 0:

   a   To this end, we set the number of queries a BayesOpt policy can make in each experiment as 50 and designate that each policy needs to run 10 repeated experiments.

   b   The default value quantifying optimization progress if no feasible solution is found should be set to −2.

4 Run the constrained EI policy as well as the regular EI policy on this problem,
and then visualize and compare their average progress (along with error bars).
The plot should look similar to figure 8.9.

Summary

- Constrained optimization is an optimization problem in which, in addition to optimizing the objective function, we need to satisfy other constraints to have practical solutions to the optimization problem. Constrained optimization is common in materials and drug discovery as well as hyperparameter tuning, where the objective function's optimum is too difficult or dangerous to be used in practice.

- A data point that satisfies the constraints in a constrained optimization problem is called a feasible point, while a data point that violates the constraints is called infeasible. We aim to find the point that maximizes the objective function among the feasible points.

- Constraints can vastly change the solution to an optimization problem, cutting off or even excluding a region with high objective values. We, therefore, need to actively account for the constraints when optimizing the objective function.

- In the framework of constrained BayesOpt, we train a GP on each of the functions that define the constraints. These GPs allow us to reason about whether a data point will satisfy the constraints in a probabilistic manner. Specifically, the probability that a given data point is feasible is easy to compute thanks to the fact that the predictive distributions from a GP are normal distributions.

- We can modify the EI policy to account for the constraints by adding the probability of feasibility to its acquisition score. The constrained EI policy can balance optimizing the objective function and satisfying the constraints.

- BoTorch provides a class implementation of the constrained EI policy. When implementing constrained EI, we need to pass in the GPs modeling the objective and constraint functions as well as declare the constraint lower and upper bounds.

9

Balancing utility and cost with multifidelity optimization

This chapter covers

- The problem of multifidelity optimization with variable cost
- Training a GP on data from multiple sources
- Implementing a cost-aware multifidelity BayesOpt policy

Consider the following questions:

- Should you trust the online reviews saying that the newest season of your favorite TV show isn't as good as the previous ones and you should quit watching the show, or should you spend your next few weekends watching it to find out for yourself whether you will like the new season?
- After seeing that their neural network model doesn't perform well after being trained for a few epochs, should an ML engineer cut their losses and switch to a different model, or should they keep training for more epochs in the hope of achieving better performance?
- When a physicist wants to understand a physical phenomenon, can they use a computer simulation to gain insights, or are real, physical experiments necessary to study the phenomenon?

222

These questions are similar in that they demand that the person in question choose between two possible actions that can help them answer a question they're interested in. On one hand, the person can take an action with a relatively low cost, but the answer generated from the action might be corrupted by noise and, therefore, not necessarily true. On the other hand, the person can opt for the action with a higher cost, which will help them arrive at a more definite conclusion:

- Reading the online reviews about the newest season of your TV shows would only take a few minutes, but there's a chance the reviewers don't have the same taste as you and you will still enjoy the show anyway. The only way to know for sure is to watch it yourself, but it's a huge time commitment to do so.
- The performance of a neural network after being trained for a few epochs may be, but is not necessarily, indicative of its true performance. However, more training means more time and resources spent on a potentially non-value-adding task if the model ends up performing poorly in the end.
- A computer simulation can tell a physicist many things about a phenomenon but cannot capture everything in the real world, so it's possible the simulation cannot offer the right insight. Performing physical experiments, on the other hand, will certainly answer the physicist's question but will cost a lot of money and effort.

These situations belong to a class of problems called *multifidelity* decision-making, where we can decide to observe some phenomenon at various levels of granularity and cost. Observing the phenomenon on a shallow level may be inexpensive and easy to do, but it doesn't give us as much information as possible. On the other hand, inspecting the phenomenon closely might entail more effort. The term *fidelity* here refers to how closely an observation reflects the truth about the phenomenon in question. An inexpensive, low-fidelity observation is noisy and, thus, can lead us to the wrong conclusion, while high-quality (or high-fidelity) observations are expensive and, therefore, cannot be made liberally. Black box optimization has its own multifidelity variant.

> **DEFINITION** *Multifidelity optimization* is an optimization problem where in addition to the true objective function to be maximized, we can observe approximations that do not exactly match but still offer information about the objective function. These low-fidelity approximations can be evaluated at lower costs than the true objective function.

In a multifidelity optimization, we need to use these multiple sources of data simultaneously to gain the most information about what we're interested in, which is the optimum of the objective function. In this chapter, we go into more detail about the problem of multifidelity optimization and how to approach it from the angle of BayesOpt. We learn about a strategy that balances learning about the objective function and cost, which results in a cost-aware BayesOpt policy for the multifidelity setting. We then see how to implement this optimization problem and the cost-aware policy in Python. By the end of this chapter, we learn how to perform multifidelity BayesOpt and see that our cost-aware strategy is more efficient at optimization than algorithms that only use the ground-truth function.

9.1   *Using low-fidelity approximations to study expensive phenomena*

We first discuss the motivation of a multifidelity BayesOpt problem, its setup, and real-world examples of the problem. This discussion will help clarify what we look for in a decision-making policy for this setting.

In the simplest setting of BayesOpt, we evaluate the objective function at each search iteration, each time carefully reasoning about where to make this evaluation to make the most optimization progress. The need for this careful reasoning stems from the high cost of making function evaluations, as is typical in an expensive black box optimization problem. This cost can refer to the amount of time we spend waiting for a large neural network to finish training while searching for the best network architecture or, in a drug discovery procedure, the money and effort needed to synthesize an experimental drug and conduct experiments to test its effectiveness.

But what if there are ways to gauge the result of a function evaluation without actually evaluating the objective function, denoted as $f(x)$? That is, in addition to the objective function, we can query an inexpensive surrogate $\bar{f}(x)$. This surrogate $\bar{f}(x)$ is an inexact approximation to the objective function, so evaluating it won't tell us everything about the true objective function $f(x)$. However, since $\bar{f}(x)$ is an approximation of $f(x)$, knowledge about the former still offers us insight into the latter. The question we need to ask ourselves is this: How should we balance using the true objective function $f(x)$, which is expensive to query but offers exact information, and using the surrogate $\bar{f}(x)$, which is inaccurate but inexpensive to query? This balance is illustrated in figure 9.1, where the ground truth $f(x)$ is the high-fidelity data source and the surrogate $\bar{f}(x)$ is the low-fidelity approximation.

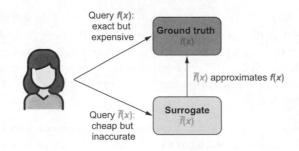

Figure 9.1   Model of a multifidelity decision-making problem, where the agent needs to balance querying the true objective function $f(x)$ for accurate information and querying the inexpensive surrogate $\bar{f}(x)$

As noted in the introduction, using a low-fidelity approximation is common in the real world, as in the following examples:

- *Training a neural network only for a small number of epochs to gauge its performance on some dataset.* The performance of the neural network over, for example, 5 epochs is a low-fidelity approximation of its optimized performance that can be achieved after 50 epochs.

- *Running a computer simulation in lieu of a real experiment to study some scientific phenomenon.* This computer simulation imitates the physical processes happening in the real world and approximates the phenomenon the physicist wants to study. However, this approximation is low fidelity because the computer cannot accurately mirror the real world.

In a multifidelity optimization problem where we aim to optimize the objective function $f(x)$, we get to choose between querying the high-fidelity $f(x)$ or the low-fidelity $\overline{f}(x)$ to best learn about and optimize $f(x)$. Of course, querying $f(x)$ will offer more information about $f(x)$ itself, but the querying cost prevents us from making such queries many times. Instead, we can choose to take advantage of the low-fidelity approximation $\overline{f}(x)$ to learn as much as possible about our target $f(x)$ while minimizing our querying cost.

> ### Having multiple low-fidelity approximations
>
> To keep things simple, we only work with one low-fidelity approximation $\overline{f}(x)$ in the examples in this chapter. However, many real-world settings offer multiple low-fidelity approximations $\overline{f}_1(x)$, $\overline{f}_2(x)$, ..., $\overline{f}_k(x)$ to the objective function, each having its own querying cost and accuracy.
>
> The Bayesian approach we learn in the next section doesn't limit how many low-fidelity approximations we have access to, and we solve a multifidelity optimization with two low-fidelity approximations $\overline{f}_1(x)$ and $\overline{f}_2(x)$ in this chapter's exercise 2.
>
> Having multiple low-fidelity approximations is applicable when, for example, the computer simulation approximating the real experiment has a setting that controls the quality of the approximation. If one were to set the simulation quality to low, the computer program would run a coarse simulation of the real world and return the result more quickly. On the other hand, if the simulation quality is set to high, the program might need to run for a longer duration to better approximate a real experiment. For now, we stick with one objective function and one low-fidelity approximation.

Consider figure 9.2, where in addition to the Forrester function as an example objective function in BayesOpt, denoted as the solid line, we also have a low-fidelity approximation to the objective, denoted as the dotted line. Here, although the low-fidelity approximation doesn't exactly match the ground truth, the former captures the general shape of the latter and can, therefore, be helpful in the search for the objective's optimum.

For example, since the low-fidelity approximation is informative of the true objective function, we could query the approximation many times to study its behavior across the search space, only querying the ground truth when we want to "zero in" on the objective's optimum. Our goal in this chapter is to design a BayesOpt policy that

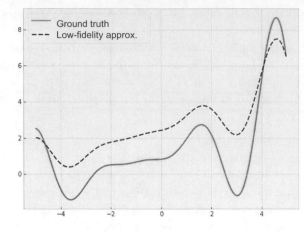

Figure 9.2   **The Forrester function (solid line) and a low-fidelity approximation to the function (dotted line). Although the low-fidelity approximation doesn't exactly match the ground truth, the former offers information about the latter, as the two functions have roughly the same shape.**

navigates this search for us and decides where and which function to query to optimize our objective function as quickly and cheaply as possible.

The multifidelity BayesOpt loop is summarized in figure 9.3 with the following notable changes from the traditional BayesOpt loop in figure 1.6:

- In step 1, the GP is trained on data from *both* sources: the high-fidelity, or ground truth, function and the low-fidelity approximation. That is, our data is split into two sets: the set of data points evaluated on the ground truth $f(x)$ and the set of points evaluated on the approximation $\overline{f}(x)$. Training on both datasets ensures the predictive model can reason about the objective function in regions where there is low-fidelity data but no high-fidelity data.

- In step 2, the BayesOpt policy generates an acquisition score for each data point in the search space to quantify the data point's value in helping us identify the

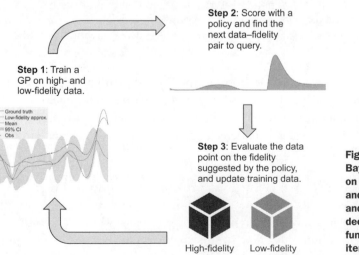

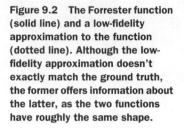

Step 2: Score with a policy and find the next data–fidelity pair to query.

Step 1: Train a GP on high- and low-fidelity data.

Step 3: Evaluate the data point on the fidelity suggested by the policy, and update training data.

High-fidelity   Low-fidelity

Figure 9.3   **The multifidelity BayesOpt loop. The GP trains on data from both the high- and low-fidelity functions, and the BayesOpt policy decides where and which function to query at each iteration of the loop.**

objective's optimum. However, it's not just the data points that are scored but the data point–fidelity pairs; that is, the policy quantifies the value of querying a given data point on a particular function (either the high- or low-fidelity function). This score needs to balance the optimization of the objective and the querying cost.

- In step 3, we query the data point on the fidelity corresponding to the pair maximizing the acquisition score of the BayesOpt policy. We then update our training datasets with the new observation and loop back to step 1 to continue our BayesOpt procedure.

For the remainder of this chapter, we learn about the components of the multifidelity BayesOpt loop and how to implement them in Python, starting with training a GP on a dataset that includes both high- and low-fidelity observations.

9.2   *Multifidelity modeling with GPs*

As noted in figure 9.3, our GP model is trained on a combined dataset that includes observations from multiple fidelities. This combined training allows the GP to make predictions about the objective function, even in regions where there are only low-fidelity observations, which subsequently informs the BayesOpt policy that makes optimization-related decisions. In the next section, we learn how to represent a multifidelity dataset and train a special variant of the GP on the dataset; the code we use is included in CH09/01 - Multifidelity modeling.ipynb.

9.2.1   *Formatting a multifidelity dataset*

To set up the multifidelity optimization problem, we use the following code for our one-dimensional Forrester objective function and its low-fidelity approximation in figure 9.2; our search space is between –5 and 5:

```
def objective(x):
    y = -((x + 1) ** 2) * torch.sin(2 * x + 2) / 5 + 1 + x / 3
    return y
```
The true objective function

```
def approx_objective(x):
    return 0.5 * objective(x) + x / 4 + 2
```
The low-fidelity approximation to the objective function

```
lb = -5
ub = 5
bounds = torch.tensor([[lb], [ub]], dtype=torch.float)
```
Bounds of the search space, to be used by optimization policies later on

Of particular importance is a PyTorch tensor that stores the information about the correlation between each fidelity function we have access to and the true objective function, which we aim to maximize. We assume we know the values of these correlations and declare this tensor `fidelities` as follows:

```
fidelities = torch.tensor([0.5, 1.0])
```

This tensor has two elements corresponding to the two fidelities we have access to: 0.5, which we use to indicate the correlation between the Forrester function $f(x)$ and its low-fidelity approximation $\overline{f}(x)$ (the solid and dotted lines in figure 9.2), and exactly 1, which is the correlation between the Forrester function and itself.

These correlation values are important because they inform how much the GP we will train later should rely on data from a particular fidelity:

- If the correlation to the true objective function of a low-fidelity approximation is high, then that approximation offers a lot of information about the objective. An extreme example of this is the objective function itself, which offers perfect information about what we're interested in and, therefore, has a correlation value of 1.
- A low-fidelity approximation with a correlation value of 0.5, which we have in our example, offers information about the objective that is inexact but still valuable.
- At the other end of the spectrum, an approximation with a correlation value of 0 doesn't tell us anything about the objective function; a perfectly horizontal line is an example, since this "approximation" is constant across the domain.

Figure 9.4 illustrates this scale of correlation: the higher a correlation is, the more information about the ground truth a low-fidelity approximation offers.

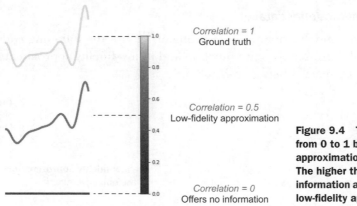

Figure 9.4 **The scale of correlation from 0 to 1 between a low-fidelity approximation and the ground truth. The higher the correlation, the more information about the ground truth the low-fidelity approximation offers.**

Setting the fidelities variable

In general, `fidelities` is a tensor with k elements, where k is the number of functions we can query, including the objective. The elements are numbers between 0 and 1 denoting the correlation between the functions and the objective. It's more convenient for the subsequent learning and decision-making tasks to have 1, the correlation between the true objective and itself, at the end of the tensor.

Unfortunately, there is no concrete rule on how to set these fidelity values; the decision is left to the BayesOpt engineer. If these values are not known in your own use case, you can make a rough estimate based on figure 9.4 by estimating where your low-fidelity function lies between the high-fidelity function (the ground truth) and an uninformative data source.

With the functions and correlation values in hand, let's now create an example training dataset. We first randomly sample 10 locations inside the search space and store them as a tensor in `train_x`:

```
n = 10          ◁——|  The size of the
                     training set
torch.manual_seed(0)                    ◁——
train_x = bounds[0] + (bounds[1] - bounds[0]) * torch.rand(n, 1)          ◁——
```

The size of the training set

Fixes the random seed for reproducibility

Draws points uniformly at random from the space

The tensor `train_x` has 10 rows and 1 column since we have 10 data points within a one-dimensional space. Each of these data points is associated with a fidelity from which the observation comes (that is, each data point is either a high-fidelity or a low-fidelity observation). We encode this information in our dataset by adding in an extra column to `train_x` to indicate the fidelity of each data points, as illustrated in figure 9.5.

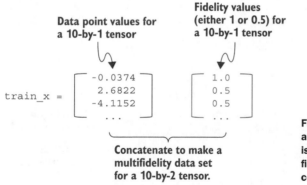

Data point values for a 10-by-1 tensor

Fidelity values (either 1 or 0.5) for a 10-by-1 tensor

$$train\_x = \begin{bmatrix} -0.0374 \\ 2.6822 \\ -4.1152 \\ \dots \end{bmatrix} \quad \begin{bmatrix} 1.0 \\ 0.5 \\ 0.5 \\ \dots \end{bmatrix}$$

Concatenate to make a multifidelity data set for a 10-by-2 tensor.

Figure 9.5 Formatting the features in a multifidelity dataset. Each data point is associated with a fidelity; these fidelity values are stored in an extra column in the training set.

NOTE Remember that we aim to train a GP on data coming from both sources: the ground truth and the low-fidelity function. To this end, we will randomly assign each of the 10 data points we have to either fidelity.

We use `torch.randint(2)` to randomly pick out an integer between 0 (inclusive) and 2 (exclusive), effectively choosing between 0 and 1. This number determines from which function each data point comes: 0 means that the data point is evaluated on the low-fidelity approximation $\bar{f}(x)$; 1 means the data point is evaluated on the objective function $f(x)$. We then extract the corresponding correlation values in `fidelities` for each data point and concatenate this array of correlation values to our training data:

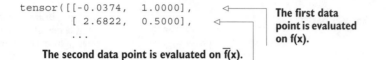

Randomly selects the fidelity (and therefore the correlation value) of each data point

```
train_f = fidelities[torch.randint(2, (n, 1))]
train_x_full = torch.cat([train_x, train_f], dim=1)
```

Adds the correlation values to the training data

Taking a look at the full training data `train_x_full`, we see the first two data points are

```
tensor([[-0.0374,  1.0000],
        [ 2.6822,  0.5000],
        ...
```

The first data point is evaluated on f(x).

The second data point is evaluated on $\overline{f}(x)$.

The first column of `train_x_full` contains the locations of the data points between –5 and 5, while the second column contains the correlation values. This output means our first training point is at –0.0374, and it's evaluated on $f(x)$. On the other hand, the second training point is at 2.6822, this time evaluated on $\overline{f}(x)$.

Now, we need to generate the observations `train_y` appropriately so that the observations are computed with the correct function: the first element of `train_y` is equal to $f(-0.0374)$, the second element is $\overline{f}(2.6822)$, and so on. To do this, we write a helper function that takes in the full training set, where the last column contains the correlation values, and call the appropriate function to generate `train_y`. That is, if the correlation value is 1, we call `objective()`, which is $f(x)$, as previously defined; if the correlation value is 0.5, we call `approx_objective()` for $\overline{f}(x)$:

```
def evaluate_all_functions(x_full):
    y = []
    for x in x_full:
        if torch.isclose(x[-1], torch.ones(1)):
            y.append(objective(x[:-1]))
        else:
            y.append(approx_objective(x[:-1]))

    return torch.tensor(y).unsqueeze(-1)
```

Iterates through the data points

Queries f(x) if the correlation value is 1

Queries $\overline{f}(x)$ if the correlation value is 0.5

Reshapes the observation tensor to be of the correct shape

Calling `evaluate_all_functions()` on `train_x_full` gives us the observed value `train_y`, evaluated on appropriate functions. Our training set is visualized in figure 9.6, where there are three high-fidelity observations and seven low-fidelity observations.

That's how we generate and format a training set in multifidelity BayesOpt. Our next task is to train a GP on this dataset in a way that uses both the ground truth and the low-fidelity approximation.

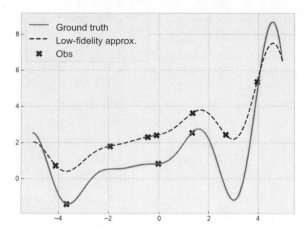

Figure 9.6 **A randomly sampled, multifidelity training dataset from the Forrester function and its low-fidelity approximation. This training set contains three high-fidelity observations and seven low-fidelity observations.**

9.2.2   *Training a multifidelity GP*

Our goal in this section is to have a GP that takes in a set of multifidelity observations and outputs probabilistic predictions about the target function—that is, the objective function $f(x)$ to be maximized.

Remember from section 2.2 that a GP is an MVN distribution of infinitely many variables. The GP models the covariance (and, therefore, correlation) between any pair of variables using the covariance function. It's with this correlation between any two variables that the GP can make predictions about one variable when the value of the other is observed.

> **A refresher on correlation and updated belief about a variable**
>
> Say there are three variables *A*, *B*, and *C*, jointly modeled with a tri-variate Gaussian distribution, where the correlation between *A* and *B* is high, but the correlation between *A* and *C* and between *B* and *C* are both low.
>
> Now, when we observe the value of *A*, the uncertainty in our updated belief about *B* (represented as the posterior distribution of the value of *B*) significantly reduces. This is because the correlation between *A* and *B* is high, so observing the value *A* gives us a lot of information about the value of *B*. This is not the case for *C*, however, since the correlation between *A* and *C* is low, so the updated belief about *C* still has considerable uncertainty. See section 2.2.2 for a similar and detailed discussion about housing prices.

As we learned in section 2.2.2, as long as we have a way to model the correlation between any pair of variables (that is, the function values at any two given locations), we can update the GP accordingly to reflect our updated belief about the function anywhere in the domain. This is still true in the multifidelity setting: as long as we have a way to model the correlation between two observations, even if one is from the high fidelity $f(x)$ and the other is from the low fidelity $\bar{f}(x)$, we can update the GP on the objective function $f(x)$.

What's left for us to do is use a covariance function that can compute the covariance between two given observations, which may or may not be from the same fidelity. Fortunately for us, BoTorch offers a modified version of the Matérn kernel that accounts for the fidelity correlation value associated with each data point in our training set:

- If the correlation value of a data point is high, the kernel will produce a high covariance between that observed data point and any nearby point, thus allowing us to reduce the GP's uncertainty with an informative observation.
- If the correlation value is low, the kernel will output a low covariance, and the posterior uncertainty will remain high.

NOTE We first learned about the Matérn kernel in section 3.4.2. While we won't go into the details about the multifidelity Matérn kernel here, the interested reader can find more information in BoTorch's documentation (http://mng.bz/81ZB).

Since the GP with the multifidelity kernel is implemented as a special GP class, we can import it from BoTorch without having to write our own class implementation. Specifically, this GP is an instance of the `SingleTaskMultiFidelityGP` class, which takes in a multifidelity training set `train_x_full` and `train_y`. The initialization also has a `data_fidelity` argument, which should be set to the index of the column in `train_x_full` that contains the correlation values; this, in our case, is `1`:

```
from botorch.models.gp_regression_fidelity          Imports the GP class
  import SingleTaskMultiFidelityGP                    implementation

model = SingleTaskMultiFidelityGP(                    Initializes a
  train_x_full, train_y, data_fidelity=1)             multifidelity GP
```

After initializing the model, we now need to train it by maximizing the likelihood of the observed data. (Refer to section 3.3.2 for more on why we choose to maximize the likelihood to train a GP.) Since the GP we have is an instance of a special class from BoTorch, we can take advantage of BoTorch's helper function `fit_gpytorch_mll()`, which facilitates the training process behind the scenes. All we need to do is initialize a (log) likelihood object as our training objective and pass it to the helper function:

```
from gpytorch.mlls.exact_marginal_log_likelihood import    Imports the log likelihood
  ExactMarginalLogLikelihood                                objective and the helper
from botorch.fit import fit_gpytorch_mll                    function for training

mll = ExactMarginalLogLikelihood(model.likelihood,         Initializes the log
  model)                                                    likelihood objective
fit_gpytorch_mll(mll);          Trains the GP to maximize
                                the log likelihood
```

These surprisingly few lines of code are all we need to train a multifidelity GP on a set of observations.

BoTorch warnings about data type and scaling

When running the previous code, newer versions of GPyTorch and BoTorch might display two warnings, the first of which is

```
UserWarning: The model inputs are of type torch.float32. It is strongly
recommended to use double precision in BoTorch, as this improves both
precision and stability and can help avoid numerical errors. See
https://github.com/pytorch/botorch/discussions/1444
  warnings.warn(
```

This warning indicates that we should use a different data type for `train_x` and `train_y` from the default `torch.float32` to improve numerical precision and stability. To do this, we can add the following to our code (at the beginning of the script):

```
torch.set_default_dtype(torch.double)
```

The second warning concerns scaling the input features `train_x` to be in the unit cube (each feature value being between 0 and 1) and the response values `train_y` to be standardized to have zero mean and unit variance:

```
InputDataWarning: Input data is not
 contained to the unit cube. Please consider min-max scaling the input data.
  warnings.warn(msg, InputDataWarning)
InputDataWarning: Input data is not standardized. Please consider scaling
the input to zero mean and unit variance.
  warnings.warn(msg, InputDataWarning)
```

Scaling `train_x` and `train_y` this way helps us fit the GP more easily and in a more numerically stable way. To keep our code simple, we won't implement such scaling here and will be filtering out these warnings using the `warnings` module. The interested reader can refer to chapter 2's exercise for more details.

Now, to verify whether this trained GP is able to learn about the training set, we visualize the GP's predictions about $f(x)$ between −5 and 5 with the mean and the 95% CIs.

Our test set `xs` is a dense grid (with over 200 elements) between −5 and 5:

```
xs = torch.linspace(-5, 5, 201)
```

Unlike what we've seen in previous chapters, we need to augment this test set with an extra column denoting the fidelity on which we'd like to predict. In other words, the test set `xs` needs to be in the same format as the training set `train_x_full`. Since we're interested in the GP's predictions about $f(x)$, we add in an extra column full of ones (as 1 is the correlation value of $f(x)$):

```
with torch.no_grad():
    pred_dist = model(torch.vstack([xs, torch.ones_like(xs)]).T)
    pred_mean = pred_dist.mean
    pred_lower, pred_upper = pred_dist.confidence_region()
```

**Augments the test set with the fidelity
column and passes it to the model**

Computes the 95% CIs

Computes the mean predictions

Disables gradient tracking

These predictions are visualized in figure 9.7, which illustrates a number of important features about our multifidelity GP:

1 The mean predictions about $f(x)$ go through the high-fidelity observations at roughly –3.6, 0, and 1.3. This interpolation makes sense as these data points were indeed evaluated on $f(x)$.

2 In regions where we have low-fidelity observations but not high-fidelity observations (e.g., at –2 and around 2.7), our uncertainty about $f(x)$ still decreased. This is because the low-fidelity observations offer information about $f(x)$, even though they weren't evaluated on $f(x)$.

3 Among these low-fidelity observations, we see that the data point at 4 could offer valuable information to an optimization policy since the data point captures the upward trend of the objective function around that region. By exploiting this information, an optimization policy could discover the global optimum nearby, around 4.5.

**1. The mean goes
through high-fidelity
observations.**

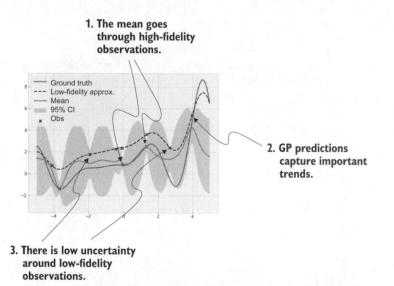

**2. GP predictions
capture important
trends.**

**3. There is low uncertainty
around low-fidelity
observations.**

**Figure 9.7   The multifidelity GP's predictions about the objective function
(ground truth). The mean predictions appropriately go through the high-
fidelity observations, but uncertainty is still reduced around low-fidelity
observations.**

Figure 9.7 shows that the GP successfully learned from a multifidelity data set. To push our ability to learn from low-fidelity observations and predict $f(x)$ to the extreme, we could modify the way we generate our training set so it only contains low-fidelity observations. We do this by setting the correlation values in the extra column in `train_x_full` to `0.5`:

```
train_f = torch.ones_like(train_x) * fidelities[0]
train_x_full = torch.cat([train_x, train_f], dim=1)
```

The correlation values are all 0.5.

Adds the correlation values to the training set

Rerunning the last of the code so far will generate the left panel of figure 9.8, where we see that all data points are, indeed, from the low-fidelity approximation $\bar{f}(x)$. Compared to figure 9.7, we are more uncertain about our predictions here, which is appropriate because having observed only low-fidelity observations, the GP doesn't learn as much about the objective function $f(x)$.

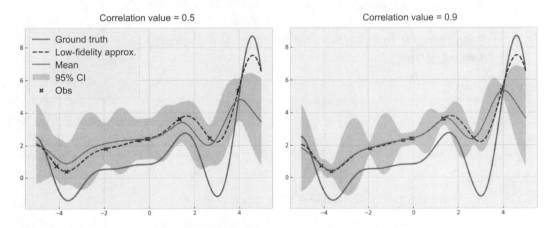

Figure 9.8   The predictions about the objective function (ground truth) by a GP trained on only low-fidelity observations. The left panel shows the result when the correlation value is 0.5; the right shows the result when the correlation value is 0.9, which exhibits less uncertainty.

To further show the flexibility of our multifidelity GP, we can play around with the correlation values stored in `fidelities` (while assuming we know how to appropriately set these correlation values). As we learned in section 9.2.1, the first element in this tensor denotes the correlation between $f(x)$ and $\bar{f}(x)$, which roughly translates to how much the GP should "trust" the low-fidelity observations. By setting this first element to 0.9 (as opposed to 0.5, as we currently do), we can assign more importance to the low-fidelity observations. That is, we are telling the GP to learn more from the low-fidelity data, as it offers a lot of information about $f(x)$. The right panel of figure 9.8 shows the resulting GP, where our uncertainty is, indeed, lower than in the left panel.

Aside from the flexibility of the multifidelity GP model, figure 9.8 also shows how important it is to have the correct correlation values in the `fidelities` tensor. Comparing the two panels in figure 9.8, we see that 0.5 is a better value for the correlation value between two fidelities than 0.9:

- In the right panel, our predictions miss the true objective $f(x)$ in most of the space due to our overreliance on and trust in the low-fidelity observations.
- In the left panel, the 95% CIs are appropriately wider to reflect our uncertainty about $f(x)$.

In other words, we don't want to overestimate how informative the low-fidelity approximation $\bar{f}(x)$ is about the objective $f(x)$.

At this point, we have learned how to model a function with a multifidelity GP. For the remainder of this chapter, we discuss the second part of the multifidelity optimization problem: decision-making. More specifically, we learn how to design a multifidelity optimization policy that selects at which location and which function to query at each step of the BayesOpt loop.

9.3   Balancing information and cost in multifidelity optimization

To be able to trade off between the informativeness of a query (low or high fidelity) and the cost of running that query, we need to have a way to model and reason about the querying cost. In the next section, we learn how to represent the cost of querying a given fidelity with a linear model. Using this cost model, we then implement a multifidelity BayesOpt policy that trades off cost and making optimization progress. The code we use is stored in the CH09/02 - Multi-fidelity optimization.ipynb notebook.

9.3.1   Modeling the costs of querying different fidelities

In the multifidelity optimization problem, we assume we know how much it costs to query each of the functions we have access to, either the objective function $f(x)$ itself or the low-fidelity approximation $\bar{f}(x)$. To facilitate a modular optimization workflow, we need to represent this information about the cost of querying each function as a cost model. This model takes in a given data point (with an extra feature containing the correlation value, as we saw in section 9.2.1) and returns the known cost of querying that data point on the specified fidelity.

> **NOTE**   Since the cost of querying a fidelity is known, there's no prediction involved in this cost model. We just need this model formulation to keep the optimization procedure we learn about in the next section.

BoTorch provides the class implementation for a linear cost model named `Affine-FidelityCostModel` from the `botorch.models.cost` module. This linear cost model assumes the querying costs obey the relationships shown in figure 9.9, where the cost of querying a data point on a fidelity scales linearly with the correlation between that fidelity and the ground truth $f(x)$. The slope of this linear trend is the weight parameter in figure 9.9, and there's a fixed cost to making any query.

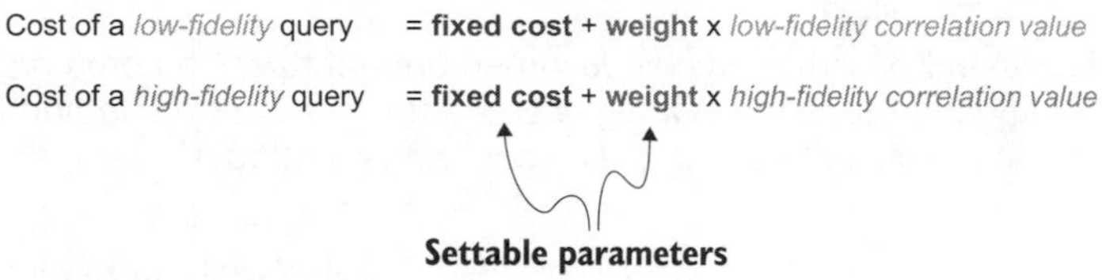

Cost of a *low-fidelity* query   = **fixed cost** + **weight** x *low-fidelity correlation value*

Cost of a *high-fidelity* query   = **fixed cost** + **weight** x *high-fidelity correlation value*

Settable parameters

Figure 9.9 **The linear cost model for multifidelity optimization. The cost of querying a data point on a fidelity scales linearly with the correlation between that fidelity and the ground truth $f(x)$.**

We initialize this linear cost model with the following code, where we set the fixed cost at 0 and the weight at 1. This means querying a low-fidelity data point will cost us exactly the correlation value of the low-fidelity approximation, which is 0.5 (units of cost). Similarly, querying a high-fidelity data point will cost 1 (unit of cost). Here, the `fidelity_weights` argument takes in a dictionary mapping the index of the column containing the correlation values in `train_x_full` (1 in our case) to the weight:

```
from botorch.models.cost import AffineFidelityCostModel
```

```
cost_model = AffineFidelityCostModel(
  fixed_cost=0.0,
  fidelity_weights={1: 1.0},
)
```

The fixed querying cost

The linear weight to be multiplied with the correlation values

> **NOTE** The unit of cost being used depends on the specific application. This cost comes down to the difference in "convenience" between querying the objective and querying the low-fidelity approximation, which can be time (the unit would be minutes, hours, or days), money (in dollars), or some measure of effort, and should be set by the user.

The linear trend captures the relationship between the correlation value and cost: a high-fidelity function with a high correlation value should have a high querying cost, while a low-fidelity function should have a lower cost to query. The two settable parameters—the fixed cost and weight—allow us to flexibly model many types of querying costs. (We see how different types of querying costs can lead to different decisions being made in the next section.) With this cost model in hand, we are now ready to learn how to balance cost and progress in a multifidelity optimization problem.

Modeling nonlinear querying costs

We only use the linear cost model in this chapter. If your use case demands the querying costs to be modeled by a nonlinear trend (e.g., a quadratic or an exponential trend), you can implement your own cost model.

(continued)

This is done by extending the `AffineFidelityCostModel` class we are using and rewriting its `forward()` method. The implementation of the `AffineFidelityCost-Model` class is shown in BoTorch's official documentation (https://botorch.org/api/_modules/botorch/models/cost.html), where we see the `forward()` method implements the linear relationship between querying cost and correlation value, as in figure 9.9:

```
def forward(self, X: Tensor) -> Tensor:
    lin_cost = torch.einsum(
        "...f,f", X[..., self.fidelity_dims], self.weights.to(X)
    )
    return self.fixed_cost + lin_cost.unsqueeze(-1)
```

Multiplies the correlation values with the weight

Adds the fixed cost

In a new class for the custom cost model, you can then rewrite this `forward()` method to implement the relationship between querying cost and correlation value that you need. Even with a custom cost model, the rest of the code we use in this chapter doesn't need to be modified, which illustrates the benefit of BoTorch's modular design.

9.3.2   *Optimizing the amount of information per dollar to guide optimization*

We now return to the question posed at the beginning of this chapter: How should we balance the amount of information we can gain by querying a function and the cost of querying that function? In multifidelity optimization, a high-fidelity function (the ground truth) offers us exact information about the objective $f(x)$ to optimize $f(x)$, but the querying cost is high. On the other hand, a low-fidelity approximation is inexpensive to evaluate but can only provide inexact information about $f(x)$. It is the job of a multifidelity BayesOpt policy to decide how this balancing is done.

In multifidelity optimization, we need to balance learning about the objective function and the cost of querying data.

Info about objective function

Querying cost

We already have a model from section 9.3.1 that computes the cost of querying any given data point. As for the other side of the scale, we need a method of quantifying how much we will learn about the objective function from a given query that can either be from the objective $f(x)$ itself or from the low-fidelity approximation $\overline{f}(x)$.

NOTE How much information about $f(x)$ or, more specifically, about the optimum of $f(x)$, we will gain from a query is exactly what the Max-value Entropy Search (MES) policy, which we learned about in chapter 6, uses to rank its queries. MES chooses the query that gives us the most information about the highest value of $f(x)$ in the single-fidelity setting, where we can only query the objective.

As this information gain measure is a general information-theoretic concept, it can be applied to the multifidelity setting as well. In other words, we use MES as the base policy to compute how much information about the optimum of $f(x)$ we gain with each query during optimization. With both components, cost and information gain, available to us, we now need to design a way to balance the two, which gives us a *cost-aware* measure of utility of a query.

> **The return on investment quantity**
> To quantify the cost-aware utility of a query, we use a common metric in economics, called the return on investment (ROI) measure, which is calculated by dividing the profit from an investment by the investing cost. In the context of using MES in multifidelity optimization, the profit is the amount of information gained from querying a data point, and the cost is the querying cost.

Remember that the acquisition score of a BayesOpt policy is the score the policy assigns to each data point within the search space to quantify the point's value in helping us optimize the objective function. With the ROI acquisition score we use here, each data point is scored by the amount of information it provides about the objective's optimum for each unit of cost. This calculation is visualized in figure 9.10.

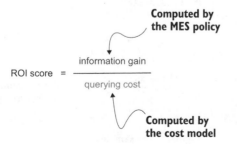

Figure 9.10 The formula of the ROI acquisition score for multifidelity optimization. This score quantifies the amount of information a query provides about the objective's optimum for each unit of cost.

We see that this ROI score is an appropriate measure that weights the information gained from a query by how inexpensive it is to make that query:

- If two queries we can potentially make have the same cost but result in different information gains, we should pick the one offering more information.
- If two queries provide the same amount of information about the objective's optimum, we should pick the one that's less expensive to make.

This tradeoff allows us to acquire information about the objective function $f(x)$ from inexpensive, low-fidelity approximations if these approximations are, indeed, informative. On the other hand, if and when the low-fidelity queries stop offering information about $f(x)$, we will switch to high-fidelity data points. Essentially, we always choose the optimal cost-aware decision that gives "the most bang for our buck."

To implement this cost-aware variant of MES, we can make use of BoTorch's `qMulti-FidelityMaxValueEntropy` class implementation. This implementation requires a number of components, which it takes in as arguments:

- *A cost utility object that does the ROI computation in figure 9.10.* This object is implemented with the `InverseCostWeightedUtility` class, which weights the utility of a query by the inverse of its cost. The initialization takes in the cost model we made earlier:

```
from botorch.acquisition.cost_aware import InverseCostWeightedUtility

cost_aware_utility = InverseCostWeightedUtility(cost_model=cost_model)
```

- *A Sobol sequence that acts as the candidate set for the entropy computation of MES.* We first learned about using Sobol sequences with MES in section 6.2.2, and the procedure is the same here, where we draw a 1,000-element Sobol sequence from the unit cube (it's just the segment going from 0 to 1, in our one-dimensional case) and scale it to our search space. One more thing we need to do in the multi-fidelity setting is augment this candidate set with the extra column for the correlation value of 1 (corresponding to the objective function $f(x)$) to denote that we want to measure entropy in our target $f(x)$:

```
torch.manual_seed(0)                              ⟵  Fixes the random seed
                                                      for reproducibility

sobol = SobolEngine(1, scramble=True)             ⟵  Draws 1,000 points from a Sobol
candidate_x = sobol.draw(1000)                        sequence within the unit cube

candidate_x = bounds[0] + (bounds[1] - bounds[0]) *
➥candidate_x                                      ⟵  Scales the samples
                                                      to our search space

candidate_x = torch.cat([candidate_x, torch.ones_like(
➥candidate_x)], dim=1)         ⟵  Augments the samples with
                                   the index of the ground truth
```

■ *Finally, a helper function that projects a given data point from any fidelity to the ground truth.* This projection is necessary in the computation of entropy that our policy uses to calculate the acquisition scores. Here, BoTorch provides that helper function `project_to_target_fidelity`, which doesn't need any further parameterization if the last column in our training set contains the correlation values and the correlation value of the ground truth is 1, both of which are true in our code.

Using the preceding components, we implement our cost-aware, multifidelity MES policy as follows:

```
from botorch.acquisition.utils import project_to_target_fidelity

policy = qMultiFidelityMaxValueEntropy(
    model,
    candidate_x,
    num_fantasies=128,
    cost_aware_utility=cost_aware_utility,
    project=project_to_target_fidelity,
)
```

The samples from the Sobol sequence → `candidate_x`

The cost utility object that weights utility by the inverse of the cost → `cost_aware_utility=cost_aware_utility`

The projection helper function → `project=project_to_target_fidelity`

At this point, we can use this policy object to score each data point from any fidelity by its cost-adjusted value in helping us find the objective's optimum. The last piece of the puzzle is the helper function we use to optimize the acquisition score of this policy to find the point with the highest ROI score at each iteration of the search. In previous chapters, we use `optimize_acqf` from the `botorch.optim.optimize` module to optimize the acquisition score in the single-fidelity setting, which only works if our search space is continuous.

> **NOTE**   In our current multifidelity setting, the search space for the location of the query is still continuous, but the choice for the function with which to query is discrete. In other words, our search space is mixed. Fortunately, BoTorch offers the analogous helper function for a mixed search space: `optimize_acqf_mixed`.

In addition to the usual arguments that `optimize_acqf` takes, the new helper function, `optimize_acqf_mixed`, also has a `fixed_features_list` argument, which should be a list of dictionaries, each mapping the index of a discrete column in `train_x_full` to the possible values the column contains. In our case, we only have one discrete column, the last column containing the correlation values, so we use `[{1: cost.item()} for cost in fidelities]` for the `fixed_features_list` argument. Further, the `bounds` variable we usually pass to the helper function now needs to contain the bounds for the correlation values as well. Overall, we optimize our multifidelity MES acquisition score with

```
from botorch.optim.optimize import optimize_acqf_mixed

next_x, acq_val = optimize_acqf_mixed(
    policy,
```

```
bounds=torch.cat(
    [bounds, torch.tensor([0.5, 1.0]).unsqueeze(-1)], dim=1
),
fixed_features_list=[{1: cost.item()} for cost in fidelities],
q=1,
num_restarts=20,
raw_samples=50,
)
```

The discrete values the correlation column could contain

Bounds for the search space, including those for the correlation values

This helper function completes the code we need to use the multifidelity MES policy. The bottom panel of figure 9.11 visualizes the acquisition scores computed by this policy with the multifidelity GP we trained in section 9.2.2. In this bottom panel, the boundary of the shaded region (denoting the scores of low-fidelity queries) exceeds that of the hatch-pattern region (the scores of high-fidelity queries), meaning low-fidelity queries are more cost-effective than high-fidelity ones, given our current knowledge. Ultimately, the best query we make, denoted as the star, is around 3.5 on the low-fidelity approximation $\bar{f}(x)$.

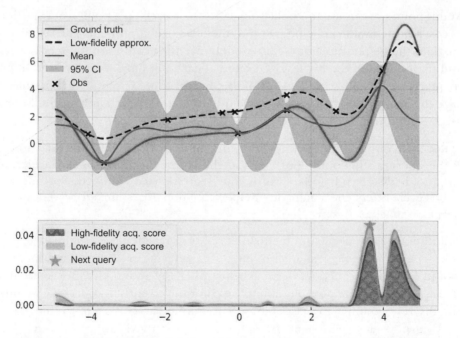

Figure 9.11 **The current GP belief about the objective function (top) and the acquisition scores computed by the multifidelity MES policy (bottom). In this example, low-fidelity queries are preferred to high-fidelity ones thanks to their low cost.**

A low-fidelity query is the optimal kind to make in figure 9.11, as it offers more information relative to its cost than any high-fidelity query. However, this is not always the case. By modifying our data generation procedure from section 9.2.2 to generate an all-low-fidelity-observation training set and rerunning our code, we obtain the left panel of figure 9.12, where this time, the optimal decision is to query the high-fidelity function $f(x)$. This is because according to our GP belief, we have sufficiently learned from low-fidelity data, and it's time we inspected the ground truth $f(x)$.

As a final analysis of the behavior of our policy, we can study the effect of the querying costs on how decisions are made. To do this, we change our querying costs, so a low-fidelity query won't be much less expensive than a high-fidelity one, specifically by increasing the fixed querying cost described in section 9.3.1 from 0 to 10. This change means a low-fidelity query now costs 10.5 units of cost, and a high-fidelity query now costs 11. Compared to the costs of 0.5 and 1 from before, 10.5 and 11 are much closer to each other, making the denominators in figure 9.10 for the two fidelities almost equal. This means the low-fidelity approximation $\overline{f}(x)$ is almost as expensive to query as the objective function $f(x)$ itself. Given these querying costs, the right panel of figure 9.12 shows how the MES policy scores potential queries. This time, because high-fidelity queries aren't much more expensive than low-fidelity ones, the former are preferred, as they give us more knowledge about $f(x)$.

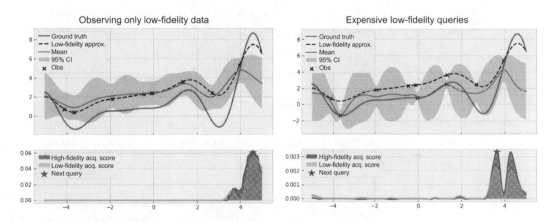

Figure 9.12 Situations where high-fidelity queries are preferred to low-fidelity ones. On the left, the training set contains only low-fidelity observations. On the right, low-fidelity queries are almost as expensive as high-fidelity queries.

These examples show that MES can identify the optimal decision that balances information and cost appropriately. That is, the policy assigns higher scores to low-fidelity queries when they are inexpensive to make and can offer substantial information about the objective function. If, on the other hand, high-fidelity queries are either significantly more informative or not much more expensive, these high-fidelity queries will be preferred by the policy.

9.4   *Measuring performance in multifidelity optimization*

Our previous discussion shows that the multifidelity MES policy is able to make appropriate decisions when choosing between the two fidelities to query. But is this policy better than regular BayesOpt policies that only query the ground truth $f(x)$, and if so, how much better is it? In this section, we learn how to benchmark the performance of a BayesOpt policy within the multifidelity setting, which requires additional considerations. The code we show can be found in the CH09/03 - Measuring performance.ipynb notebook.

> **NOTE**   To measure optimization progress in previous chapters, we recorded the highest objective values (aka the *incumbents*) we have collected in the training set throughout the search. If the incumbent values collected by policy *A* exceed those collected by policy *B*, we say that policy *A* is more effective at optimization than policy *B*.

Recording the incumbent values doesn't work here in the multifidelity setting. First, if we were to record the incumbent value in a training set, it would only make sense to pick the high-fidelity data point with the highest-valued label. However, this strategy ignores any contribution toward learning about the objective $f(x)$ that low-fidelity queries make. Take the two possible scenarios visualized in figure 9.13, for example:

- In the first scenario, on the left, we have made three high-fidelity observations, and the highest observed value is roughly 0.8. Objectively speaking, we have made no optimization progress in this situation; we haven't even explored the region where *x* is greater than 0.
- In the second scenario, on the right, we have only made low-fidelity observations, so recording the high-fidelity incumbent value isn't even applicable.

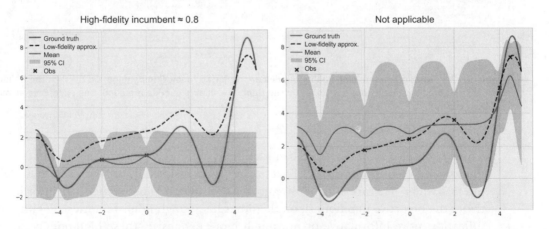

Figure 9.13   Measuring performance with the high-fidelity incumbent is inappropriate in multifidelity optimization. On the left, the high-fidelity incumbent is roughly 0.8, while we haven't discovered the objective's optimum. On the right, even though we are close to locating the objective's optimum, there's no high-fidelity query to record the incumbent value with.

However, we see that we are very close to finding the objective function's optimum here as our queries have discovered the function's peak around 4.5.

In other words, we should prefer the second scenario to the first, as one illustrates near success at optimization, while the other shows little optimization progress. However, using the high-fidelity incumbent as a measure of progress doesn't help us make this distinction between the two scenarios. Thus, we need another way of measuring optimization progress.

NOTE A common progress measure in the BayesOpt community is the objective function's value at the location that currently gives the highest posterior mean. This measure corresponds to the answer to this question: If we were to stop running BayesOpt and recommend a point as the solution to the optimization problem, which point should we choose? Intuitively, we should choose the point that, in the most plausible scenario (according to our GP belief), gives the highest value, which is the posterior mean maximizer.

We see that the posterior mean maximizer facilitates the comparison we made in figure 9.13, where on the left, the posterior mean maximizer is at 0, which still gives an objective value of 0.8 (the mean maximizer usually corresponds to the incumbent in the single-fidelity case), while on the right, the mean maximizer is around 4.5. In other words, the posterior-mean-maximizer metric successfully helps us distinguish between the two scenarios and shows that the one on the left is less preferable than the one on the right.

To implement this metric, we make a helper policy that uses the posterior mean as its acquisition score. Then, just as we optimize a regular policy's acquisition score in BayesOpt, we optimize the posterior mean using this helper policy. This policy requires two components:

- The class implementation of the BayesOpt policy that uses the posterior mean as its acquisition score. This class is `PosteriorMean`, which can be imported from `botorch.acquisition`.
- A *wrapper* policy that only optimizes high-fidelity metrics. This wrapper is required because our GP model is a multifidelity one, and we always need to specify which fidelity we'd like to work with when passing this model to an optimization policy. This wrapper policy is implemented as an instance of `Fixed-FeatureAcquisitionFunction` from `botorch.acquisition.fixed_feature`.

Overall, we make the posterior-mean-maximizer metric with the following helper policy, where the wrapper policy takes in an instance of `PosteriorMean`, and we specify the other arguments as the following:

- *The dimension of the search space is* `d = 2`—Our actual search space is one-dimensional, and there's an additional dimension for the correlation values (that is, the fidelity to query).

- *The index of the dimension to be fixed during optimization,* columns = [1] *and its fixed value* values = [1]—Since we only want to find the posterior mean maximizer corresponding to the objective function, the high-fidelity function, we specify that the second column (index 1) should always have the value 1:

```
from botorch.acquisition.fixed_feature
➥import FixedFeatureAcquisitionFunction
from botorch.acquisition import PosteriorMean
```

Optimizes the posterior mean
The index of the fixed column

```
post_mean_policy = FixedFeatureAcquisitionFunction(
    acq_function=PosteriorMean(model),
    d=2,
    columns=[1],
    values=[1],
)
```

The number of dimensions of the search space
The value of the fixed column

We then use the familiar helper function optimize_acqf to find the point that maximizes the acquisition score, which is the posterior mean of the objective function (we first learned about this helper function in section 4.2.2):

```
final_x, _ = optimize_acqf(
    post_mean_policy,
    bounds=bounds,
    q=1,
    num_restarts=20,
    raw_samples=50,
)
```

Optimize the posterior mean.
The other arguments are the same as when we optimize another policy.

This final_x variable is the location that maximizes the posterior mean of the objective function. In our Jupyter notebook, we put this code in a helper function that returns final_x, augmented with a correlation value of 1, indicating the true objective function:

```
def get_final_recommendation(model):
    post_mean_policy = FixedFeatureAcquisitionFunction(...)
    final_x, _ = optimize_acqf(...)

    return torch.cat([final_x, torch.ones(1, 1)], dim=1)
```

Makes the wrapper policy
Optimizes the acquisition score
Augments the final recommendation with a correlation value of 1

Now, during the BayesOpt loop, instead of recording the incumbent value as an indication of optimization progress, we call this get_final_recommendation helper function. Further, instead of a maximum number of queries to be made in each run, we now have a maximum budget, which can be spent on either low- or high-fidelity queries. In other words, we keep running our optimization algorithm until the cumulative cost exceeds our budget limit. The skeleton of our multifidelity BayesOpt loop is as follows:

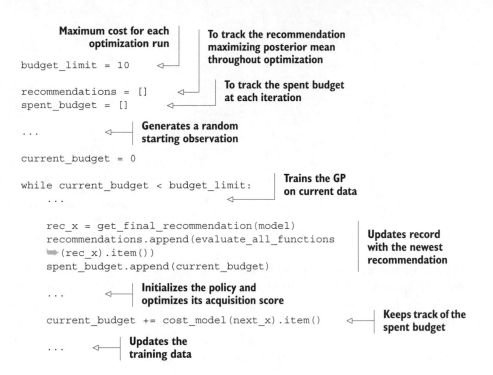

We are now ready to run multifidelity MES to optimize the Forrester objective function. As a benchmark, we will also run the single-fidelity MES policy, which only queries the ground truth $f(x)$. The GP model we have is a multifidelity one, so to run a single-fidelity BayesOpt policy with this model, we need a wrapper policy of the `FixedFeatureAcquisitionFunction` class to restrict the fidelity the policy can query:

```
policy = FixedFeatureAcquisitionFunction(
    acq_function=qMaxValueEntropy(model, candidate_x, num_fantasies=128),  ◁─┐
    d=2,
    columns=[1],    Fixes the correlation value in the     The wrapped policy is
    values=[1],     second column (index 1) at 1           the single-fidelity MES.
)

next_x, acq_val = optimize_acqf(...)    ◁─┤ Optimizes the acquisition score using
                                           the helper function optimize_acqf
```

Running the two policies generates the result in figure 9.14, where we observe that multifidelity MES greatly outperforms the single-fidelity version. The cost-effectiveness of multifidelity MES illustrates the benefit of balancing between information and cost. However, we note that this is only the result of a single run; in exercise 1, we run this experiment multiple times with different initial datasets and observe the average performance of these policies.

In this chapter, we have learned about the problem of multifidelity optimization, in which we balance optimizing the objective function with the cost of gaining knowledge

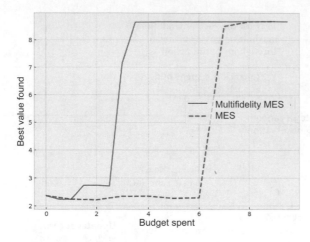

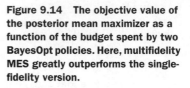

Figure 9.14 The objective value of the posterior mean maximizer as a function of the budget spent by two BayesOpt policies. Here, multifidelity MES greatly outperforms the single-fidelity version.

about the objective. We learned how to implement a GP model that can learn from multiple sources of data. This model then allowed us to reason about the information-theoretic value of making a query in terms of locating the optimal value of the objective. By combining this information-theoretic quantity with the querying cost in a return-on-investment measure, we devised a cost-aware, multifidelity variant of the MES policy that can trade off knowledge and cost automatically.

9.5 *Exercise 1: Visualizing average performance in multifidelity optimization*

To compare the performance of our policies, figure 9.14 visualizes the objective value of the posterior mean maximizer throughout optimization against the amount of budget spent. However, this is the result from just one optimization run, and we'd like to show the average performance by each policy from multiple experiments. (We first discussed the idea of repeated experiments in exercise 2 of chapter 4.) In this exercise, we run the optimization loop multiple times and learn how to take the average performance to obtain a more holistic comparison. By the end of the exercise, we will see that multifidelity MES balances well between information and cost and optimizes the objective function more effectively than its single-fidelity counterpart. The solution is stored in the CH09/04 - Exercise 1.ipynb notebook.

Take the following steps:

1 Copy the problem setup and the multifidelity optimization loop from the CH09/03 - Measuring performance.ipynb notebook, and add another variable denoting the number of experiments we want to run (10, by default).

2 To facilitate repeated experiments, add an outer loop to the optimization loop code. This should be a `for` loop with 10 iterations where a different random observation is generated each time. (This random generation could be done by setting PyTorch's random seed to the iteration number, which ensures the

random number generator returns the same data across different runs with the same seed.)

3 The code in the CH09/03 - Measuring performance.ipynb notebook uses two lists, `recommendations` and `spent_budget`, to keep track of optimization progress. Make each of these variables a list of lists where each inner-list serves the same purpose as the corresponding list in the CH09/03 - Measuring performance.ipynb notebook. These lists of lists allow us to keep track of optimization progress over the 10 experiments and compare different optimization policies in later steps.

4 Run the multifidelity MES policy and its single-fidelity version on our optimization problem.

5 Since the cost of querying the low-fidelity function is different from that of querying the high-fidelity function, it's likely that the lists in `spend_budget` don't exactly match with each other. In other words, the points in the curves in figure 9.14 don't have the same x-coordinates across the runs. This mismatch prevents us from taking the average progress stored in `recommendations` across the multiple runs.

   To address this problem, we use a linear interpolation for each progress curve, which allows us to "fill in" the progress values on a regular grid. It is on this regular grid that we will average out the performance of each policy across runs. For the linear interpolation, use `np.interp` from NumPy, which takes in a regular grid as its first argument; this grid can be an array of integers between 0 and `budget_limit`: `np.arange(budget_limit)`. The second and third arguments are the x- and y-coordinates of the points making up each progress curve—that is, each inner-list in `spend_budget` and `recommendations`.

6 Use the linearly interpolated values to plot the average performance and error bars of the two policies we ran, and compare their performance.

7 Due to the way we're currently measuring optimization performance, it's possible that the list of recommendations we keep track of throughout each run is not monotonically increasing. (That is, we might end up with a recommendation that performs worse than the previous iteration's recommendation.) To inspect this phenomenon, we can plot the linearly interpolated curves representing individual runs' optimization progress, along with the average performance and error bars. Implement this visualization for the two policies we ran, and inspect the nonmonotonicity of the resulting curves.

9.6 Exercise 2: Multifidelity optimization with multiple low-fidelity approximations

The approach we learned in this chapter can generalize to scenarios where there is more than one low-fidelity approximation to the objective function that we can query. Our strategy is the same: divide the amount of information we gain from each query by its cost, and then pick the query that gives the highest return on investment. This exercise shows us that our multifidelity MES policy can balance between multiple low-fidelity functions. The solution is stored in the CH09/05 - Exercise 2.ipynb notebook.

Take the following steps:

1 For our objective function, we use the two-dimensional function named `Branin`, which is a common test function for optimization, like the Forrester function. BoTorch comes with a multifidelity version of Branin, so we import it to our code with `from botorch.test_functions.multi_fidelity import Augmented-Branin`. For convenience, we scale the domain and output of this function using the following code, which makes `objective` the function to call when we evaluate a query:

```
problem = AugmentedBranin()        ⟵─┤  Imports the Branin
                                        function from BoTorch

def objective(X):
    X_copy = X.detach().clone()
    X_copy[..., :-1] = X_copy[..., :-1] * 15 - 5
    X_copy[..., -2] = X_copy[..., -2] + 5
    return (-problem(X_copy) / 500 + 0.9).unsqueeze(-1)
```

Processes the input and output of the function, mapping the values to a nice range (annotation for code above)

2 Define the bounds of our search space to be the unit square. That is, the two lower bounds are 0, and the two upper bounds are 1.
3 Declare the `fidelities` variable that stores the correlation values of the different functions we can query. Here, we have access to two low-fidelity approximations with correlation values of 0.1 and 0.3, so `fidelities` should contain these two numbers and 1 as the last element.

The three functions are visualized in figure 9.15, where bright pixels denote high objective values. We see that both low-fidelity approximations follow the general trend exhibited by the ground truth, and the resemblance to the ground truth increases with the fidelity value. That is, the second approximation with

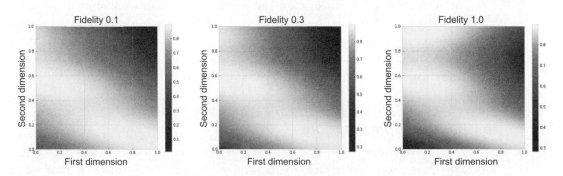

Figure 9.15   The objective function Branin (right) and two low-fidelity approximations

fidelity 0.3 (middle) is more similar to the true objective function (right) than the first approximation with fidelity 0.1 (left).

4 Set the fixed cost of the linear cost model to 0.2 and the weight to 1. This means the cost of querying the low-fidelity function on the left of figure 9.15 is $0.2 + 1 \times 0.1 = 0.3$. Similarly, the cost of querying the middle function is 0.5, and that of querying the true objective function is 1.2. Set the limit of our budget in each experiment to 10 and the number of repeated experiments to 10 as well.

5 Set the number of candidates drawn from the Sobol sequence to 5,000, and use 100 restarts and 500 raw samples when using helper functions to optimize the acquisition score of a given policy.

6 Redefine the helper function `get_final_recommendation` that finds the posterior mean maximizer so that the arguments are appropriately set for our two-dimensional objective function: `d = 3` and `columns = [2]`.

7 Run the multifidelity Max-value Entropy Search policy and its single-fidelity version on the optimization problem, and plot the average optimization progress and error bars of each policy using the method described in exercise 1. Note that when creating the wrapper policy for the single-fidelity policy, the arguments `d` and `columns` need to be set in the same way as in the previous step. Verify that the multifidelity policy performs better than the single-fidelity one.

Summary

- Multifidelity optimization is an optimization setting in which we have access to multiple sources of information, each with its own level of accuracy and cost. In this setting, we need to balance the amount of information gained from taking an action and the cost of taking that action.
- In multifidelity optimization, a high-fidelity function offers exact information but is costly to evaluate, while a low-fidelity function is inexpensive to query but might give inexact information. At each iteration of the optimization loop, we need to decide where and which function to query to find the objective function's optimum as quickly as possible.
- The level of information each fidelity provides is quantified by the correlation between itself and the ground truth, which is a number between 0 and 1. The higher the correlation, the more closely the fidelity matches the ground truth. In Python, we store the correlation value of each data point as an extra column in the feature matrix.
- A GP with a kernel that can process the correlation values of the training data points can be trained on a multifidelity dataset; we can use the multifidelity variant of the Matérn kernel for this task. The uncertainty in the predictions of the GP depends on which function each observation comes from and, if it comes from a low-fidelity function, what the correlation value of that function is.

- We use a linear model to encode the querying cost of each fidelity we have access to during optimization. By setting the parameters of this model—the fixed cost and the weight—we can model the positively correlated relationship between querying cost and the quality of the data. Nonlinear cost models can also be implemented using BoTorch.

- To balance between informativeness and cost, we use a variant of the MES policy that weights the amount of information resulting from each query by the inverse of the querying cost. This measure is analogous to the return-on-investment concept in economics and is implemented with the `InverseCost-WeightedUtility` class from BoTorch.

- Exact calculation of information gain for the objective function's optimal value, the core task of MES, is intractable due to the non-Gaussian distribution of the optimal value. To approximate the information gain, we use a Sobol sequence to represent the entire search space, alleviating the computational burden in the calculation.

- The multifidelity MES policy successfully balances information and cost and prioritizes cost-effective queries.

- To optimize the acquisition score of a multifidelity policy, we use the `optimize_acqf_mixed` helper function, which can work with a mixed search space whose dimensions can be either continuous or discrete.

- To accurately measure performance in the multifidelity setting, we use the maximizer of the posterior mean at each iteration as a final recommendation before termination. This quantity captures what we know about the objective function better than the high-fidelity incumbent value.

- To optimize a single-fidelity acquisition score in a multifidelity setting, we use a wrapper policy that is an instance of the `FixedFeatureAcquisitionFunction` class. To initialize a wrapper policy, we declare which dimension in the search space is fixed and at what value.

Learning from pairwise comparisons with preference optimization

This chapter covers

- The problem of learning about and optimizing preferences using only pairwise comparison data
- Training a GP on pairwise comparisons
- Optimization policies for pairwise comparisons

Have you ever found it difficult to rate something (food, a product, or an experience) on an exact scale? Asking for the customer's numerical score for a product is a common task in A/B testing and product recommendation workflows.

DEFINITION The term *A/B testing* refers to the method of measuring a user's experience in two environments (referred to as *A* and *B*) via randomized experiments and determining which environment is more desirable. A/B testing is commonly conducted by technology companies.

A/B testers and product recommendation engineers often have to deal with a high level of noise in the feedback collected from their customers. By *noise*, we mean any type of corruption that the feedback collected from customers is subject to. Example sources of noise in product rating include the number of advertisements served on an online streaming service, the quality of the delivery service for a package, or the general mood of the customer when they consume a product. These factors affect how the customer rates their product, potentially corrupting the signal that is the customer's true evaluation of the product.

Uncontrollable external factors make it hard for the customer to report their true evaluation of a product. Customers, therefore, often find it hard to choose a numerical score as their evaluation of a product when rating on a scale. The prevalence of feedback noise in A/B testing and product recommendation means a service platform cannot rely on a few data points collected from their users to learn about their preferences. Instead, the platform needs to collect more data from the customers to become more certain about what the customers truly want.

However, just as in other settings of black box optimization, such as hyperparameter tuning and drug discovery, querying the objective function is expensive. In product recommendation, every time we query a customer asking for their rating of a product, we run the risk of intruding on the customer's experience and discouraging them from continuing to use the platform. Hence, there's a natural tension between the need for a large amount of data to better learn customers' preferences and being intrusive, potentially leading to a loss of customers.

Luckily, there's a way around this problem. Research in the field of psychology (http://mng.bz/0KOl) has found the intuitive result that we humans are much better at giving preference-based responses in the form of pairwise comparisons (e.g., "product A is better than product B") than rating products on a scale (e.g., "product A is an 8 out of 10").

> **DEFINITION** A *pairwise comparison* is a method of collecting preference data. Each time we want to elicit information about a customer's preference, we ask the customer to pick (from two items) the item they prefer. Pairwise comparisons are different from numerical ratings, where we ask the customer to rate an item on a scale.

The reason for the difference in difficulty between pairwise comparisons and ratings is that comparing two items is a less cognitively demanding task, and we, therefore, can compare two objects while being consistent with our true preference better than we can provide numerical ratings. In figure 10.1, consider two example interfaces of an online shopping site that is trying to learn about your preference for Hawaiian shirts:

- The first interface asks you to rate the shirt on the scale from 1 to 10. This can be difficult to do, especially if you don't have a frame of reference.
- The second interface asks you to instead pick the shirt that you like better. This task is easier to complete.

Given the potential of high-quality data we can collect using pairwise comparisons, we'd like to apply this preference elicitation technique to BayesOpt of a user's preference. The question becomes, "How can we train a ML model on pairwise comparison data, and afterwards, how should we present new comparisons to the user to best learn and optimize their preference?" We answer these questions in this chapter,

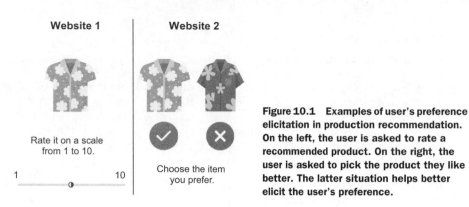

Website 1

Rate it on a scale
from 1 to 10.

1   10

Website 2

Choose the item
you prefer.

Figure 10.1   Examples of user's preference elicitation in production recommendation. On the left, the user is asked to rate a recommended product. On the right, the user is asked to pick the product they like better. The latter situation helps better elicit the user's preference.

first by using a GP model that can effectively learn from pairwise comparisons. We then develop strategies that pit the best data point (representing a product) we have found so far against a promising rival, allowing us to optimize the user's preference as quickly as possible. In other words, we assume the user's preference is the objective function defined over a search space, and we'd like to optimize this objective function.

This setting of learning and optimizing a user's preference from pairwise comparisons is a unique task that lies at the intersection of black box optimization and product recommendation and has been gaining interest in both communities. By the end of this chapter, we learn how to approach this problem from the BayesOpt, trading off exploitation and exploration as we collect data from the user.

10.1   *Black-box optimization with pairwise comparisons*

In this section, we further discuss the usefulness of pairwise comparisons in the task of eliciting preference. We then examine the BayesOpt loop that is modified for this preference-based optimization setting.

In addition to exact numerical evaluations as ratings, pairwise comparisons offer a method of collecting information about a customer in a production recommendation application. Compared to numerical ratings, pairwise comparisons pose less of a cognitive burden on the user and are, therefore, likely to result in higher-quality data (feedback that is consistent with the user's true preference).

Pairwise comparisons in multiobjective optimization

A setting where pairwise comparisons are particularly useful is decision-making when multiple criteria need to be considered. For example, say you are looking to buy a car and are choosing between car A and car B. To make your decision, you list out the different characteristics you care about in a car: appearance, practicality, energy efficiency, cost, and so on. You then score both cars on each of these criteria, hoping to find a clear winner. Unfortunately, car A scores higher than car B on some of the criteria but not all, and car B scores higher than car A on the rest of the criteria.

(continued)

So, there's no clear winner between the two cars, and combining the scores for the different criteria into a single score could be difficult. You care about some criteria more than others, so those criteria that you care about more need to be weighted more heavily when being combined with the other criteria to produce a single number. However, working out the exact values for these weights could pose an even greater challenge than choosing between the two cars themselves! It can be much easier to ignore the specifics, view each car as a whole, and compare the two cars "head-to-head."

The ease of using pairwise comparisons has, therefore, been exploited in optimization situations where there are multiple criteria to be considered. For example, a research project by Edward Abel, Ludmil Mikhailov, and John Keane (http://mng.bz/KenZ) used pairwise comparisons to tackle group decision-making.

Of course, pairwise comparisons are not objectively better than numerical evaluations. While the former are easier to elicit from users, they contain considerably less information than the latter. The response that you like the orange shirt better than the red shirt in figure 10.1 contains exactly one bit of information (the outcome of the comparison is binary; either orange is better than red or red is better than orange, so observing the outcome information theoretically constitutes gaining one bit of information). Meanwhile, if you were to report that you rate the orange shirt 8 out of 10 and the red 6 out of 10, we would have much more information than simply knowing that orange is valued more highly than red.

In other words, there's always a tradeoff in choosing the method of eliciting feedback from users. Numerical evaluations contain more information, but they are prone to noise and can place a larger cognitive burden on the user. Pairwise comparisons, on the other hand, offer less information but are easier for the user to report. These pros and cons are summarized in figure 10.2.

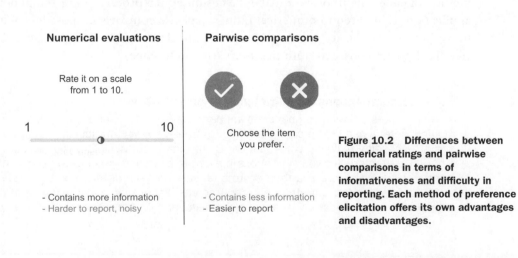

Numerical evaluations

Rate it on a scale from 1 to 10.

1   10

- Contains more information
- Harder to report, noisy

Pairwise comparisons

Choose the item you prefer.

- Contains less information
- Easier to report

Figure 10.2   **Differences between numerical ratings and pairwise comparisons in terms of informativeness and difficulty in reporting. Each method of preference elicitation offers its own advantages and disadvantages.**

Keeping the tradeoff between information and difficulty of reporting in mind, we should stick to numerical evaluations if we are willing to ask users to complete a more cognitively demanding task to gain more information and if we can account for noise. On the other hand, if we place more importance on having customers accurately express their true preferences and are willing to gain less information, pairwise comparisons should be our method of choice to elicit customers' feedback.

> **Other ways of eliciting customers' preferences**
>
> Pairwise comparisons are not the only form of relieving the cognitive burden of numerical evaluations. For example, the online streaming service Netflix collects viewers' ratings by asking them to choose between three options: "thumbs down" to indicate they dislike something, "thumbs up" to indicate they like something, and "double thumbs up" to indicate they *love* something (http://mng.bz/XNgl). This setting constitutes an ordinal classification problem in which items are classified into different categories and there's an inherent order among the categories. The production recommendation problem in this setting is just as interesting to consider, but we keep our focus on pairwise comparisons in this chapter.

In this chapter, we learn how to facilitate the task of using pairwise comparisons to learn and optimize a customer's preference using BayesOpt. First, we examine a modified version of the BayesOpt loop we saw in figure 1.6, as shown in figure 10.3:

1 In step 1, the GP is trained on pairwise comparison data instead of numerical evaluations. The key challenge is to ensure that the GP belief about the objective function (the user's true preference function) reflects information in the observed comparisons.

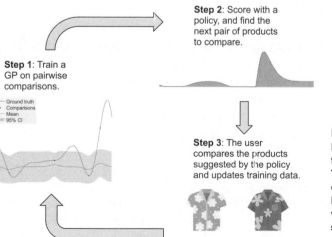

Step 1: Train a GP on pairwise comparisons.

Step 2: Score with a policy, and find the next pair of products to compare.

Step 3: The user compares the products suggested by the policy and updates training data.

Product A   Product B

Figure 10.3 The BayesOpt loop with pairwise comparisons for preference optimization. The GP trains on pairwise comparison data, and the BayesOpt policy decides which pair of data points it should ask the user to compare.

2 In step 2, the BayesOpt policy computes acquisition scores to quantify how useful each potential new query to the user is. A query to the user needs to come in the form of a pair of products for the user to compare. Just as in other settings, the policy needs to balance exploiting a region where we know the user's preference is high and exploring other regions where we don't know a lot about the user's preference.

3 In step 3, the user compares the two products presented to them by the BayesOpt policy and reports the product they prefer. This new information is then added to our training set.

We seek to address two main questions in the remainder of this chapter:

1 How can we train a GP only on pairwise comparisons? A GP, when trained on numerical responses, produces probabilistic predictions with quantified uncertainty, which is crucial in decision-making. Can we use the same model here with pairwise comparison responses?

2 How should we generate new product pairs for the user to compare so as to identify the maximizer of the user's preference as quickly as possible? That is, how do we best elicit the user's feedback using pairwise comparisons to optimize their preference?

10.2 Formulating a preference optimization problem and formatting pairwise comparison data

Before we start tackling these questions, this section introduces the product recommendation problem we'll be solving throughout the chapter and how we simulate the problem in Python. Setting up the problem properly will help us more easily integrate the BayesOpt tools we will learn about in subsequent sections. The code we use here is included in the first portion of the CH10/01 - Learning from pairwise comparisons.ipynb Jupyter notebook.

As hinted at in figures 10.1 and 10.3, the scenario we're in is a product recommendation problem for Hawaiian shirts. That is, imagine we run an online shopping site for Hawaiian shirts, and we are trying to determine the product that maximizes the preference of a specific customer who is currently shopping for a shirt.

For simplicity's sake, let's assume that after a brief survey, we learn that the factor that matters the most to the customer is the number of flowers printed on the shirt. Other factors, such as style and color, matter too, but the most important thing about a Hawaiian shirt to this customer is how floral the shirt is. Further, assume we have many Hawaiian shirts in our stock with varying numbers of flowers, so we can roughly find a shirt with any given specified degree of "floral-ness." So our goal is to find the shirt with the optimal number of flowers, which is unknown to us, with respect to the customer's preference. We conduct this search in a one-dimensional search space, where the lower bound of the space corresponds to shirts without floral patterns and the upper bound of the space contains shirts covered in flowers.

Figure 10.4 visualizes our setup in more detail. In the top portion, the figure shows the customer's true preference and how it changes with respect to how floral a shirt is:

- The *x*-axis indicates the number of flowers a shirt has. On one end of the spectrum, we have shirts without any flowers; on the other are shirts covered in flowers.
- The *y*-axis is the customer's preference for each shirt. The higher the customer's preference for a shirt, the more the customer likes the shirt.

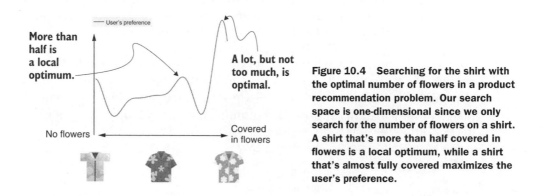

Figure 10.4   Searching for the shirt with the optimal number of flowers in a product recommendation problem. Our search space is one-dimensional since we only search for the number of flowers on a shirt. A shirt that's more than half covered in flowers is a local optimum, while a shirt that's almost fully covered maximizes the user's preference.

We see that this customer likes floral shirts: there's a local optimum in preference past the middle point of the shirt, and the global optimum of the preference function is located near the upper bound of the search space. This means that a shirt that has a lot of flowers but is not completely covered in them maximizes the customer's preference.

Since what we have is a black box optimization problem, the customer's preference curve in figure 10.4 is actually inaccessible to us in the real world, and we need to learn about this preference function using pairwise comparisons and optimize it as quickly as possible. Now, let's see how we can set up this optimization problem in Python.

You might have already noticed that we are using the Forrester function used in previous chapters to simulate the objective function, the customer's true preference, in figure 10.4. As a result, the code for this function doesn't change from what we had in other chapters, which is the following formula, defined as between –5 and 5, the lower and upper bounds of our search space:

```
def objective(x):
    y = -((x + 1) ** 2) * torch.sin(2 * x + 2) /
    ➡5 + 1 + x / 3
    return y
```
The objective function

```
lb = -5
ub = 5
bounds = torch.tensor([[lb], [ub]], dtype=torch.float)
```
The bounds of the search space

Remember from previous chapters that where the labels of our data have numerical values, each data point in the training set, stored in variable `train_x`, has a corresponding label in `train_y`. Our current setting is a little different. As our data is in the form of pairwise comparisons, each observation results from comparing two data points in `train_x`, and the label of the observation indicates which data point is valued more by the customer.

> **NOTE**   We follow BoTorch's convention to encode the result of each pairwise comparison between two data points in `train_x` as a PyTorch tensor of two elements: the first is the index of the data point that is preferred within `train_x`, and the second is the index of the data point not preferred.

For example, say that based on two queries to the user, we know that the user prefers $x = 0$ to $x = 3$ (that is, $f(0) > f(3)$, where $f(x)$ is the objective function), and the user also prefers $x = 0$ to $x = -4$ (so $f(0) > f(-4)$). A way for us to represent these two pieces of information expressed as a training data set is with `train_x` having the following values:

```
                Represents x = 0
tensor([[ 0.],   ←──┘   Represents x = 3
        [ 3.],    ←──────┘
        [-4.]])    ←──────┘   Represents x = −4
```

These values are the three *x* values we have used to query the user. The training labels `train_comp`, on the other hand, should be

```
tensor([[0, 1],   ←──┘   Represents f(0) > f(3)
        [0, 2]])   ←────┐   Represents f(0) > f(−4)
```

Each row in `train_comp` is a two-element tensor representing the result of a pairwise comparison. In the first row, `[0, 1]` says that the data point with index `0` in `train_x`, which is $x = 0$, is preferred to the point with index `1`, which is $x = 3$. Similarly, the second row `[0, 2]` encodes the comparison that $f(0) > f(-4)$.

To help streamline the process of comparing any pair of data points within our search space, we write a helper function that takes in the objective values of any two data points and returns `[0, 1]` if the first objective value is the greater of the two and `[1, 0]` otherwise:

```
def compare(y):
    assert y.numel() == 2     ←── Makes sure we only
                                  have two objective
                                  values to compare

    if y.flatten()[0] > y.flatten()[1]:     ── If the first value
        return torch.tensor([[0, 1]]).long()    is greater
    else:                                    ── If the second
        return torch.tensor([[1, 0]]).long()    value is greater
```

Let's use this function to generate a sample training set. We first randomly draw two data points within our search space:

```
torch.manual_seed(0)                          ◄── Fixes the random seed
                                                  for reproducibility
train_x = bounds[0] + (bounds[1] - bounds[0]) * torch.rand(2, 1)   ◄──┐
                                              Draws two numbers between 0 and 1 and
                                                  scales them to our search space
```

The variable `train_x` here contains the following two points:

```
tensor([[-0.0374],
        [ 2.6822]])
```

Now, we obtain the result of the comparison between these two points by evaluating the user's true preference function and calling `compare()`:

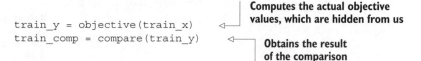

```
train_y = objective(train_x)      ◄── Computes the actual objective
                                      values, which are hidden from us
train_comp = compare(train_y)     ◄── Obtains the result
                                      of the comparison
```

The result of the comparison between the objective values of the data points in `train_x` is stored in `train_comp`, which is

```
tensor([[0, 1]])
```

This result means the first data point in `train_x` is valued by the customer more than the second point.

We also write another helper function named `observe_and_append_data()` whose role is to take in a pair of data points, compare them, and add the result of the comparison to a running training set:

1   The function first calls the helper function `compare()` to obtain either `[0, 1]` or `[1, 0]` and then adjusts the values of the indices stored in the two-element tensor so that the indices point to the correct locations of the data points in the training set:

```
def observe_and_append_data(x_next, f, x_train, comp_train, tol=1e-3):
    x_next = x_next.to(x_train)       Evaluates the
    y_next = f(x_next)                comparison according
    comp_next = compare(y_next)       to the user's preference

    n = x_train.shape[-2]
    new_x_train = x_train.clone()            Keeps track
    new_comp_next = comp_next.clone() + n    of the indices
```

2   The function also checks for data points within the training set that are close enough to each other to be considered the same point (e.g., $x = 1$ and $x = 1.001$).

These very similar data points can cause the training of the preference-based GP we learn in the next section to become numerically unstable. Our solution is to flag these similar data points, treat them as duplicates, and remove one of them:

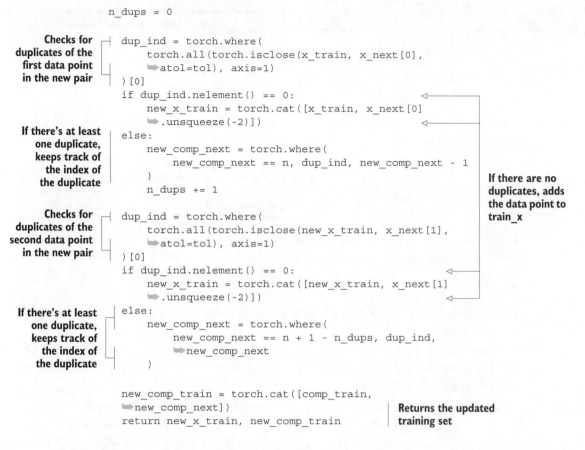

```
n_dups = 0

                        dup_ind = torch.where(
Checks for                  torch.all(torch.isclose(x_train, x_next[0],
duplicates of the           ➥atol=tol), axis=1)
first data point        )[0]
in the new pair         if dup_ind.nelement() == 0:                          ◁
                            new_x_train = torch.cat([[x_train, x_next[0]
                            ➥.unsqueeze(-2)])                               ◁
If there's at least     else:
one duplicate,              new_comp_next = torch.where(
keeps track of                 new_comp_next == n, dup_ind, new_comp_next - 1
the index of               )
the duplicate              n_dups += 1                                           If there are no
                                                                                 duplicates, adds
                        dup_ind = torch.where(                                   the data point to
Checks for                  torch.all(torch.isclose(new_x_train, x_next[1],      train_x
duplicates of the           ➥atol=tol), axis=1)
second data point       )[0]
in the new pair         if dup_ind.nelement() == 0:                          ◁
                            new_x_train = torch.cat([new_x_train, x_next[1]
                            ➥.unsqueeze(-2)])                               ◁
If there's at least     else:
one duplicate,             new_comp_next = torch.where(
keeps track of                 new_comp_next == n + 1 - n_dups, dup_ind,
the index of                   ➥new_comp_next
the duplicate              )

                        new_comp_train = torch.cat([comp_train,
                        ➥new_comp_next])                               Returns the updated
                        return new_x_train, new_comp_train            training set
```

We make use of these two helper functions in our downstream tasks of training GPs and optimizing the user's preference function, the first of which we explore in the next section.

10.3   *Training a preference-based GP*

We continue to use the code in the CH10/01 - Learning from pairwise comparisons.ipynb notebook to implement our GP model in this section.

We learned in section 2.2.2 that under the Bayesian update rule (which allows us to update our belief in light of data), we can obtain the exact posterior form of an MVN distribution, given that we have observed the values of some of the variables. This ability to compute a posterior MVN distribution exactly is the basis for updating a

GP in light of new observations. Unfortunately, this exact update is only applicable under numerical observations. That is, we can only exactly update a GP with observations in the form of $y = f(x)$, where x and y are real-valued numbers.

Under our current setting, observations come in the form of pairwise comparisons, and the posterior form of a GP when conditioned on this type of preference-based data is *not* a GP anymore, which rules out most of the methods we have developed in this book that rely on the fact that our predictive model is a GP. However, this doesn't mean we have to abandon the entire project.

> ### Approximating the posterior GP under pairwise comparisons
> A common theme in ML (and computer science, in general) is trying to approximately solve a task when we can't accomplish it exactly. Within our context, this approximation equates to finding a posterior form for our GP that gives the highest likelihood for the observed pairwise comparisons. The interested reader can find more details about this approach in the research paper by Wei Chu and Zoubin Ghahramani that proposed it: http://mng.bz/9Dmo.

Of course, the distribution that truly maximizes the likelihood of the data is a non-GP posterior distribution. But as we'd like to have a GP as our predictive model, enabling the BayesOpt policies we have learned, our goal is to find the GP with the highest data likelihood. Note that finding the GP maximizing the likelihood of the data is also what we do when we train a GP: we find the best hyperparameters for the GP (e.g., length scale and output scale) that maximize the data likelihood. (See section 3.3.2, where we first discuss this method.)

In terms of implementation, we can initialize and train a GP on pairwise comparisons using the following code:

- BoTorch provides a special class implementation for this GP model named `PairwiseGP`, which can be imported from the `botorch.models.pairwise_gp` module.

- The likelihood of pairwise comparison data requires a different computation from that of the likelihood of real-valued data. For this computation, we use `PairwiseLaplaceMarginalLogLikelihood`, imported from the same module as the class implementation.

- To be able to visualize and inspect the predictions made by the GP, we fix its output scale so that it retains its default value of 1 during training. We do this by disabling its gradient with `model.covar_module.raw_outputscale.requires_grad_(False)`. This step is only for visualization purposes and is, therefore, optional; we won't do this when running our optimization policies later in the chapter.

- Finally, we use the helper function `fit_gpytorch_mll` from `botorch.fit` to obtain the posterior GP that maximizes the likelihood of our training data:

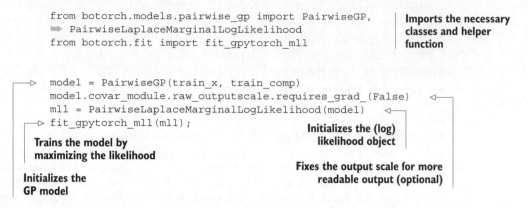

```
from botorch.models.pairwise_gp import PairwiseGP,     |  Imports the necessary
➥  PairwiseLaplaceMarginalLogLikelihood              |  classes and helper
from botorch.fit import fit_gpytorch_mll               |  function
```

```
model = PairwiseGP(train_x, train_comp)
model.covar_module.raw_outputscale.requires_grad_(False)
mll = PairwiseLaplaceMarginalLogLikelihood(model)
fit_gpytorch_mll(mll);
```

Trains the model by
maximizing the likelihood

Initializes the (log)
likelihood object

Fixes the output scale for more
readable output (optional)

Initializes the
GP model

Using this trained GP model, we can now make and visualize predictions across our search space in figure 10.5. We note a few interesting points about these predictions:

- The mean predictions obey the relationship expressed in the training data that $f(-0.0374) > f(2.6822)$, in that the mean prediction at $x = -0.0374$ is greater than 0, while at $x = 2.6822$, it is less than 0.
- The uncertainty in our predictions at -0.0374 and 2.6822 is also lower than in the rest of the predictions. This difference in uncertainty reflects the fact that upon observing $f(-0.0374) > f(2.6822)$, we have gained some information about $f(-0.0374)$ and $f(2.6822)$, and our knowledge about these two objective values should increase.

  However, the uncertainty at these points doesn't significantly decrease to zero, as we see in settings where we train on numerical observations (e.g., in figure 2.14). This is because, as we remarked in section 10.1, pairwise comparisons don't offer as much information as numerical evaluations, so a significant level of uncertainty remains. Figure 10.5 shows that the GP we trained can effectively learn from a pairwise comparison where the mean function obeys the observed comparison and the uncertainty is well calibrated.

BoTorch warning when making predictions

You might encounter a warning from BoTorch similar to the following when making predictions with the GP we just trained:

```
NumericalWarning: A not p.d., added jitter of 1.0e-06 to the diagonal
  warnings.warn(
```

This warning indicates that the covariance matrix produced by the GP is not positive definite, causing numerical stability-related problems, and BoTorch has automatically added a "jitter" to the diagonal of the matrix as a fix, so we, the users, don't need to do anything further. Refer to section 5.3.2 for the instance in which we encounter this warning.

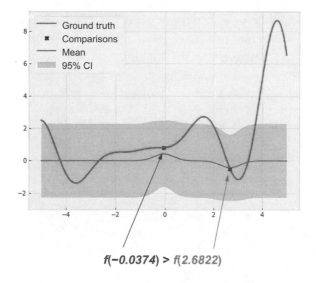

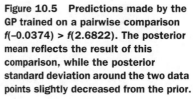

f(−0.0374) > f(2.6822)

Figure 10.5 **Predictions made by the GP trained on a pairwise comparison** f(−0.0374) > f(2.6822). **The posterior mean reflects the result of this comparison, while the posterior standard deviation around the two data points slightly decreased from the prior.**

To play around with this model further and see how it can learn from more complicated data, let's create a slightly larger training set. Specifically, say we'd like to train the GP on three individual comparisons: $f(0) > f(3)$, $f(0) > f(-4)$, and $f(4) > f(-0)$, all of which are true for the objective function we have in figure 10.5. To this end, we set our training data points stored in `train_x` as

```
train_x = torch.tensor([[0.], [3.], [-4.], [4.]])
```

This set contains all the data points involved in the preceding observed comparisons. Now, as for `train_comp`, we encode the three comparisons using two-element tensors in the way we discussed in section 10.2:

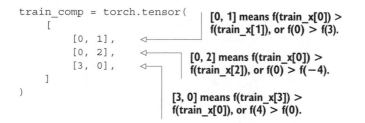

Now, we simply redeclare the GP and refit it on this new training data:

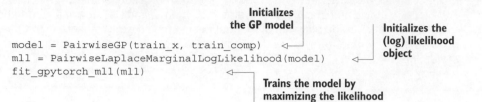

```
model = PairwiseGP(train_x, train_comp)
mll = PairwiseLaplaceMarginalLogLikelihood(model)
fit_gpytorch_mll(mll)
```

The GP model produces the predictions shown in figure 10.6, where we see that all three comparison results in the training data are reflected in the mean predictions, and uncertainty, once again, decreases around the training data points.

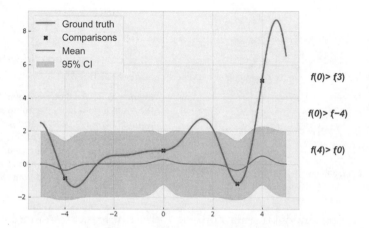

Figure 10.6   Predictions made by the GP trained on the pairwise comparisons are shown on the right. The posterior mean reflects the result of this comparison, while the posterior standard deviation around the data points in the training set decreased from the prior.

Figure 10.6 shows that our GP model can effectively train on pairwise comparison data. We now have a means to learn from preference-based data and make probabilistic predictions about the user's preference function. This leads us to the final topic of this chapter: decision-making in preference optimization. That is, how should we select data pairs to have the user compare them to find the most preferred data point as quickly as possible?

The range of the objective function in preference learning

An interesting advantage of training a GP on pairwise comparisons compared to doing so with numerical evaluations is that the range of the objective function doesn't need to be accounted for during training. This is because all we care about are the *relative comparisons* between objective values. In other words, learning about $f(x)$ is equivalent to learning about $f(x) + 5$, or $2 f(x)$, or $f(x) / 10$.

Meanwhile, when training a traditional GP with numerical evaluations, it's crucial to account for the range of the objective function because only by doing so can we have a model with a well-calibrated uncertainty quantification. (For example, to model an objective function that ranges from −1 to 1, an output scale that's equal to 1 is appropriate, while for an objective function that ranges from −10 to 10, we need a larger output scale.)

10.4   *Preference optimization by playing king of the hill*

In this section, we learn to apply BayesOpt to preference learning. The code we use is included in the CH10/02 - Optimizing preferences.ipynb notebook.

The question we need to address is how to select the best pair of data points, present them to the user, and ask for their preference to find the data point the user prefers the most. As with any BayesOpt optimization policy, our strategy needs to achieve a balance between exploitation (zeroing in on a region in the search space where we know the user's value is high) and exploration (inspecting the regions we don't know much about).

The BayesOpt policies we learned in chapters 4 through 6 effectively address this exploitation–exploration tradeoff using various heuristics. We will, therefore, develop a strategy to repurpose these policies for our preference-based setting. Remember that in previous chapters, a BayesOpt policy computes an acquisition score for each data point within the search space, quantifying the data point's value in helping us optimize the objective function. By finding the data point maximizing this acquisition score, we obtain the next point to evaluate the objective function with.

Using a BayesOpt policy to suggest pairwise comparisons

In our current preference-based setting, we need to present a pair of data points to the user for them to compare. At each iteration of the optimization loop, we assemble this pair with, first, the data point that maximizes the acquisition score of a given BayesOpt policy and, second, the best point we have seen so far.

The strategy we use resembles the popular children's game king of the hill, where at each iteration, we attempt to "beat" the best data point we have collected so far (the current "king of the hill"), using a challenger chosen by a BayesOpt policy, as illustrated in figure 10.7.

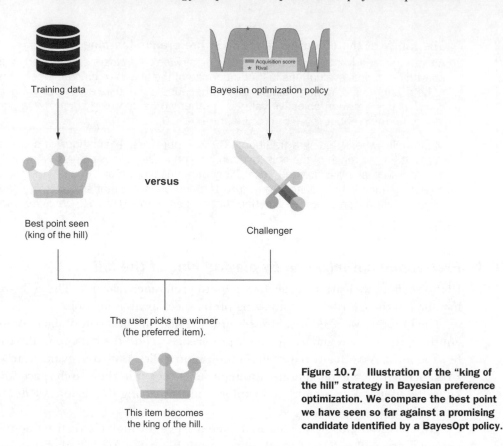

Figure 10.7   Illustration of the "king of the hill" strategy in Bayesian preference optimization. We compare the best point we have seen so far against a promising candidate identified by a BayesOpt policy.

By using this "king of the hill" strategy, we are outsourcing the task of constructing a pair of data points for the user to compare to a regular BayesOpt policy that can balance the exploitation–exploration tradeoff well and that we already know how to work with.

Code-wise, this strategy is straightforward to implement. We simply declare a BayesOpt policy object and optimize its acquisition score using the helper function `optimize_acqf()`. For example, the following code uses the Upper Confidence Bound (UCB) policy, which we learned about in section 5.2. The UCB policy uses upper bounds of the predictive normal distributions made by the GP as acquisition scores to quantify the value of inspecting a data point:

```
policy = UpperConfidenceBound(model, beta=2)     ◁——  Initializes the
                                                       BayesOpt policy

challenger, acq_val = optimize_acqf(
    policy,
    bounds=bounds,
    q=1,                            Finds the data
    num_restarts=50,                point maximizing
    raw_samples=100,                the acquisition
)                                   score
```

Another policy we use is Expected Improvement (EI), which we learned about in section 4.3. An attribute of EI that makes it suitable for our setting is that the motivation of the policy matches exactly with the "king of the hill" strategy we employ. That is, EI aims to search for data points that, on average, lead to the biggest improvement (in terms of the value of the objective function, our optimization goal) from the best point seen so far. Exceeding the best value found so far is exactly what the "king of the hill" strategy is all about. To implement EI in our setting, we use a different class implementation that can handle noisy observations, named `qNoisyExpectedImprovement`.

Noisy observations in BayesOpt

The term *noisy observations* in BayesOpt refers to the situation in which we suspect the labels we observe are corrupted by noise in the same way described in the beginning of this chapter.

As shown in figures 10.5 and 10.6, we still have substantial uncertainty in our GP predictions, even at locations included in our training data `train_x`. The noisy version of EI should be used here because this policy handles this type of uncertain prediction better than the regular EI policy. We implement noisy EI as follows:

```
policy = qNoisyExpectedImprovement(model, train_x)          ⟵  Initializes the
                                                               BayesOpt policy
challenger, acq_val = optimize_acqf(
    policy,
    bounds=bounds,             Finds the data
    q=1,                       point maximizing
    num_restarts=50,           the acquisition
    raw_samples=100,           score
)
```

As a point of comparison, let's also include a naïve strategy of picking the challenger for the best point seen so far uniformly at random within the search space:

```
challenger = bounds[0] + (bounds[1] - bounds[0]) * torch.rand(1, 1)    ⟵

                                    Picks a random point between 0 and 1 and
                                      scales the point to our search space
```

This random strategy serves as a benchmark to determine whether the BayesOpt policies we have can work better than random selection. With these policies in hand, we are now ready to run our BayesOpt loop to optimize a user's preference in our example problem. The code for this loop resembles what we used in previous chapters, except for the step where we present the pair of data points to the user for their feedback to append the result to our training set. This is done with the `observe_and_append_data()` helper function we wrote in section 10.2:

```
incumbent_ind = train_y.argmax()          ◁────────  Finds the best
                                                      point seen so far
next_x = torch.vstack([train_x[incumbent_ind,
   ➡:], challenger])

train_x, train_comp = observe_and_append_data(       Updates our
    next_x, objective, train_x, train_comp           training
)                                                     data
train_y = objective(train_x)
```

**Assembles the batch with the best point
and the point suggested by a policy**

In the code in the CH10/02 - Optimizing preferences.ipynb notebook, each BayesOpt run starts out with a randomly generated pair of data points and the feedback from the objective function comparing those two points. Each run then proceeds with 20 pairwise comparisons (that is, 20 queries to the user). We also repeat the experiment 10 times for each policy so that we can observe the aggregated performance of each strategy.

Figure 10.8 shows the average best value (and error bars) found by the optimization strategies we have. EI performs the best, consistently discovering the global optimum. Perhaps a large part of EI's success can be attributed to the agreement between our "king of the hill" method and the algorithmic motivation behind EI. More surprisingly, UCB fails to outperform the random strategy; perhaps a different value for the tradeoff parameter β can improve UCB's performance.

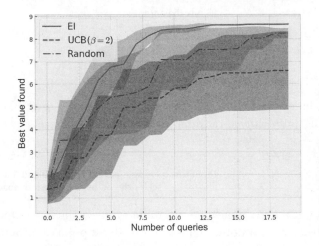

Figure 10.8   Optimization performance of various BayesOpt policies, aggregated across 10 experiments. EI performs the best, consistently discovering the global optimum. Surprisingly, UCB fails to outperform the random strategy.

NOTE   UCB's tradeoff parameter β directly controls how the policy balances between exploration and exploitation. Refer to section 5.2.2 for more discussion on this parameter.

In this chapter, we covered the problem of preference learning and optimization using pairwise comparisons. We learned about the motivation behind this particular method of data collection and the advantages it has over requiring users to report numerical evaluations. We then tackled the optimization problem using BayesOpt, first training a GP on pairwise comparisons using an approximate method. This GP model can effectively learn about the relations between data points expressed in the training set, while still offering a well-calibrated quantification of uncertainty. Finally, we learned to apply BayesOpt policies to this problem by pitting the best data point we have seen against the point recommended by a given BayesOpt policy. In the next chapter, we learn about a multiobjective variant of the black box optimization problem where there are multiple competing objective functions we need to balance during optimization.

Summary

- In production recommendation applications, comparing two items can help us obtain feedback that is more consistent with the user's true preference than ratings on a numerical scale. This is because the former poses a less cognitively demanding task.

- Pairwise comparisons contain less information than numerical evaluations, so there's a tradeoff between relieving the user's cognitive burden and obtaining information when choosing between the two methods of eliciting preference.

- A GP can be trained to maximize the likelihood of a dataset of pairwise comparisons. This model approximates the true posterior non-GP model when conditioned on pairwise comparison data.

- A GP trained on pairwise comparisons produces mean predictions consistent with the comparison results in the training set. In particular, the mean predictions at preferred locations are greater than the mean predictions at locations not preferred.

- The uncertainty of the GP trained on pairwise comparisons slightly decreases from the prior GP but doesn't collapse to zero, which appropriately reflects our uncertainty about the user's preference function because pairwise comparisons offer less information than numerical evaluations.

- A strategy for optimizing the user's preference using BayesOpt involves pitting the best data point found against the candidate recommended by a BayesOpt policy. The motivation of this strategy is to constantly try to improve from the best point we have found so far.

- The result of a pairwise comparison is represented as a two-element tensor in BoTorch where the first element is the index of the data point that is preferred within the training set, and the second element is the index of the data point not preferred.

- To use the EI policy in the optimization setting with pairwise comparisons, we use the noisy version of the policy that can handle high levels of uncertainty in the trained GP better than regular EI.

11
Optimizing multiple objectives at the same time

This chapter covers

- The problem of optimizing multiple objectives at the same time
- Training multiple GPs to learn about multiple objectives at the same time
- Jointly optimizing multiple objectives

Every day, we are faced with optimization tradeoffs:

- "This coffee tastes good, but there's too much sugar."
- "That shirt looks great, but it's out of my price range."
- "The neural network I just trained has a high accuracy, but it is too big and takes too long to train."

In an attempt to achieve a good performance on some objective, we sacrifice another criterion that's just as important: a coffee drinker with a sweet tooth might optimize the taste of their coffee while using an unhealthy amount of sugar; a shopper scores a clothing article high on looks and low on affordability; an ML engineer develops a neural network that has good predictive performance but is too large to be used in a real-time application. By focusing on one optimization objective, we might perform badly on another objective that needs to be accounted for. We should instead model *all* objective functions that are to be optimized into our optimization procedure and attempt to jointly optimize them all. For example, we should look for coffee recipes that are both tasty and low in sugar, clothing items that are both fashionable and affordable, or ML models that perform well and are practical to implement. This type of optimization problem is called *multiobjective optimization*.

> **DEFINITION** A multiobjective optimization problem, as the name suggests, involves multiple objective functions that are to be optimized *at the same time*. The goal is to find data points that achieve high values on all of the objectives.

Of course, in any nontrivial multiobjective optimization problem, we might have *competing* objectives, for which the only way to achieve good performance on one objective function is to sacrifice performance on another objective. This inherent conflict between optimization objectives gives rise to the need to balance these objectives (very much like the need to balance exploitation and exploration, discussed in section 4.1.2, which are the two "objectives" we need to optimize for inside the BayesOpt loop).

In this chapter, we learn about multiobjective optimization, how to successfully address it by finding data points whose performance on one objective cannot be improved without sacrificing another objective, and how to apply BayesOpt to this problem when the objective functions are expensive-to-query black boxes. Multiobjective optimization is a common problem across many fields, and by the end of this chapter, we add the ability to tackle this problem to our toolkit using Bayesian methods.

11.1 Balancing multiple optimization objectives with BayesOpt

Applications of multiobjective optimization are ubiquitous:

- In engineering and manufacturing, engineers often face a tradeoff between multiple objectives, such as the quality of a product versus the manufacturing cost. For example, car manufacturers are constantly optimizing their production line to maximize quality and minimize cost.
- In resource allocation problems, such as the distribution of monetary and medical aid across poor communities or to those affected by natural disasters, decision-makers need to balance having the largest effect on these communities and the various logistical difficulties in distribution.
- Similar to the examples of the cost-constrained optimization problem we discussed in section 8.1.1, scientists developing drugs to treat a certain disease need to balance maximizing effectiveness against the disease and minimizing side effects on patients.
- More relevant to ML engineers, a practical ML model that can be deployed in the real world needs to achieve good performance while maintaining a low training cost.

Unlike optimization settings discussed in previous chapters, we no longer have a single optimization objective to focus on. In many of these problems, the objectives we need to optimize are in conflict with each other: only by sacrificing our performance on one metric can we improve on another. One way to think about this inherent conflict between the optimization objectives is that we have to "juggle" the various objectives at the same time: we can't simply focus on certain objectives while ignoring the others. This need to juggle multiple objectives at the same time is visualized in figure 11.1. Fortunately, the fact that there is now more than one objective function doesn't affect most of the BayesOpt workflow we have developed throughout this book.

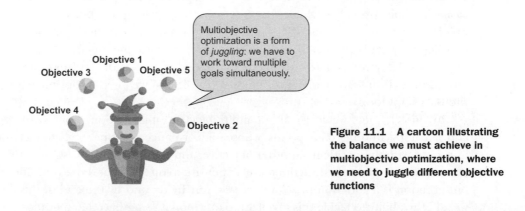

Figure 11.1   A cartoon illustrating the balance we must achieve in multiobjective optimization, where we need to juggle different objective functions

Modeling multiple objective functions using multiple GPs

In previous chapters, we trained a GP model on observed data to model our belief about the single objective function to be optimized. In this chapter, we have multiple objective functions to model, but each of these objectives can still be modeled as a GP. By maintaining these multiple GPs, we have a way to reason about all objective functions in a probabilistic manner.

Figure 11.2 shows the BayesOpt loop in which there are two objective functions to be optimized. Compared to figure 1.6, step 1 now has a GP for each of the objectives, and each data point identified by the BayesOpt policy is evaluated on all objective functions at step 3.

   Training a GP on data from each objective is straightforward to implement; in fact, we've already done this for constrained optimization in chapter 8, where we train one GP on the objective function and another on the constraint function. In other words, we only need to focus on the design of the BayesOpt policy in step 2 of figure 11.2 to help us make effective decisions during optimization. We focus on learning how the BayesOpt policy should address the balance between the multiple objectives so that we can find high-performing data points as quickly as possible in the rest of this chapter.

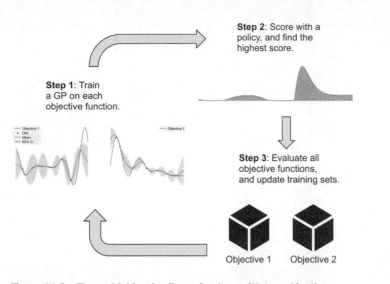

Figure 11.2   **The multiobjective BayesOpt loop with two objective functions. A GP trains on data from each objective function, and the BayesOpt policy decides which data point to evaluate the objective functions with next.**

11.2   *Finding the boundary of the most optimal data points*

In this section, we learn about mathematical concepts that are commonly used in multiobjective optimization to quantify how much progress we have made during optimization. These concepts help us establish the target of the optimization strategy we develop later in this chapter. To make our discussion concrete, we use the code in the CH11/01 - Computing hypervolume.ipynb notebook.

We start out with the two objective functions that we need to optimize at the same time:

- The first objective is the familiar Forrester function used in previous chapters. The global optimum of this objective function is located on the right side of the search space. This function is implemented as `objective1()` in the following code.

- We also have another objective function, implemented as `objective2()`, which has a different functional form and behavior from Forrester. Crucially, the global optimum of this objective is located on the left side of the search space—the mismatch in the locations of the global optima of the two objective functions simulates the tradeoff that is common in multiobjective optimization problems.

- We write a helper function `joint_objective()` that returns the values of the two objective functions in a PyTorch tensor for a given input data point x. This function helps keep our code concise.

- Finally, we define the search space of our optimization problem to be between −5 and 5:

```
def objective1(x):
    return -((x + 1) ** 2) * torch.sin(2 * x + 2)
    ⮕/ 5 + 1 + x / 20
```
The first objective function

```
def objective2(x):
    return (0.1 * objective1(x) + objective1(x - 4))
    ⮕/ 3 - x / 3 + 0.5
```
The second objective function

```
def joint_objective(x):
    y1 = objective1(x)
    y2 = objective2(x)
    return torch.vstack([y1.flatten(), y2.flatten()])
    ⮕.transpose(-1, -2)
```
The helper function that calls both objective functions

```
lb = -5
ub = 5
bounds = torch.tensor([[lb], [ub]], dtype=torch.float)
```
The bounds of the search space

Figure 11.3 shows these two objective functions in our search space. We see that the data points that maximize the two objectives are different from each other: the solid curve is maximized around $x = 4.5$, while the dashed curve is maximized around $x = -4.5$. This difference means that we have two conflicting objectives, and the joint optimization of these two functions requires trading off their objective values.

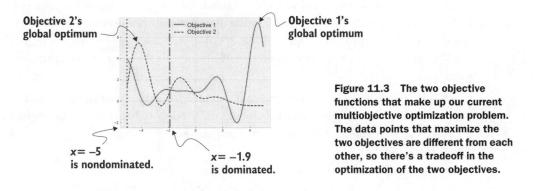

Objective 2's global optimum

Objective 1's global optimum

$x= -5$ is nondominated.

$x= -1.9$ is dominated.

Figure 11.3   The two objective functions that make up our current multiobjective optimization problem. The data points that maximize the two objectives are different from each other, so there's a tradeoff in the optimization of the two objectives.

By "trading off," we mean there exist points x in our search space whose values for the first objective (denoted as $f_1(x)$) cannot be improved unless their values for the second objective (denoted as $f_2(x)$) are lowered. In other words, there are data points that optimize one objective function in the sense that their values cannot be exceeded unless we sacrifice another objective function.

As an example, consider $x = -5$ as indicated in figure 11.3. This is the data point on the very far left of the search space. This point has an objective value $f_1(-5)$ of roughly 4 and an objective value $f_2(-5)$ of roughly 1.5. Now, $x = -5$ is one of the data points where, if we want to do better than 4 on the first objective $f_1(x)$, we will have to do worse than 1.5 on $f_2(x)$. Indeed, the only way for us to achieve a higher $f_1(x)$ value than 4 is to query on the rightmost portion of the search space where $x > 4$. Here, the values of $f_2(x)$ fall below 0.

Conversely, the region on the right ($x > 4$) is also where the tension between $f_1(x)$ and $f_2(x)$ exists: to increase the value of $f_2(x)$, we would have to move away to the left of the space, in which case the value of $f_1(x)$ would suffer.

> **DEFINITION** A data point whose value for an objective cannot be exceeded unless its value for another objective decreases is called *nondominated*. The opposite, a *dominated* point x_1, is one such that there exists another point x_2, whose objective values all exceed those of x_1. A nondominated point can also be called a *Pareto optimal*, *Pareto efficient*, or *noninferior*.

The point $x = -5$, therefore, is a nondominated point, and so are some of the points where $x > 4$. An example of a dominated point is $x = -1.9$ in figure 11.3, which gives $f_1(-1.9) \approx f_2(-1.9) \approx 1$. This point is dominated by $x = -5$ since the former's objective values are lower than those of the latter: $f_1(-1.9) < f_1(-5)$ and $f_2(-1.9) < f_2(-5)$.

In many cases, we have infinitely many nondominated points. Figure 11.4 shows the nondominated points in our current problem as dash-shaded regions (we talk about how to find these nondominated points later in this section; for now, let's focus on the behavior of these nondominated points):

- We see that $x = -5$ is, indeed, a nondominated point, along with many points around that region that give high values for the second objective $f_2(x)$. The points outside this region don't yield higher $f_2(x)$ values, so the points inside the region are nondominated. We call this set of points *group 1*.
- A smaller region on the right that gives high values for the first objective $f_1(x)$ is also nondominated. This set of points is called *group 2*.

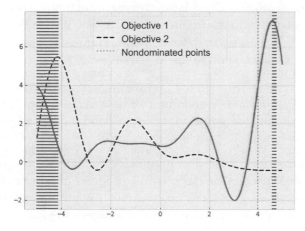

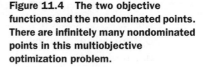

Figure 11.4 The two objective functions and the nondominated points. There are infinitely many nondominated points in this multiobjective optimization problem.

- There's a third, smallest region around $x = 4$ that's also nondominated, whose values for $f_1(x)$ are not exceeded by the nondominated points on the far left of the search space. Though this region doesn't contain the global optimum of either objective function, the region trades off between the values of the two objectives and is, therefore, nondominated. We call these points *group 3*.

The nondominated points are valuable in multi objective optimization because they, themselves, are solutions to the optimization problem, as we cannot improve upon them without sacrificing at least one objective. Further, by studying the nondominated points, their relationship with one another, and how they are spread out within the search space, we can understand more about the tradeoff between the multiple objectives in our optimization problem. Hence, a reasonable goal of multiobjective optimization is to find many nondominated points.

However, it's not immediately clear how we should concretely quantify this goal of finding nondominated points. We shouldn't simply seek to uncover as many nondominated points as possible, since there can be, and often are, infinitely many of them. Instead, we use a quantity that is easier to think about if we were to visualize the data points in a different space.

In figures 11.3 and 11.4, the *x*-axis corresponds to the data points themselves, and the *y*-axis corresponds to the objective values of these data points. To study the tradeoff between two conflicting objectives, we can also use a scatter plot, where the *x*-coordinate of a given data point x is the value for the first objective $f_1(x)$, and the *y*-coordinate is the value for the second objective $f_2(x)$.

Figure 11.5 shows this scatter plot for each point in a dense grid of 201 equally spaced points between –5 and 5, where dominated points are denoted as dots and nondominated points as stars. We see that whether a point is dominated or not is more easily determined in this space: for each data point x_1, if there's another data point x_2 that's placed above and to the right of x_1, then x_1 is a dominated point; conversely, if there isn't any point x_2 that's simultaneously above and to the right of x_1, then x_1 is nondominated. We also see in figure 11.5 the three groups of nondominated points corresponding to those in the discussion regarding figure 11.4.

From the set of nondominated points, visualized in the space of the objective values, we now introduce another concept: the *Pareto frontier*. Figure 11.6 visualizes the Pareto frontier of our current optimization problem.

> **DEFINITION** The curve that traces through the nondominated points is called the *Pareto frontier*. It's called a *frontier* because when we view all data points as a set, this curve of the nondominated points makes up a boundary, or a frontier, of the set beyond which no data point lies.

The concept of the Pareto frontier is crucial in multiobjective optimization because the frontier directly leads to a metric that can quantify progress in a multiobjective optimization problem. In particular, we focus on how much of the space—the one defined by the collected objective values from multiple objectives—the Pareto frontier

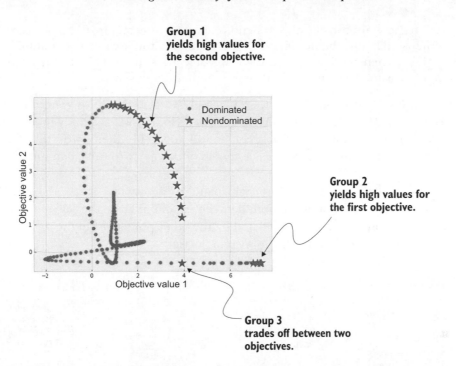

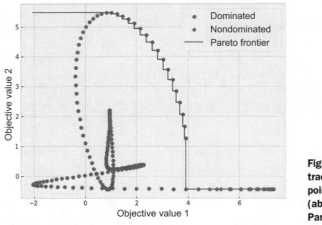

Figure 11.5   Scatter plot of data points based on their values for the two objective functions. Dominated points are denoted as dots; nondominated points are stars. The three groups of nondominated points correspond to those in the discussion regarding figure 11.4.

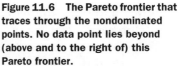

Figure 11.6   The Pareto frontier that traces through the nondominated points. No data point lies beyond (above and to the right of) this Pareto frontier.

covers; that is, the area inside (below and to the left) of the Pareto frontier. This area is shown as the shaded region in the left panel of figure 11.7.

DEFINITION   We use the term *dominated hypervolume* (or, sometimes, simply *hypervolume*) to denote how much of the space is covered by the Pareto frontier.

When there are two objective functions, like in our example, the space is two-dimensional and the dominated hypervolume is the area of the dominated region. When there are more than two objectives, the dominated hypervolume measures the same quantity but in higher dimensions.

The scattered points shown in the left panel of figure 11.7 are generated using a dense grid of 201 points across the search space so that we can study the behavior of the Pareto frontier and its hypervolume in full detail. In other words, this dense grid represents the result of an exhaustive search of the space to fully map out the Pareto frontier.

As a point of comparison, the right panel of figure 11.7 shows the result of 20 points selected uniformly at random between –5 and 5. From the selected points, we, again, find those that aren't dominated by any other points within the set of 20 points and draw the Pareto frontier of this second dataset.

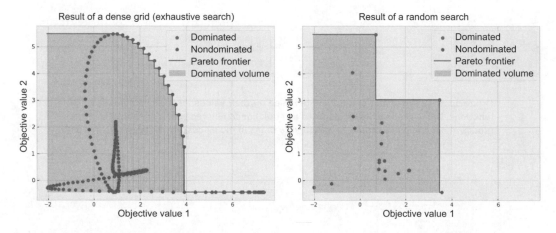

Figure 11.7   The dominated hypervolume of a dense grid (left), which is equivalent to an exhaustive search, and that of 20 data points randomly selected at random (right). The first dataset has a larger dominated volume and, therefore, does a better job at multiobjective optimization than the second dataset.

Unlike the case on the left, where we fully cover the search space, the small dataset on the right only has four nondominated points. In the context of multiobjective optimization, we make more progress with the first dataset (from the exhaustive search) than we do with the second (from the random search).

Compared to the dataset from the exhaustive search, these four nondominated points make up a more jagged Pareto frontier, which, in turn, has a much smaller dominated hypervolume. In other words, this measure of dominated hypervolume can be used to quantify optimization progress in a multiobjective optimization problem.

NOTE   In a multiobjective optimization problem, we measure optimization progress by the hypervolume of the dominated region resulting from the

current collected data. The bigger the dominated hypervolume of our collected data, the more progress we have made in simultaneously optimizing
our objective functions.

According to the hypervolume metric, figure 11.7 shows that an exhaustive search
does a better job than a random search (with fewer queries) at optimization, which is
an expected result. But to quantify *how much* better the former search strategy is, we
need a way to compute this hypervolume metric. For this computation, a *reference point*
is needed; this reference point acts as an endpoint for the dominated region, setting a
lower-left bound for the region. We can think of this reference point as the worst possible outcome we can observe under a multiobjective optimization setting, so the hypervolume of the region between this reference point and the Pareto frontier quantifies
how much we have improved from this worst possible outcome. (The worst possible
outcome for each objective function, if not known to us, the BayesOpt users, can be
set at a particular value that we think is the bare minimum each query can achieve.)

> **NOTE**   In multiobjective optimization, a common reference point is an *array*,
> each of whose elements corresponds to the lowest value of an objective func-
> tion to be maximized.

For example, the reference point for our current optimization problem is [−2.0292,
−0.4444] since the first element, −2.0292, is the minimum value of the first objective
function (the solid curve in figure 11.3), and −0.4444 is the minimum value of the second objective (the dashed curve in figure 11.3). This reference point is visualized in
figure 11.8 as the star, which, again, sets a lower bound for the dominated space.

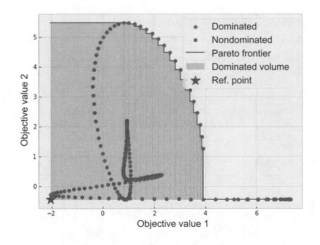

Figure 11.8   The reference point in a
multiobjective optimization problem,
which sets a lower bound for the
dominated space. The hypervolume is
computed to be the volume of the
region between the reference point
and the Pareto frontier.

With this reference point, we can compute the hypervolume of the dominated region of
a dataset collected by a multiobjective optimization policy. The algorithm to complete
this computation involves dividing the dominated region into multiple nonintersecting

hyperrectangles that collectively make up the dominated region. From there, we can easily compute the hypervolume of each hyperrectangle and sum them up to obtain the hypervolume of the entire region. The interested reader can refer to the research paper by Renaud Lacour, Kathrin Klamroth, and Carlos M. Fonseca that proposes this algorithm (http://mng.bz/jPdp).

With BoTorch, we can import and run this algorithm without the need to implement the low-level details. More specifically, assume we have stored the collected labels found during optimization in variable `train_y`. As we have two objective functions in our example, `train_y` should have a shape of *n*-by-2, where *n* is the number of data points in the collected set. We can then use the following code to compute the hypervolume measure, where

- The `DominatedPartitioning` class implements the partitioning of a dominated region. To initialize this object, we pass in the reference point and the collected labels `train_y`.
- We then call the `compute_hypervolume()` method on the dominated region object to compute its hypervolume:

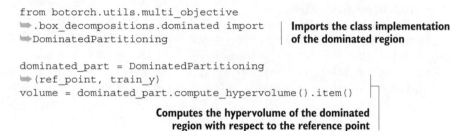

```
from botorch.utils.multi_objective
➡.box_decompositions.dominated import
➡DominatedPartitioning
```
Imports the class implementation of the dominated region

```
dominated_part = DominatedPartitioning
➡(ref_point, train_y)
volume = dominated_part.compute_hypervolume().item()
```
Computes the hypervolume of the dominated region with respect to the reference point

Using this method, we can compute the hypervolumes of the exhaustive and random search, as shown in the left and middle panels of figure 11.9. We see that the exhaustive search does achieve a higher hypervolume (31.49) than that of the random search (25.72).

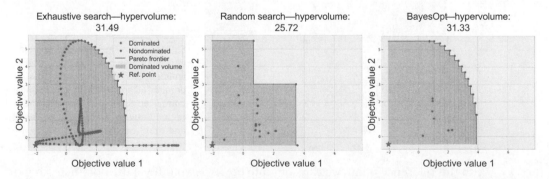

Figure 11.9   The multiobjective optimization results of various search strategies and the corresponding hypervolumes. BayesOpt achieves almost the same hypervolume as an exhaustive search, with significantly fewer queries.

In the right panel of figure 11.9, we also see the corresponding result achieved by the BayesOpt strategy we learn about in the next section with just 20 data points. With only one-tenth of the budget (20 versus 201), BayesOpt achieves almost the same hypervolume as the exhaustive search. Compared to the random search with the same budget, BayesOpt is able to map out the true Pareto frontier more fully and achieve a much higher hypervolume.

11.3 *Seeking to improve the optimal data boundary*

How should a BayesOpt policy aim to maximize the hypervolume of the dominated region within its collected data? A simple strategy is to alternate between optimizing each of the objectives in an iteratively manner: at this iteration of the BayesOpt loop, we seek to maximize the first objective $f_1(x)$; at the next iteration, we aim to maximize the second objective $f_2(x)$; and so on. During an iteration, we have a specific objective we want to optimize, which we can achieve by using the various BayesOpt policies we learned in chapters 4 through 6. For the remainder of this chapter, we use Expected Improvement (EI), which we learned in section 4.3. EI is a policy commonly used in practice, thanks to its algorithmic simplicity and consistent performance.

Assume that in our multiobjective optimization problem, we have observed the data points indicated by the Xs in the top panels of figure 11.10. By training a GP on the dataset belonging to each objective function, we obtain the GP predictions for the first objective (top-left panel) and the second objective (top-right panel).

In the bottom panels of figure 11.10, we show the acquisition scores of the individual EI policies on the corresponding objective functions. The bottom-left EI seeks to maximize the first objective $f_1(\mathrm{x})$, while the bottom-right EI searches for the optimum of the second objective $f_2(x)$. We see that the conflict between the two objectives is clear here when the first EI focuses on the right region of the search space, where $f_1(x)$ is maximized, while the second EI looks at the left region, where $f_2(x)$ is maximized.

> **NOTE** The acquisition score of a datapoint, as computed by a BayesOpt policy, quantifies how valuable the data point is to our search for an objective function's optimum. The higher the acquisition score, the more valuable the data point, and the point giving the highest acquisition score is the point the policy recommends to be queried.

In the alternating strategy we came up with previously, we either follow the first EI policy and query the point around $x = 4.5$ or follow the second EI and query the point around $x = -4.5$, depending on whether it's $f_1(x)$'s or $f_2(x)$'s turn to be optimized. We use this alternating strategy as a baseline to compare our final solution against.

What should this solution be to allow us to do better than the simple strategy of alternating between different objective functions? We note that by having a GP to model each of the objectives to be maximized, we have a way to probabilistically reason about the value each potential new query gives on each objective *simultaneously*. Specifically, we know that the value each potential new query gives on each objective follows a

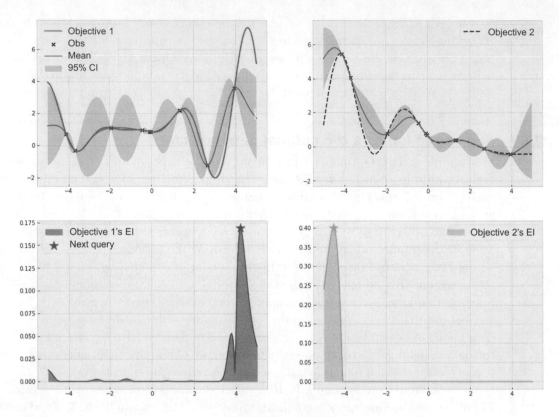

Figure 11.10   The current GP belief about each of the two objective functions (top) and the corresponding EI acquisition scores (bottom). Each EI policy seeks to optimize its own objective function and focuses on separate regions.

known normal distribution; this normal distribution is our prediction about the value of the query.

This prediction allows us to reason about whether each potential new query is a nondominated point and if so, how much it will increase the hypervolume of the dominated region. Each newly observed nondominated point extends the boundary of the dominated region (that is, the Pareto frontier) and, therefore, increases the dominated hypervolume. We, therefore, can use the increase in the hypervolume that each new query leads to, on average, as the acquisition score to quantify how valuable the query is. The bigger the increase in hypervolume that we can expect from a query, the more it will help us make optimization progress.

Of course, we can't know for sure how much of an increase in hypervolume we will obtain from a query until we actually make the query on the objective functions. However, again, we can reason about this hypervolume increase in a probabilistic manner. That is, we can compute the *expected value* of the increase in hypervolume that will result from a potential query.

Like the algorithm that determines the hypervolume of a dominated region, this computation of the expected increase in hypervolume involves dividing the dominated region into hyperrectangles and is quite complicated. We, once again, won't go into the mathematical details here, but you can refer to the research paper by Kaifeng Yang, Michael Emmerich, André Deutz, and Thomas Bäck that proposes the corresponding BayesOpt policy, which is called *Expected Hypervolume Improvement* (EHVI), for more details (http://mng.bz/WzYw).

DEFINITION   The Expected Hypervolume Improvement policy uses the expected value of the increase in hypervolume of the dominated region that a new data point will result in as the acquisition score of that data point. This policy is the generalization of EI to the multiobjective setting, where we aim to maximize the dominated hypervolume.

Figure 11.11 shows the acquisition scores of EHVI in the bottom-right panel on the same dataset as in figure 11.10. We see that compared to the individual EI policies, EHVI nicely balances the two objectives by assigning high acquisition scores to multiple

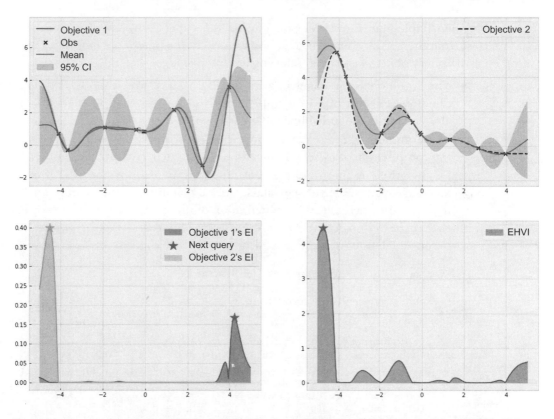

Figure 11.11   The current GP belief about each of the two objective functions (top), the corresponding EI acquisition scores (bottom left), and the EHVI acquisition scores (bottom right). EHVI balances the two objectives, assigning high acquisition scores to multiple regions that likely extend the Pareto frontier.

regions that likely extend the Pareto frontier: the leftmost region of the search space has the highest score, but the rightmost region, along with other regions in between, also has nonnegligible acquisition scores.

To verify that this EHVI strategy does, indeed, give us an advantage in multiobjective optimization, we implement the policy and run it on our current problem. The code we use is included in the CH11/02 - Multi-objective BayesOpt loop.ipynb notebook.

First, we need the class implementation of the GP model and a helper function `fit_gp_model()` that facilitates the training of each GP on observed data. As we have implemented these components in previous chapters, we won't show the code for them here again; you can refer to section 4.1.1 for a refresher on this code. At each step of the BayesOpt loop, we call the helper function to initialize and train a GP on each objective function's data. In our case, we have two objective functions, so we call the helper function twice, each time with either `train_y[:, 0]`, which are the labels observed from the first objective $f_1(x)$, or `train_y[:, 1]`, the labels from the second objective $f_2(x)$:

```
model1, likelihood1 = fit_gp_model(train_x, train_y[:, 0])
model2, likelihood2 = fit_gp_model(train_x, train_y[:, 1])
```

We then implement the EHVI policy using the `ExpectedHypervolumeImprovement` class from the `botorch.acquisition.multi_objective.analytic` module. To initialize the policy object, we set the following arguments:

- The argument `model` takes in a list of GPs, each of which models an objective function. This list of GPs is implemented as an instance of the `ModelListGP` class, taking in the individual GP objects (`model1`, `model2`).
- The argument `ref_point` takes in the reference point, which is necessary for the computation of hypervolume and potential hypervolume increases.
- Finally, the argument `partitioning` takes in an instance of the `Fast-NondominatedPartitioning` class, which facilitates the computation of hypervolume increases. The initialization of this object, similar to a `Dominated-Partitioning` object we saw previously, takes in a reference point and the observed labels `train_y`:

```
from botorch.acquisition.multi_objective
➡.analytic import
➡ExpectedHypervolumeImprovement                         Imports the
from botorch.utils.multi_objective.box_decompositions   necessary classes
➡.non_dominated import
➡FastNondominatedPartitioning
from botorch.models.model_list_gp_regression import ModelListGP

                 policy = ExpectedHypervolumeImprovement(
The                    model=ModelListGP(model1, model2),          The list of GP models,
reference              ref_point=ref_point,                        each for one objective
point                  partitioning=FastNondominatedPartitioning   function
                 ➡(ref_point, train_y)                             The nondominated partitioning
                 )                                                  object to compute the
                                                                    hypervolume increase
```

Using the `policy` object for the EHVI policy, we can then compute the acquisition score, denoting the expected hypervolume increase, which results from a potential new observation. We can then find the data point that gives the highest score, using the helper function `optimize_acqf()`:

```
next_x, acq_val = optimize_acqf(
    policy,
    bounds=bounds,
    q=1,
    num_restarts=20,
    raw_samples=50
)
```

The variable `next_x` stores the location of the query we will make our objective functions with next: `next_y = joint_objective(next_x)`.

That's all we need to run EHVI on our current optimization problem. As a point of reference, we also test the previously discussed alternating optimization strategy, in which we use regular EI to optimize a selected objective function. As we have two objectives, we simply switch back and forth between the two (`num_queries`, here, is the total number of evaluations we can make in a BayesOpt run):

```
for i in range(num_queries):
    if i % 2 == 0:            ◁─ If the current iteration
        model = model1            number is even, optimizes
        best_f = train_y[:, 0].max()   the first objective
    else:                     ◁─ If the current iteration
        model = model2            number is odd, optimizes
        best_f = train_y[:, 1].max()   the second objective

    policy = ExpectedImprovement(model=model,
    ⇥best_f=best_f)           ◁─── Creates the EI
                                   policy accordingly
```

Finally, to quantify our optimization progress, we record the hypervolume of the dominated region resulting from the current dataset collected throughout the search. This recording is done with a tensor named `hypervolumes`, which stores the current dominated hypervolume at each step during an experiment, across many experiments. Overall, our BayesOpt loop is the following, where for each policy, we run the experiment multiple times, each with an initial dataset chosen uniformly at random:

```
                              The history of hypervolumes
                              found throughout optimization

hypervolumes = torch.zeros((num_repeats, num_queries))   ◁─

for trial in range(num_repeats):
  torch.manual_seed(trial)
  train_x = bounds[0] + (bounds[1] - bounds[0]) * torch    Initializes a
  ⇥.rand(1, 1)                                             random initial
  train_y = joint_objective(train_x)                       training set
```

```
for i in range(num_queries):
    dominated_part = DominatedPartitioning(ref_point,
    ➥train_y)
    hypervolumes[trial, i] = dominated_part
    ➥.compute_hypervolume().item()
```
◁———— **Records the current hypervolume**

```
    ...
```
◁———— **Retrains the models, initializes a policy, and finds the next query**

The CH11/02 - Multi-objective BayesOpt loop.ipynb notebook runs the two BayesOpt policies we have for 10 experiments, each with a budget of 20 queries to the objective functions. Figure 11.12 shows the average hypervolume and error bars as a function of the number of queries made by the two policies. We see that EHVI consistently outperforms the alternating EI policy, which illustrates the benefits of the hypervolume-based approach.

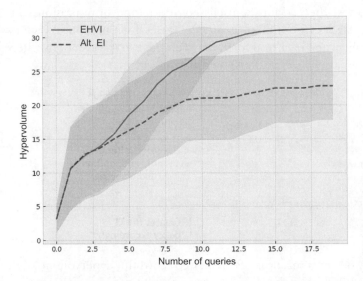

Figure 11.12   Average hypervolume and error bars as a function of the number of queries made by two BayesOpt policies. EHVI consistently outperforms the alternating EI policy.

In this chapter, we have learned about the multiobjective optimization problem and how to approach it using BayesOpt. We discussed the concept of hypervolume as a measure of optimization performance, quantifying how much progress we have made in optimizing the objective functions. By using a variant of the EI policy to optimize the increase in hypervolume, we obtained an EHVI policy that achieves strong performance.

Unfortunately, there are other aspects of multiobjective BayesOpt that can't be covered in this chapter. Specifically, in addition to EHVI, we can consider other optimization policies. One common technique is *scalarization*, which combines multiple competing objectives into one by taking a weighted sum. This strategy is a generalization of the alternating EI policy, which we can think of as assigning a weight of 1 to one objective and a weight of 0 to the other at each iteration. The interested reader can refer to the BoTorch documentation (see https://botorch.org/docs/multi_objective and https://botorch.org/tutorials/multi_objective_bo), which provides a brief summary of different multiobjective optimization policies that BoTorch offers.

11.4 Exercise: Multiobjective optimization of airplane design

In this exercise, we apply the multiobjective optimization techniques we have learned to the problem of optimizing the aerostructural design of an airplane. This problem was first introduced in exercise 2 of chapter 7 and was modified as a cost-constrained problem in exercise 2 of chapter 8. We reuse the code from chapter 8 here. This exercise allows us to observe the performance of the Expected Hypervolume Improvement (EHVI) policy in a multidimensional problem. The solution is included in the CH11/03 - Exercise 1.ipynb notebook.

Take the following steps:

1   Copy the code for the objective functions `flight_utility()` and `flight_cost()` from exercise 2 of chapter 8. Negate the sign of the returned value of the second function, `flight_cost()`. We use these two functions as objectives for our multiobjective optimization problem.

2   Write a helper function that takes in an input `x` (which could contain multiple data points) and returns the values of `x` evaluated on the two objective functions. The returned value should be a tensor of size n-by-2, where n is the number of data points in `x`.

3   Declare the search space to be the four-dimensional unit square. That is, the four lower bounds are 0, and the four upper bounds are 1.

4   To compute the hypervolume of a dataset collected by an optimization algorithm, we need a reference point. Declare this reference point to be $[-1.5, -2]$, which are the corresponding lowest values of the two objective functions.

5   Implement the class for the GP model, which should have a constant mean and a four-dimensional Matérn 2.5 kernel with automatic relevance determination (ARD; see section 3.4.2) and a helper function `fit_gp_model()` that initializes and trains a GP on a training set. Refer to section 4.1.1 for details on implementing these components.

6   Set the number of experiments to be run to 10 and the budget (the number of queries to be made) in each experiment to 50.

7   Run the EHVI policy to optimize the two objective functions we have as well as the alternating EI strategy discussed in section 11.3. Plot the average hypervolume and error bars achieved by these two policies (similar to figure 11.2), and compare their performance.

Summary

- The multiobjective optimization problem arises when there are multiple potentially conflicting objectives that need to be optimized at the same time. This problem is common in the real world as we often contend with multiple competing goals in many real-life tasks.

- When using BayesOpt for multiobjective optimization, we use multiple GPs to model our belief about the objective functions (one model for each objective). We can use these GPs to reason about the objective functions simultaneously in a probabilistic manner.

- A nondominated point achieves objective values that cannot be improved upon unless we sacrifice performance on at least one objective. Discovering nondominated data points is a goal of multiobjective optimization as they allow us to study the tradeoff between the objective functions.

- Nondominated data points make up the Pareto frontier, which sets the boundary that represents optimality in multiobjective optimization. No data point lies beyond the Pareto frontier of all nondominated points.

- The hypervolume of the dominated space—that is, the region covered by the Pareto frontier—measures optimization performance of a dataset collected by an algorithm. The larger the hypervolume, the better the algorithm's performance will be. The hypervolume of a dataset can be computed by calling the `compute_hypervolume()` method on an instance of BoTorch's `Dominated-Partitioning` class.

- To compute the hypervolume of a dataset, we need a reference point that serves as the endpoint of the dominated space. We usually set the reference point to be the lowest values of the objective functions to be optimized.

- As the GPs allow us to make predictions about the objective functions, we can seek to improve upon the hypervolume of our current dataset. This strategy corresponds to the EHVI policy, which is a variant of EI in multiobjective optimization. This policy successfully balances the competing objectives.

Part 4

Special Gaussian process models

Gaussian processes (GPs), outside of the context of BayesOpt, are a powerful class of ML models in their own right. While the main topic of this book is BayesOpt, it would be a missed opportunity not to give GPs more attention. This part shows us how to extend GPs and make them more practical in various ML tasks, while retaining their most valuable feature: the quantification of uncertainty in the predictions.

In chapter 12, we learn how to accelerate the training of GPs and scale them to large data sets. This chapter helps us address one of the biggest disadvantages of GPs: their training cost.

Chapter 13 shows how to take the GP's flexibility to another level by combining them with neural networks. This combination offers the best of both worlds: the ability of neural networks to approximate any function and the quantification of uncertainty by GPs. This chapter is also where we can truly appreciate having a streamlined software ecosystem in PyTorch, GPyTorch, and BoTorch, which makes working with neural networks and GPs together seamless.

Scaling Gaussian processes to large datasets

This chapter covers

- Training a GP on a large dataset
- Using mini-batch gradient descent when training a GP
- Using an advanced gradient descent technique to train a GP faster

So far, we have seen that GPs offer great modeling flexibility. In chapter 3, we learned that we can model high-level trends using the GP's mean function as well as variability using the covariance function. A GP also provides calibrated uncertainty quantification. That is, the predictions for datapoints near observations in the training dataset have lower uncertainty than those for points far away. This flexibility sets the GP apart from other ML models that produce only point estimates, such as neural networks. However, it comes at a cost: speed.

Training and making predictions with a GP (specifically, computing the inverse of the covariance matrix) scales cubically with respect to the size of the training data. That is, if our dataset doubles in size, a GP will take eight times as long to train and predict. If the dataset increases tenfold, it will take a GP 1,000 times longer.

This poses a challenge to scaling GPs to large datasets, which are common in many applications:

- If we aim to model housing prices across an entire country, such as the United States, where each data point represents the price of a single house at a given time, the size of our dataset would contain hundreds of millions of points. As an illustration, the online database Statista keeps track of the number of housing units in the United States from 1975 to 2021; this report can be accessed at https://www.statista.com/statistics/240267/number-of-housing-units-in-the-united -states/. We see that this number has been steadily rising since 1975, exceeding 100 million in 1990, and is now at more than 140 million.

- In the drug discovery applications we discussed in section 1.1.3, a database of possible molecules that could potentially be synthesized into drugs could have billions of entries.

- In weather forecasting, low-cost monitoring devices make it easy to collect weather data on a large scale. A dataset could contain by-minute measurements across multiple years.

Given the cubic running time of the normal GP model, it's infeasible to train it on datasets of this scale. In this chapter, we learn how we can use a class of GP models called *variational Gaussian process* (VGPs) to tackle this problem of learning from big data.

> **DEFINITION**   A variational Gaussian process picks out a small subset of the data that represents the entire set well. It does this by seeking to minimize the difference between itself and the regular GP that is trained on the full data. The term *variational* refers to the subfield of mathematics that studies the optimization of functionals.

This idea of choosing to train on only a small subset of these representative points is quite natural and intuitive. Figure 12.1 shows a VGP in action, where by learning from a few selective data points, the model produces almost identical predictions to those produced by a regular GP.

We cover how to implement this model and observe its computational benefits in this chapter. Further, when working with a VGP, we can use a more advanced version of gradient descent, which, as we saw in section 3.3.2, is used to optimize the hyperparameters of a GP. We learn to use this version of the algorithm to train faster and more effectively and, ultimately, scale our GPs to large datasets. The code accompanying this chapter can be found in the CH11/01 - Approximate Gaussian process inference.ipynb notebook.

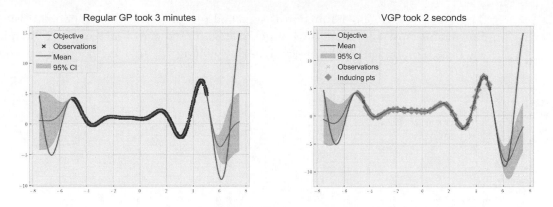

Figure 12.1 Predictions made by a regular GP and those by a VGP. The VGP produces almost identical predictions as the GP, while taking significantly less time to train.

12.1   Training a GP on a large dataset

In this section, to see firsthand how training a GP on a large dataset poses a difficult challenge, we attempt to apply the GP model that we used in chapters 2 and 3 to a medium-sized dataset of 1,000 points. This task will make clear that using a regular GP is infeasible and motivate what we learn in the next section: variational GPs.

12.1.1   Setting up the learning task

We first create our dataset in this subsection. We reuse the one-dimensional objective function we saw in chapters 2 and 3, the Forrester function. Again, we implement it as follows:

```
def forrester_1d(x):
    y = -((x + 1) ** 2) * torch.sin(2 * x + 2) / 5 + 1
    return y.squeeze(-1)
```

Similar to what we did in section 3.3, we will also have a helper function that takes in a GP model and visualizes its predictions across the domain. The function has the following header and takes in three parameters—the GP model, the corresponding likelihood function, and a Boolean flag denoting whether the model is a VGP:

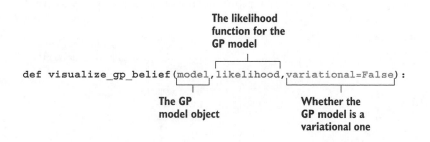

The logic of this helper function is sketched out in figure 12.2, which consists of four main steps: computing the predictions, plotting the ground truth and the training data, plotting the predictions, and, finally, plotting the inducing points if the model is a VGP.

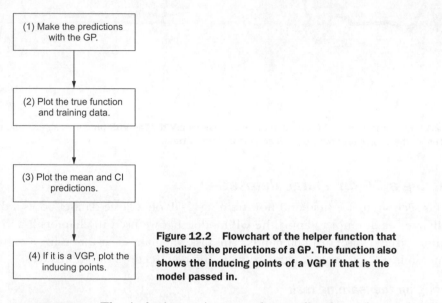

Figure 12.2   Flowchart of the helper function that visualizes the predictions of a GP. The function also shows the inducing points of a VGP if that is the model passed in.

DEFINITION   The inducing points are the small subset chosen by the VGP model to represent the entire dataset to train on. As the name suggests, these points aim to *induce* knowledge about all of the data.

We now go through the steps in greater detail. In the first step, we compute the mean and CI predictions with the GP:

```
with torch.no_grad():
    predictive_distribution = likelihood(model(xs))
    predictive_mean = predictive_distribution.mean
    predictive_upper, predictive_lower =
    ➥predictive_distribution.confidence_region()
```

In the second step, we make the Matplotlib plot and show the true function stored in xs and ys (which we generate shortly) and our training data train_x and train_y:

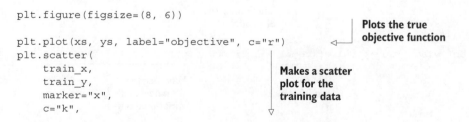

```
plt.figure(figsize=(8, 6))

plt.plot(xs, ys, label="objective", c="r")
plt.scatter(
    train_x,
    train_y,
    marker="x",
    c="k",
```

Plots the true objective function

Makes a scatter plot for the training data

```
    alpha=0.1 if variational else 1,
    label="observations",
)
```
Makes a scatter plot for the training data

Here, if the model is a VGP (if `variational` is set to `True`), then we plot the training data with lower opacity (by setting `alpha = 0.1`), making them look more transparent. This is so we can plot the representative points learned by the VGP more clearly later.

The predictions made by the GP are then shown with the solid mean line and the shaded 95% CI region in the third step:

```
plt.plot(xs, predictive_mean, label="mean")
plt.fill_between(
    xs.flatten(),
    predictive_upper,
    predictive_lower,
    alpha=0.3,
    label="95% CI"
)
```

Finally, we plot the representative points selected by the VGP by extracting out `model.variational_strategy.inducing_points`:

```
if variational:
  inducing_points =
    model.variational_strategy.inducing_points.detach().clone()
  with torch.no_grad():
      inducing_mean = model(inducing_points).mean

  plt.scatter(
      inducing_points.squeeze(-1),
      inducing_mean,
      marker="D",
      c="orange",
      s=100,
      label="inducing pts"
  )
```
Scatters the inducing points

Now, to generate our training and dataset, we randomly select 1,000 points between −5 and 5 and compute the function values at these points:

```
torch.manual_seed(0)
train_x = torch.rand(size=(1000, 1)) * 10 - 5
train_y = forrester_1d(train_x)
```

To make our test set, we compute a dense grid between −7.5 and 7.5 using the `torch.linspace()` function. This test set includes −7.5, 7.4, −7.3, and so on to 7.5:

```
xs = torch.linspace(-7.5, 7.5, 151).unsqueeze(1)
ys = forrester_1d(xs)
```

To visualize what our training set looks like, we can once again make a scatter plot with the following:

```
plt.figure(figsize=(8, 6))
plt.scatter(
    train_x,
    train_y,
    c="k",
    marker="x",
    s=10,
    label="observations"
)
plt.legend();
```

This code produces figure 12.3, where the black dots denote the individual data points in our training set.

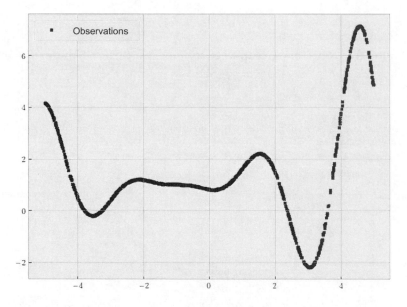

Figure 12.3   The training dataset for our learning task, containing 1,000 data points. It takes considerable time to train a regular GP on this set.

12.1.2 *Training a regular GP*

We are now ready to implement and train a GP model on this dataset. First, we implement the GP model class, which has a constant function (an instance of `gpytorch.means.ConstantMean`) as its mean function and the RBF kernel with an output scale (implemented with `gpytorch.kernels.ScaleKernel(gpytorch.kernels.RBFKernel())`) as its covariance function:

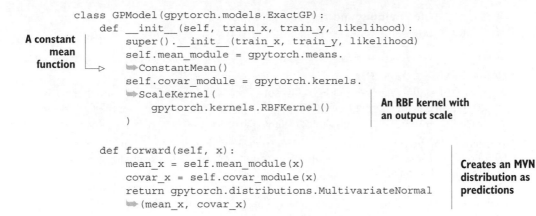

```
class GPModel(gpytorch.models.ExactGP):
    def __init__(self, train_x, train_y, likelihood):
        super().__init__(train_x, train_y, likelihood)
        self.mean_module = gpytorch.means.
        ➥ConstantMean()
        self.covar_module = gpytorch.kernels.
        ➥ScaleKernel(
            gpytorch.kernels.RBFKernel()
        )

    def forward(self, x):
        mean_x = self.mean_module(x)
        covar_x = self.covar_module(x)
        return gpytorch.distributions.MultivariateNormal
        ➥(mean_x, covar_x)
```

A constant mean function →

An RBF kernel with an output scale

Creates an MVN distribution as predictions

Now, we initialize this GP model with our training data and a `GaussianLikelihood` object:

```
likelihood = gpytorch.likelihoods.GaussianLikelihood()
model = GPModel(train_x, train_y, likelihood)
```

Finally, we train our GP by running gradient descent to minimize the loss function defined by the likelihood of the data. At the end of training, we obtain the hyperparameters of the model (e.g., the mean constant, length scale, and output scale) that give a low loss value. Gradient descent is implemented with the optimizer Adam (`torch.optim.Adam`), which is one of the most commonly used gradient descent algorithms:

The gradient descent algorithm Adam

The loss function, which computes the likelihood of the data from the hyperparameters

```
optimizer = torch.optim.Adam(model.parameters(), lr=0.01)
mll = gpytorch.mlls.ExactMarginalLogLikelihood(likelihood, model)

model.train()
likelihood.train()

for i in tqdm(range(500)):
    optimizer.zero_grad()

    output = model(train_x)
    loss = -mll(output, train_y)

    loss.backward()
    optimizer.step()

model.eval()
likelihood.eval()
```

Enables training mode

Runs 500 iterations of gradient descent

Enables prediction mode

NOTE As a reminder, when training a GP, we need to enable training mode for both the model and the likelihood (using `model.train()` and `likelihood`

`.train()`). After training and before making predictions, we need to enable prediction mode (with `model.eval()` and `likelihood.eval()`).

> ### Using GPUs to train GPs
>
> A method of scaling up GPs to large datasets that is not the focus of this chapter is to use graphics processing units (GPUs). GPUs are often used to parallelize matrix multiplications and speed up training neural networks.
>
> The same principle applies here, and GPyTorch keeps training GPs on GPUs simple by following PyTorch's syntax of transferring objects to the GPU (by calling the `cuda()` method on the objects). In particular, we call `train_x = train_x.cuda()` and `train_y = train_y.cuda()` to put our data onto the GPU, and `model = model.cuda()` and `likelihood = likelihood.cuda()` to put the GP model and its likelihood onto the GPU.
>
> You can find more details on this topic in GPyTorch's documentation at http://mng.bz/lW8B.

We also ran gradient descent for 500 iterations, but as our current dataset is significantly larger, this loop might take a while to complete (so grab a coffee while you wait!). Once training is done, we call the `visualize_gp_belief()` helper function we wrote earlier to show the predictions made by our trained GP, which produces figure 12.4:

```
visualize_gp_belief(model, likelihood)
```

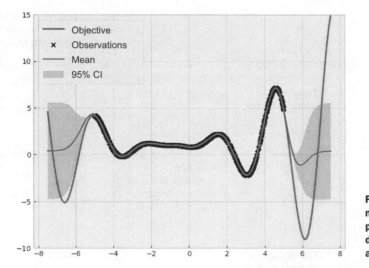

Figure 12.4   Predictions made by a regular GP. The predictions match the training data well, but training takes a long time.

We see that our GP's predictions match the training data points well—an encouraging sign that our model successfully learned from the data. However, there are several problems with this procedure.

12.1.3 Problems with training a regular GP

In this subsection, we discuss some of the challenges of training a GP on a large dataset. The first challenge, as we've mentioned, is that training takes quite a long time. On my MacBook, the 500 iterations of gradient descent could take up to 45 seconds, which is significantly longer than what we observed in chapters 2 and 3. This is a direct result of the GP's cubic running time that we mentioned earlier, and this long training time only becomes more prohibitive as our dataset gets larger and larger, as indicated by table 12.1.

Table 12.1 Estimated training time of a GP given the size of the training dataset. Training quickly becomes prohibitive.

Size of the training set	Training time
500 points	45 seconds
2,000 points	48 minutes
3,000 points	2.7 hours
5,000 points	12.5 hours
10,000 points	4 days

The second, and perhaps more concerning, problem stems from the fact that computing the loss function (the marginal log likelihood of the training data) used in gradient descent becomes more and more difficult as the size of the training data increases. This is indicated by the warning messages GPyTorch prints out during training:

```
NumericalWarning: CG terminated in 1000 iterations with average
   residual norm...
```

These messages tell us that we are encountering numerical instability in the computation of the loss.

> **NOTE** Computing the loss across many data points is a computationally unstable operation.

Numerical instability prevents us from correctly calculating the loss and, therefore, effectively minimizing that loss. This is illustrated by how this loss changes across the 500 iterations of gradient descent, shown in figure 12.5.

Unlike what we saw in chapters 2 and 3, our loss here jumps up and down erratically, indicating that gradient descent is not doing a good job of minimizing that loss. In fact, as we go through more iterations, our loss actually increases, which means we have arrived at a suboptimal model! This phenomenon is understandable: if we are miscalculating the loss of our model, then by using that miscalculated term to guide learning in gradient descent, we likely obtain a suboptimal solution.

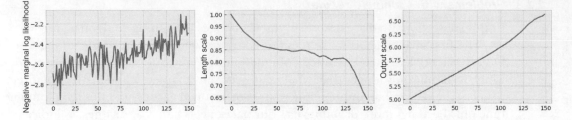

Figure 12.5   Progressive loss of a regular GP during gradient descent. Due to numerical instability, the loss curve is jagged and not effectively minimized.

You might be familiar with the analogy of gradient descent as climbing down a mountain. Say you are at the top of a mountain and want to come down. At every step along the way, you find a direction to walk along that will allow you to get to a lower place (that is, descend). Eventually, after taking enough steps, you arrive at the bottom of the mountain. Similarly, in gradient descent, we start out with a relatively high loss, and by adjusting the hyperparameters of our model at each iteration, we iteratively decrease the loss. With enough iterations, we arrive at the optimal model.

> **NOTE**   An excellent discussion on gradient descent and how it is analogous to descending a mountain is included in Luis Serrano's *Grokking Machine Learning.*

This process works well only if we can compute the loss accurately—that is, if we can see exactly which direction will get us to a lower place on the mountain. If, however, this computation is prone to errors, we naturally won't be able to effectively minimize the loss of our model. This is similar to trying to descend the mountain with a blindfold on! As we see in figure 12.5, we actually ended up at a higher place on the mountain (our loss is higher than its value before gradient descent).

Overall, training a regular GP on a large dataset is not a good approach. Not only does training scale cubically with the size of the training data, but the computation of the loss value to be optimized is also unstable. In the remainder of this chapter, we learn about variational GPs, or VGPs, as the solution to this problem.

12.2   *Automatically choosing representative points from a large dataset*

The idea behind VGPs is to select a set of points that are representative of the whole dataset and train a GP on this smaller subset. We have learned to train a GP on a small dataset well. The hope is that this smaller subset captures the general trend of the entire dataset, so minimal information is lost when a GP is trained on the subset.

This approach is quite natural. It's common for a large dataset to contain redundant information, so if we can learn only from the most informative data points, we

Figure 12.6   Running gradient descent with a numerically unstable loss computation is similar to descending a mountain with a blindfold on.

can avoid having to process these redundancies. We have noted in section 2.2 that a GP, like any ML model, works under the assumption that similar data points produce similar labels. When a large dataset contains many similar data points, a GP needs only to focus on one of them to learn about their trend. For example, even though by-minute weather data is available, a weather forecasting model can effectively learn from just hourly measurements. In this section, we learn how to do this automatically by making sure that learning from the small subset leads to minimal information loss compared with when we learn from the large set, as well as how to implement this model with GPyTorch.

12.2.1   Minimizing the difference between two GPs

How can we best select this smaller subset so that the final GP model can gain the most information from the original dataset? In this subsection, we discuss the high-level idea of how this is done by a VGP. The process equates to finding the subset of inducing points that, when a GP is trained on this subset, will induce a posterior GP that is as close as possible to the posterior GP trained on the entire dataset.

Diving into some mathematical details, when training a VGP, we aim to minimize the difference between the posterior GP conditioned on the inducing points and the posterior GP conditioned on the entire dataset. This requires a way to measure the difference between two distributions (the two GPs), and the measure chosen for this is the Kullback–Leibler divergence, or the KL divergence.

> **DEFINITION**   The *Kullback–Leibler (KL) divergence* is a statistical distance that measures the distance between two distributions. In other words, the KL divergence computes how different a probability distribution is from another distribution.

Supplementary material for the KL divergence

An intuitive explanation of the KL divergence can be found in Will Kurt's excellent "Kullback-Leibler Divergence Explained" blog post (https://www.countbayesie.com/blog/ 2017/5/9/kullback-leibler-divergence-explained). The mathematically inclined reader may refer to chapter 2 of David MacKay's *Information Theory, Inference, and Learning Algorithms* (Cambridge University Press, 2003).

Just as the Euclidean distance between point A and point B (that is, the length of the segment connecting the two points) measures how far apart those two points are in Euclidean space, the KL divergence measures how far apart two given distributions are in the space of probability distributions—that is, how different they are from each other. This is illustrated in figure 12.7.

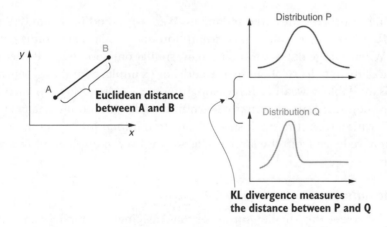

Figure 12.7   Euclidean distance measures the distance between two points on a plane, while the KL divergence measures the distance between two probability distributions.

> **NOTE**   As a mathematically valid distance measure, the KL divergence is non-negative. In other words, the distance between any two distributions is at least zero, and when it is equal to zero, the two distributions exactly match up.

So, if we could easily compute the KL divergence between the posterior GP trained on the inducing points and the posterior GP trained on the entire dataset, we should choose the inducing points that make the KL divergence zero. Unfortunately, in a similar manner to how computing the marginal log likelihood is computationally unstable, computing the KL divergence is not easy either. However, due to its mathematical properties, we can rewrite the KL divergence as the difference between two quantities, as illustrated in figure 12.8.

Figure 12.8   The KL divergence is decomposed into the difference between the marginal log likelihood and the evidence lower bound (ELBO). The ELBO is easy to compute and, therefore, chosen as the metric to be optimized.

The third term in this equation, the evidence lower bound, or ELBO for short, is exactly the difference between the marginal log likelihood and the KL divergence. Even though these two terms, the marginal log likelihood and the KL divergence, are hard to compute, the ELBO has a simple form and can be computed easily. For this reason, instead of minimizing the KL divergence so that the posterior GP trained on the inducing points is as close as possible to the posterior GP trained on the complete dataset, we can maximize the ELBO as a way to indirectly maximize the marginal log likelihood.

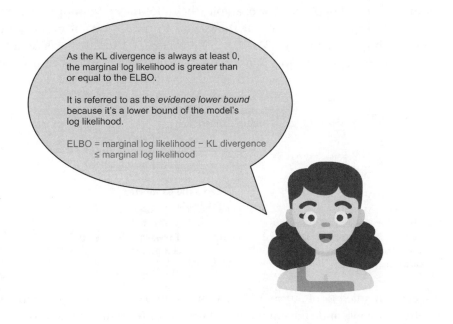

To summarize, to find the set of inducing points that will give us a posterior GP that is the most similar to the GP we would obtain if we were able to train on the large dataset, we aim to minimize the KL divergence between the two GPs. However, this KL divergence is difficult to compute, so we choose to optimize a proxy of the KL divergence, the ELBO of the model, which is easier to compute. As we see in the next subsection, GPyTorch provides a convenient loss function that computes this ELBO term for us. Before we cover implementation, there's one more thing for us to discuss: how to account for all data points in a large training set when maximizing the ELBO term.

12.2.2 *Training the model in small batches*

As we aim to find the set of inducing points that best represents the entire training dataset, we still need to include all points in the training set in the computation of the ELBO. But we said earlier that computing the marginal log likelihood across many data points is numerically unstable, so gradient descent becomes ineffective. Do we face the same problem here? In this subsection, we see that when training a VGP by optimizing the ELBO term, we can avoid this numerical instability problem by using a modified version of gradient descent that is more amenable to large datasets.

The task of computing the loss function of an ML model across many data points is not unique to GPs. For example, neural networks usually train on thousands and millions of data points, and computing the loss function of the network for all data points is not feasible either. The solution to this problem, for both neural networks and VGPs, is to *approximate* the true loss value across all data points using the loss value across a random subset of points. For example, the following code snippet is from the official PyTorch documentation, and it shows how to train a neural network on an image dataset (http://mng.bz/8rBB). Here, the inner loop iterates over small subsets of the training data and runs gradient descent on the loss values computed on these subsets:

```
for epoch in range(2):          ⟵──┤ Loops over the dataset
                                     multiple times

    running_loss = 0.0                       Gets the inputs;
    for i, data in enumerate(trainloader, 0):  data is a list of
        inputs, labels = data    ⟵──┤         [inputs, labels]

        optimizer.zero_grad()    ⟵──┤ Zeros the parameter
                                      gradients

        outputs = net(inputs)
        loss = criterion(outputs, labels)     Forward + backward
        loss.backward()                       + optimize
        optimizer.step()
```

When we calculate the loss of our model on a small number of points, the computation can be done in a stable and efficient manner. Further, by repeating this approximation many times, we can approximate the true loss well. Finally, we run gradient descent on this approximated loss, which hopefully also minimizes the true loss across all data points.

> **DEFINITION** The technique of running gradient descent on the loss computed with a random subset of the data is sometimes called *mini-batch gradient descent*. In practice, instead of randomly choosing a subset in each iteration of gradient descent, we often split the training set into small subsets and iteratively compute the approximate loss using each of these small subsets.

For example, if our training set contains 1,000 points, we can split it into 10 small subsets of 100 points. Then, we compute the loss with each subset of 100 for gradient descent and iteratively repeat for all 10 subsets. (This is exactly what we do in our code example later.) Again, while this approximate loss, computed from a subset of the data, is not exactly equal to the true loss, in gradient descent, we repeat this approximation many times, which, in aggregation, points us in the correct descent direction.

The difference between gradient descent minimizing the true loss and mini-batch gradient descent minimizing the approximate loss is illustrated by the example in figure 12.9. Compared to gradient descent (which, again, isn't possible to run with large data), the mini-batch version might not point to the most effective descent direction, but by repeating the approximation multiple times, we are still able to reach the goal.

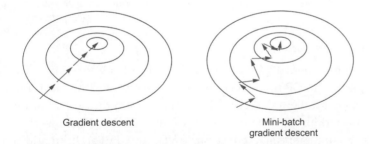

Gradient descent   Mini-batch gradient descent

Figure 12.9   An illustration of gradient descent and mini-batch gradient descent within a loss "valley," where the center of the valley gives the lowest loss. Gradient descent, if feasible to compute, leads straight to the target. Mini-batch gradient descent goes in directions that are not optimal but still reaches the target in the end.

If we were thinking in terms of the climbing-down-the-mountain-while-blindfolded analogy, mini-batch gradient descent would be similar to being blindfolded with a thin cloth that can be partially seen through. It's not always guaranteed that with every step we take, we arrive at a lower location, but given enough time, we will be able to descend successfully.

NOTE   Not all loss functions can be approximated by the loss on a subset of the data. In other words, not all loss functions can be minimized using mini-batch gradient descent. The negative marginal log likelihood of a GP is an example; otherwise, we could have run mini-batch gradient descent on this function. Fortunately, mini-batch gradient descent is applicable to the ELBO of a VGP.

To recap, training a VGP follows a roughly similar procedure as training a regular GP, in which we use a version of gradient descent to minimize the appropriate loss of the model. Table 12.2 summarizes the key differences between the two model classes: a regular GP should be trained on small datasets by running gradient descent to minimize the exact negative marginal log likelihood, while a VGP can be trained on large datasets by running mini-batch gradient descent to optimize the ELBO, which is an approximation of the true log likelihood.

Table 12.2   Training a GP vs. training a VGP. The high-level procedure is similar; only the specific components and settings are replaced.

Training procedure	GP	VGP
Training data size	Small	Medium to large
Training type	Exact training	Approximate training
Loss function	Negative marginal log likelihood	ELBO
Optimization	Gradient descent	Mini-batch gradient descent

12.2.3 Implementing the approximate model

We are now ready to implement a VGP in GPyTorch. Our plan is to write a VGP model class, which is similar to the GP model classes we have worked with, and minimize its ELBO using mini-batch gradient descent. The differences in our workflow described in table 12.2 are reflected in our code in this subsection. Table 12.3 shows the components required when implementing a GP versus a VGP in GPyTorch. In addition to a mean and covariance module, a VGP requires two other components:

- *A variational distribution*—Defines the distribution over the inducing points for the VGP. As we learned in the previous section, this distribution is to be optimized so that the VGP resembles the GP trained on the full dataset.
- *A variational strategy*—Defines how predictions are produced from the inducing points. In section 2.2, we saw that a multivariate normal distribution may be updated in light of an observation. This variational strategy facilitates the same update for the variational distribution.

Table 12.3   Necessary components when implementing a GP vs. a VGP in GPyTorch. A VGP requires a mean and covariance module like a GP but additionally needs a variational distribution and a variational strategy.

Components	GP	VGP
Mean module	Yes	Yes
Covariance module	Yes	Yes
Variational distribution	No	Yes
Variational strategy	No	Yes

With these components in mind, we now implement the VGP model class, which we name `ApproximateGPModel`. We don't take in the training data and a likelihood function in the `__init__()` method anymore. Instead, we take in a set of inducing points that will be used to represent the entire dataset. The rest of the `__init__()` method consists of declaring the learning pipeline that will be used to learn which set of inducing points is best:

- *The* `variational_distribution` *variable is an instance of the* `Cholesky-VariationalDistribution` *class, which takes in the number of inducing points during initialization.* The variational distribution is the core of a VGP.

- *The* `variational_strategy` *variable is an instance of the* `VariationalStrategy` *class.* It takes in the set of inducing points as well as the variational distribution. We set `learn_inducing_locations = True` so that we can learn the best locations for these inducing points during training. If this variable is set to `False`, the points passed to `__init__()` (stored in `inducing`) will be used as the inducing points:

Instead of an ExactGP object, our VGP is an approximate GP.   **Takes in a set of initial inducing points**

```
class ApproximateGPModel(gpytorch.models.ApproximateGP):
    def __init__(self, inducing_points):
        variational_distribution =
        gpytorch.variational.CholeskyVariationalDistribution(
            inducing_points.size(0)
        )
        variational_strategy = gpytorch.variational.VariationalStrategy(
            self,
            inducing_points,
            variational_distribution,
            learn_inducing_locations=True,
        )
        super().__init__(variational_strategy)

    ...
```

Sets up variational parameters necessary for training

... ◁——— **To be continued**

As the last step in the __init__() method, we declare the mean and covariance functions for the VGP. They should be whatever we'd like to use in a regular GP if it were to be trained on the data. In our case, we use the constant mean and the RBF kernel with an output scale:

```
class ApproximateGPModel(gpytorch.models.ApproximateGP):
    def __init__(self, inducing_points):
        ...

        self.mean_module = gpytorch.means.ConstantMean()
        self.covar_module = gpytorch.kernels.ScaleKernel(
            gpytorch.kernels.RBFKernel()
        )
```

We also declare the forward() method in the same way as in a regular GP, which we do not show here. Let's now initialize this model with the first 50 data points in the training set as the inducing points:

```
model = ApproximateGPModel(train_x[:50, :])     ◁
likelihood = gpytorch.likelihoods.GaussianLikelihood()
```

> **The sliced tensor train_x[:50, :] gives the first 50 data points in train_x.**

There is nothing special about these first 50 data points, and their values, stored internally in the VGP model, will be modified during training. The most important part of this initialization is that we are specifying that the model should use 50 inducing points. If we'd like to use 100, we could pass train_x[:100, :] to the initialization.

It's hard to say exactly what number of inducing points is sufficient for a VGP. The fewer points we use, the faster the model will train but the less effective those inducing points will be at representing the whole set. As the number of points increases, a VGP has more freedom in spreading out the inducing points to cover the whole set, but training will become slower.

> **NOTE** A general rule is not to go over 1,000 inducing points. As we discuss shortly, 50 points is enough for us to approximate the trained GP in the previous subsection with high fidelity.

To set up mini-batch gradient descent, we first need an optimizer. We, once again, use the Adam optimizer:

```
optimizer = torch.optim.Adam(
    [
        {"params": model.parameters()},
        {"params": likelihood.parameters()}     ◁
    ],
    lr=0.01
)
```

> **Optimizes the parameters of the likelihood together with those of the GP**

> ### Parameters to optimize
> Previously, we only needed to pass `model.parameters()` to Adam. Here, the likelihood is not coupled with the VGP model—a regular GP is initialized with a likelihood, while a VGP isn't. So, it's necessary to pass `likelihood.parameters()` to Adam in this case.

For the loss function, we use the `gpytorch.mlls.VariationalELBO` class, which implements the ELBO quantity we aim to optimize with a VGP. During initialization, an instance of this class takes in the likelihood function, the VGP model, and the size of the full training set (which we can access with `train_y.size(0)`). With that, we declare this object as follows:

```
mll = gpytorch.mlls.VariationalELBO(
    likelihood,
    model,                              The size of the
    num_data=train_y.size(0)    ◁──┘   training data
)
```

With the model, the optimizer, and the loss function set up, we now need to run mini-batch gradient descent. To do this, we split our training dataset into batches, each containing 100 points, using PyTorch's `TensorDataset` and `DataLoader` classes:

```
train_dataset = torch.utils.data.TensorDataset(train_x, train_y)
train_loader = torch.utils.data.DataLoader(train_dataset, batch_size=100)
```

This `train_loader` object allows us to iterate through mini batches of size 100 of our dataset in a clean way when running gradient descent. The loss—that is, the ELBO—is computed with the following syntax:

```
output = model(x_batch)
loss = -mll(output, y_batch)
```

Here, `x_batch` and `y_batch` are a given batch (small subset) of the full training set. Overall, gradient descent is implemented as follows:

```
model.train()            Enables
likelihood.train()       training mode         Iterates through the entire
                                               training dataset 50 times
for i in tqdm(range(50)):               ◁──
    for x_batch, y_batch in train_loader:   ◁──┤  In each iteration, iterates through
        optimizer.zero_grad()                      the mini batches in train_loader

        output = model(x_batch)             Mini-batch gradient
        loss = -mll(output, y_batch)        descent, running gradient
                                            descent on the batches
        loss.backward()
        optimizer.step()
```

```
model.eval()          Enables
likelihood.eval()     prediction mode
```

While running this mini-batch gradient descent loop, you will notice it is significantly faster than the loop with the regular GP. (On the same MacBook, this process took less than one second, a major improvement in speed!)

> ### The speed of a VGP
> You might think that our comparison between the 500 iterations of gradient descent with the regular GP and the 50 iterations of mini-batch gradient descent with the VGP is not a fair one. But remember that in each iteration of the outer `for` loop of mini-batch gradient descent, we also iterate over 10 mini batches in `train_loader`, so in the end, we did take 500 gradient steps in total. Further, even if we did run 500 iterations of mini-batch gradient descent, it would take less than 1 second times 10, still a 4x speedup from 45 seconds.

So with mini-batch gradient descent, our VGP model can be trained much more efficiently. But what about the quality of the training? The left panel of figure 12.10 visualizes the progressive ELBO loss during our mini-batch gradient descent run. Compared with figure 12.5, although the loss didn't consistently decrease at every step (there is a zigzag trend), the loss was effectively minimized throughout the entire procedure.

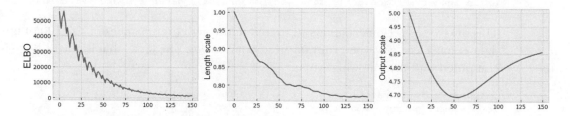

Figure 12.10 Progressive loss and the corresponding length scale and output scale of a VGP during mini-batch gradient descent

This shows that every step during the optimization might not be the best direction to take to minimize the loss, but the mini-batch gradient descent is, indeed, effective at minimizing the loss. This is shown more clearly in figure 12.11.

Now, let's visualize the predictions made by this VGP model to see if it produces reasonable results. Using the `visualize_gp_belief()` helper function, we obtain figure 12.12, which shows that we have obtained a high-quality approximation of the GP trained on the true loss at a small fraction of the time cost.

To end our discussion on VPGs, let's visualize the locations of the inducing points our VGP model has learned. We have said that these inducing points should

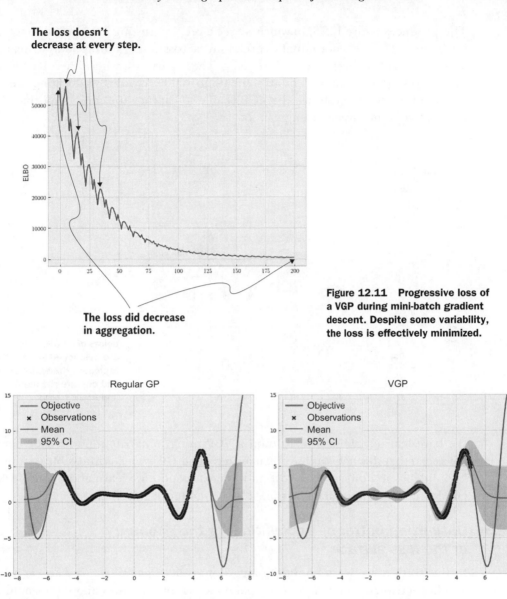

**The loss doesn't
decrease at every step.**

**The loss did decrease
in aggregation.**

**Figure 12.11   Progressive loss of
a VGP during mini-batch gradient
descent. Despite some variability,
the loss is effectively minimized.**

**Figure 12.12   Predictions made by a GP and a VGP. The predictions made by the VGP roughly match those
by the GP.**

be representative of the whole dataset and capture its trend well. To plot the inducing points, we can access their locations with `model.variational_strategy.inducing_points.detach()` and plot them as scattered points along the mean prediction. Our `visualize_gp_belief()` helper function already has this implemented, and the only thing we need to do is to set `variational = True` when calling this function:

```
visualize_gp_belief(model, likelihood, variational=True)
```

This produces figure 12.13, in which we see a very interesting behavior in these inducing points. They are not equally spread out across our training data; instead, they
cluster around different parts of the data. These parts are where the objective function curves up or down or exhibits some nontrivial behavior. By allocating the inducing points to these locations, the VGP is able to capture the most important trends
embedded in the large training dataset.

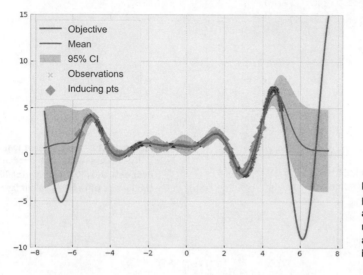

Figure 12.13   The inducing
points of a VGP. These points
are positioned so that they
represent the entire data
and capture the most
important trends.

We have learned about how to train a VGP using mini-batch gradient descent and
have seen that this helps us approximate a regular GP, which is infeasible to train, with
high fidelity at a much lower cost. In the next section, we learn about another gradient descent algorithm that can train a VGP even more effectively.

12.3   *Optimizing better by accounting for the geometry of the loss surface*

In this section, we learn about the algorithm called *natural gradient descent,* which is
another version of gradient descent that reasons more carefully about the geometry of
the loss function when computing the descent step. As we see shortly, this careful reasoning allows us to quickly descend the loss function, ultimately leading to more effective optimization with fewer iterations (that is, faster convergence).

To understand the motivation for natural gradient descent and why it works better
than what we already have, we first distinguish between the two types of parameters of
a VGP:

- The first type is the regular parameters of a GP, such as the mean constant and
  the length and output scales of the covariance function. These parameters take
  on regular numerical values that exist in the Euclidean space.

- The second type consists of the *variational* parameters that only a VGP has. These have to do with the inducing points and the various components necessary to facilitate the approximation with the variational distribution. In other words, these parameters are associated with probability distributions and have values that cannot be represented well within the Euclidean space.

> **NOTE** The difference between these two types of parameters is somewhat similar, although not exactly analogous, to how the Euclidean distance can measure the distance between two points in that space, but it can't measure the difference between two probability distributions.

Although mini-batch gradient descent as we used it in the previous section worked sufficiently well, the algorithm assumes that all parameters exist in Euclidean space. For example, from the perspective of the algorithm, the difference between a length scale of 1 and a length scale of 2 is the same as the difference between an inducing point's mean value of 1 and a mean value of 2. However, this is not true: going from a length scale of 1 to a length scale of 2 would affect the VGP model very differently from going from an inducing point's mean value of 1 to a mean value of 2. This is illustrated in the example of figure 12.14, where the behavior of the loss with respect to the length scale is quite different than that with respect to the inducing mean.

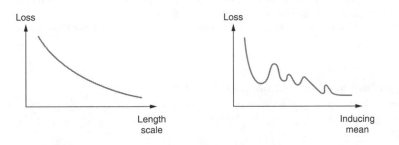

Figure 12.14   An example of how the loss to be minimized might behave very differently with respect to a regular parameter and a variational parameter. This gives rise to the need to take into account the geometry of the loss.

This difference in behavior exists because the geometry of the loss function with respect to the regular parameters of a VGP is fundamentally different from that with respect to the variational parameters. If mini-batch gradient descent could account for this geometric difference when computing a descent direction of the loss, the algorithm would be more effective at minimizing that loss. This is where natural gradient descent comes in.

> **DEFINITION** *Natural gradient descent* uses information about the geometry of the loss function with respect to the variational parameters to compute better descent directions for these parameters.

By taking better descent directions, natural gradient descent can help us optimize our VGP model more effectively and quickly. The end result is that we converge to our final model in fewer steps. Continuing with our two-dimensional illustration of the different gradient descent algorithms, figure 12.15 shows how this geometric reasoning helps natural gradient descent reach the goal faster than mini-batch gradient descent. That is, natural gradient descent tends to require fewer steps during training to achieve the same loss as mini-batch gradient descent. In our climbing-down-the-mountain analogy, with natural gradient descent, we are still blindfolded by a thin cloth when trying to climb down the mountain, but we are now wearing special hiking shoes that help us traverse the terrain more effectively.

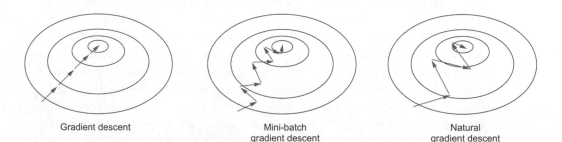

Gradient descent   Mini-batch   Natural
                      gradient descent   gradient descent

Figure 12.15   An illustration of gradient descent, mini-batch gradient descent, and natural gradient descent within a loss "valley," where the center of the valley gives the lowest loss. By accounting for the geometry of the loss function, natural gradient descent reaches the loss minimum more quickly than mini-batch.

> ## Supplementary material for natural gradient descent
> For a more math-heavy explanation of natural gradient descent, I recommend the excellent "Natural Gradient Descent" blog post by Agustinus Kristiadi: http://mng .bz/EQAj.

NOTE   It is important to note that the natural gradient descent algorithm only optimizes the variational parameters of a VGP. The regular parameters, such as the length and output scales, could still be optimized by a regular mini-batch gradient descent algorithm. We see this when we implement our new training procedure next.

And with that, let's use natural gradient descent to train our VGP model. With the same one-dimensional objective function in previous sections, we implement a VGP model that works with natural gradient descent. The model class in this case is similar to `ApproximateGPModel`, which we implemented for mini-batch gradient descent in the previous section, in that it

- Still extends `gpytorch.models.ApproximateGP`
- Needs a variational strategy to manage the learning process

- Has a mean function, covariance function, and `forward()` method like a regular GP model

The only difference here is that the variational distribution needs to be an instance of `gpytorch.variational.NaturalVariationalDistribution` for us to use natural gradient descent when training the model. The entire model class is implemented as follows:

```
class NaturalGradientGPModel(gpytorch.models.ApproximateGP):
  def __init__(self, inducing_points):
    variational_distribution =
      gpytorch.variational.
      ➥NaturalVariationalDistribution(
        inducing_points.size(0)
    )

    variational_strategy = gpytorch.variational.
    ➥VariationalStrategy(
        self,
        inducing_points,
        variational_distribution,
        learn_inducing_locations=True,
    )
    super().__init__(variational_strategy)
    self.mean_module = gpytorch.means.ConstantMean()
    self.covar_module = gpytorch.kernels.ScaleKernel(
        gpytorch.kernels.RBFKernel()
    )

  def forward(self, x):
    ...
```

The variational distribution needs to be a natural one to work with natural gradient descent.

Declaring the rest of the variational strategy is the same as before.

The forward() method is the same as before.

We, once again, initialize this VGP model with 50 inducing points:

```
model = NaturalGradientGPModel(train_x[:50, :])
likelihood = gpytorch.likelihoods.GaussianLikelihood()
```

50 inducing points

Now comes the important part, in which we declare the optimizers for our training. Remember that we use the natural gradient descent algorithm to optimize the variational parameters of our model. However, the other parameters, such as the length and output scales, still must be optimized by the Adam optimizer. We, thus, use the following code:

```
ngd_optimizer = gpytorch.optim.NGD(
  model.variational_parameters(), num_data=train_y.
  ➥size(0), lr=0.1
)
```

Natural gradient descent takes in the VGP's variational parameters, model.variational_parameters().

```
hyperparam_optimizer = torch.optim.Adam(
  [{"params": model.parameters()}, {"params":
  ➥likelihood.parameters()}],
  lr=0.01
)
```

Adam takes in the VGP's other parameters, model.parameters() and likelihood.parameters().

```
mll = gpytorch.mlls.VariationalELBO(
  likelihood, model, num_data=train_y.size(0)
)
```

Now, during training, we still compute the loss using

```
output = model(x_batch)
loss = -mll(output, y_batch)
```

While computing the loss, we loop through mini-batches (`x_batch` and `y_batch`) of our training data. However, now that we have two optimizers running at the same time, we need to manage them by calling `zero_grad()` (to clear out the gradients from the previous step) and `step()` (to take a descent step) on each of them at each iteration of training:

```
model.train()          │ Enables
likelihood.train()     │ training mode

for i in tqdm(range(50)):
    for x_batch, y_batch in train_loader:
        ngd_optimizer.zero_grad()              │ Clears out the gradients
        hyperparam_optimizer.zero_grad()       │ from the previous step

        output = model(x_batch)
        loss = -mll(output, y_batch)

        loss.backward()

        ngd_optimizer.step()                   │ Takes a descent step
        hyperparam_optimizer.step()            │ with each optimizer

model.eval()           │ Enables
likelihood.eval()      │ prediction mode
```

> **NOTE** As always, we need to call `model.train()` and `likelihood.train()` prior to gradient descent, and `model.eval()` and `likelihood.eval()` after training has finished.

Notice that we call `zero_grad()` and `step()` on both the natural gradient descent optimizer and Adam to optimize the respective parameters of a VGP model. The training loop, once again, takes a very short time to finish, and the trained VGP produces the predictions shown in figure 12.16. We see very similar predictions as those of a regular GP in figure 12.4 and those of a VGP trained with mini-batch gradient descent in figure 12.13.

We can further inspect the progressive ELBO loss during training. Its progress is visualized in the left panel of figure 12.17.

Remarkably, our ELBO loss dropped to a low value almost immediately during training, indicating natural gradient descent was able to help us converge to a good

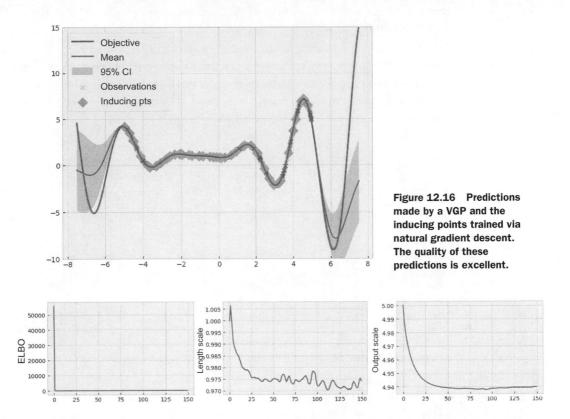

Figure 12.16 Predictions made by a VGP and the inducing points trained via natural gradient descent. The quality of these predictions is excellent.

Figure 12.17 Progressive loss of a VGP during natural gradient descent. The loss was effectively minimized after a few number of iterations.

model quickly. This illustrates the benefits of this variant of the gradient descent algorithm when training VGPs.

We have now reached the end of chapter 12. In this chapter, we learned to scale GP models to large datasets by using inducing points, which are a set of representative points that aim to capture the trends exhibited by a large training set. The resulting model is called a VGP, which is amenable to mini-batch gradient descent and, therefore, can be trained without the computation of the model loss across all data points. We also examined natural gradient descent as a more effective version of the mini-batch algorithm, allowing us to optimize more effectively. In chapter 13, we cover another advanced usage of GPs, combining them with neural networks to model complex, structured data.

12.4 Exercise

This exercise demonstrates the improvement in efficiency when going from a regular GP model to a VGP one on a real-life dataset of housing prices in California. Our goal is to observe the computational benefits of a VGP—this time, in a real-world setting.

Complete the following steps:

1 Use the `read_csv()` function from the Pandas library to read in the dataset stored in the spreadsheet named `data/housing.csv`, obtained from Kaggle's California Housing Prices dataset (http://mng.bz/N2Q7) under a Creative Common Public Domain license. Once read in, the Pandas dataframe should look similar to the output in figure 12.18.

	longitude	latitude	housing_median_age	total_rooms	total_bedrooms	population	households	median_income	median_house_value
0	-117.08	32.70	37	2176	418.0	1301	375	2.8750	98900
1	-117.91	34.11	20	3158	684.0	2396	713	3.5250	153000
2	-117.10	32.75	11	2393	726.0	1905	711	1.3448	91300
3	-117.22	32.74	52	1260	202.0	555	209	7.2758	345200
4	-121.99	37.29	32	2930	481.0	1336	481	6.4631	344100
...	...	...	...	...	...	...	...	...	...
4995	-118.41	34.19	42	779	145.0	450	148	3.9792	193800
4996	-122.96	38.42	50	2530	524.0	940	361	2.9375	122900
4997	-118.00	33.77	24	1324	267.0	687	264	3.4327	192800
4998	-122.81	38.54	12	2289	611.0	919	540	1.1553	139300
4999	-118.08	33.84	25	3696	953.0	2827	860	3.3438	153300

Figure 12.18   The housing price dataset shown as a Pandas dataframe. This is the training set for this exercise.

2 Visualize the `median_house_value` column, which is our prediction target, in a scatter plot whose *x*- and *y*-axes correspond to the `longitude` and `latitude` columns. The location of a dot corresponds to the location of a house, and the color of the dot corresponds to the price. The visualization should look similar to figure 12.19.

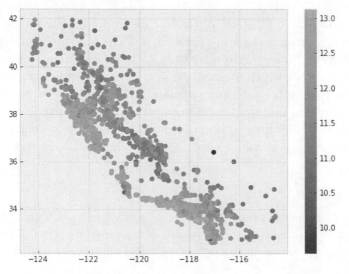

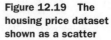
Figure 12.19   The housing price dataset shown as a scatter

3 Extract all the columns, except the last (`median_house_value`), and store them as a PyTorch tensor. This will be used as our training features, `train_x`.

4 Extract the `median_house_value` column, and store its log transformation as another PyTorch tensor. This is our training target, `train_y`.

5 Normalize the training labels `train_y` by subtracting the mean and dividing by the standard deviation. This will make training more stable.

6 Implement a regular GP model with a constant mean function and a Matérn 5/2 kernel with automatic relevance determination (ARD) with an output scale. For a refresher on Matérn kernels and ARD, refer to sections 3.4.2 and 3.4.3, respectively.

7 Make a likelihood whose noise is constrained to be at least 0.1 using the following code:

```
likelihood = gpytorch.likelihoods.GaussianLikelihood(
    noise_constraint=gpytorch.constraints.GreaterThan(1e-1)    ◁
)
```

The constraint forces the noise to be at least 0.1.

This constraint helps us smooth out the training labels by raising the noise tolerance.

8 Initialize the previously implemented GP model and train it with the likelihood using gradient descent for 10 iterations. Observe the total training time.

9 Implement a variational GP model with the same mean and covariance functions as the GP. This model looks similar to the `ApproximateGPModel` class we implemented in the chapter, except we now need the Matérn 5/2 kernel with ARD.

10 Train this VGP with the similarly initialized likelihood and 100 inducing points, using natural gradient descent for 10 iterations. For mini-batch gradient descent, you could split the training set into batches of size 100.

11 Verify that training the VGP takes less time than training the GP. For timing functionalities, you can use `time.time()` to record the start and end time of training each model, or you can use the `tqdm` library to keep track of the duration of training, like in the code we've been using.

The solution is included in the `CH11/02 - Exercise.ipynb` notebook.

Summary

- The computation cost of a GP scales cubically with the size of the training dataset. Therefore, training the model becomes prohibitive as the size of the dataset grows.
- Computing the loss of an ML model across a large number of data points is numerically unstable. A loss computed in an unstable way may mislead optimization during gradient descent, leading to poor predictive performance.

- A VGP scales to a large dataset by only training on a small set of inducing points. These inducing points need to be representative of the dataset, so the trained model can be as similar as possible to the GP trained on the whole dataset.

- To produce an approximate model that is as close as possible to the model trained on all of the training data, the Kullback–Leibler divergence, which measures the difference between two probability distributions, is used in the formulation of a VGP.

- The evidence lower bound (ELBO) acts as a proxy for the true loss when training a VGP. More specifically, the ELBO lower-bounds the marginal log likelihood of the model, which is what we aim to optimize. By optimizing the ELBO, we indirectly optimize the marginal log likelihood.

- Training a VGP may be done in small batches, allowing for a more stable computation of the loss. The gradient descent algorithm used in this procedure is mini-batch gradient descent.

- Although each step of mini-batch gradient descent is not guaranteed to completely minimize loss, the algorithm, when a large number of iterations are run, can effectively reduce the loss. This is because many steps of mini-batch gradient descent, in aggregation, can point toward the right direction to minimize the loss.

- Natural gradient descent accounts for the geometry of the loss function with respect to the variational parameters of a VGP. This geometric reasoning allows the algorithm to update the variational parameters of the trained model and minimize the loss more effectively, leading to faster convergence.

- Natural gradient descent optimizes the variational parameters of a VGP. Regular parameters such as the length and output scales are optimized by mini-batch gradient descent.

13

Combining Gaussian processes with neural networks

This chapter covers

- The difficulty of processing complex, structured data with common covariance functions
- Using neural networks to handle complex, structured data
- Combining neural networks with GPs

In chapter 2, we learned that the mean and covariance functions of a Gaussian process (GP) act as prior information that we'd like to incorporate into the model when making predictions. For this reason, the choice for these functions greatly affects how the trained GP behaves. Consequently, if the mean and covariance functions are misspecified or inappropriate for the task at hand, the resulting predictions won't be useful.

As an example, remember that a *covariance function*, or *kernel*, expresses the correlation—that is, similarity—between two points. The more similar the two points are, the more likely they are to have similar values for the labels we're trying to predict. In our housing price prediction example, similar houses are likely to go for similar prices.

How does a kernel exactly compute the similarity between any two given houses? Let's consider two cases. In the first, a kernel only considers the color of the front door and outputs 1 for any two houses of the same door color and 0 otherwise. In other words, this kernel thinks two houses are similar if and only if they have the same color for their front doors.

This kernel, as illustrated by figure 13.1, is a bad choice for a housing price prediction model. The kernel thinks that the house on the left and the one in the middle should have similar prices, while the house on the right and the one in the middle should have different prices. This is not appropriate, as the left house is much bigger than the other two, which are of similar size. The misprediction happens because the kernel is wrong about which characteristic of a house is a good predictive feature for how much the house costs.

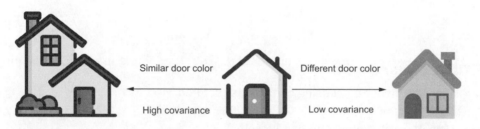

Figure 13.1   The covariance between houses computed by an inappropriate kernel. Because it looks only at the color of the front door, this kernel doesn't produce appropriate covariances.

The other kernel is more sophisticated and accounts for relevant factors, such as location and living area. This kernel is more appropriate as it can describe the similarity between the prices of two houses more reasonably. Having the appropriate kernel—that is, the correct measure of similarity—is paramount for GPs. If the kernel can correctly describe how similar or different a given pair of data points are, the GP using the covariance will be able to produce well-calibrated predictions. Otherwise, the predictions will be of low quality.

You might think a kernel for houses that only considers door color is inappropriate, and no reasonable kernels in ML would behave this way. However, as we show in this chapter, some common kernels we have used thus far (e.g., RBF and Matérn) fall apart in the same way when processing structured input data, such as images. Specifically, they fail to adequately describe the similarity between two images, which poses a challenge for training GPs on these structured data types. The approach we take is to use neural networks. Neural networks are flexible models that can approximate any function well, given enough data. We learn to use a neural network to transform input data that a GP's kernel isn't able to process well. In doing this, we get the best of both worlds: flexible modeling with a neural network *and* uncertainty-calibrated predictions from a GP.

In this chapter, we show that our usual RBF kernel doesn't capture the structure of a common dataset well, resulting in bad predictions from the GP. We then combine a neural network model with this GP and see that the new kernel can successfully reason about similarity. By the end of the chapter, we obtain a framework to help a GP handle structured data types and improve predictive performance.

13.1 Data that contains structures

In this section, we explain what exactly we mean by *structured data*. Unlike the type of data we have been using to train our GPs in previous chapters, where each feature (column) in the dataset could take on values within a continuous range, in many applications, data has more complexity. Take the following, for instance:

- The number of stories in a house can only be a positive integer.
- In computer vision tasks, the pixel value in an image is an integer between 0 and 255.
- In molecular ML, a molecule is often represented as a graph.

That is, there are *structures* embedded in the data points in these applications, or requirements that the data points need to follow: no house can have a negative number of stories; a pixel cannot take a fraction as its value; a graph denoting a molecule will have nodes and edges representing chemicals and bindings. We call these kinds of data *structured data*. Throughout this chapter, we use the popular MNIST handwritten digit dataset (see https://huggingface.co/datasets/mnist) as a case study for our discussions.

DEFINITION The Modified National Institute of Standards and Technology (MNIST)) dataset contains images of handwritten digits. Each image is a 28-by-28 matrix of integers between 0 and 255.

An example data point from this set is shown in figure 13.2, where a pixel is shown with a shade corresponding to its value; 0 corresponds to a white pixel, and 255 corresponds to a dark pixel. We see that this data point is an image of the number five.

NOTE While this handwritten digit recognition task is technically a classification problem, we use it to simulate a regression problem (which is the type of problem we aim to solve in BayesOpt). Since each label is a number (a digit), we pretend these labels exist in a continuous range and directly use them as our prediction target.

Our task is to train a GP on a dataset of image labels (each label here is the value of the digit written in the corresponding image) and then use it to predict on a test set. This distinction is illustrated in figure 13.3, which shows that unlike classification, where we choose one of the classes as a prediction for each data point, each prediction here is a number inside a continuous range in a regression task.

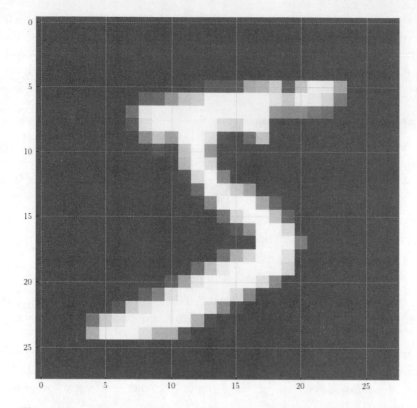

Figure 13.2   A data point from the MNIST dataset, which is an image with 28 rows and 28 columns of pixels, represented as a PyTorch tensor

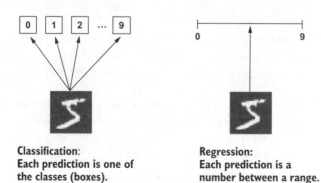

Classification:
Each prediction is one of
the classes (boxes).

Regression:
Each prediction is a
number between a range.

Figure 13.3   Classification vs. regression in the context of the MNIST data. Each prediction is a classification task that corresponds to one of the classes; each prediction in regression is a number inside a continuous range.

There are many real-world applications that follow this form of regression problem on structured data:

- In product recommendation, we want to predict the probability that someone will click on a customized ad. The ads, which are images one can customize, are the structured data, and the click probability is the prediction target. This probability can be any number between 0 and 1.

- In materials science, a scientist may want to predict the energy level of a molecular composition when that composition is synthesized in a laboratory. Each molecular composition can be represented as a graph of a specific structure with nodes and edges, and the energy level can be any number between the theoretical minimum and maximum energy levels that a composition can exhibit.

- In drug discovery, we want to predict the effectiveness of a drug that could be produced. As illustrated in figure 13.4, each drug corresponds to a chemical compound, which can also be represented as a graph. Its effectiveness can be a real number on a scale (say from 0 to 10).

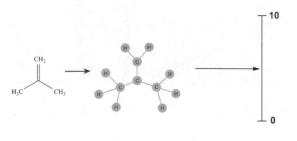

Figure 13.4 Drug discovery as an example of a structured regression problem. Each compound is represented as a structured graph, and we aim to predict the effectiveness of the compound in treating some disease on a scale from 0 to 10.

Each data point (input) is a molecule represented as a graph.   Each prediction (output) is a real number inside a range.

In all of these applications, the input data we'd like to perform a prediction on is structured, and our prediction target is a real-valued number. In short, they are regression problems on structured data. Using the MNIST dataset, we simulate one such problem.

13.2 Capturing similarity within structured data

In this section, we explore how common kernels, such as the radial basis function (RBF) kernel (see section 2.4), fail to describe similarity within structured data. The output of the kernel for any two inputs x_1 and x_2, which quantifies the covariance of the two inputs, is defined as follows:

$$K(x_1, x_2) = \exp\left(-\frac{\|x_1 - x_2\|^2}{2l^2}\right)$$

This output, which is the covariance between the two variables, is the exponential of the negated difference in values between the two inputs divided by a scale. The output is always between 0 and 1, and the bigger the difference in values, the smaller the output.

This makes sense in many cases since if the two inputs have similar values, and hence a small difference, their covariance will be high, and if they have different values, the covariance will be low. Two houses with roughly equal living area are likely to have similar prices—that is, their prices have a high covariance; the prices of a very large house and very small one, on the other hand, are likely to have a low covariance.

13.2.1 *Using a kernel with GPyTorch*

Let's verify this with code. We usually initialize an `RBFKernel` object when creating a GP model. Here, we work directly with this kernel object. To do this, we first create an RBF kernel object with GPyTorch:

```
import gpytorch

rbf_kernel = gpytorch.kernels.RBFKernel()
```

> **NOTE**   As always, GPyTorch is our library of choice for implementing GP-related objects in Python. Refer to section 2.4 for a refresher on how a kernel object is used by a GP in GPyTorch.

To compute the covariance between two inputs, we simply pass them to this kernel object. For example, let's compute the covariance between 0 and 0.1:

```
>>> rbf_kernel(torch.tensor([0.]), torch.tensor([0.1])).evaluate().item()
0.9896470904350281
```

These two numbers are close to each other on the real number line (that is, they are similar), so their covariance is very high—almost 1. Let's now compute the covariance between 0 and 10, two numbers that are different:

```
>>> rbf_kernel(torch.tensor([0.]), torch.tensor([10.])).evaluate().item()
0.0
```

This time, as the difference between the two numbers is much larger, their covariance drops to 0. This contrast, which is a reasonable behavior to have, is illustrated by figure 13.5.

Figure 13.5   The covariance between various numbers. When the difference between two numbers is small, the covariance increases. When the difference is large, the covariance decreases.

The problem arises when the difference in value between two inputs doesn't capture the structural difference in the meaning of the data. This is often the case for structured data such as images, as we will see now.

13.2.2 *Working with images in PyTorch*

In this subsection, we see how images are imported and stored as PyTorch tensors as well as how value-based similarity metrics, such as the RBF kernel, break down when processing this kind of data. First, we redefine our RBF kernel with a large-length scale so that higher covariances are more likely:

```
rbf_kernel = gpytorch.kernels.RBFKernel()
rbf_kernel.lengthscale = 100
```
The large-length scale leads to higher covariances.

Now, we need to import images from the MNIST dataset into our Python code. We can do this using PyTorch and its popular add-on library, torchvision:

```
import torch
from torchvision import datasets, transforms


transform = transforms.Compose([
    transforms.ToTensor(),
    transforms.Normalize((0.1307,), (0.3081,))
])

dataset = datasets.MNIST(
    "../data", train=True, download=True, transform=transform
)

train_x = dataset.data.view(-1, 28 * 28)
```
Defines the transformation to normalize the pixel values

Downloads and imports the dataset

Extracts the pixel values as a flattened tensor

We won't go deeply into this code, as it's not the focus of our discussion. All we need to know is that `train_x` contains the images in the MNIST dataset, each of which is stored as a PyTorch tensor containing the pixel values that represent an image of a handwritten digit.

As the data points are images, we can visualize them as heat maps, using the familiar `imshow()` function from Matplotlib. For example, the following code visualizes the first data point in `train_x`:

```
plt.figure(figsize=(8, 8))

plt.imshow(train_x[0, :].view(28, 28));
```
Each image has 28 rows and 28 columns of pixels, so we need to reshape it into a 28-by-28 square tensor.

This code produces figure 13.2, which we see is an image of the digit 5. When we print out the actual values of this first data point, we see that it's a $28 \times 28 = 784$-element PyTorch tensor:

```
>>> train_x[0, :]
tensor([ 0,    0,    0,    0,    0,    0,    0,    0,    0,    0,    0,    0,    0,    0,
         0,    0,    0,    0,    0,    0,    0,    0,    0,    0,    0,    0,    0,    0,
         0,    0,    0,    0,    0,    0,    0,    0,    0,    0,    0,    0,    0,    0,
         0,    0,    0,    0,    0,    0,    0,    0,    0,    0,    0,    0,    0,    0,
         0,    0,    0,    0,    0,    0,    0,    0,    0,    0,    0,    0,    0,    0,
```

```
     0,   0,   0,   0,   0,   0,   0,   0,   0,   0,   0,   0,   0,   0,
     0,   0,   0,   0,   0,   0,   0,   0,   0,   0,   0,   0,   0,   0,
     0,   0,   0,   0,   0,   0,   0,   0,   0,   0,   0,   0,   0,   0,
     0,   0,   0,   0,   0,   0,   0,   0,   0,   0,   0,   0,   0,   0,
     0,   0,   0,   0,   0,   0,   0,   0,   0,   0,   0,   0,   0,   0,
     0,   0,   0,   0,   0,   0,   0,   0,   0,   0,   0,   0,   3,  18,
    18,  18, 126, 136, 175,  26, 166, 255, 247, 127,   0,   0,   0,   0,
     0,   0,   0,   0,   0,   0,   0,   0,  30,  36,  94, 154, 170, 253,
   253, 253, 253, 253, 225, 172, 253, 242, 195,  64,   0,   0,   0,   0,
     0,   0,   0,   0,   0,   0,   0,  49, 238, 253, 253, 253, 253, 253,
   253, 253, 253, 251,  93,  82,  82,  56,  39,   0,   0,   0,   0,   0,
     0,   0,   0,   0,   0,   0,   0,  18, 219, 253, 253, 253, 253, 253,
   198, 182, 247, 241,   0,   0,   0,   0,   0,   0,   0,   0,   0,   0,
     0,   0,   0,   0,   0,   0,   0,   0,  80, 156, 107, 253, 253, 205,
    11,   0,  43, 154,   0,   0,   0,   0,   0,   0,   0,   0,   0,   0,
     0,   0,   0,   0,   0,   0,   0,   0,   0,  14,   1, 154, 253,  90,
[output truncated]
```

Each element in this tensor, ranging between 0 and 255, represents a pixel we see in figure 13.2. A value of 0 corresponds to the lowest signal, the background in the figure, while higher values correspond to the bright spots.

13.2.3   *Computing the covariance of two images*

That's all the background information we need to explore the problem that common GP kernels face when processing structured data. To highlight the problem, we single out three specific data points, which we call point A, point B, and point C, respectively, indexed by the following numbers:

```
ind1 = 304      ⌐┘  Point A
ind2 = 786      ◁────── Point B
ind3 = 4        ◁─┐  Point C
```

Before checking the actual digits these images show, let's compute their covariance matrix using our RBF kernel:

```
>>> rbf_kernel(train_x[[ind1, ind2, ind3], :]).evaluate()
tensor([[1.0000e+00, 4.9937e-25, 0.0000e+00],
        [4.9937e-25, 1.0000e+00, 0.0000e+00],
        [0.0000e+00, 0.0000e+00, 1.0000e+00]], ...)
```

This is a 3-by-3 covariance matrix with a familiar structure: the diagonal elements take on the value of 1, representing the variances of the individual variables, while the off-diagonal elements represent the different covariances. We see that the points A and C are completely uncorrelated, having a covariance of zero, while points A and B are slightly correlated. According to the RBF kernel, points A and B are similar to each other and are completely different from point C.

We should, then, expect points A and B to share the same label. However, this is not the case! Once again, we visualize these data points as heat maps, and we obtain figure 13.6.

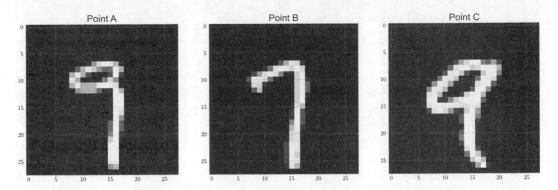

Figure 13.6 Three specific data points from the MNIST dataset. The first and second points have a nonzero covariance, despite having different labels. The first and third points have a zero covariance, despite having the same label.

Here, it's points A and C that share the same label (digit 9). So why does the RBF kernel think points A and B are correlated? Looking at figure 13.6, we can make a good guess that while points A and B have different labels, the images themselves are similar in the sense that many of the pixels match. In fact, the stroke that makes up the tail of the digits almost matches exactly in the two images. So, in a sense, the RBF kernel is doing its job, computing the difference between the images and outputting a number representing their covariance based on that difference. However, the difference is computed by comparing the pixels in and of themselves, which is not a metric that is indicative of what we're trying to learn: the values of the digits.

By only looking at the pixel values, the RBF kernel is overestimating the covariance between points A and B, which have different labels, and underestimating the covariance between points A and C, which share the same label, as illustrated by figure 13.7. An analogy can be used here to demonstrate the inappropriate house kernel we mentioned at the introduction of the chapter: this kernel looks only at the color of the front door to decide whether two houses are correlated, leading to inaccurate predictions of their prices. In a similar (but not as extreme) manner, the RBF kernel only considers the values of the pixels, rather than the higher-level patterns, when comparing two images, which leads to inferior predictive performance.

Figure 13.7 The covariance between handwritten digits computed by the RBF kernel. Because it only looks at the pixel values, the RBF kernel doesn't produce appropriate covariances.

13.2.4 *Training a GP on image data*

By using the wrong metric for similarity, RBF confuses which of points B and C is the one correlated to point A, which, as we see next, leads to poor results when training a GP. We once again use the MNIST dataset, this time extracting 1,000 data points to make up the training set and another 500 points as the test set. Our data preparation and learning workflow is summarized in figure 13.8, the distinct steps of which we go through in detail.

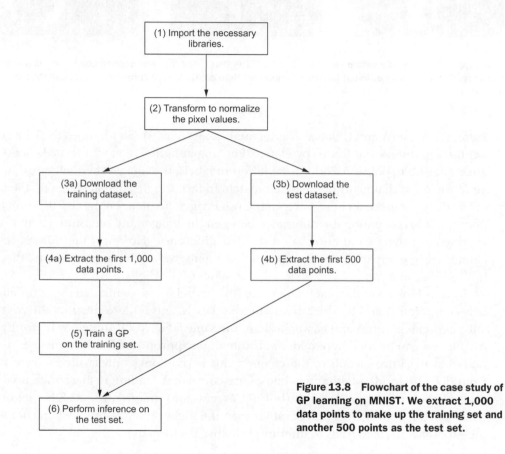

Figure 13.8   Flowchart of the case study of GP learning on MNIST. We extract 1,000 data points to make up the training set and another 500 points as the test set.

First, we import PyTorch and torchvision—the latter of which is an extension of PyTorch that manages computer-vision–related functionalities and datasets, such as MNIST. From torchvision, we import the modules `datasets` and `transforms`, which help us download and manipulate the MNIST data, respectively:

```
import torch
from torchvision import datasets, transforms
```

In the second data preparation step, we again use the object that transforms the images to PyTorch tensors (which is the data structure that GPs implemented in GPyTorch can process) and normalizes the pixel values. This normalization is done by subtracting the pixel values by 0.1307 (the mean of the data) and dividing the values by 0.3081 (the standard deviation of the data). This normalization is considered common practice for the MNIST dataset, and more details on this step can be found in PyTorch's official forum discussion (http://mng.bz/BmBr):

```
transform = transforms.Compose([          Transforms the data
    transforms.ToTensor(),                to PyTorch tensors
    transforms.Normalize((0.1307,), (0.3081,))        Normalizes
])                                                    the tensors
```

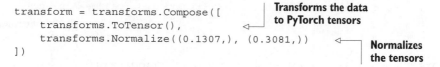

This transformation object stored in `transform` can now be passed to a call to any torchvision dataset initialization, and the transformations (conversion to PyTorch tensors and normalization) will be applied to our data. We initialize the MNIST dataset with this transformation object as follows. Note that we create the dataset twice, once setting `train = True` to create the training set and once setting `train = False` for the test set:

```
dataset1 = datasets.MNIST(                              Downloads and
    "../data", train=True, download=True, transform=transform    imports the
)                                                       training set

dataset2 = datasets.MNIST(                              Downloads and
    "../data", train=False, download=True, transform=transform   imports the
)                                                       test set
```

As the last step of data preparation, we extract the first 1,000 data points from the training set and 500 points from the test set. We do this by accessing from the dataset objects `dataset1` and `dataset2`:

- The `data` attribute to obtain the features, the pixel values making up the image for each data point
- The `targets` attribute to obtain the labels, the values of the handwritten digits:

```
train_x = dataset1.data[:1000, ...].view(1000, -1)
    .to(torch.float)              Gets the first 1,000 points
train_y = dataset1.targets[:1000]  in the training set

test_x = dataset2.data[:500, ...].view(500, -1)
    .to(torch.float)              Gets the first 500 points
test_y = dataset2.targets[:500]   in the test set
```

We also implement a simple GP model with a constant mean and an RBF kernel with an output scale:

```
class GPModel(gpytorch.models.ExactGP):                 A constant
    def __init__(self, train_x, train_y, likelihood):   mean
        super().__init__(train_x, train_y, likelihood)  function
        self.mean_module = gpytorch.means.ConstantMean()
```

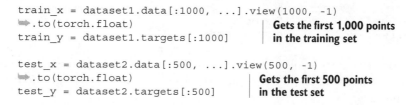

```
    self.covar_module = gpytorch.kernels.ScaleKernel(
        gpytorch.kernels.RBFKernel()
    )
```

An RBF covariance function with an output scale

```
def forward(self, x):
    mean_x = self.mean_module(x)
    covar_x = self.covar_module(x)
    return gpytorch.distributions.MultivariateNormal(mean_x, covar_x)
```

Makes an MVN distribution as the prediction for input x

> **NOTE** The forward() method of a GPyTorch GP model was first discussed in section 2.4.

Then, we initialize our GP and train it on the 1,000-point training set, using gradient descent with the Adam optimizer. This code will optimize the values of the hyperparameters of the GP (e.g., the mean constant and the length and output scale) so that we achieve a high marginal likelihood of the data we observe:

```
likelihood = gpytorch.likelihoods.GaussianLikelihood()
model = GPModel(train_x, train_y, likelihood)
```

Declares the likelihood function and the GP model

```
optimizer = torch.optim.Adam(model.parameters(), lr=0.01)
mll = gpytorch.mlls.ExactMarginalLogLikelihood
⮕(likelihood, model)
```

Declares the gradient descent algorithm and the loss function

```
model.train()
likelihood.train()
```

Enables training mode

```
for i in tqdm(range(500)):
    optimizer.zero_grad()

    output = model(train_x)
    loss = -mll(output, train_y)

    loss.backward()
    optimizer.step()
```

Runs five hundred iterations of gradient descent

```
model.eval()
likelihood.eval()
```

Enables prediction mode

> **NOTE** Refer to section 2.3.2 for a discussion of how gradient descent optimizes the likelihood of the data we observe—that is, how gradient descent trains a GP.

Finally, to see how well our model performs on the test set, we compute the average absolute difference between the GP's prediction and the ground truth (the value of label of each data point). This metric is often called the *mean absolute error*.

> **NOTE** The typical metric for the MNIST dataset is the percentage of the test set that the model predicts correctly (that is, the accuracy), which is the norm

for a classification problem. As we are using this dataset to simulate a regression problem, the mean absolute error is appropriate.

This is done by comparing the mean predictions against the true labels stored in test_y:

```
with torch.no_grad():
    mean_preds = model(test_x).mean

print(torch.mean(torch.abs(mean_preds - test_y)))

Output: 2.7021167278289795
```

This output means that, on average, the GP's prediction for the value of the digit depicted in an image is off by almost 3. This performance is quite low, given that there are only 10 values to learn in this task. This result highlights regular GP models' incapability of dealing with structured data, such as images.

13.3   Using neural networks to process complex structured data

The root cause of our GP's inferior performance, as we have seen, is that the kernels aren't equipped to process the complex structure of the input data, leading to poor covariance calculation. The RBF kernel specifically has a simple form that only accounts for the difference in numeric values between two inputs. In this section, we learn to address this problem by using a neural network to process structured data, before feeding that processed data to a GP's mean function and kernel.

13.3.1   Why use neural networks for modeling?

We noted at the beginning of the book that neural networks aren't great at making uncertainty-calibrated predictions, especially when data is expensive to obtain. (This is the whole reason why GPs are used in BayesOpt.) However, what neural networks are good at is learning complex structures. This flexibility is a result of having multiple layers of computation (specifically, matrix multiplication) in a neural network, as illustrated in figure 13.9.

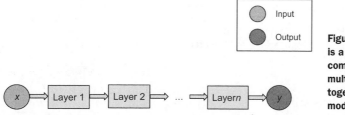

Figure 13.9   A neural network is a collection of layered computations. By chaining multiple layers of computations together, a neural network can model complex functions well.

In a neural network, each layer corresponds to a matrix multiplication whose output is then put through a nonlinear activation function. By having many such layers chained together in one forward pass, the input of the network can be processed and manipulated in a flexible manner. The end result is that a neural network can model complex functions well. For a thorough explanation of neural networks and their usage, refer to François Chollet's excellent book, *Deep Learning with Python, Second Edition* (Manning, 2021)

The flexibility that neural networks possess can help us tackle the problem described in the previous section. If a GP's kernel, such as the RBF kernel, cannot process complex data structures well, we could leave that job to a neural network and only feed the processed input to the GP's kernel. This procedure is visualized in figure 13.10, where the input *x* first goes through the neural network layers before being passed to the mean function and the kernel of the GP.

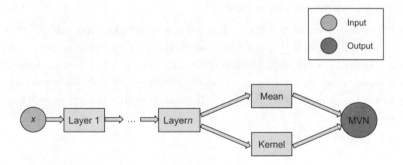

Figure 13.10 Combining a neural network with a GP. The neural network processes the structured data input *x* first and then feeds the output to the mean function and the kernel of the GP.

While the end result is still an MVN distribution, the input of the mean function and the kernel is now the *processed input* produced by a neural network. This approach is promising because with its flexible modeling capability, the neural network will be able to extract the important features from the structured input data (which is important in terms of providing information for the similarity calculation) and boil them down to numerical values that are amenable to the GP's kernel.

> **DEFINITION** The neural network is often called the *feature extractor* of the combined model because the network *extracts* features that are conducive to GP modeling from the structured data.

In this way, we can take advantage of a neural network's flexible learning, while maintaining the ability to make uncertainty-calibrated predictions with a GP. It's the best of both worlds! Further, training this combined model follows the same procedure of training a regular GP: we define our loss function, which is the negative log likelihood, and use gradient descent to find the values for our hyperparameters that best explain our data (by minimizing the loss). Instead of optimizing only the mean constant and the length and output scales, we now additionally optimize the weights of the neural networks. In the next subsection, we see that implementing this learning procedure with GPyTorch requires minimal changes from what we have been doing in previous chapters.

> **NOTE** This combined framework is a method of *dynamically learning* how to process structured data, purely from our training dataset. Previously, we only used a fixed kernel that processed data the same way across multiple applications. Here, we learn "on the fly" the best way to process our input data unique to the task at hand. This is because the weights of the neural network are optimized with respect to the training data.

13.3.2 *Implementing the combined model in GPyTorch*

Finally, we now implement this framework and apply it to our MNIST dataset. Here, defining our model class is more involved, as we need to implement the neural network and hook it into the GP model class. Let's tackle the first part—implementing the neural network—first. We design a simple neural network with the architecture in figure 13.11. This network has four layers with 1,000, 5,000, 50, and 2 nodes, respectively, as indicated in the figure. This is a common architecture for the MNIST dataset.

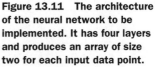

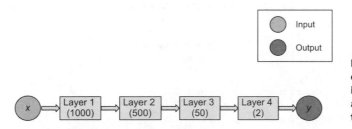

Figure 13.11 The architecture of the neural network to be implemented. It has four layers and produces an array of size two for each input data point.

> **NOTE** We need to pay attention to the size of the last layer (2), which denotes the dimensionality of the processed output to be fed into the mean function

and the kernel of the GP. By setting the size of this layer to 2, we aim to learn a representation of the images that exists in a two-dimensional space. Values other than 2 can also be used, but we opt for 2 here for the purpose of visualization.

We implement this architecture using the `Linear()` and `ReLU()` classes from PyTorch. Here, each layer of our network is implemented as a `torch.nn.Linear` module with the appropriate size, as defined by figure 13.11. Each module is also coupled with a `torch.nn.ReLU` activation function module, which implements the nonlinear transformation mentioned earlier. This is illustrated in figure 13.12, which annotates each component of the network architecture with the corresponding code that implements it.

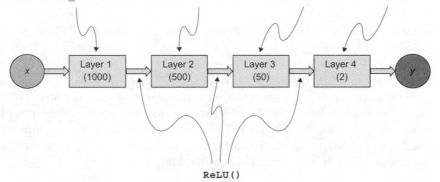

Figure 13.12   The architecture of the neural network to be implemented and the corresponding PyTorch code. Each layer is implemented with `torch.nn.Linear` and each activation function with `torch.nn.ReLU`.

By using the convenient `add_module()` method, we are implicitly defining the logic of the `forward()` method of our neural network model. We implement the model with the `LargeFeatureExtractor` class next. This class passes its input x sequentially through the layers we implement in the `__init__()` method, which takes in `data_dim`, the dimensionality of the input data. In our case, this number is 28 × 28 = 784, which we compute with `train_x.size(-1)`:

```
data_dim = train_x.size(-1)        ◁—— The dimensionality
                                         of the data
```

```
class LargeFeatureExtractor(torch.nn.Sequential):
    def __init__(self, data_dim):
        super(LargeFeatureExtractor, self).__init__()

        self.add_module('linear1', torch.nn.Linear
        ➥(data_dim, 1000))                              The first layer of
        self.add_module('relu1', torch.nn.ReLU())       the network
```

```
        self.add_module('linear2', torch.nn.Linear
      (1000, 500))                                          | The second layer
        self.add_module('relu2', torch.nn.ReLU())

        self.add_module('linear3', torch.nn.Linear
      (500, 50))                                            | The third layer
        self.add_module('relu3', torch.nn.ReLU())

        self.add_module('linear4', torch.nn.Linear
      (50, 2))                                   ◁──     The fourth layer
```

```
feature_extractor = LargeFeatureExtractor(data_dim)    ◁──  Initializes the
                                                             network
```

Next, we discuss the combined model, which is a GP model class that makes use of `feature_extractor`, the neural network feature extractor we just initialized. We implement its `__init__()` method first, which comprises several components:

1. The covariance module is wrapped around by a `gpytorch.kernels.Grid-InterpolationKernel` object, which offers computational speedup for our mid-sized training set of 1,000 points. We declare the number of dimensions of the input data to be two, as that is the dimensionality of the output produced by the feature extractor.
2. The feature extractor itself is the `feature_extractor` variable we declared earlier.
3. The output of the feature extractor could take on extreme values (negative or positive infinity) if the weights of the neural network are badly initialized. To address this, we scale these output values to the range between –1 and 1, using the `gpytorch.utils.grid.ScaleToBounds` module.

The `__init__()` method is implemented as follows:

```
class GPRegressionModel(gpytorch.models.ExactGP):
    def __init__(self, train_x, train_y, likelihood):
        super(GPRegressionModel, self).__init__(train_x, train_y, likelihood)

        self.mean_module = gpytorch.means.ConstantMean()

        self.covar_module = gpytorch.kernels
      .GridInterpolationKernel(
            gpytorch.kernels.ScaleKernel(
                gpytorch.kernels.RBFKernel                 An RBF kernel with
              (ard_num_dims=2)                             two dimensions with
            ),                                             computational
            num_dims=2,                                    speedup
            grid_size=100
        )

        self.feature_extractor = feature_extractor    ◁──  The neural network
                                                             feature extractor

        self.scale_to_bounds = gpytorch.utils.grid
      .ScaleToBounds(-1., 1.)
```

A module to scale the neural network's output to reasonable values └▷

In our `forward()` method, we bring all of these components together. First, we use our neural network feature extractor to process the input. We then feed the processed input to the mean and covariance modules of our GP model. In the end, we still end up with an MVN distribution as what the `forward()` method returns:

```
class GPRegressionModel(gpytorch.models.ExactGP):
  def forward(self, x):
    projected_x = self.feature_extractor(x)
    projected_x = self.scale_to_bounds(projected_x)

    mean_x = self.mean_module(projected_x)
    covar_x = self.covar_module(projected_x)
    return gpytorch.distributions.MultivariateNormal
    ➥(mean_x, covar_x)
```

> Scaled output of the neural network feature extractor

> Creates an MVN distribution object from the processed input

Finally, to train this combined model using gradient descent, we declare the following objects. Here, in addition to the regular GP hyperparameters, such as the mean constant and the length and output scales, we also want to optimize the weights of our neural network feature extractor, which are stored in `model.feature_extractor.parameters()`:

> The likelihood function, the GP model, and the loss function are the same as before.

```
likelihood = gpytorch.likelihoods.GaussianLikelihood()
model = GPRegressionModel(train_x, train_y, likelihood)
mll = gpytorch.mlls.ExactMarginalLogLikelihood(likelihood, model)

optimizer = torch.optim.Adam([
    {'params': model.feature_extractor.parameters()},
    {'params': model.covar_module.parameters()},
    {'params': model.mean_module.parameters()},
    {'params': model.likelihood.parameters()},
], lr=0.01)
```

> The gradient descent optimizer Adam now needs to optimize the weights of the feature extractor and the GP's hyperparameters.

And with that, we are ready to run gradient descent the same way as before:

```
model.train()
likelihood.train()
```

> Enables training mode

```
for i in tqdm(range(500)):
    optimizer.zero_grad()

    output = model(train_x)
    loss = -mll(output, train_y)

    loss.backward()
    optimizer.step()
```

> Runs 500 iterations of gradient descent

```
model.eval()
likelihood.eval()
```

> Enables prediction mode

NOTE As a reminder, when training a GP, we need to enable training mode for both the model and the likelihood (using `model.train()` and `likelihood.train()`). After training and before making predictions, we then need to enable prediction mode (with `model.eval()` and `likelihood .eval()`).

We have now trained the GP model combined with a neural network feature extractor. Before we make our predictions on the test set using this model, we can take a peek inside the model and see whether the neural network feature extractor has learned to process our data well. Remember that each image is transformed into a two-element array by the feature extractor. So, we can pass our training data through this feature extractor and visualize the output using a scatter plot.

NOTE Training this combined model takes more time than training a regular GP. This is because we now have many more parameters to optimize. However, as we see shortly, this cost is well worth it, as we achieve a much higher performance gain.

In this scatter plot, if we see points with the same label (that is, images depicting the same digit) cluster together, that will be an indication that the feature extractor was able to effectively learn from data. Again, we do this by passing the training data through the feature extractor the same way that data is processed in the `forward()` method of the model class:

```
with torch.no_grad():
    extracted_features = model.feature_extractor(train_x)
    extracted_features = model.scale_to_bounds(extracted_features)
```

Here, `extracted_features` is a 1,000-by-2 PyTorch tensor that stores the two-dimensional extracted features of the 1,000 data points in our training set. To visualize this tensor in a scatter plot, we use `plt.scatter()` from the Matplotlib library, making sure each label corresponds to a color:

```
for label in range(10):              ┌ Filters the data points
    mask = train_y == label      ◁──┘  with a specific label

    plt.scatter(
        extracted_features[mask, 0],
        extracted_features[mask, 1],      Creates a scatter plot
        c=train_y[mask],                  for the current data
        vmin=0,                           points, which share
        vmax=9,                           the same color
        label=label,
    )
```

This code produces figure 13.13, although your result might vary, depending on the library versions and the system your code runs on. Just as we expected, data points of the same label cluster around one another. This means our neural network feature extractor is successfully grouping points with the same label together. After being processed by the network, two images of the same label become two points that are close to each other in a two-dimensional plane, which will then have a high covariance if computed by the RBF kernel. This is exactly what we wanted our feature extractor to help us do!

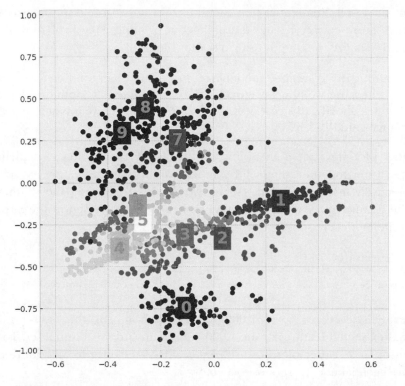

Figure 13.13   Features extracted from the MNIST dataset by a neural network. Not only do data points of the same label cluster together, but there is also a label gradient across the plot: going from the bottom to the top, the value of the label increases.

Another interesting aspect of figure 13.13 is that there is a clear gradient with respect to the label value: going from the bottom to the top cluster, the value of the corresponding label gradually increases from 0 to 9. This is a great feature to have in a feature extractor, as it indicates our model has found a smooth representation of the MNIST images that respects the label values.

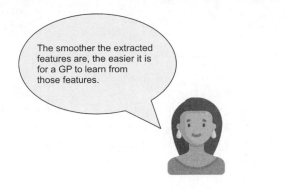

The smoother the extracted features are, the easier it is for a GP to learn from those features.

For example, consider the comparison in figure 13.14, where the left panel shows figure 13.13 and the right panel shows a random swapping of the labels of the same scatter plot, making the features "rougher." By "rough," we mean that the label values jump around erratically: the bottom cluster contains the 0s, some of the clusters in the middle correspond to 7s and 9s, and the top cluster contains the 5s. In other words, the trend of the labels with rough features is not monotonic, making it more difficult to train a GP.

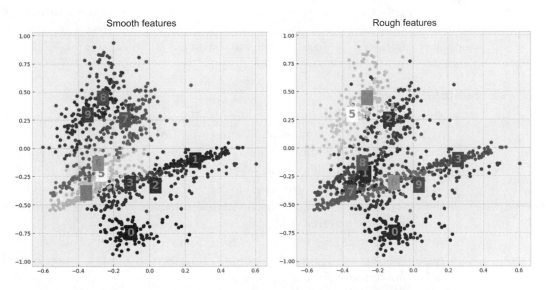

Figure 13.14   A comparison between the smooth extracted features from figure 13.13 (left) and a random swapping of the labels, making the features less smooth (right). The smooth features are easier to learn with a GP than the rough features.

So, it seems that the neural network is doing a good job extracting useful features from images. To see whether this actually leads to better predictive performance, we again compute the mean absolute error (MAE):

```
with torch.no_grad():
    mean_preds = model(test_x).mean

print(torch.mean(torch.abs(mean_preds - test_y)))
```

Output: 0.8524129986763

This result tells us that on average, our prediction is off by 0.85; this is a significant improvement from the vanilla GP we had in the previous section, whose MAE was roughly 2.7. This improvement illustrates the superior performance of the combined model, which stems from the flexible modeling capability of neural networks.

As we said at the beginning, this framework doesn't only apply to handwritten digits but also to various types of structured data that a neural network can learn from, including other types of images and graph structures, such as molecules and proteins. All we need to do is define an appropriate DL architecture that extracts features from these structured data, which are then passed to the GP's mean function and kernel.

This concludes chapter 12. Throughout this chapter, we have learned about the difficulty of learning from structured data, such as images, where common kernels cannot effectively compute covariances between data points. By attaching a neural network feature extractor in front of a GP, we learn to transform this structured data into a form that the GP's kernel can then process. The end result is a combined model that can flexibly learn from structured data but still produces probabilistic predictions with uncertainty quantification.

Summary

- Structured data is data whose features need to satisfy constraints, such as being an integer or being nonnegative, and cannot be treated as continuous, real-valued data. Examples include data from common applications, such as images in computer vision and protein structures in drug discovery.
- Structured data poses a challenge to common kernels for GPs. This is because these kernels only consider the numerical values of input data, which may be poor predictive features.
- A kernel using the wrong features to compute covariances could lead to low-quality predictions from the resulting GP. Using the wrong features is particularly common with structured data.
- For image data specifically, the raw values of the pixels are not an informative feature. A kernel that computes covariances using the raw pixel values can lead to a low-quality GP.
- Having multiple layers of nonlinear computation, neural networks are effective at learning complex functions and can extract features from structured data. By using a neural network to extract continuous, real-valued features from structured data, a GP can still learn effectively.

- In combining a neural network with a GP, we dynamically learn a way to process data that is dedicated to the problem at hand. This flexibility allows this model to generalize to many kinds of structured data.

- It's important to scale the output of a neural network to a small range before passing it to a GP. In doing this, we avoid extreme values that could result from a badly initialized neural network feature extractor.

- The representation learned from a neural network feature extractor exhibits a smooth gradient with respect to the labels. This smooth gradient makes the extracted features more amenable to learning with a GP.

appendix
Solutions to the exercises

A.1 *Chapter 2: Gaussian processes as distributions over functions*

In this exercise, we train a GP on a real-world dataset we saw in chapter 1. The solution is included in the CH02/02 - Exercise.ipynb notebook. Complete the following steps:

1 Create the four-dimensional dataset.

  We first import the necessary libraries: PyTorch for array/tensor manipulation, GPyTorch for GP modeling, and Matplotlib for visualization:

```
import torch
import gpytorch
import matplotlib.pyplot as plt
```

  We then store the numbers in the table in two PyTorch tensors, `train_x` and `train_y`, which, respectively, contain the features and labels of our dataset:

```
train_x = torch.tensor(
    [
        [1 / 2, 1 / 2, 0, 0],
        [1 / 3, 1 / 3, 1 / 3, 0],
        [0, 1 / 2, 1 / 2, 0],
        [0, 1 / 3, 1 / 3, 1 / 3],
    ]
)

train_y = torch.tensor([192.08, 258.30, 187.24, 188.54])
```

2 Normalize the fifth column by subtracting the mean from all values and dividing the results by their standard deviation.

We normalize the labels as follows:

```
# normalize the labels
train_y = (train_y - train_y.mean()) / train_y.std()
```

When printed out, `train_y` should contain the following values: `tensor([-0.4183,` `1.4974, -0.5583, -0.5207])`.

3 Treat the first four columns as features and the fifth as labels. Train a GP on this data.

We reimplement our GP model class as follows:

```
class BaseGPModel(gpytorch.models.ExactGP):
    def __init__(self, train_x, train_y, likelihood):
        super().__init__(train_x, train_y, likelihood)
        self.mean_module = gpytorch.means.ZeroMean()
        self.covar_module = gpytorch.kernels.RBFKernel()

    def forward(self, x):
        mean_x = self.mean_module(x)
        covar_x = self.covar_module(x)
        return gpytorch.distributions.MultivariateNormal(mean_x, covar_x)
```

We then initialize an object of this class with our training data:

```
lengthscale = 1
noise = 1e-4

likelihood = gpytorch.likelihoods.GaussianLikelihood()
model = BaseGPModel(train_x, train_y, likelihood)

model.covar_module.lengthscale = lengthscale
model.likelihood.noise = noise

model.eval()
likelihood.eval()
```

4 Create a test dataset containing compositions with zero percent germanium and manganese.

To assemble our test dataset, we first create a mesh grid for the first and second columns that spans over the unit square:

```
grid_x = torch.linspace(0, 1, 101)

grid_x1, grid_x2 = torch.meshgrid(grid_x, grid_x, indexing="ij")
```

These first two columns are stored in `grid_x1` and `grid_x2`. We then append two additional, all-zero columns to `grid_x1` and `grid_x2`, completing the test set with four columns:

```
First          xs = torch.vstack(
column             [
                       grid_x1.flatten(),
Second                 grid_x2.flatten(),
column                 torch.zeros(101 ** 2),
                       torch.zeros(101 ** 2),
                   ]
               ).transpose(-1, -2)
```

First column → grid_x1.flatten(),
Second column → grid_x2.flatten(),
Third column, containing all zeros → torch.zeros(101 ** 2),
Forth column, containing all zeros → torch.zeros(101 ** 2),

5 Predict the mixing temperature on this test set.

To make predictions on this test set, we simply pass xs through our GP model under the torch.no_grad() context:

```
with torch.no_grad():
    predictive_distribution = likelihood(model(xs))
    predictive_mean = predictive_distribution.mean
    predictive_stddev = predictive_distribution.stddev
```

6 Visualize the predictions.

To visualize these predictions, we first create a figure with two panels (that is, two Matplotlib subplots):

```
fig, ax = plt.subplots(1, 2, figsize=(16, 6))
```

We then use plt.imshow() to visualize the mean and standard deviation vectors as heat maps, making sure to reshape the two vectors into square matrices:

```
c = ax[0].imshow(
    predictive_mean.detach().reshape(101, 101).transpose(-1, -2),
    origin="lower",
    extent=[0, 1, 0, 1],
)
```

Heat map for the predictive mean

```
c = ax[1].imshow(
    predictive_stddev.detach().reshape(101, 101).transpose(-1, -2),
    origin="lower",
    extent=[0, 1, 0, 1],
)
plt.colorbar(c, ax=ax[1])
```

Heat map for the predictive standard deviation

This will create plots similar to those in figure A.1.

NOTE   If you are using a different GP implementation, it's entirely possible to produce heat maps that are slightly different from those in figure A.1. As long as the general trend of the heat maps is the same, your solution is correct.

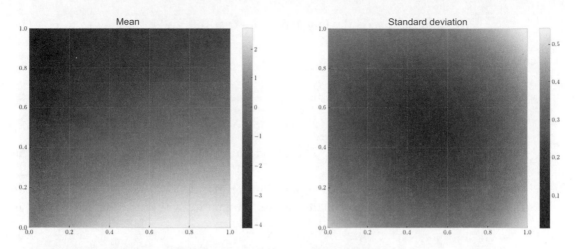

Figure A.1   Predictions made by a GP on a 2-dimensional space

A.2   Chapter 3: Incorporating prior knowledge with the mean and covariance functions

This exercise provides practice for implementing a GP model with automatic relevance determination (ARD). The solution is included in CH03/03 - Exercise.ipynb. Complete the following steps:

1   Implement the two-dimensional function in Python using PyTorch.

We first import the necessary libraries—PyTorch for array/tensor manipulation, GPyTorch for GP modeling, and Matplotlib for visualization:

```
import torch
import gpytorch
import matplotlib.pyplot as plt
```

We then implement the objective function using the given formula:

```
def f(x):
    return (
        torch.sin(5 * x[..., 0] / 2 - 2.5) * torch.cos(2.5 - 5 * x[..., 1])
        + (5 * x[..., 1] / 2 + 0.5) ** 2 / 10
    ) / 5 + 0.2
```

2   Visualize the function over the domain $[0, 2]^2$.

To visualize the function, we need to create a mesh grid the domain. We store this grid in xs:

```
lb = 0
ub = 2
xs = torch.linspace(lb, ub, 101)          ⟵  One-dimensional
                                                grid
x1, x2 = torch.meshgrid(xs, xs)                               Two-dimensional
                                                                        grid
xs = torch.vstack((x1.flatten(), x2.flatten())).transpose(-1, -2)   ⟵
```

We then can obtain the function values over this grid by passing `xs` to `f()`. The results are stored in `ys`:

```
ys = f(xs)
```

We use `plt.imshow()` to visualize `ys` as a heat map:

```
plt.imshow(ys.reshape(101, 101).T, origin="lower", extent=[lb, ub, lb, ub])
```

3   Randomly draw 100 data points from the domain $[0, 2]^2$. This will be used as our training data.

　　To randomly sample 100 points within the domain, we use `torch.rand()` to sample from the unit square, and then we multiply the result by 2 to scale it to our domain:

```
torch.manual_seed(0)
train_x = torch.rand(size=(100, 2)) * 2
```

The function values of these points can be obtained by calling `f(train_x)`:

```
train_y = f(train_x)
```

4   Implement a GP model with a constant mean function and a Matérn 5/2 kernel with an output scale implemented as a `gpytorch.kernels.ScaleKernel` object. We implement our GP model as specified:

```
class GPModel(gpytorch.models.ExactGP):
    def __init__(self, train_x, train_y, likelihood):
        super().__init__(train_x, train_y, likelihood)
        self.mean_module = gpytorch.means.ConstantMean()
        self.covar_module = gpytorch.kernels.ScaleKernel(
            gpytorch.kernels.MaternKernel(
                nu=2.5,
                ard_num_dims=None        ⟵─┐  Set to None to
            )                                  disable ARD and
        )                                      2 to enable ARD.

    def forward(self, x):
        mean_x = self.mean_module(x)
        covar_x = self.covar_module(x)
        return gpytorch.distributions.MultivariateNormal(mean_x, covar_x)
```

5   Don't specify the `ard_num_dims` parameter when initializing the kernel object or set the parameter to `None`.

　　This is done in the previous code.

6   Train the hyperparameters of the GP model using gradient descent, and inspect the length scale after training.

　　We initialize our GP and train it using gradient descent for 500 iterations as follows:

```
noise = 1e-4

likelihood = gpytorch.likelihoods.GaussianLikelihood()
model = GPModel(train_x, train_y, likelihood)

model.likelihood.noise = noise

optimizer = torch.optim.Adam(model.parameters(), lr=0.01)
mll = gpytorch.mlls.ExactMarginalLogLikelihood(likelihood, model)

model.train()              │  Enables the
likelihood.train()         │  training model

losses = []
for i in tqdm(range(500)):
    optimizer.zero_grad()

    output = model(train_x)     │  Gradient descent to
    loss = -mll(output, train_y)│  optimize the GP's
                                │  hyperparameters
    loss.backward()
    losses.append(loss.item())

    optimizer.step()

model.eval()               │  Enables the
likelihood.eval()          │  prediction model
```

After these 500 iterations, we inspect the length scale by printing out the following value:

```
>>> model.covar_module.base_kernel.lengthscale
tensor([[1.1535]])
```

In other words, the optimized length scale is equal to roughly 1.15.

7 Redefine the GP model class, this time setting `ard_num_dims = 2`.

Setting `ard_num_dims=2` in the `GPModel` class and rerunning all the code cells, we obtain the following values for the length scales:

```
>>> model.covar_module.base_kernel.lengthscale
tensor([[1.6960, 0.8739]])
```

Here, the length scale of the first dimension is large (roughly 1.70), while the length scale of the second dimension is small (roughly 0.87). This corresponds to the fact that the objective function varies more along the second dimension.

A.3   Chapter 4: Refining the best result with improvement-based policies

There are two exercises in this chapter:

1   The first covers a way of refining the Probability of Improvement (PoI) policy, allowing it to better explore the search space.
2   The second applies the two BayesOpt policies we have learned to a simulated real-world task of hyperparameter tuning.

A.3.1   Exercise 1: Encouraging exploration with Probability of Improvement

This exercise, implemented in the CH04/02 - Exercise 1.ipynb notebook, walks us through how to modify PoI to encourage exploration. Complete the following steps:

1   Recreate the BayesOpt loop in the CH04/01 - BayesOpt loop notebook, which uses the one-dimensional Forrester function as the optimization objective.
2   Before the `for` loop that implements BayesOpt, declare a variable named `epsilon`:

```
epsilon = 0.1
```

3   Inside the `for` loop, initialize the PoI policy as before, but this time, specify that the incumbent threshold, set by the `best_f` argument, is the incumbent value *plus* the value stored in `epsilon`:

```
policy = botorch.acquisition.analytic.ProbabilityOfImprovement(
    model, best_f=train_y.max() + epsilon
)
```

4   Rerun the notebook, and observe whether this modification leads to better optimization performance than the original PoI policy by encouraging more exploration, as shown in figure A.2.

Here, the modified PoI has found the optimum.

5   How much more explorative PoI becomes heavily depends on the minimum improvement threshold stored in `epsilon`. Setting this variable to 0.001 doesn't sufficient encourage exploration, and the policy once again gets stuck. Setting this variable to 0.5 works well.

6   Implement a relative minimum improvement threshold with a 110% improvement requirement:

```
epsilon_pct = 0.1

for i in range(num_queries):                        ⟵┘ Omitted
    ...

        policy = botorch.acquisition.analytic.ProbabilityOfImprovement(
            model, best_f=train_y.max() * (1 + epsilon_pct)
        )
```

Relative improvement └⟶

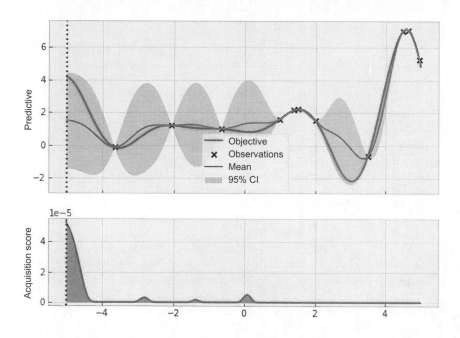

Figure A.2   Optimization progress of the modified PoI at the last iteration. The policy has found the optimum.

A.3.2   *Exercise 2: BayesOpt for hyperparameter tuning*

This exercise, implemented in CH04/03 - Exercise 2.ipynb, applies BayesOpt to an objective function that simulates the accuracy surface of a support-vector machine model in a hyperparameter tuning task. Complete the following steps:

1 Recreate the BayesOpt loop in CH04/01 - BayesOpt loop.ipynb. Our objective function is implemented as

```
def f(x):
    return (
        torch.sin(5 * x[..., 0] / 2 - 2.5)
        * torch.cos(2.5 - 5 * x[..., 1])
        + (5 * x[..., 1] / 2 + 0.5) ** 2 / 10
    ) / 5 + 0.2
```

2 Declare the corresponding test data with xs for a two-dimensional grid representing the domain and ys for the function values of xs:

```
lb = 0
ub = 2
num_queries = 20

bounds = torch.tensor([[lb, lb], [ub, ub]], dtype=torch.float)
```

```
xs = torch.linspace(lb, ub, 101)
x1, x2 = torch.meshgrid(xs, xs)
xs = torch.vstack((x1.flatten(), x2.flatten())).transpose(-1, -2)
ys = f(xs)
```

3 Modify the helper function that visualizes optimization progress. We declare this function as `visualize_progress_and_policy()`, which only needs to take in a policy object and `next_x` as the next point to query. First, the function computes the acquisition scores for the test data `xs`:

```
def visualize_progress_and_policy(policy, next_x=None):
    with torch.no_grad():
        acquisition_score = policy(xs.unsqueeze(1))
```

   ...   ◁—— **To be continued**

Next, we declare the two Matplotlib subplots and, for the first, plot the ground truth stored in `ys`:

Heat map showing the ground truth

```
c = ax[0].imshow(
    ys.reshape(101, 101).T, origin="lower", extent=[lb, ub, lb, ub]
)
ax[0].set_xlabel(r"$C$", fontsize=20)
ax[0].set_ylabel(r"$\gamma$", fontsize=20)
plt.colorbar(c, ax=ax[0])

ax[0].scatter(train_x[..., 0], train_x[..., 1], marker="x", c="k")
```

Scattered points showing labeled data

Finally, we plot another heat map in the second subplot, showing the acquisition scores:

```
c = ax[1].imshow(
    acquisition_score.reshape(101, 101).T,
    origin="lower",
    extent=[lb, ub, lb, ub]
)
ax[1].set_xlabel(r"$C$", fontsize=20)
plt.colorbar(c, ax=ax[1])
```

Heat map showing the acquisition scores

We optionally show `next_x`:

```
if next_x is not None:
    ax[1].scatter(
        next_x[..., 0],
        next_x[..., 1],
        c="r",
        marker="*",
        s=500,
        label="next query"
    )
```

4   Copy the GP class from the exercise in chapter 3, which implements a Matérn 2.5 kernel with ARD. Further modify this class to make it integratable with BoTorch:

```
class GPModel(gpytorch.models.ExactGP,
  botorch.models.gpytorch.GPyTorchModel):          BoTorch-related
    _num_outputs = 1                               modifications

    def __init__(self, train_x, train_y, likelihood):
        super().__init__(train_x, train_y, likelihood)
        self.mean_module = gpytorch.means.ConstantMean()
        self.covar_module = gpytorch.kernels.
        ➥ScaleKernel(
            gpytorch.kernels.MaternKernel(          Matérn 2.5
                nu=2.5,                             kernel with
                ard_num_dims=2                      ARD
            )
        )

    def forward(self, x):
        ...                          ⟵—— Omitted
```

5   Reuse the helper function `fit_gp_model()` and the `for` loop that implements BayesOpt. We copy `fit_gp_model()` and declare the initial dataset:

```
train_x = torch.tensor([
    [1., 1.],
])
train_y = f(train_x)
```

We then declare the BayesOpt loop:

```
num_queries = 20

for i in range(num_queries):
    print("iteration", i)
    print("incumbent", train_x[train_y.argmax()], train_y.max())

    model, likelihood = fit_gp_model(train_x, train_y)

    policy = ...          ⟵—| Placeholder for
                             | policy initialization

    next_x, acq_val = botorch.optim.optimize_acqf(
        policy,
        bounds=bounds,
        q=1,
        num_restarts=40,     | Making the search
        raw_samples=100,     | more exhaustive
    )

    visualize_progress_and_policy(policy,
    ➥next_x=next_x)          ⟵————| Calling the new
                                   | visualization
    next_y = f(next_x)             | helper function
```

```
train_x = torch.cat([train_x, next_x])
train_y = torch.cat([train_y, next_y])
```

6 Run the PoI policy on this objective function. Observe that the policy once again gets stuck at a local optimum. Replace the line that initializes the BayesOpt policy with

```
policy = botorch.acquisition.analytic.ProbabilityOfImprovement(
    model, best_f=train_y.max()
)
```

Running the entire notebook shows that the policy once again gets stuck at a local optimum, as shown in figure A.3.

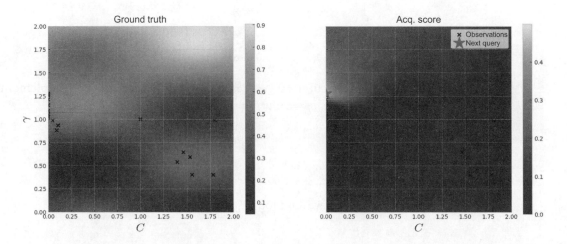

Figure A.3   Optimization progress of PoI at the last iteration. The policy is stuck at a local optimum.

7 Run the modified version of PoI, where the minimum improvement threshold is set at 0.1. Replace the line that initializes the BayesOpt policy with

```
policy = botorch.acquisition.analytic.ProbabilityOfImprovement(
    model, best_f=train_y.max() + 0.1
)
```

This policy is more explorative and outperforms regular PoI. Figure A.4 shows the progress of this policy at iteration 17, where it first achieves an accuracy of at least 90%.

Here, C = 1.6770 and γ = 1.9039 are the parameters giving this accuracy.

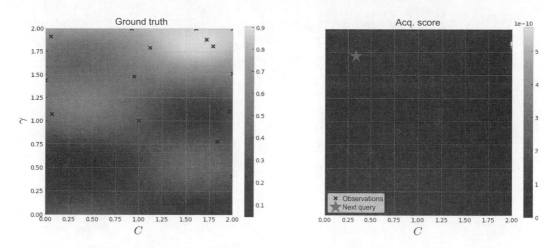

Figure A.4 Optimization progress of the modified PoI at iteration 17, where the policy first achieves an accuracy of at least 90%

8   Run the Expected Improvement (EI) policy on this objective function. Replace the line that initializes the BayesOpt policy with

```
policy = botorch.acquisition.analytic.ExpectedImprovement(
    model, best_f=train_y.max()
)
```

This policy performs well on our objective function, finding an accuracy of at least 90% at iteration 15, as shown in figure A.5.

Here, $C = 1.6331$ and $\gamma = 1.8749$ are the parameters giving this accuracy.

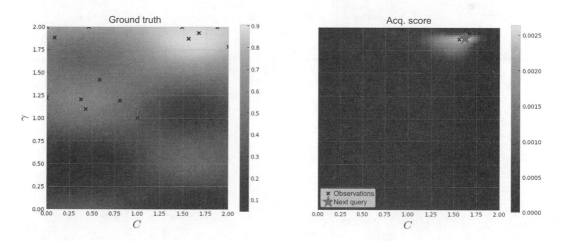

Figure A.5 Optimization progress of EI at iteration 4, where the policy first achieves an accuracy of at least 90%

9 Implement repeated experiments, and visualize the average incumbent values and error bars across 10 experiments. We first put the code that implements our BayesOpt loop in an outer loop that iterates over multiple experiments. We store the best-seen value at each step across the experiments in `incumbents`:

```python
num_repeats = 10

incumbents = torch.zeros((num_repeats, num_queries))

for trial in range(num_repeats):
    print("trial", trial)

    torch.manual_seed(trial)
    train_x = bounds[0] + (bounds[1] - bounds[0])      # Uniformly samples
    ⇒* torch.rand(1, 2)                                #  a data point in the
    train_y = f(train_x)                               #  search space as the
                                                       #  starting point

    for i in tqdm(range(num_queries)):
        incumbents[trial, i] = train_y.max()    ◁——  Keeps track of the
                                                      best-seen value
        ...     ◁——  The mitted code is
                      the same as before.
torch.save(incumbents, [path to file])   ◁——  Saves results to a file so that
                                               we can visualize them later
```

We then implement a helper function that plots the average incumbent values and error bars. This function reads in a PyTorch tensor saved at `path`, which should be the saved version of `incumbents` in the previous step:

```python
def show_agg_progress(path, name):
    def ci(y):
        return 2 * y.std(axis=0) / np.sqrt(num_repeats)   # Helper subfunction to
                                                           # compute the error bars

    incumbents = torch.load(path)   ◁——  Loads saved
                                          optimization results
    avg_incumbent = incumbents.mean(axis=0)   # Computes the mean
    ci_incumbent = ci(incumbents)             # results and error bars

    plt.plot(avg_incumbent, label=name)
    plt.fill_between(
        np.arange(num_queries),          # Visualizes the
        avg_incumbent + ci_incumbent,    # mean results
        avg_incumbent - ci_incumbent,    # and error bars
        alpha=0.3,
    )
```

We then can run the preceding policies we have in the previous code and compare their performance:

```python
plt.figure(figsize=(8, 6))

show_agg_progress([path to EI data], "EI")
show_agg_progress([path to PoI data], "PoI")
show_agg_progress([path to modified PoI data], "PoI" + r"$(\epsilon = 0.1)$")
```

```
plt.xlabel("# queries")
plt.ylabel("accuracy")

plt.legend()

plt.show()
```

This generates figure A.6, which shows the optimization performance of PoI, the modified version of PoI, and EI.

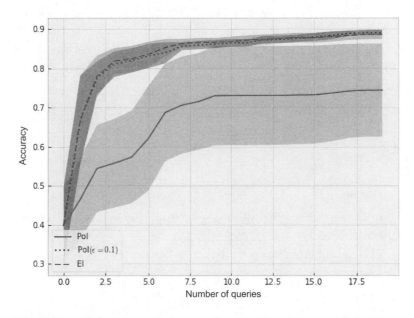

Figure A.6   Optimization progress of various policies, aggregated across 10 repeated experiments

We see that figure A.6 gives us more insight than inspecting the policies in a single run. Here, not only does PoI perform worse than the other two policies, but its performance is also less robust, as seen from the large error bars. The modified PoI and EI perform comparably, and it's hard to tell if one is better than the other, as their error bars overlap.

A.4   Chapter 5: Exploring the search space with bandit-style policies

There are two exercises in this chapter:

1   The first exercise explores a potential method to set the tradeoff parameter for the UCB policy that considers how far along we are in optimization.

2 The second exercise applies the two policies we have learned in this chapter to the hyperparameter tuning problem seen in previous chapters.

A.4.1 *Exercise 1: Setting an exploration schedule for Upper Confidence Bound*

This exercise, implemented in CH05/02 - Exercise 1.ipynb, discusses a strategy of adaptively setting the value of the tradeoff parameter β of the UCB policy. Complete the following steps:

1 Recreate the BayesOpt loop in CH04/02 - Exercise 1.ipynb, which uses the one-dimensional Forrester function as the optimization objective.

Since there are 10 iterations in the BayesOpt loop, β is multiplied by the multiplier m 10 times to go from 1 to 10. That is, $1 \times m^{10} = 10$. Solving this equation gives the code for the multiplier:

```
num_queries = 10

start_beta = 1
end_beta = 10

multiplier = (end_beta / start_beta) ** (1 / num_queries)
```

2 Implement this scheduling logic, and observe the resulting optimization performance.

We modify the BayesOpt loop as follows:

```
num_queries = 10

start_beta = 1
end_beta = 10

multiplier = (end_beta / start_beta) ** (1 / num_queries)

beta = start_beta

for i in range(num_queries):
    ...                          ◁──  Obtains the
                                      trained GP

    policy = botorch.acquisition.analytic.UpperConfidenceBound(
        model, beta=beta
    )

                                      Finds the point that maximizes the
    ...               ◁──             acquisition score, queries the objective
                                      function, and updates the training data

    beta *= multiplier
```

This code produces figure A.7.

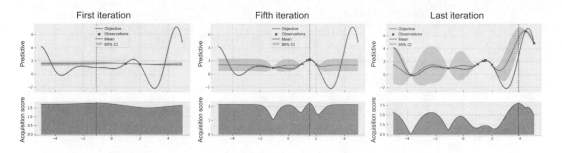

Figure A.7   Progress made by the adaptive version of the UCB policy. The policy is able to escape the local optimum and get closer to the global optimum.

We see that the policy inspects a local optimum at the fifth iteration but ultimately is able to escape and get closer to the global optimum at the end.

A.4.2   Exercise 2: BayesOpt for hyperparameter tuning

This exercise, implemented in CH05/03 - Exercise 2.ipynb, applies BayesOpt to an objective function that simulates the accuracy surface of a support-vector machine model in a hyperparameter tuning task. Complete the following steps:

1   Recreate the BayesOpt loop in CH04/03 - Exercise 2.ipynb, including the outer loop that implements repeated experiments.
2   Run the UCB policy, setting the value of the tradeoff parameter to $\beta \in \{ 1, 3, 10, 30 \}$, and observe the values' aggregated performance.

   The value of the tradeoff parameter can be set when the policy object is initialized:

```
policy = botorch.acquisition.analytic.UpperConfidenceBound(
    model, beta=[some value]
)
```

Figure A.8 shows the optimization performance of the four versions of UCB. We see that when $\beta = 1$, the policy is too exploitative and achieves the worst performance.

   As the value of the tradeoff parameter increases, performance increases, but when $\beta = 30$, over-exploration causes UCB to be slower at locating an accuracy of 90%. Overall, $\beta = 10$ achieves the best performance.

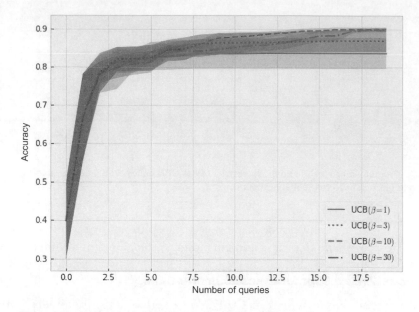

Figure A.8　Progress made by the various UCB policies

3　Run the adaptive version of UCB (see Exercise 1).

We modify the BayesOpt loop as follows:

```
num_repeats = 10

start_beta = 3
end_beta = 10

multiplier = (end_beta / start_beta) ** (1 / num_queries)

incumbents = torch.zeros((num_repeats, num_queries))

for trial in range(num_repeats):
    ...                                    ◁─── Randomly generates the
                                                initial training data
    beta = start_beta

    for i in tqdm(range(num_queries)):
        ...                                ◁─── Records the incumbent value
                                                and retrains the model

        policy = botorch.acquisition.analytic.UpperConfidenceBound(
            model, beta=beta
        )
        ...             ◁─── Finds the point maximizing the acquisition
                             score, queries the objective function, and
                             updates the training data
        beta *= multiplier
```

Figure A.9 shows the optimization performance of the two adaptive versions against the best performing fixed value $\beta = 10$.

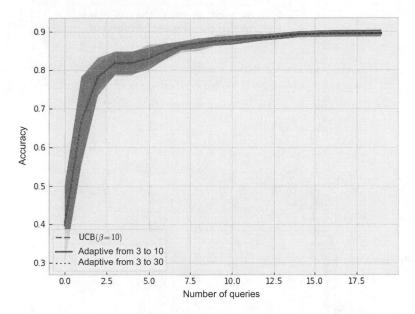

Figure A.9   Progress made by two adaptive versions of the UCB policy. The policy is robust against the end value of the tradeoff parameter.

These versions are comparable, and changing the end value from 10 to 30 doesn't affect optimization performance much.

4 Run the Thompson sampling (TS) policy, and observe its aggregated performance. We implement TS as follows:

```
num_candidates = 2000
num_repeats = 10

incumbents = torch.zeros((num_repeats, num_queries))

for trial in range(num_repeats):          | Randomly generates
    ...                                    | the initial training data

  for i in tqdm(range(num_queries)):       | Records the incumbent value
    ...                                    | and retrains the model

    sobol = torch.quasirandom.SobolEngine(1, scramble=True)
    candidate_x = sobol.draw(num_candidates)
    candidate_x = bounds[0] + (bounds[1] - bounds[0]) * candidate_x
```

```
ts = botorch.generation.MaxPosteriorSampling(model,
⮡replacement=False)
next_x = ts(candidate_x, num_samples=1)
```

... ◁—— **Finds the point maximizing the acquisition score, queries the objective function, and updates the training data**

Figure A.10 shows the optimization performance of TS. We see that the policy makes significant progress at the beginning and is comparable to EI from chapter 6 and slightly worse than the best version of UCB.

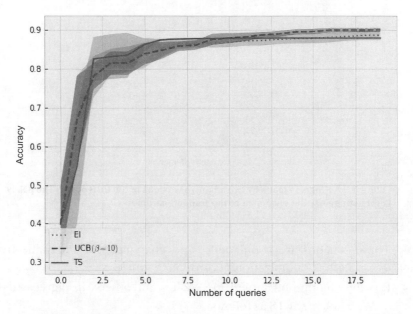

Figure A.10   Progress made by TS. The policy is comparable to EI and slightly worse than the best version of UCB.

A.5   *Chapter 6: Using information theory with entropy-based policies*

There are two exercises in this chapter:

1 The first exercise covers a variant of binary search in which prior information can be taken into account when making decisions.
2 The second walks us through the process of implementing Max-value Entropy Search (MES) in the hyperparameter tuning problem seen in previous chapters.

A.5.1   *Exercise 1: Incorporating prior knowledge into entropy search*

This exercise, implemented in CH06/02 - Exercise 1.ipynb, shows us an instance of using different priors when finding the information-theoretically optimal decision and will ultimately help us further appreciate the elegance and flexibility of entropy search as a generic decision-making-under-uncertainty procedure:

1 Prove that $Pr(X = 1) + Pr(X = 2) + ... + Pr(X = 10) = 1$.

We can do this by simply adding the probabilities together:

$$1 / 2 + 1 / 4 + ... + 1 / 2^9 + 1 / 2^9 = 1 / 2 + 1 / 4 + ... + 1 / 2^8 + 1 / 2^8 = ...$$
$$= 1 / 2 + 1 / 2 = 1.$$

2 Calculate the entropy of this prior distribution.

Remember the formula for the entropy is $-\Sigma_i\, p_i \log p_i$. We can write a Python function that computes this sum:

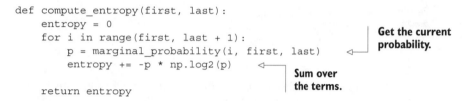

```
def compute_entropy(first, last):
    entropy = 0
    for i in range(first, last + 1):
        p = marginal_probability(i, first, last)      ◁── Get the current
        entropy += -p * np.log2(p)   ◁──                  probability.
                                        Sum over
    return entropy                      the terms.
```

This function takes `first` and `last` as parameters, which correspond to the smallest and biggest numbers X could be (which start out as 1 and 10), respectively. We then iterate through the numbers between `first` and `last` and add up the $-p_i \log p_i$ terms. Here, `marginal_probability()` is a helper function that computes $Pr(X = n)$, which we implement as

```
def marginal_probability(floor, first, last):
    if floor == last:                    An edge case when the floor
        return 2 ** -(last - first)      is the highest possible floor

    return 2 ** -(floor - first + 1)
```

Running `compute_entropy(1, 10)` gives us 1.99609375. This is the entropy of the prior distribution for X.

3 Given the prior distribution defined between 1 and 10, what is the probability the phone will break when dropped from the second floor? What is this probability for the fifth floor? How about the first floor?

The probability that the phone will break when dropped from the second floor is exactly $Pr(X = 1)$, which is 0.5.

The probability that the phone will break from the fifth floor is the probability that $X \leq 4$, which is $Pr(X = 1) + Pr(X = 2) + Pr(X = 3) + Pr(X = 4) = 15/16 = 0.9375$.

These two calculations could be implemented as a function:

```
def cumulative_density(floor, first, last):
    return sum(
        [
            marginal_probability(i, first, last)
            for i in range(first, floor)
        ]
    )
```

Sum over the probabilities for X less than the threshold.

Since our prior knowledge dictates that the phone won't break if dropped from the first floor, this probability is 0.

4 Compute the entropy of the fictitious posterior distribution in the two cases where we conduct a trial on the fifth floor.

Using the `compute_entropy()` function we implemented, we can compute the entropy in two cases. If the phone breaks, we set `first = 1` and `last = 4`; otherwise, we set `first = 5` and `last = 10`:

```
>>> compute_entropy(1, 4)
Output: 1.75
>>> compute_entropy(5, 10)
Output: 1.9375
```

5 Given the prior distribution, compute the expected posterior entropy after you conduct a trial on the fifth floor.

We have already done the necessary calculations for this expected posterior entropy computation. First, the probability that the phone will break from the fifth floor is 0.9375, in which case the posterior entropy is 1.75. Second, the probability that the phone won't break from the fifth floor is $1 - 0.9375 = 0.0625$, in which case the posterior entropy is 1.9375.

Taking the average of the two cases gives $(0.9375)\ 1.75 + (0.0625)\ 1.9375 = 1.76171875$. This is the expected posterior entropy after you conduct a trial on the fifth floor.

6 Compute this expected posterior entropy for other floors.

We can implement a function that does the calculation we just went over:

```
def compute_expected_posterior_entropy(floor, first, last):
    break_probability = cumulative_density
    (floor, first, last)

    return (
        break_probability * compute_entropy
        (first, floor - 1)
        + (1 - break_probability) * compute_entropy
        (floor, last)
    )
```

The probability that the phone will break from a given floor

Takes the average of the two cases

Using this function, we can plot out the expected posterior entropy for numbers between 1 and 10.

This plot is shown in figure A.11, which tells us that the information-theoretically optimal location for our first trial is the second floor, since 2 gives us the lowest expected posterior entropy (and, therefore, uncertainty).

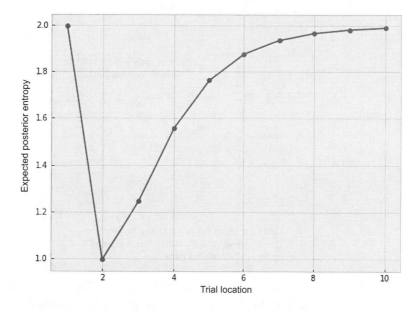

Figure A.11   The expected posterior entropy as a function of the location to conduct the trial

We see that this is not the same as the decision binary search suggests, 5. This is a direct effect of the domain knowledge we are encoding using the prior distribution for X: since there's a high chance that $X = 2$ (50%), it's actually better to simply try out that number first in case we can immediately find our answer if the phone breaks.

Interestingly, dropping the phone from the first floor gives us no reduction in entropy. This is because we know for sure that the phone won't break from this floor, so our knowledge of the world won't change after conducting this trial.

A.5.2   *Exercise 2: BayesOpt for hyperparameter tuning*

This exercise, implemented in the CH06/03 - Exercise 2.ipynb notebook, applies BayesOpt to an objective function that simulates the accuracy surface of a support-vector machine model in a hyperparameter tuning task:

1   Recreate the BayesOpt loop in CH04/03 - Exercise 2.ipynb, including the outer loop that implements repeated experiments.
2   Run the MES policy.

Since our objective function is two-dimensional, we should set the size of the Sobol sequence used by MES as 2,000:

```
num_candidates = 2000
num_repeats = 10

incumbents = torch.zeros((num_repeats, num_queries))

for trial in range(num_repeats):          Randomly generates the
    ...                                    initial training data

    for i in tqdm(range(num_queries)):     Records the incumbent value
        ...                                and retrains the model

        sobol = torch.quasirandom.SobolEngine(1, scramble=True)
        candidate_x = sobol.draw(num_candidates)
        candidate_x = bounds[0] + (bounds[1] - bounds[0]) * candidate_x

        policy = botorch.acquisition.max_value_entropy_search.qMaxValueEntropy(
            model, candidate_x
        )
                             Finds the point maximizing the acquisition
        ...                  score, queries the objective function, and
                             updates the training data
```

Figure A.12 shows the optimization performance of MES. We see that the policy is competitive against all the BayesOpt policies we have learned thus far.

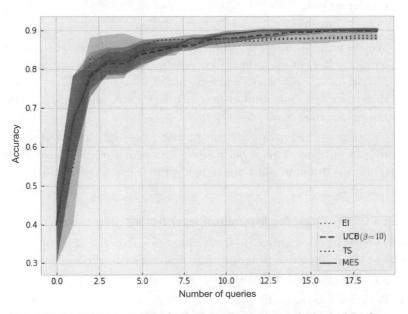

Figure A.12   Progress made by MES. The policy performs the best of the four policies shown.

A.6   Chapter 7: Maximizing throughput with batch optimization

There are two exercises in this chapter:

1 The first covers the implementation of TS under the batch setting.
2 The second shows us how to run BayesOpt policies on a four-dimensional aero-structural optimization problem.

A.6.1   Exercise 1: Extending TS to the batch setting via resampling

Remember that TS in the sequential setting, which we learned in section 5.3, draws one sample from the current GP belief about the objective function and queries the data point that maximizes that sample. In the batch setting, we simply repeat this process of sampling from the GP and maximizing the sample multiple times to assemble a batch of queries of the desired size. The code for this exercise can be found in the CH07/02 - Exercise 1.ipynb notebook:

1 Recreate the batch BayesOpt loop in CH05/01 - BayesOpt loop.ipynb notebook.
2 Implement TS with a Sobol sampler, as described in section 5.3.

   We implement the policy as follows, where we use a 2,000-element Sobol sequence and specify the number of samples as the batch size:

```
num_candidates = 2000          ◁──┐ Specifies the length of
                                   │ the Sobol sequence

...          ◁──┐ Randomly picks the
                │ initial training data

for i in tqdm(range(num_iters)):
    ...                ◁──┐ Retrains
                          │ the GP

    sobol = torch.quasirandom.SobolEngine
    ⮡(2, scramble=True)
    candidate_x = sobol.draw(num_candidates)       │ Initializes the
    candidate_x = (bounds[1] - bounds[0]) *        │ Sobol sequence
    ⮡candidate_x + bounds[0]

    ts = botorch.generation.MaxPosteriorSampling(model,    │ Draws multiple
    ⮡replacement=False)                                    │ samples from
    next_x = ts(candidate_x, num_samples=batch_size)  ◁──┘ the GP

    ...          ◁──┐ Queries the objective function
                    │ and updates the training data
```

3 Run this TS policy on the hyperparameter tuning objective function, and observe its performance.

After running batch TS, we can plot the progress made by the policy against other policies we have learned, as shown in figure A.13. Here, TS is able to make significant progress after only the first batch of queries.

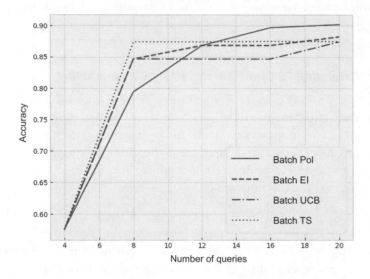

Figure A.13   Progress made by batch TS in the hyperparameter tuning example. The policy makes significant progress after only the first batch of queries.

A.6.2   *Exercise 2: Optimizing airplane designs*

This exercise provides an objective function that simulates this process of benchmarking the performance of an airplane design. The code is provided in the CH07/04 - Exercise 2.ipynb notebook. Complete the following steps:

1 Implement the objective function that simulates the performance benchmarking.
   The code for the objective function is already provided, so we simply copy and paste it in our program:

```
def flight_utility(X):
  X_copy = X.detach().clone()
  X_copy[:, [2, 3]] = 1 - X_copy[:, [2, 3]]
  X_copy = X_copy * 10 - 5

  return -0.005 * (X_copy**4 - 16 * X_copy**2 + 5 * X_copy).sum(dim=-1) + 3
```

2 Implement a GP model with a constant mean function and a Matérn 2.5 kernel with an output scale implemented as a `gpytorch.kernels.ScaleKernel` object.

The class implementation of this GP model is mostly the same as before, except that we need to specify the correct number of dimensions in the ARD kernel:

```
class GPModel(
    gpytorch.models.ExactGP,
    botorch.models.gpytorch.GPyTorchModel,
    botorch.models.model.FantasizeMixin
):
    _num_outputs = 1

    def __init__(self, train_x, train_y, likelihood):
        super().__init__(train_x, train_y, likelihood)
        self.mean_module = gpytorch.means.ConstantMean()
        self.covar_module = gpytorch.kernels.ScaleKernel(
            gpytorch.kernels.MaternKernel(
                nu=2.5,                         A Matérn 2.5 kernel
                ard_num_dims=4                  for four dimensions
            )
        )

    def forward(self, x):
        ...
```

3   Implement a helper function that trains the GP on a given training dataset.

We can simply copy the same helper function `fit_gp_model()` from other notebooks in this chapter, namely 02 - Exercise 1.ipynb, as we don't need to modify anything in this helper function.

4   Define the settings of our optimization problem.

We first define the bounds of our search space:

```
lb = 0
ub = 1

bounds = torch.tensor([[lb] * 4, [ub] * 4], dtype=torch.float)
```

We then specify how many queries can be made, the batch size, and the number of experiments to repeat for each policy:

```
num_experiments = 5

num_queries = 100
batch_size = 5
num_iters = num_queries // batch_size
```

5   Run each batch BayesOpt policy we learn in this chapter on the objective function implemented previously.

We first use this code to implement the optimization loop and the outer loop that repeats the experiments for each policy. Specifically, for each individual experiment, we randomly sample one data point inside the search space and then run each BayesOpt policy until we run out of queries. We see how each policy is defined in the next step:

```
incumbents = torch.zeros((num_experiments, num_iters))

pbar = tqdm(total=num_experiments * num_iters)

for exp in range(num_experiments):
    torch.manual_seed(exp)
    train_x = bounds[0] + (bounds[1] -        # Randomly initializes the training data
    ➡bounds[0]) * torch.rand(1, 4)
    train_y = flight_utility(train_x)

    for i in range(num_iters):
        incumbents[exp, i] = train_y.max()    # Keeps track of optimization progress and updates the predictive model

        model, likelihood = fit_gp_model
        ➡(train_x, train_y)

        ...                                    # Defines the policy and finds the next batch to query

        next_y = flight_utility(next_x)        # Queries the points recommended by the policy and updates the training data

        train_x = torch.cat([train_x, next_x])
        train_y = torch.cat([train_y, next_y])

        pbar.update()
```

For the PoI policy, we use the following code:

```
policy = botorch.acquisition.monte_carlo.qProbabilityOfImprovement(
    model, best_f=train_y.max()
)
```

For the EI policy, we use the following code:

```
policy = botorch.acquisition.monte_carlo.qExpectedImprovement(
    model, best_f=train_y.max()
)
```

For the UCB policy, we use the following code:

```
policy = botorch.acquisition.monte_carlo.qUpperConfidenceBound(
    model, beta=2
)
```

These three policies can then be optimized using the helper function `optimize_acqf()` as follows:

```
next_x, acq_val = botorch.optim.optimize_acqf(
    policy,
    bounds=bounds,
    q=batch_size,
    num_restarts=100,
    raw_samples=200,
)
```

Otherwise, for either TS or MES, we first need to define the Sobol sequence:

Specifies the number of dimensions to be 4

```
sobol = torch.quasirandom.SobolEngine(4, scramble=True)   <──┘
candidate_x = sobol.draw(5000)
candidate_x = (bounds[1] - bounds[0]) * candidate_x + bounds[0]
```

For the TS policy, we use the following code:

```
ts = botorch.generation.MaxPosteriorSampling(model, replacement=False)
next_x = ts(candidate_x, num_samples=batch_size)
```

For the MES, we use the following code, which uses the helper function `optimize_acqf_cyclic()` to implement cyclic optimization. Note that we are specifying that cyclic optimization should only take a maximum of 5 iterations:

```
policy = botorch.acquisition.max_value_entropy_search.qMaxValueEntropy(
    model, candidate_x
)
```

```
next_x, acq_val = botorch.optim.optimize_acqf_cyclic(
    policy,
    bounds=bounds,
    q=batch_size,
    num_restarts=40,
    raw_samples=100,
    cyclic_options={"maxiter": 5}   <──┘
)
```

Specifies the maximum number of iterations in cyclic optimization

6 Plot the optimization progress of the BayesOpt policies we have run and observe their performance.

Figure A.14 shows the optimization results obtained by the policies we've implemented. We see that most policies are comparable, except for TS; batch PoI has a slight edge.

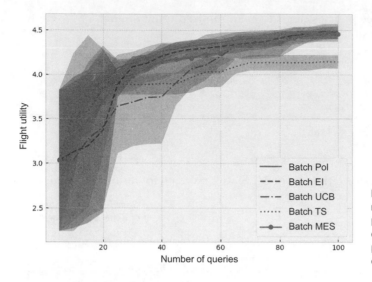

Figure A.14 Progress made by various BayesOpt policies in the airplane design optimization example. Most policies are comparable, except for TS.

A.7   Chapter 8: Satisfying extra constraints with constrained optimization

There are two exercises in this chapter:

1 The first verifies that the result we obtain from BoTorch's implementation of the constrained EI policy is the same as the product of the regular EI score and the probability of feasibility.
2 The second shows us how to run constrained BayesOpt on a four-dimensional aerostructural optimization problem.

A.7.1   Exercise 1: Manual computation of constrained EI

The acquisition score of the constrained EI policy is the product of the EI score and the probability of feasibility. Although the `ConstrainedExpectedImprovement` class from BoTorch provides an implementation of the constrained EI score, we can, in fact, perform the computation manually. In this exercise, we explore this manual computation and verify our result against that of the `ConstrainedExpectedImprovement` class. The solution of this exercise is in the CH08/02 - Exercise 1.ipynb notebook amd can be explained as follows:

1 Recreate the constrained BayesOpt problem used in CH08/01 - Constrained optimization.ipynb, including the objective function, the cost function, the GP implementation, and the helper function that trains a GP on some training data `fit_gp_model()`.
2 Create a PyTorch tensor that is a dense grid between -5 and 5. This tensor will act as our test set. We use `torch.linspace()` to create a dense grid:

```
lb = -5
ub = 5

xs = torch.linspace(lb, ub, 201)
```

3   Create a toy training dataset by randomly sampling three data points from our search space (between –5 and 5), and evaluate the objective and cost functions at these points. We use `torch.rand()` to randomly sample between 0 and 1 and scale the samples to our search space:

```
n = 3                                              Fixes the seed for
torch.manual_seed(0)                               reproducibility
train_x = bounds[0] + (bounds[1] - bounds[0]) * torch.rand(n)

train_utility = objective(train_x)                 Samples between 0 and 1
train_cost = cost(train_x)                         and then scales the samples
                                                   to our search space
```

4   Train a GP on the data from the objective function and another GP on the data from the cost function using the helper function `fit_gp_model()`.

```
utility_model, utility_likelihood = fit_gp_model(      Trains a GP on the
    train_x.unsqueeze(-1), train_utility               objective function's
)                                                      data

cost_model, cost_likelihood = fit_gp_model(
    train_x.unsqueeze(-1), train_cost                  Trains a GP on the
)                                                      cost function's data
```

5   Use the GP trained on the data from the cost function to compute the probability of feasibility for each point in the test set.

   We first compute the predictive distribution of the cost GP on our test set:

```
with torch.no_grad():
    cost_pred_dist = cost_likelihood(cost_model(xs))
    cost_pred_mean = cost_pred_dist.mean
    cost_pred_lower, cost_pred_upper = \
        cost_pred_dist.confidence_region()
```

We then initialize a normal distribution object, with the mean and standard deviation corresponding to the means and standard deviations of `cost_pred_dist`:

```
normal = torch.distributions.Normal(cost_pred_mean, cost_pred_dist.stddev)
```

Finally, we call the `cdf()` method on this object to compute the probability of feasibility. The argument this method takes is the upper bound of our cost constraint, which is 0:

```
feasible_prob = normal.cdf(torch.zeros(1))
```

6   Initialize a regular EI policy, with the `model` argument being the GP trained on the data from the objective function and the `best_f` argument being the current feasible incumbent.

    We compute the current feasible incumbent with `train_utility[train_cost <= 0].max()`:

```
ei = botorch.acquisition.analytic.ExpectedImprovement(
    model=utility_model,
    best_f=train_utility[train_cost <= 0].max(),
)
```

We then compute the EI score by calling the EI policy object on `xs[:, None, None]`, which is the test dense grid reshaped to make sure it's of appropriate shape:

```
with torch.no_grad():
    ei_score = ei(xs[:, None, None])
```

7   Initialize a constrained EI policy, and compute the constrained EI score for each point in the test set:

```
constrained_ei =
botorch.acquisition.analytic.ConstrainedExpectedImprovement(
    model=botorch.models.model_list_gp_regression.ModelListGP(
        utility_model, cost_model
    ),
    best_f=train_utility[train_cost <= 0].max(),
    objective_index=0,
    constraints={1: [None, 0]}
)
```

We also compute the constrained EI score with the reshaped test set:

```
with torch.no_grad():
    constrained_ei_score = constrained_ei(xs[:, None, None])
```

8   Compute the product of the EI scores and the probabilities of feasibility, and verify that this manual computation leads to the same results as those from BoTorch's implementation. Run an assertion to make sure all corresponding terms match up:

```
assert torch.isclose(
    ei_score * feasible_prob, constrained_ei_score, atol=1e-3
).all()
```

9   Plot the EI scores and the constrained EI scores in a graph, and visually verify that the former is always greater than or equal to the latter. Prove this is the case.

We plot out the scores we have computed thus far as follows:

```
plt.plot(xs, ei_score, label="EI")
plt.plot(xs, constrained_ei_score, label="BoTorch constrained EI")
```

This code generates figure A.15, which shows that the EI score is, indeed, always at least the constrained EI score.

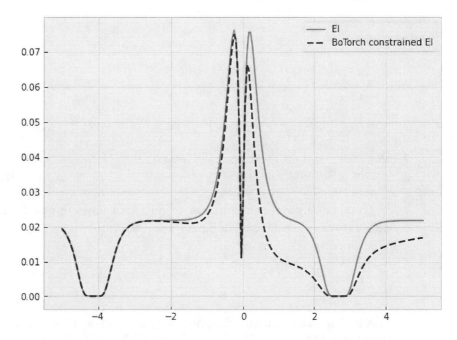

Figure A.15   The acquisition score of EI (solid line) and constrained EI (dashed line). The former is always greater than or equal to the latter.

We can mathematically prove this by noting that the constrained EI score is equal to the regular EI score multiplied by the probability of feasibility. This probability of feasibility is always a maximum of 1, so the EI score is always greater than or equal to the constrained EI score.

A.7.2   *Exercise 2: Constrained optimization of airplane design*

In this exercise, we tackle a constrained optimization problem using the airplane-utility objective function in exercise 2 of chapter 7. This process allows us to run constrained BayesOpt on a higher-dimensional problem in which it's not obvious where the feasibility optimal solution is. The solution to this exercise is included in the CH08/03 - Exercise 2.ipynb notebook:

1 Recreate the BayesOpt problem used in the CH07/04 - Exercise 2.ipynb notebook, including the airplane-utility objective function named `flight_utility()`,

the bounds of our search space (the four-dimensional unit hypercube), the GP implementation, and the helper function that trains a GP on some training data `fit_gp_model()`.

2 Implement the following cost function, which simulates the cost of making the airplane design specified by a four-dimensional input:

```
def flight_cost(X):
  X = X * 20 - 10

  part1 = (X[..., 0] - 1) ** 2

  i = X.new(range(2, 5))
  part2 = torch.sum(i * (2.0 * X[..., 1:] ** 2 - X[..., :-1]) ** 2,
  ➥dim=-1)

  return -(part1 + part2) / 100_000 + 2
```

3 Our goal is to maximize the objective function `flight_utility()`, while following the constraint that the cost, as computed by `flight_cost()`, is less than or equal to 0.

To this end, we set the number of queries a BayesOpt policy can make in each experiment as 50, and designate that each policy needs to run 10 repeated experiments:

```
num_queries = 50
num_repeats = 10
```

The default value quantifying optimization progress if no feasible solution is found should be set to –2.

```
default_value = -2
feasible_incumbents = torch.ones((num_repeats, num_queries)) * default_value
```

4 Run the constrained EI policy as well as the regular EI policy on this problem; visualize and compare their average progress (along with error bars).

We implement the constrained EI policy in the same way as we did in chapter 8, where we set `best_f` to be either the current feasible incumbent if a feasible solution has been found or the default value –2 otherwise. Our model list contains the objective GP, which has an index of 0, and the cost GP, which has an index of 1:

```
if (train_cost <= 0).any():
    best_f = train_utility[train_cost <= 0].max()
else:
    best_f = torch.tensor(default_value)
```

Finds the appropriate value of the current incumbent

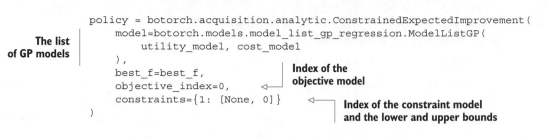

```
policy = botorch.acquisition.analytic.ConstrainedExpectedImprovement(
    model=botorch.models.model_list_gp_regression.ModelListGP(
        utility_model, cost_model
    ),
    best_f=best_f,
    objective_index=0,
    constraints={1: [None, 0]}
)
```

The list of GP models

Index of the objective model

Index of the constraint model and the lower and upper bounds

We implement the regular EI policy as follows:

```
policy = botorch.acquisition.analytic.ExpectedImprovement(
    model=utility_model,
    best_f=train_utility.max(),
)
```

Figure A.16 shows the optimization results obtained by the two preceding policies we implemented. We see that constrained EI completely dominates the regular EI policy by accounting for the cost constraint we impose.

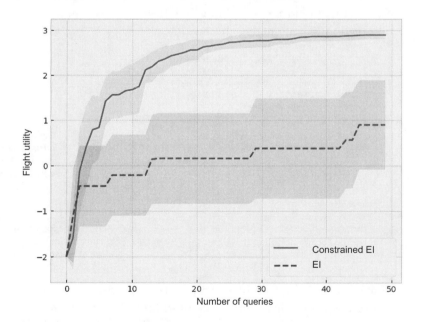

Figure A.16   Progress made by various Bayesian optimization policies in the constrained airplane design optimization example. Compared to the regular EI, the constrained variant finds a more feasible solution on average.

A.8   Chapter 9: Balancing utility and cost with multifidelity optimization

There are two exercises in this chapter:

1 Exercise 1 walks through the process of measuring and visualizing the average performance of an optimization policy across multiple experiments.
2 Exercise 2 applies the optimization policies we know to a two-dimensional problem with three functions we can query from.

A.8.1   Exercise 1: Visualizing average performance in multifidelity optimization

In this exercise, we run the optimization loop multiple times and learn how to take the average performance to obtain a more holistic comparison:

1 Copy the problem setup and the multifidelity optimization loop from the CH09/03 - Measuring performance.ipynb notebook, and add another variable denoting the number of experiments we want to run (10, by default).
2 To facilitate repeated experiments, add an outer loop to the optimization loop code. This should be a `for` loop with 10 iterations, where a different random observation is generated each time:

```
num_repeats = 10        ⟵───  Repeats the
                              experiment 10 times

for trial in range(num_repeats):
    torch.manual_seed(trial)
    train_x = bounds[0] + (bounds[1] - bounds[0])
    ➡* torch.rand(1, 1)                              Generates a random
    train_x = torch.cat(                             initial training set
        [train_x, torch.ones_like(train_x)           specific to the
        ➡* fidelities[0]], dim=1                     current iteration
    )
    train_y = evaluate_all_functions(train_x)

    current_budget = 0                          The inner loop that
    while current_budget < budget_limit:        runs optimization until
        ...                                     we exhaust our budget
```

3 Make each of the variables `recommendations` and `spent_budget` a list of lists, where each inner-list keeps track of optimization performance of an individual experiment. We add to the code for the nested loop in the previous step as follows:

```
num_repeats = 10
recommendations = []        Each variable is a (currently
spent_budget = []           empty) list of lists.

for trial in range(num_repeats):
    torch.manual_seed(trial)
```

```
train_x = bounds[0] + (bounds[1] - bounds[0]) * torch.rand(1, 1)
train_x = torch.cat(
    [train_x, torch.ones_like(train_x) * fidelities[0]], dim=1
)
train_y = evaluate_all_functions(train_x)

current_budget = 0
recommendations.append([])              Appends an empty list to each list
spent_budget.append([])                 of lists for the next experiment

while current_budget < budget_limit:
    ...

    rec_x = get_final_recommendation(model)
    recommendations[-1].append              Adds the optimization
    ⇨ (evaluate_all_functions(rec_x).item())  progress statistics to the
    spent_budget[-1].append(current_budget)   newest list in each variable

    ...
```

4 Run the multifidelity MES policy and its single-fidelity version on our optimization problem.

5 We first make the regular grid and the currently empty interpolated recommended values that we will fill in later:

```
xs = np.arange(budget_limit)
interp_incumbents = np.empty((num_repeats, budget_limit))
```

We then iterate through each list in `recommendations` (renamed to `incumbents` in our code) and `spend_budget`, compute the linear interpolation, and then fill in the values in `interp_incumbents`:

```
for i, (tmp_incumbents, tmp_budget) in enumerate(
    zip(incumbents, spent_budget)
):
    interp_incumbents[i, :] = np.interp(xs, tmp_budget, tmp_incumbents)
```

6 Use the linearly interpolated values to plot the average performance and error bars of the two policies we ran and compare their performance. The comparison is visualized in figure A.17, where we see that the multifidelity MES policy greatly outperforms its single-fidelity competitor.

7 Plot the linearly interpolated curves representing individual runs' optimization progress, along with the average performance and error bars. The comparison is visualized in figure A.18. Indeed, our optimization progress in each run, as measured by the maximum posterior mean recommendation, is not monotonically increasing.

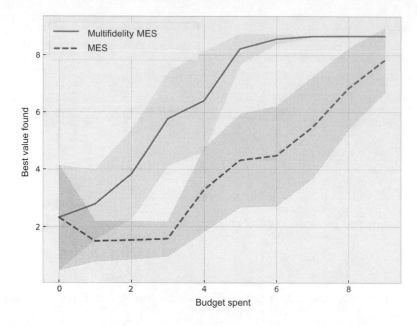

Figure A.17 Average optimization progress of the single- and multifidelity MES policies on the Forrester function across 10 experiments. The multifidelity policy greatly outperforms the single-fidelity one.

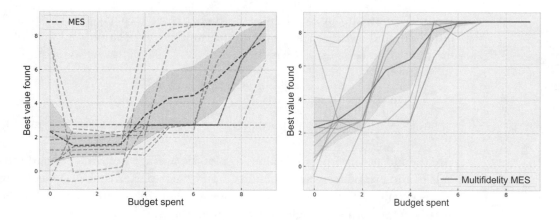

Figure A.18 Linearly interpolated curves representing individual runs' optimization progress across 10 experiments. Our optimization progress in each run, as measured by the maximum posterior mean recommendation, is not monotonically increasing.

A.8.2 *Exercise 2: Multifidelity optimization with multiple low-fidelity approximations*

This exercise shows us that our multifidelity Max-value Entropy Search policy can balance between multiple low-fidelity functions. The solution, found in the CH09/05 - Exercise 2.ipynb notebook, can be explained as follows:

1 Implement the objective function. The code for this step has already been provided in the instructions.

2 Define the bounds of our search space as the unit square:

```
bounds = torch.tensor([[0.0] * 2, [1.0] * 2])
```

3 Declare the `fidelities` variable that stores the correlation values of the different functions we can query:

```
fidelities = torch.tensor([0.1, 0.3, 1.0])
bounds_full = torch.cat(
    [
        bounds,
        torch.tensor([fidelities.min(), fidelities.max()]).unsqueeze(-1)
    ],
    dim=1
)
```

4 Set the fixed cost of the linear cost model to 0.2 and the weight to 1:

```
from botorch.models.cost import AffineFidelityCostModel

cost_model = AffineFidelityCostModel(fixed_cost=0.2)
```

Set the limit of our budget in each experiment to 10 and the number of repeated experiments to 10 as well:

```
budget_limit = 10
num_repeats = 10
```

5 Set the number of candidates drawn from the Sobol sequence to 5,000, and use 100 restarts and 500 raw samples when using helper functions to optimize the acquisition score of a given policy:

```
num_samples = 5000

num_restarts = 100
raw_samples = 500
```

6 Redefine the helper function `get_final_recommendation` that finds the posterior mean maximizer:

```
from botorch.acquisition.fixed_feature import
➡FixedFeatureAcquisitionFunction
```

```
from botorch.acquisition import PosteriorMean
from botorch.optim.optimize import optimize_acqf, optimize_acqf_mixed


def get_final_recommendation(model):
    post_mean_policy = FixedFeatureAcquisitionFunction(
        acq_function=PosteriorMean(model),
        d=3,
        columns=[2],              The necessary changes
        values=[1],
    )

    final_x, _ = optimize_acqf(
        post_mean_policy,
        bounds=bounds,
        q=1,
        num_restarts=num_restarts,
        raw_samples=raw_samples,
    )

    return torch.cat([final_x, torch.ones(1, 1)], dim=1)
```

7   Run the multifidelity MES policy and its single-fidelity version on our optimization problem, and plot the average optimization progress and error bars of each policy, using the method described in exercise 1. Figure A.19 shows the comparison between the two policies.

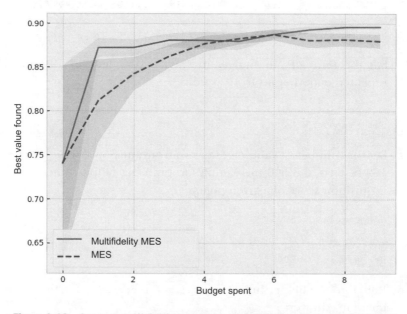

Figure A.19   Average optimization progress of the single- and multifidelity MES policy on the Branin function across 10 experiments. The multifidelity policy, once again, outperforms the single-fidelity one.

A.9   Chapter 11: Optimizing multiple objectives at the same time

In this exercise, we apply the multiobjective optimization techniques we have learned to the problem of optimizing the aerostructural design of an airplane. This exercise allows us to observe the performance of the Expected Hypervolume Improvement (EHVI) policy in a multidimensional problem:

1 We copy the code for the objective functions as follows:

```
def objective1(X):
  X_copy = X.detach().clone()
  X_copy[:, [2, 3]] = 1 - X_copy[:, [2, 3]]
  X_copy = X_copy * 10 - 5
  return (
    -0.005
    * (X_copy ** 4 - 16 * X_copy ** 2 + 5 * X_copy)
    ⟹.sum(dim=-1)
      + 3
  )
```

The first objective function

The second objective function, negated from the code in exercise 2 of chapter 8

```
def objective2(X):
  X = X * 20 - 10
  part1 = (X[..., 0] - 1) ** 2
  i = X.new(range(2, 5))
  part2 = torch.sum(i * (2.0 * X[..., 1:] ** 2 - X[..., :-1]) ** 2,
    ⟹ dim=-1)
  return (part1 + part2) / 100_000 - 2
```

2 We implement the helper function as follows:

```
def joint_objective(X):
    return torch.vstack(
        [
            objective1(X).flatten(),
            objective2(X).flatten(),
        ]
    ).transpose(-1, -2)
```

3 We declare the bounds of the search space:

```
bounds = torch.tensor([[0.0] * 4, [1.0] * 4])
```

4 We declare the reference point:

```
ref_point = torch.tensor([-1.5, -2.0])
```

5 The class implementation and helper function can be implemented using the same code as, for example, in CH08/03 - Exercise 2.ipynb.

6   We set the experimental settings:

```
num_queries = 50
num_repeats = 10
```

7   We implement the two BayesOpt policies in the same way as in CH11/02 - Multi-objective BayesOpt loop.ipynb. Figure A.20 shows the performance of the two policies aggregated across 10 experiments. EHVI, once again, outperforms the alternating EI policy.

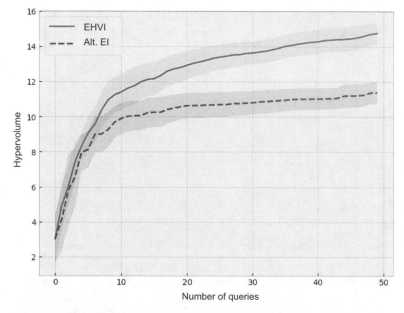

Figure A.20   **Average hypervolume and error bars as a function of the number of queries made by two Bayesian optimization policies. EHVI consistently outperforms the alternating EI policy.**

A.10   *Chapter 12: Scaling Gaussian processes to large data sets*

This exercise demonstrates the improvement in efficiency when going from a regular GP model to a VGP one on a real-life dataset of housing prices in California. Our goal is to observe the computational benefits of a VGP—this time, in a real-world setting.

Complete the following steps:

1   We use the Pandas library to read in the dataset:

```
import pandas as pd

df = pd.read_csv("../data/housing.csv")
```

Once read in, the Pandas dataframe should look similar to the output in figure A.21.

	longitude	latitude	housing_median_age	total_rooms	total_bedrooms	population	households	median_income	median_house_value
0	-117.08	32.70	37	2176	418.0	1301	375	2.8750	98900
1	-117.91	34.11	20	3158	684.0	2396	713	3.5250	153000
2	-117.10	32.75	11	2393	726.0	1905	711	1.3448	91300
3	-117.22	32.74	52	1260	202.0	555	209	7.2758	345200
4	-121.99	37.29	32	2930	481.0	1336	481	6.4631	344100
...	...	...	...	...	...	...	...	...	...
4995	-118.41	34.19	42	779	145.0	450	148	3.9792	193800
4996	-122.96	38.42	50	2530	524.0	940	361	2.9375	122900
4997	-118.00	33.77	24	1324	267.0	687	264	3.4327	192800
4998	-122.81	38.54	12	2289	611.0	919	540	1.1553	139300
4999	-118.08	33.84	25	3696	953.0	2827	860	3.3438	153300

Figure A.21   The housing price dataset shown as a Pandas dataframe. This is the training set for this exercise.

2   We create the scatter plot as follows:

```
plt.figure(figsize=(8, 6))
plt.scatter(df.longitude, df.latitude, c=np.log(df.median_house_value))
plt.colorbar();
```

The visualization should look similar to figure A.22.

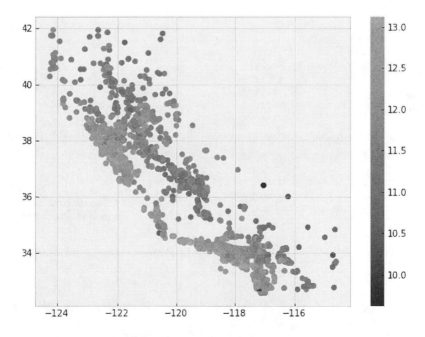

Figure A.22   The housing price dataset shown as a scatter

3   To extract our training features, we use the `torch.from_numpy()` method to convert a NumPy array to a PyTorch tensor:

```
train_x = torch.from_numpy(df.drop(["median_house_value"], axis=1).values)
```

4   We similarly do this for the log of the house prices, which are our training labels:

```
train_y = torch.from_numpy(
    df.median_house_value.values
).log().to(train_x.dtype)
```

5   We normalize the training labels `train_y` as follows:

```
train_y = (train_y - train_y.mean()) / train_y.std()
```

6   We implement the GP model as follows:

```
class GPModel(gpytorch.models.ExactGP):
    def __init__(self, train_x, train_y, likelihood):
        super().__init__(train_x, train_y, likelihood)
        self.mean_module = gpytorch.means.ConstantMean()
        self.covar_module = gpytorch.kernels.ScaleKernel(
            gpytorch.kernels.MaternKernel(
                nu=2.5,
                ard_num_dims=train_x.shape[1]
            )
        )

    def forward(self, x):
        mean_x = self.mean_module(x)
        covar_x = self.covar_module(x)
        return gpytorch.distributions.MultivariateNormal(mean_x, covar_x)
```

The constant mean function → `self.mean_module = gpytorch.means.ConstantMean()`

An ARD Matern 5/2 kernel with an output scale

7   Make a likelihood whose noise is constrained to be at least 0.1, using the following code:

```
likelihood = gpytorch.likelihoods.GaussianLikelihood(
    noise_constraint=gpytorch.constraints
    ➥.GreaterThan(1e-1)
)
```

The constraint forces the noise to be at least 0.1.

8   We train the previously implemented GP model using gradient descent as follows:

```
model = GPModel(train_x, train_y, likelihood)

optimizer = torch.optim.Adam(model.parameters(),
➥lr=0.01)
mll = gpytorch.mlls.ExactMarginalLogLikelihood
➥(likelihood, model)
```

The gradient descent optimizer Adam

The (negative) marginal log likelihood loss function

```
model.train()                    Enable
likelihood.train()               training mode

for i in tqdm(range(10)):
    optimizer.zero_grad()

    output = model(train_x)
    loss = -mll(output, train_y)

    loss.backward()
    optimizer.step()
```

The total training time was 24 seconds on a MacBook.

9 We implement the VGP model as follows:

```
class ApproximateGPModel(gpytorch.models.ApproximateGP):
  def __init__(self, inducing_points):
    variational_distribution =
    ⟹gpytorch.variational
    ⟹.NaturalVariationalDistribution(
        inducing_points.size(0)
    )
    variational_strategy = gpytorch.variational     Variational
    ⟹.VariationalStrategy(                          parameters
        self,
        inducing_points,
        variational_distribution,
        learn_inducing_locations=True,
    )
    super().__init__(variational_strategy)
    self.mean_module = gpytorch.means.ConstantMean()
    self.covar_module = gpytorch.kernels.ScaleKernel(
        gpytorch.kernels.MaternKernel(
            nu=2.5,
            ard_num_dims=inducing_points.shape[1]
        )
    )

  def forward(self, x):     The same
    ...                     as the GP
```

10 This VGP is trained as follows:

```
num_datapoints = 100
torch.manual_seed(0)                          Randomly picks
model = ApproximateGPModel(                    100 points as the
  train_x[torch.randint(train_x.shape[0],      initial inducing
  ⟹(num_datapoints,)), :]                      points
)

likelihood = gpytorch.likelihoods.GaussianLikelihood(
  noise_constraint=gpytorch.constraints.GreaterThan(1e-1)
)
```

```
train_dataset = torch.utils.data.Tensordataset
➥(train_x, train_y)
train_loader = torch.utils.data.DataLoader(
  train_data set,
  batch_size=100,
  shuffle=True
)
```
**Prepares the
mini batches**

```
ngd_optimizer = gpytorch.optim.NGD(
  model.variational_parameters(),
  ➥num_data=train_y.size(0), lr=0.1
)
```
**Natural gradient
descent for variational
parameters**

```
hyperparam_optimizer = torch.optim.Adam(
  [{"params": model.parameters()}, {"params":
  ➥likelihood.parameters()}],
  lr=0.01
)
```
**Adam for
the other
parameters**

```
mll = gpytorch.mlls.VariationalELBO(
  likelihood, model, num_data=train_y.size(0)
)

model.train()
likelihood.train()

for i in tqdm(range(10)):
  for x_batch, y_batch in train_loader:
    ngd_optimizer.zero_grad()

    output = model(x_batch)
    loss = -mll(output, y_batch)

    loss.backward()

    ngd_optimizer.step()
    hyperparam_optimizer.step()
```

11 On the same MacBook, training took 6 seconds—a 400% improvement in speed.

The solution is included in the CH12/02 - Exercise.ipynb notebook.

index